John—

Without your help and encouragement through the years, this book would never have been written.

Thanks for everything.

Love,
Cathy

Frontier Expansion and Peasant Protest
in Colombia, 1850-1936

Frontier Expansion
and
Peasant Protest in Colombia,
1850–1936

Catherine LeGrand

University of New Mexico Press
Albuquerque

Library of Congress Cataloging in Publication Data

LeGrand, Catherine, 1947–
Frontier expansion and peasant protest in Colombia, 1850–1936.

Bibliography: p.
Includes index.
1. Land tenure—Colombia—History.   2. Peasantry—
Colombia—History.   3. Colombia—Rural conditions.
I. Title.
HD515.L44 1986   333.1′6′09861   85-24244
ISBN 0-8263-0851-1

To My Parents

Contents

Illustrations

Figures

Maps

Acknowledgments

It gives me pleasure to acknowledge the many debts I have incurred in researching and writing this study. I particularly want to thank the many Colombian scholars who, in their concern to make known the reality of the Colombian rural past, shared their knowledge and their enthusiasms. Early conversations with Hermes Tovar Pinzón, Darío Fajardo, Eduardo Santa, and the late Jorge Villegas gave direction and purpose to my research, while later talks with Marco Palacios, Germán Colmenares, Jaime Jaramillo Uribe, Mario Valderrama, and José Antonio OCampo lent insight into the complexities of Colombian rural life. Humberto Rojas Ruiz of the Oficina Para Investigaciones Socio-económicas y Legales (OFISEL) provided warm encouragement and a congenial place to work. Meanwhile, throughout the two years I spent in Bogotá, the stimulating intellectual companionship of Gonzalo Sánchez and Terry Horgan was a constant source of new ideas and materials. It was Terry who discovered the then uncatalogued Public Land Correspondence in the Colombian National Archive and generously informed me of its existence.

Back in North America, friends and teachers helped me toward a more coherent and communicable understanding of my material. Alan Tully, Barbara Nunberg, Jean Barman, Roderick Barman, Charles Bergquist, John Wirth, Thomas Holloway, Frank Safford, Renato Rosaldo, and Chris De-Bresson contributed much appreciated comments and suggestions. Two other individuals have been particularly important in my formation as a historian. John J. Johnson, who supervised the dissertation that became this book, urged his students to take on important subjects and gave us the autonomy to explore them. I am deeply grateful to him. I also want to thank Charles Gibson, who read and criticized the dissertation and who has been for me a humane example of what a scholar can be. The original maps and figures were drawn by Paul Patmore with his customary skill and good humor; they have been redone for the book by Paul Jance and Frank Flynn's computer wizardry.

While this study could not have been completed in its present form without the assistance of those mentioned above, the conclusions and limitations are my own. The research was made possible by fellowships from the Fulbright-Hays Commission and the Social Science Research Council and by grants from the Weter Memorial Fund at Stanford University and the Humanities and Social Sciences Fund of the Canadian Social Science and Humanities Research Council at The University of British Columbia.

Introduction

When I was a university student, a campus-wide trivia game was held. Following several witty and appropriately petty queries, someone piped up: "There are forty million peasants starving in Asia. Name one." A long silence ensued. Most of us have never met a peasant. We know little of how they live, even less how they think and what they care about. Yet a majority of the world's people are peasants. If economic development is to take place, their problems and viewpoints must be understood.

In many parts of the globe, peasants are making their concerns known forcefully in protest movements. They have played a major role in the social upheavals shaping the contemporary world. While rural revolts have occurred throughout history, in this century peasant protests have for the first time taken on wide political significance. The Mexican Revolution, the Russian Revolution, the Indian Independence Movement, the Chinese Revolution, the War in Vietnam, and the crisis of the 1980s in El Salvador all originated in part in agrarian problems. What, then, are the roots of conflict in the countryside? Why do peasants protest? Against whom? And what do they want? These are the questions we must answer in order to make sense of social conflict in the Third World and the social implications of economic development.

Today around one third of the people of Latin America live in the countryside. The rural areas of Latin America are characterized on the one hand by great estates, producing commodities for commercial and often export markets, and on the other by peasant subsistence agriculture. Known as the *latifundia/minifundia* system, this landholding structure has long been regarded as one of the basic causes of economic underdevelopment and social inequality in Latin America. Most students of the region have maintained that this structure originated in the colonial period and that it has remained fundamentally unchanged ever since.

This static image of a traditional countryside informs much of the development literature on Latin America. In the 1950s and 1960s, modernization theorists commonly applied the term *traditional* both to the structure of landholding and to the country people. By *traditional*, they meant archaic, resistant to change, and lacking in economic values. Thus, it was said, the great landlords were more concerned with social prestige than with economic profits, while the peasants, passive and fatalistic, cared only for economic subsistence. Given this fixed picture of the countryside, modernization theorists insisted that the impulse for change, whether it be economic modernization or political mobilization, must come from without.[1]

Despite its popular appeal, this approach provides little real insight into the genesis of rural conflict in Latin America. The problem is that it denies the country people their own history. Most important, it disregards the transformations in rural life that accompanied the growth of the agricultural export economy after 1850.[2] Exporters of primary materials under Iberian rule, the nations of Latin America continued to perform a similar economic role in the world economy following independence. In the nineteenth century, however, a major shift occurred in the kind of raw materials exported. Whereas in colonial times the great wealth of Latin America lay in her mineral resources, particularly silver and gold, after 1850 agricultural produce became a major source of export earnings. From 1850 through 1930, economic growth in Latin America occurred in large part through the expansion of commercial agriculture and stockbreeding to provision the burgeoning industrial centers of Europe and the United States. Population growth and urbanization in Europe and North America gave rise to sustained demands for foods like coffee, sugar, wheat, bananas, and beef that new transport systems made it possible for the Americas to supply. The growth of production for export markets profoundly affected land tenure and social relations in the Latin American countryside.

Economic growth is not a unilinear process generated solely by objective forces like trade, markets, or population growth. It is also a social process shaped by the often conflicting interests of the various social classes involved.[3] The crucial questions in agrarian society center on access to land—that is, on the definition of property rights—and on control of labor power. What appears to have happened in Latin America after 1850 is that the growth of overseas markets generated new economic opportunities to which both peasants and landlords responded. The result was competition for land and labor. In some places, landlords succeeded in expanding their properties and creating a dependent labor force by pressuring peasants off the land. In others, overt conflicts between peasants and landlords erupted. The patterns of land tenure and the types of economic activity that emerged in any given region reflected the outcome of this struggle. The basic antagonism between peasants and landlords has nowhere been resolved: as the agricultural export economy continues to expand, the conflicts go on. Indeed, many contemporary conflicts represent at once a continuation and a transformation of earlier struggles.

The forms taken by rural conflicts in the years of agricultural export growth after 1850 were influenced by existing patterns of land use. In areas where the land was already occupied by dense Indian settlements, the disputes were caused by the emergence of large commercial estates. Whether these great estates were the sugar *haciendas* created in Morelos, Mexico, or the coffee *fincas* set up in Guatemala and El Salvador, or the sheep ranches formed in Peru and Bolivia, the conflicts pitted landlords seeking to extend private property against Indian peasant communities resolved to retain their ancestral lands.[4] As the studies of David Browning, Andrew Pearse, and others have shown, the peasants usually lost out. Some, deprived of everything, were reduced to the status of service tenants on their former holdings, while others, preserving a pittance of land which could not support them, were obliged to work part-time for wages for neighboring landlords.[5]

A second form of conflict occurred in frontier regions very different from the sedentary Indian areas. In 1850 much of Latin America still lay outside of agricultural settlement, having never been penetrated by the colonial economy. These frontier regions included the arid wastes of northern Mexico, the disease-ridden coasts of Central America, Venezuela, Colombia, and Ecuador, the Amazon basin, the vast uplands of Brazil's interior, the rich Argentine pampa, and the woodlands of southern Chile.[6] The frontier zones were sparsely inhabited and usually not held in private ownership. They were waste or public lands belonging to the national or local government. With the increasing demand for tropical and temperate crops on the world market after 1850 and the extension of transport networks, many frontier regions in Latin America began to take on economic value. Eventually some became important centers of export production. In the occupation of these areas, conflicts over access to land and control of labor power often broke out between peasant settlers and large-scale land entrepreneurs. Apart from Brazil, surprisingly few studies of frontier occupation and frontier conflicts in other areas of Latin America have been written.[7]

Colombia, one of the largest and most populous of Latin American nations, possesses a particularly complex agrarian structure and a long tradition of rural unrest. The economic development of the country in the years between 1850 and 1930 was based on the export of a number of agricultural products, of which coffee proved the most important. The intensification of commercial production, attendant on the expansion of foreign markets, occurred primarily in the western regions and on the Caribbean coast, parts of

Map 1   Political Divisions of Colombia, 1930

which were still public lands as late as 1850. Colombia thus provides an excellent example of the expansion of export agriculture into public land areas and the accompanying conflicts between peasant settlers and land entrepreneurs for control over frontier resources. The purpose of this work is to analyze the dynamics of this important but hitherto neglected form of rural conflict and to ascertain its importance in the recent history of Colombia.

Previous historical studies of Colombian frontier development have centered almost exclusively on the area of Antioqueño colonization. This region, which includes the southern part of the department of Antioquia, Old Caldas, northern Tolima and northern Valle, is today the principal area of coffee production. A sparsely inhabited frontier zone, it was populated in the 1800s by settlements *(poblaciones)* of smallholders who, migrating south from the central highlands of Antioquia, began to cultivate the mountain slopes. Today this western coffee region is characterized by a relatively wide distribution of landholding.

Many historians of the Antioqueño settlement movement have found in it the genesis of a prosperous and democratic society of family farmers.[8] The Antioqueño experience has profoundly influenced general interpretations of Colombian frontier expansion. Colonization of the public domain, it is said, provides a democratic alternative to the rigid latifundia system. Frontier settlement gives the rural poor access to land; it offers them not only independence, but also the opportunity to improve their economic situation.[9] Furthermore, some researchers suggest, the frontier functioned as a safety valve to defuse whatever social tensions may have existed in the countryside. Most historians of Colombia assume that before the 1920s no collective social protest developed in the rural areas. Some attribute this supposed lack of interclass conflict to the strength of Liberal and Conservative party identifications. Others, however, point to the existence of open frontiers which, they maintain, gave the peasants an alternative to oppressive conditions on the great estates. Tenant farmers and sharecroppers who were discontented did not have to confront the estate owners or *hacendados* directly, but could always migrate to the frontiers where land was freely available.[10]

Recently the democratic image of the Antioqueño colonization movement has been called into question by several revisionist studies that stress the pivotal role of merchants and land speculators in directing the colonization and profiting from it.[11] By using the settlement movement to enhance the value of their own properties and by controlling the processing and marketing of coffee produced by small farmers, elite groups accumulated the capital they later invested in Medellín to create the largest industrial complex in Colombia.[12]

While the studies of Antioqueño colonization have contributed greatly to our knowledge of regional history, they tell only one small part of the story of Colombian frontier expansion. In reality the Antioqueño movement was a rather exceptional fragment of a much larger process of frontier development that took place throughout the middle and lower altitudes in the late nineteenth and early twentieth centuries. By neglecting this larger process, historians have fundamentally misunderstood the character of frontier expansion in Colombia. The democratic myth has little basis in historical reality. The advance of colonization and the formation of large properties were not, as has been assumed, contradictory: indeed, between 1850 and 1930, the allocation of public lands contributed directly to the consolidation of great estates in the most economically productive areas of the country. Furthermore, social conflicts did exist in the Colombian countryside prior to 1920 and such conflicts were centered in developing frontier regions.

Generally, frontier expansion occurred in Colombia in two successive stages. First, peasant families moved into frontier areas and cleared and planted the land, increasing its value by the labor they incorporated into it.[13] These pioneers resembled peasant proprietors in other parts of the country, but with one crucial difference: they did not hold legal title to the land they farmed. In the second stage, well-to-do land entrepreneurs appeared on the scene, intending to form large estates and convert the earlier settlers into tenant farmers by asserting property ownership over the land. This basic conflict of interests between self-provisioning settler families and elite investors intent on controlling the settlers' land and labor was intrinsic to the Colombian frontier experience. Under the conditions of an expanding export economy, struggle over that most important of agricultural resources— the land itself—signified, in effect, the more fundamental competition over the benefits of economic growth.

The basic tension between settlers and land entrepreneurs in frontier regions assumed different forms in different periods of Colombian history. The specific expression of the conflict and its outcome depended on the economic, social, and, perhaps most important, political conditions that shaped the relative ability of each group to realize its ends at a given time.

Of particular importance in influencing the tactics adopted by each side was the evolving land policy of the Colombian government. Since the essential issue at stake was that of opposing definitions of proprietary right, each side naturally sought to buttress its claims by seeking government sanction. With the expansion of the scope of government action in the early twentieth century, the attitude adopted by national authorities became an increasingly important factor in determining the balance of power between landlords and settlers. As well, the growing intensity of conflicts over public lands compelled the government to intervene by moving for the first time to establish a clear legal definition of private property. The fundamental issue of debate was the structure of land tenure in former frontier areas. A decision between the landlords' and the settlers' claims became a decision between two alternate paths to rural development—one based on a system of large estates, the other on a system of family farms.

Focusing on the development of frontier regions in Colombia in the time period between 1850 and 1936 helps to explain how processes that led to the concentration of landholding generated rural conflicts and how the conflicts in turn affected both the process of change and the government's policy toward those changes. An overview in Chapter 1 of frontier regions in nineteenth century Colombia illustrates the economic forces stimulating frontier expansion and the laws intended to regulate the allocation of public lands. The next two chapters introduce the protagonists—the settlers and the land entrepreneurs—and explore their social origins, motivations, and goals. The conflicts between these two groups in the years 1870-1920, centering on the resistance of peasant settlers to the encroachments of land entrepreneurs, are examined in Chapter 4. It concludes with a description of the patterns of land tenure and labor relations that emerged in Colombian frontier regions by 1920.

The second part of the book focuses on the transformation of the conflicts as the peasants took the offensive in the late 1920s and 1930s. In Chapter 5 the economic and political changes in the 1920s that gave peasants new leverage in their struggles against the latifundia are examined. Beginning in 1928, thousands of tenant farmers and others, calling themselves settlers, invaded many of the great estates that had been formed in frontier regions during the period of agricultural export growth. The settler movements that emerged in seven different regions of Colombia between 1928 and 1936 are the topic of Chapter 6. It was during these years that the public land issue became a national political problem. Chapter 7 deals with the Colombian government's response to the conflicts by passing Law 200 of 1936, generally described as the first modern agrarian reform law in Colombian history. Commonly thought to have favored the settlers, Law 200 in fact reinforced the land claims of the large estate owners and so helped to put in place the landholding structures that prevail in the Colombian countryside to the present day.

The Land Law of 1936 closed the era of Colombian history that, beginning in 1850, had been characterized by externally oriented export growth. The basic tension between settlers and entrepreneurs over public lands did not, however, end there. A brief epilogue suggests how this tension has been acted out in recent years in still different forms in new frontier regions. It has, for instance, contributed to *La Violencia*, the anarchic civil war that took 200,000 lives in the 1950s, and it fuels the guerrilla movements that operate in Colombian frontier zones today.

The interpretation of Colombian frontier development presented here rests upon a source not previously used by historians, the Colombian Public Land Correspondence, which contains all communications concerning public lands sent from the rural localities to the national government between 1830 and 1930.[14] In addition to grant applications and reports from surveyors and government officials, the archive contains hundreds of petitions from settler families that describe their living conditions and their struggles with land-lords and speculators. These petitions provide a unique perspective on the lives of a largely illiterate and inarticulate people. The materials in the Pub-lic Land Archive of Colombia allow insight into and understanding of two related developments important not just in Colombia but throughout Latin America: the expansion of agricultural frontiers and the history of the fron-tier settler. They also shed light on the origins of the concentration of land-holding, rural poverty, and social tension that mark the Colombian countryside today.

1

The Setting

During the 1850s the Italian geographer Agustín Codazzi travelled the length and breadth of Colombia, studying the country's physical features and economy. At the end of his voyages, Codazzi concluded that approximately 75 percent of Colombian territory consisted of public land or *terrenos baldíos* to which no one claimed ownership rights.[1] The major part of the baldíos lay in regions which remain undeveloped frontier regions even today—the vast, grassy plains known as the *Llanos* stretching across the eastern half of the country and the Amazonian jungles to the south. The public domain, however, also included areas that would become the subject of much dispute over the next century—immense tracts of land in the central core of the country along the Andean mountain slopes and in the Caribbean lowlands.[2]

The Colombian Frontier

To understand why widely scattered frontier lands still existed unclaimed in Colombia in the mid-nineteenth century, a brief overview of Colombian geography and settlement patterns is necessary. The Colombian landscape presents one of the most dramatic and complex of Latin American panoramas.[3] As indicated by map 2, the western third of the country is broken by three parallel chains of the Andes mountains running from the north diagonally toward the southwest where they come together near the Ecuadorian border in a massive abutment known as the *macizo central*. Each of these mountain ranges rise to heights of between 10,000 and 18,000 feet, only to drop precipitously into the deep valleys carved by the Magdalena and Cauca rivers. Because Colombia is located near the equator, it has no seasons: rather climate varies according to elevation above sea level. The three climatic zones into which Colombians customarily divide their country—*tierra caliente* (1,000-3,000 feet), *tierra templada* (3,000-6,500 feet), and *tierra fría* (6,500-10,000 feet)—each support different forests, different crops, and different pastures and breeds of livestock. The Andean region, together with the swampy plains of the Caribbean coast, constitutes the economic core of the country. More than 95 percent of the people of Colombia have always lived in this area.

The origins of such a concentration of population can be traced to the settlement patterns of pre-Columbian times. In the centuries preceding Columbus's discovery of the New World, the Indian peoples of Colombia, like those of Ecuador and Peru, lived primarily in the highland regions. Particularly important sedentary Indian cultures were to be found in the southeast, in the present-day departments of Cauca and Nariño, and in the eastern cordillera to the north of Bogotá. When Spaniards first appeared on the scene in the sixteenth century, they naturally gravitated toward the areas of dense Indian settlement where a supply of servile labor was available. They were also drawn to the mountains of Antioquia where gold mining was profitable. It was in these areas and at a few spots along the Magdalena River and on the Caribbean coast suitable for the docking of ships that the Spanish founded urban centers.[4]

The demand for foodstuffs generated by new towns and by the mining camps soon gave rise to regional markets for agricultural produce. Some of the agricultural needs of the Spanish settlements were supplied by the Indian communities, known as *resguardos*, which received confirmation of their communal land rights from the Spanish Crown. In a few parts of the country, notably the Santanders and central Antioquia, small farmers of Spanish or mixed Spanish-Indian background also produced a variety of foodstuffs for local consumption.

The great haciendas formed by the Spanish upper classes were a third source of agricultural supply. During the late sixteenth and seventeenth centuries, Spanish elites began to consolidate large private estates near the highland urban centers, along the rivers, and around the ports. Some of these colonial landholdings originated in grants of territory awarded by the Spanish Crown. Others resulted from de facto encroachments by local notables on Crown or Indian communal lands. Using various forms of tenant labor, the haciendas raised tobacco, sugar cane, cacao, wheat, and other sundry foodstuffs as well as various kinds of livestock. A number of immense cattle ranches also emerged in the valley and coastal lowlands and in the eastern plains, producing hides for export and leather, tallow, and jerky for internal consumption.[5]

Despite a marked tendency toward the formation of private properties in response to the growth of urban markets, the land over which individuals

Map 2   Major Mountains and Rivers of Colombia

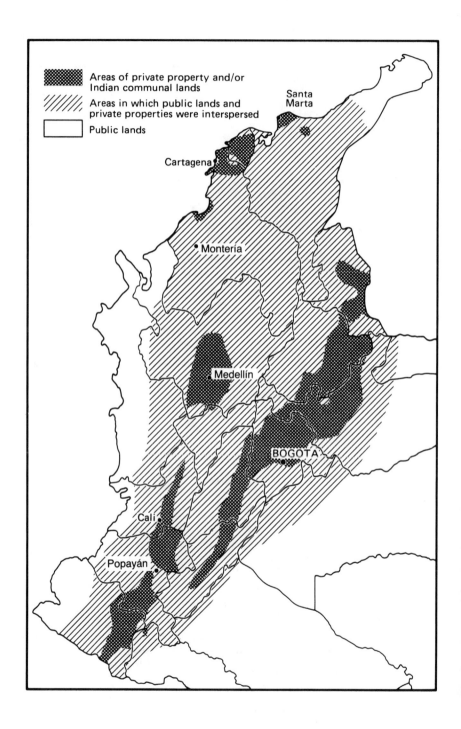

Areas of private property and/or Indian communal lands

Areas in which public lands and private properties were interspersed

Public lands

Santa Marta

Cartagena

Montería

Medellín

BOGOTA

Cali

Popayán

4

and institutions established ownership during the colonial period comprised but a small percentage of Colombian territory. Because the mountainous terrain was so formidable, the road system rudimentary, and labor scarce, territory that lay beyond a narrow radius of the populated settlements had little economic value. Such land remained unimproved wilderness throughout the colonial era, hindering trade and communications among the various regional nuclei and contributing to the crystallization of the intense regional loyalties that still divide Colombian society. Legally these wilderness lands formed part of the Spanish patrimony until 1821 when Colombia won her independence. At that time jurisdiction over the baldíos passed from the Spanish Crown to the newly constituted national government.

In Colombia, then, in the early nineteenth century there were many frontiers scattered throughout the temperate midlands and hot lowlands. Undeveloped public lands were to be found in all departments some distance beyond major population centers and transport routes. Generally these lands were the vacant territory their Spanish name, baldío, suggests. In contrast to North America, few native Indians inhabited such areas.

Map 3 shows the general location of the public domain around the time of Independence. Only in the Andean highlands and around major ports were there no public lands at all. Reconstructed from information on later land grants and disputes over public lands, this map should be regarded as but a rough approximation. The fact is that no one in the early nineteenth century knew exactly which land was privately owned and which was public domain. Private properties in the middle altitudes and lowlands often bordered on public lands, but the borders were not clearly defined. In colonial times there were no standardized measures of land and few trained surveyors. Furthermore, property limits were customarily designated by impermanent surface phenomena such as trees, stones, streambeds, mountain ridges, or neighbors' property lines. As time passed, the names of such boundary markers often were forgotten, or they shifted location or disappeared altogether. Even more confusing, many colonial deeds left the limits on one or more sides of a property completely unspecified. The result was that few people knew—or cared—exactly how much land they owned or what its true boundaries were.[6]

Map 3   Location of Public Lands in Colombia, circa 1821
Source: Reconstituted from local data in ANCB vols. 1–78 and *Memoria de Industrias*, 1931, vol. 5, pp. 249–410.

The Colombian government was no better informed. It possessed no record of land grants awarded during the colonial period or any concrete data on the extent of the public domain.[7] The technical skill, financial resources, and sustained commitment essential to a national land survey, useful as it might have been, far outstripped the capacities of the newly formed national government. The authorities openly acknowledged their ignorance in a statement appended to all land grants throughout the nineteenth and early twentieth centuries that held the applicants themselves responsible for ascertaining that the tracts they sought were truly public land and not part of someone else's property.[8]

In early nineteenth century Colombia, then, property rights in land were not clearly defined. There were, moreover, many different kinds of holdings including not only public lands, private properties, and Indian communal lands, but also Church-owned lands and municipal common lands (ejidos). This situation remained basically unchanged throughout the first half of the nineteenth century. In the aftermath of the Independence wars, exports of gold declined, without any other products to take its place. Third in population among the countries of South America, Colombia ranked seventh in export earnings until 1870. The Colombian agricultural economy, centered in the highlands, remained backward and stagnant. Agricultural markets were fragmented, and land values remained low.[9]

The Agricultural Export Economy

The colonial face of the Colombian countryside began to be transformed only with the development of an agricultural export economy after 1850. The integration of Colombia into world markets as an exporter of tropical agricultural and forest products stimulated a dramatic expansion of the rural economy into the public land regions. Between 1850 and 1885, Colombia underwent a series of brief export booms in tobacco (1854-77), cotton (1862-70), indigo (1868-76), and cinchona bark (1869-82), a forest product from which the medicine quinine, used to treat malaria, was extracted.[10] Lesser amounts of coffee, rubber, woven hats, vegetable ivory, and dye woods were also sent to Europe and the United States.[11] The many different products of this early period signalled not a healthy tendency toward diversification, but instead a multiplicity of failures.

Only after 1870 did the export crop that was to promote sustained economic growth take on significance. That crop was, of course, coffee. First cultivated in Norte de Santander in the part of the eastern cordillera near

Venezuela, coffee then spread south into Santander and Cundinamarca. In the 1890s, Cundinamarca replaced the Santanders as the major area of coffee production. In the nineteenth century coffee, like the export crops that preceded it, went through a number of cyclical expansions and recessions. After 1900 the coffee economy achieved its real importance. At this time the geographical focus of coffee cultivation shifted once again, to the west. Although the slopes of western Cundinamarca continued to produce, the major expansion of coffee in the twentieth century occurred in the central cordillera—in Antioquia, Caldas, northern Tolima, and northern Valle. Overall coffee was responsible for an increase of 450 percent in Colombian export earnings between 1870 and 1918. By 1920 coffee accounted for approximately 70 per cent of Colombian export revenues.[12]

While coffee was by far the most important export crop of the twentieth century, one further product emerged in the early 1900s along the Caribbean coast—bananas. Colombians had always produced large quantities of plantains, the long, tough, cooking bananas that could be fried, roasted, or boiled into stews. The production of sweet eating bananas for foreign markets was an innovation of the Boston-based United Fruit Company. In the years from 1899 through 1930, the United Fruit Company virtually created the Colombian banana enclave that covered five municipalities around the port of Santa Marta. By 1930, exports of bananas, directed primarily to British markets, accounted for 8 per cent of Colombian export revenues.[13] The banana economy is the prime example of foreign investment in export agriculture in Colombia. Most other export crops were developed by Colombians.

The growth of the agricultural export economy in the years 1850-1930 both encouraged and benefitted from improvements in internal transportation.[14] Until 1850, most cargos in Colombia travelled by mule back or by river raft. Such means of transport were notoriously slow, risky, and expensive. Around 1820 it still took from two to five months to travel from the port of Cartagena on the Caribbean coast to Bogotá, the capital of the country. During the twice yearly rainy seasons, river rafts often capsized, and the tortuous mule paths that wound through the mountains became virtually impassable. At such times, transport entrepreneurs occasionally substituted human cargo carriers for the less sure-footed mules.

During the period of agricultural export growth, the mule and the raft remained essential means of transport. But the introduction of the steamboat and, later, the railroad tied the country together in new ways. Steamboats were first used in the 1820s on the Magdalena River, the major route from the Caribbean coast to the interior. Regular steamboat service did not, however, begin until the tobacco export boom of mid-century. Most tobacco exported from Colombia in the 1850s and 1860s was raised on the banks of the Magdalena around Ambalema (Tolima), about half way down the river. The new tobacco shipments made investment in steam service a profitable venture to which the Colombian tobacco export houses quickly responded.

The other major transport innovation of the nineteenth century was the railroad. Although Colombian policy-makers expressed an interest in the railroad as early as 1840, not until the 1860s were the first tracks laid. The expansion of the coffee economy and the construction of railroads went hand in hand. Spurred on by government subsidies and by a Cuban entrepreneur who possessed the technical skills, Colombian investors took the initiative. Only 500 kilometers of track were laid during the economically uncertain and politically tumultuous years of the late nineteenth century. Under more propitious conditions in the first two decades of the twentieth century, another 800 kilometers were completed.[15] These railroads generally consisted of trunk lines linking areas of export production to the Magdalena River or to the nearest ocean port. Although the Colombian government also tried to encourage Colombian investors to build new roads, such efforts were less successful. Not until after 1930 when the truck and the bus became preferred forms of transport was the Colombian road system markedly improved.

While less extensive than those of many other Latin American countries, Colombian transport improvements of the 1850-1930 period were nonetheless significant. By reducing transport costs and by tying some parts of the country more closely together, the steamboat and the railroad stimulated interregional trade. These improvements, together with a growing population and the increased income from exports, also enlarged the internal market for foodstuffs, particularly meat.

The expansion of the Colombian cattle industry responded both to rising domestic meat prices and to technical improvements that transformed the ranching economy. Prior to 1870, herds of native cattle *(criollo)* ranged widely over the natural grasslands that blanketed the vast eastern plains and the Caribbean coast. The grasses native to Colombia could support no more than one steer on every two to three hectares, animals were small, and their meat tough and stringy.

In the latter part of the nineteenth century, a number of wealthy and well-educated ranchers made a concerted attempt to improve livestock productivity. Three mutually complementary innovations contributed to this end: sown pasture grasses, selective breeding, and barbed wire. New pasture seeds were introduced into Colombia from Brazil and Africa. Although their sowing required high capital investment, they allowed the pasturing of livestock on previously unusable land, supported more cattle in a smaller area, and produced heavier animals.[16] During the same years that Colombian ranchers were experimenting with new pastures, some well-to-do gentlemen began importing pure-bred brahama bulls, or *cebú*, from Europe to improve the quality of the Colombian stock. The introduction of barbed wire, which had been invented in the United States in the 1870s, permitted effective use of both the new pastures and the new breeds of cattle. By reducing costs and increasing the ease of fencing, barbed wire allowed ranchers to confine their livestock to designated pastures and begin selective breeding. The result was the development of specialized fattening ranches and a significant expansion of the livestock industry in the highlands and, even more so, in the lowlands.[17]

While most of the meat went to domestic markets, the export of hides was a small but important source of foreign earnings throughout the nineteenth century. Such exports grew steadily, from 1,400 tons in the early 1870s to 4,500 tons in 1910.[18] During two short periods in the late nineteenth century and throughout the early twentieth century, some live cattle were also sold abroad, primarily to Cuba and the other Caribbean islands. In addition, some Colombian cattle went to Venezuela and to Panama in the period 1903-1914 to feed the thousands of workers building the Panama Canal.

The expansion of agricultural production for export constituted the primary stimulus for rural economic growth in late nineteenth and early twentieth century Colombia. This period witnessed the tremendous expansion of coffee cultivation, the spread of cattle ranching, and the building of the railroads. Such growth did not, however, affect all parts of the country uniformly. The settled highland areas—the areas that had been the center of Spanish colonial life—stagnated or declined, while the new commercial activities centered in the sparsely populated and scarcely developed middle altitudes and lowlands.

The reasons for this have to do with climate. Because the Colombian highlands are cool, the crops that can be raised there are potatoes, corn, barley, and wheat, crops also produced in Europe and North America. What the industrial nations wanted and could not provide themselves were tropical products that, in Colombia, can only be raised in the middle altitudes and the lowlands. Coffee in Colombia grows on the mountain slopes of all three cordilleras at elevations from 3,000 to 6,500 feet. The cinchona bark tree flourishes in forests at similar altitudes. Colombia's other exports, such as bananas, tobacco, cotton, and rubber, are all products of the steamy lowlands.

Thus, during the period of export growth the intensification of commercial production occurred primarily in the midlands and lowlands in the western part of the country and along the Caribbean coast, areas comprised largely of public lands. This incorporation of frontier zones into the national economy was one of the most important aspects of change affecting the Colombian countryside in the late nineteenth and early twentieth centuries. People and resources flooded into frontier regions. While such individuals were responding to economic incentives afforded ultimately by the world market system, the land policy of the Colombian government played a major role in shaping the opportunities and economic activities of the various groups involved.

The Government and Public Land Legislation

When Colombia broke away from Spain in the 1820s, she became a constitutional republic with an elected president, a congress, and a judiciary. In the nineteenth century this formal governing system, however, existed more on paper than in reality. Reflecting the rugged geography, impossible communications, and regionalized economy, Colombia's political life was fragmented too. Although most laws were made in Bogotá, the central government had little effective power: it lacked the economic resources, bureaucracy, and armed might to enforce its will. The heart of politics lay in familial and local loyalties and rivalries; the way to get what one wanted was to cultivate personal connections with local and regional bosses. In the mid-nineteenth century patron-client associations took political form with the emergence of the national Liberal and Conservative parties. Each of these parties grouped together members of the upper classes, middle groups, peasants, and workers into vertical patronage networks. The significance of the Liberal/Conservative division is complex indeed; it is the subject of ongoing debate among Colombianists.[19] Regional, economic, ideological, and familial concerns all played a part. Throughout the nineteenth century and into the twentieth, the two parties struggled violently for control of the state. Recurrent civil wars pitted Liberals against Conservatives, culminating in the War of A Thousand Days (1899-1902) in which 100,000 Colombians perished. The stakes were high: to have one's party in power meant access to government jobs and contracts and influence with people in high places.

In Colombia, responsibility for the allocation of public lands lay with the national government.[20] Through legislation, Congress established the procedures by which frontier territory was to leave the public domain and specified who was eligible to claim its ownership. Until recently, such policy was the principal means by which the government sought to influence land tenure structures in the countryside. Although the laws sometimes were not enforced, they nevertheless influenced the evolution of landholding patterns and social relations in frontier regions.

Public land policy in Colombia has always manifested two fundamentally contradictory tendencies, both of which originated in Spanish colonial attitudes toward land. On the one hand, land policy was intended to foster rural economic growth and settlement by dividing the land at minimal cost among cultivators eager to till the soil. To this end, colonial authorities permitted anyone so wishing to farm or graze cattle freely on Crown lands. Those who did thereby merited legal titles to the land they had made productive.[21] The second approach to land policy views the public domain as a source of state income. From this perspective, it is logical to sell land to the highest bidder rather than giving it away. Financially strapped, the Spanish Crown resorted to such measures in the seventeenth century, selling deeds to immense tracts of undeveloped lands to whoever could pay the price.[22] This second tendency came to the fore in Colombia in the first decades after Independence.

From the 1820s through 1870, one overriding concern shaped Colombian public land policy—that of providing financial support for a bankrupt government.[23] The Independence war against Spain left Colombia saddled with the heaviest foreign debt of any South American country. The new nation found itself on the verge of collapse, forced to resort to repeated exactions from private citizens and to foreign loans to meet its obligations. The paucity of export revenues and political instability contributed to a continuing fiscal crisis that lasted throughout the nineteenth century.[24] Given the appalling financial condition of the country, it is not surprising that Congress viewed the public domain as a supplementary source of revenue. From the 1820s on, public lands provided an essential prop to the Colombian state credit system. The Colombian Congress issued certificates of public debt redeemable in public lands to back the national debt and to pay veterans of the Independence wars. Such certificates also were used to subsidize the construction of roads and railroads. Railroad companies, for example, generally received vouchers worth 200 to 300 hectares of public lands for each kilometer of rail line completed.[25]

The first emission of land certificates occurred in 1838 with several more emissions over the next sixty years. Once distributed, the land certificates did not have to be exchanged for land, but could be freely bought and sold. In Bogotá and Medellín, dealers in government debt paper known as *agiotistas* made a living specializing in such transactions. Individuals who wished to acquire a tract of public land bought as many certificates as they needed and then petitioned the government for a grant of land in whatever part of the country appealed to them. Until the 1880s the law set no limits on the number or size of land grants that could be acquired by any one certificate-holder.

Although the fiscal motive was primary, from the beginning Colombian legislators also expressed a minor interest in encouraging settlement of the public lands. As in earlier times, poor people were permitted to squat on the public domain. But they became eligible for title to their fields only under special circumstances. Colonization policy in Colombia between 1820 and 1870 was directed to three specific ends: through the offer of free land, Bogotá aimed to attract foreign immigrants, to populate the regions adjacent to its international borders, and to provide for the upkeep of national road-ways. In contrast to the large areas allotted holders of land certificates, how-ever, the legislators strictly limited the size of the parcels granted cultivators of public lands.[26]

The early colonization policy produced few concrete results. Despite the oft-expressed concern to attract North American and European farmers, the hoped-for influx of immigrants never materialized.[27] The reasons have to do with the tropical climate, the constant civil wars, and the financial debility of the state which precluded active recruiting programs. Those relatively few people of German, English, and Lebanese descent who did seek their fortunes in Colombia became merchants, storeowners, and mining engineers, not peasant farmers.[28] Intended to secure Colombia's international frontiers against her predatory neighbors, the laws providing free grants to settlers along the borders with Venezuela and Peru were no more successful.[29] These borders, which cut through the eastern plains and the Amazonian jungles, were far too isolated to attract either native or foreign settlers. Except for a few Indian groups, these areas remain virtually uninhabited today. The laws permitting free grants to settlers along national roads that passed through frontier regions also had little practical effect. The aim was to populate the roadside so as to provide food and lodging for travellers, pasturage for pack animals, and maintenance for the roadbed during the rainy months. How-ever, the handful of squatters who did come to such regions were generally too poor or too ignorant to legalize their holdings. The result was that in the 1820-1870 period few independent settlers obtained titles to the land they farmed.

Those settlers who managed to acquire property rights did so primarily as members of larger settlements known as poblaciones. During the nineteenth century, the Colombian Congress decreed a number of corporate public land grants to permit the creation of agricultural villages in frontier regions. This

type of colonization represented a continuation of Spanish colonial practices in the population of new areas.[30]

Occasionally the Congress passed laws providing land for new villages
with the aim of stimulating the migration of rural cultivators into uninhabited areas. In the 1830s, for example, Bogotá designated territory for the
formation of new poblaciones in several isolated regions of the Caribbean
coast.[31] None of these settlements, however, ever amounted to anything.

Only in the Antioqueño region did the legislation concerning corporate
settlements bear fruit. At least twenty-one important coffee-producing municipalities in the central cordillera originated in concessions of public lands
to settlements during the nineteenth century.[32] Typically, such concessions
were granted in response to petitions from large groups of settlers already
farming the territory to which they sought title. Each settlement received
from 7,500 to 12,000 hectares of land, of which 200 - 400 hectares were
reserved for the village center (area de población). A surveyor, appointed
by the departmental government and paid jointly by the settlers, measured
and mapped the land area of the grant. Then it was apportioned among qualified households by the surveyor and an agrarian committee of three respected
people selected by local authorities. Each family received both a lot in the
village large enough for a house and yard or a store and an allocation in the
countryside. Most families qualified for around 32 hectares of farmland.
Even those with many children or much land already under cultivation could
claim no more than 150 hectares.[33]

Most of the Antioqueño settlements that received corporate land grants
were founded during the years 1860-1890. After the turn of the century, as
the Antioqueño colonization movement reached its geographical limits and
the interests of those merchants and landowners who had encouraged the
migrations turned elsewhere, the settlement legislation fell into disuse.

The laws that focused on colonization in settlements aimed to discourage
the concentration of landholding and to foster the proliferation of medium-
sized, well cultivated, owner-operated farms. It must be recognized, however, that these laws were one minor part of a much larger body of legislation that, in favoring the holders of public debt certificates, also favored the
alienation of public lands in large expanses.

In sum, from 1820 through 1870 baldíos legislation primarily reflected
the fiscal preoccupations of the Colombian government. Then in the 1870s
and 1880s a significant reform of public land policy occurred: the aim of
promoting the economic exploitation of frontier areas through free grants of
land gained precedence over the financial considerations that had shaped
public land legislation previously. This policy reorientation stemmed both

directly and indirectly from the growth of the export economy. The gradual increase in export revenues, together with a timely renegotiation of the foreign debt, had somewhat eased the government's financial woes.[34] It was patently clear that, owing to the depreciation of the debt certificates, the public lands were in any case a very tiny source of income. Meanwhile, the export booms of the 1850s and 1860s convinced the Colombian upper classes of the possibilities for national development and individual profit afforded by commercial agriculture. As the export fever rose, leading merchants and politicians wrote treatises on crop production, invested in large-scale agricultural enterprises, and urged others to take part in such laudable and "patriotic" endeavors.[35] At the same time, the Colombian government itself began to take an active interest in stimulating rural economic growth. In the late 1860s national authorities commenced to subsidize the construction of railroads, and Congress established a Department of Agriculture to encourage the adoption of new crops and farming methods.[36]

The reform of public land policy represented another way by which the government endeavored to stimulate rural production. The aim was to increase commercial production by rewarding those who made economic use of the land with ownership rights. Laws 61 of 1874 and 48 of 1882 set forth the major tenets of the new policy.[37] Leaving fiscal considerations behind, these laws proposed a new criterion for landownership: "The property of public lands is acquired by its economic exploitation, whatever the extension involved," declared Law 48 of 1882. In accordance with this principle, whoever put public lands to use by sowing crops or improved pastures thereby qualified to receive a free grant of that territory plus an adjacent undeveloped tract equal in size.[38]

During the late nineteenth and early twentieth centuries, public lands could still be bought with the old land certificates. But by sanctioning "cultivators' rights," the legislative reforms created a new channel by which people might acquire property rights in public lands. These provisions opened the way for a new type of cultivator whose opportunities for legal ownership no longer were limited to a few hectares, but might well include hundreds or even thousands of hectares, depending on one's resources. In this way, the reforms of the 1870s and 1880s sought to induce wealthy individuals with capital and hired labor to found productive enterprises in frontier regions.

The reforms aimed, as well, to protect peasant settlers and to encourage others to follow their lead in populating frontier zones. The reform laws for the first time recognized the existence of independent frontier settlers who did not form part of the Antioqueño settlements. The laws endeavored to assure them title to their claims and to protect them against arbitrary dispossession. According to the 1882 statute, "Cultivators squatting on public lands with shelter and crops will be considered possessors in good faith and shall not be deprived of possession except by sentences handed down in civil court." The laws specified that even if they had not yet petitioned for legal titles, settlers by the fact of occupation thereby established rights in the land. Certificate-holders were expressly forbidden to purchase territory already opened by settler families, and in disputes over land rights, the law favored settlers who had tilled their fields for five years or more over all other claimants. Thus in the years after 1870, Colombian legislators explicitly recognized a potential conflict of interest between settlers and large-scale entrepreneurs and, in so doing, took the settlers' side. Cultivators of public lands were the only peasant group in Colombia whose rights received explicit legal definition in the late nineteenth and early twentieth centuries. At the same time, the government encouraged independent settlers to apply through legal channels for free titles to the land they tilled, for without property deeds they could not sell their plots or mortgage them. By thus reinforcing the legal privileges of cultivators and facilitating their acquisition of property rights, the Colombian government aimed to stimulate settlement and economic use of the public domain by large and small-scale producers alike.

It may seem surprising that in a continent where politics was the province of the elites, a land policy so apparently responsive to peasant interests became law. In other Latin American countries—Brazil and Chile, for example—public land policy throughout the nineteenth century reflected the concerns of the great landowners and political bosses. It is not entirely clear why Colombian policy took the direction it did. Several possible reasons, however, may be suggested. In the 1870s and 1880s when the reforms were passed, the Liberal party held power in Colombia. Colombian Liberals, like their French and Spanish counterparts, hoped to build a society of small rural capitalists. Only a wide distribution of landownership, they believed, could provide the social basis for economic progress and a stable republican political order.[39] Whereas other Liberal reforms, such as the disamortization of Church wealth, were vehemently opposed by Colombian Conservatives, the public land initiative aroused little controversy. And when the Conservatives returned to power after 1885, they did nothing to change the laws.

This apparent acceptance by the Conservatives of the Liberal initiative suggests that a land policy favorable to peasants may have reflected not just Liberal thought but an approach to rural development acceptable to both parties. Seeking to promote rural economic growth, Colombian politicians

in the 1860s and 1870s became increasingly critical of the latifundia system that kept much land in the older areas out of production. As made clear
by the congressional debates of this period that criticized the great estates
as an impediment to development, Colombian statesmen were well aware
that the mere titling of public land did not necessarily result in its economic
use. One of the primary aims of the new land policy, therefore, was to pre-
clude the formation of latifundia in new areas.[40] Seen in this light, a policy
that permitted the donation of public lands to small settlers signified public
acknowledgement of the reality of Colombian rural life. Peasants did use
their land more intensively than the great landlords[41], and smallholders in
Colombia did produce export crops like tobacco, coffee, and cacao as well
as agricultural commodities for the home market.

The concern to discourage the monopolization of frontier land by grantees unable or unwilling to make use of it was manifested in other ways. In
1882 Colombian lawmakers decided for the first time to limit the maximum
size of public land grants. Law 48 of that year set the top allocation for a
single grant at 5,000 hectares; it was reduced to 2,500 hectares in 1912.[42]
Another measure provided that all public land grants that remained unexploited for a period of ten years should automatically revert to the public
domain. Meant to oblige certificate-holders to put the grants they purchased
into production, this provision also appeared on the law books in 1882.[43]

If the public land reform of the 1870s and 1880s grew out of the government's desire to stimulate rural production, it also responded to the economic interests of the politicians themselves and the social groups they
represented. By endowing peasant pioneers with legal rights, the legislation
encouraged the rural poor to migrate toward the middle altitudes and lowlands. The peopling of the frontier zones opened opportunities for productive undertakings on a large scale. As British engineer Juan H. White observed
in 1918:

> Few mines and even fewer agricultural operations established in isolated and
> sparsely populated areas produce returns that adequately compensate the en-
> trepreneur for his investment. Only with an influx of population and the open-
> ing of transport routes can such enterprises become profitable.[44]

The presence of settlers was necessary to give value to the land, to create
regional markets, and to provide labor, not only for family farms, but also
for large-scale commercial enterprises. The fact that the legislation made
no attempt to keep resident laborers on the old highland estates only confirms what the historical literature suggests: political power in Colombia in

the 1870s and 1880s resided with those merchants, financiers, commercial agriculturalists, and land speculators whose interests lay in the dynamic expansion of the export economy.[45]

When Colombian public land policy is compared with that of other Latin American countries, some instructive similarities and differences are evident. The use of public lands to supplement government revenues, whether by the issue of debt certificates, transport allocations, or outright sale, was common throughout Latin America. Such practices contributed notably to the concentration of landholding in Mexico and elsewhere during the nineteenth century.[46] Efforts to foster the formation of a stratum of independent smallholders through free grants to immigrant families were widespread in the same period. In Argentina, southern Brazil, and southern Chile, these efforts bore results in the formation of settlements of German and Italian farmers.[47] In countries like Brazil and Argentina where immigration from Europe also contributed a significant proportion of the labor force in export agriculture, local peasants were considered lazy, backwards, and constitutionally inferior. Protective legislation providing native settlers with land rights in these countries came late or not at all.[48]

In contrast, in Colombia, where immigration did not provide an alternative source of labor, the native settler was lauded as a hardworking, determined, even heroic type whose efforts to open new lands advanced the cause of national development.[49] The prosperity of the Antioqueño colonization region contributed notably to this image, which stood in sharp contrast to the derogatory vision of the squatter in Brazil and Chile. The fact that smallholders played an important role in the cultivation of certain export crops in Colombia, particularly tobacco and coffee, lent credence to the portrait of the small cultivator as a potentially active producer of agricultural commodities both for the home market and for export.[50] Only in Costa Rica, where the conditions of export growth were similar to those of Colombia, did legislation in the nineteenth century also encourage homesteading on the part of native settlers. In Costa Rica, as in Colombia, the concentration of export agriculture in public land regions and the paucity of foreign immigration contributed to the elaboration of a public land policy favorable to peasant cultivators.[51]

These, then, were the elements particular to Colombia—a widely scattered frontier; an export economy developing on the mountain slopes and lowlands; and a land policy that encouraged both capitalist investors and peasant settlers to make use of frontier lands. We know that after a fitful start, the export economy did grow. We also know that in the late nineteenth and early twentieth centuries many frontier areas became centers of economic activity and that they were settled and carved into private properties. But the most important questions remain. How did this occur? What social groups responded to the new market and legislative incentives, and how did these groups interact? And what specific forms of land tenure, social relations, and economic activity emerged out of this interaction? To answer these questions, it is necessary to examine the process of frontier expansion as revealed through the Public Land Correspondence.

2

The Peasant Settlers

The first export crops in Colombia were raised by large landowners on private estates. The tobacco economy of the 1850s and 1860s ran its course around Ambalema (Tolima), an old cattle ranching area where there were few public lands. The first coffee trees in Norte de Santander, the Tequendama province of Cundinamarca, and southeastern Antioquia were planted on estates that dated from the colonial period. With the success of such crops and improvements in transportation, a process of frontier expansion—of incorporation of public lands into the national economy—began. Peasant settlers, who are called *colonos* in Colombia, led the way.[1]

Origins and Migrations

The origins of Colombian colonos are shrouded in obscurity. Some had lived in frontier areas for many years. Since the colonial era, the rural poor tended to build their huts and plant gardens on unclaimed territory near the haciendas or within walking distance of the village centers. Over time they gradually enlarged their holdings, and, if their claims went unchallenged, passed them on to their children. Some colonos, then, inherited their role, with some families, particularly in very remote areas, remaining squatters for generations.[2]

Colonos were of a variety of racial backgrounds. Some were black, others Indian, but the majority were of mixed ancestry. Along the Caribbean and Pacific coasts and in the Cauca River valley where a slave labor system had predominated in the colonial era, most colonos descended from African slaves. Prior to abolition, runaways sought refuge in the inaccessible baldío forests where they grouped together to form *palenques* or armed agrarian colonies. Such fortified settlements, into which whites intruded only at their own risk, were to be found in the Caribbean coast, Chocó, Antioquia, Cauca, Valle, Cundinamarca, and the eastern plains in the late eighteenth and early nineteenth centuries. Each settlement included hundreds, if not thousands, of former slaves.[3]

Other blacks who won legal manumission also withdrew from white society. Freedmen from the Chocó mining gangs moved deep into the tropical jungles along the Pacific coast where they became subsistence farmers, while Cauca Valley slaves who managed to buy their freedom formed smallholdings in the craggy mountains above the estates that monopolized the valley floor. With the formal abolition of slavery in 1851, the movement of blacks and mulattos toward the public lands assumed even greater proportions. Many ex-slaves resisted their former masters' attempts to induce them to remain on the haciendas. Seeking economic independence, they struck out on their own to till public lands nearby.[4]

Some squatters in other regions were of pure Indian blood. Various Indian communities in western Colombia and along the Caribbean coast lacked titles to the territory on which they had lived since colonial times, whether because the Spanish never created resguardos there or because provincial governments had decreed their dissolution. Although they formed closed corporate communities with their own political authorities, in their legal relationship to the land, these Indians were colonos occupying baldíos.[5] In the eastern highlands, it was the final breakdown of the Indian communities in the first half of the nineteenth century that gave rise to a population of Indian colonos. The encroachments of outsiders, the fragmentation of the resguardos, and finally, the Liberal laws of the 1850s that decreed an end to communal land tenure deprived many of the Indians of Boyacá and Cundinamarca of their traditional holdings.[6] Some of these people eventually found their way to public lands part-way down the mountains.

In the early decades of the twentieth century, the number of Indian colonos in the central and western cordilleras also began to grow. Cattle haciendas expanded into the surviving resguardos, forcing some Indians to move onto baldíos further up the mountains or else south into the jungles of Caquetá and Putumayo.[7] This situation gave rise to a strong Indian resistance movement determined to defend the resguardos, a movement which continues active in western Colombia today. Beyond their efforts to defend the resguardos, the original leaders of this movement, Manuel Quintín Lamé and José Gonzalo Sánchez, also petitioned the national government to protect Indian colonos of public lands.[8]

If black or Indian colonos predominated in some areas, the majority were of mixed Spanish-Indian heritage reflecting the primarily *mestizo* composition of the Colombian population. Many of these settlers were the sons and daughters of small proprietors, tenant farmers, sharecroppers, or artisans from the highlands.[9] They had turned to the public lands either because adverse conditions at home compelled them to migrate or because they envisaged in the life of the independent colono prospects for a better future.

In the latter part of the nineteenth century both push and pull factors combined to direct the attention of the laboring classes toward settlement of the public lands. With the growth of the export economy, the densely inhabited eastern highlands underwent relative economic decline. Artisans in the towns and rural areas of Santander and Boyacá lost their markets as cheap imports replaced home industry. In some areas an increasing concentration of landholding occurred, and agricultural land was turned into pastures for cattle which required less labor. The real wages of tenants and day laborers on large estates tended to decline, while hacendados imposed more onerous work obligations. Meanwhile in those upland zones with a multitude of small properties, continued subdivision through inheritance accentuated the problem of *minifundismo* or excessive fragmentation of land holding to the point where some families had hardly enough land to support themselves.[10] In the highlands of Cauca and Antioquia, similar conditions prevailed. One observer, a priest writing in 1890, attributed migration away from central Antioquia where he lived to the monopolization of the land by the rich, exploitative terms of tenancy, soil exhaustion, and soaring food prices.[11]

As well as economic hardship, political tensions pushed some people out of the highlands toward the public lands. The civil wars between Liberals and Conservatives caused many rural people to abandon their homes. Some left to evade military conscription, while others fled from the threat of political retaliation or the actual destruction wrought by war.[12]

In the same period that living conditions worsened in the areas of colonial settlement, public lands in the middle and lower altitudes became increasingly attractive. Economic growth in those regions and the concomitant construction of transport routes heightened the appeal of the baldíos. By cultivating public lands in areas where communications and proximity to markets allowed scope for productive activity, former tenants, artisans, and *minifundistas* could aspire to improve their economic situation. The new legislation passed in the 1870s and 1880s that promised state support and protection for settlers of public lands probably also encouraged some to assume colono status.

For these reasons, the migration of the rural poor to public lands accelerated after 1850. The trickle of colonos became a steady stream. For some families, the occupation of public lands involved a displacement of only a few miles from their place of origin. Others moved over greater

distances, apparently aware in advance where to find unclaimed land apt
for colonization.

Some, it seems, were alerted to possibilities for settlement by the induce-
ments of land entrepreneurs and colonizing companies. Typically in nineteenth century Colombia, the government paid road contractors in tolls and
in grants of public lands along the roadside. Only with the quickening of
commercial activity that came from a rise in population could they hope for
a return on their investment. Particularly in the Antioqueño region, but also
in some other parts of Colombia, road contractors and individuals who owned
real estate in isolated zones tried to stimulate an influx of settlers so as to
increase the value of their properties. For example, merchants from Medellín who had purchased 10,000 hectares of undeveloped land in central Caldas
around 1900 posted broadsides shortly thereafter in the village of Támesis
advertising free land for settlement to the south. The response was enormous:
in the years 1890-1910, several thousand colonos converged on the area
and the new municipality of Belalcázar took form. [13] Another merchant group
who built a road connecting Bogotá to the eastern plains made a concerted
effort to populate the land through which the road passed. The activities of
this particular company in encouraging colonization gave rise to the present-
day municipalities of Colombia (Huila) and Uribe (Meta). [14] It should be
noted that in order to attract settlers, such companies sometimes portrayed
land that had already been titled to be public land, free for the taking. Consequently, in the early stages of frontier development some colonos unwittingly squatted on titled properties, often with the tacit consent of the owners. [15]

Although privately directed colonization schemes were not uncommon in
Colombia in the nineteenth and early twentieth centuries, relatively few outside of the Antioqueño region bore fruit. Not many entrepreneurs, foreign
or Colombian, had the resources, know-how, or sustained commitment to
implement them. And so such colonization efforts account for but a minor
part of the settlement movements that took place.

Another way that peasants learned of areas to settle was by involvement
in the civil wars. If some settlers moved into frontier regions seeking refuge
from the struggles, others became acquainted with such zones through active participation in the interminable wars of the nineteenth century. The
fighting took the rural poor, who were conscripted by the government or swept
up by rebel forces, out of their home communities into new areas that some
found preferable to the places they had left behind. And so they remained
to open small farms after the wars subsided. New agricultural villages of a
single political affiliation emerged in this way in Huila, Tolima, Valle, and
Bolívar. [16] The last and bloodiest of the nineteenth century conflicts, the

War of a Thousand Days (1899-1902), also precipitated important colonization movements in the Sumapaz region of Cundinamarca and around the
Caribbean port of Santa Marta where the United Fruit Company had just
made its appearance.[17]

The example of the United Fruit Company suggests one further incentive
for migration into public land regions. Numerous highland peasants first
moved into the middle and lower altitudes in response to employment opportunities in export agriculture, mining, or the forest industry. Some of
these entered the dense forests which blanketed much of the public domain
to forage for cinchona bark and other forest products that could be sold to
exporters. Others responded to the lure of higher wages and more attractive
work contracts in tobacco production, the coffee haciendas, or the banana
plantations. Once such people had become familiar with the area and accumulated some savings, they left the plantations and became independent
producers on public lands nearby. There was, thus, a radiating effect as
new land was being brought into production.

The settlement of El Líbano (Tolima), a frontier area in the central cordillera, provides one example of this kind of step migration. The collapse of
the Ambalema tobacco boom around 1870 sent many migrants into the previously unsettled Líbano area, some forty miles to the northwest. Aided by
a Liberal partisan and coffee entrepreneur with access to tobacco money,
these migrants, who were of Antioqueño origin, founded a new municipality. El Líbano soon became a major center of coffee production. By the first
decades of the twentieth century, coffee producers had become accustomed
to send recruiters to the eastern highlands to contract migrant harvest workers. Once they arrived, some of these coffee pickers stayed on for a few
years as tenant farmers, after which they moved out of the temperate coffee
zone toward the cold mountain region of Murillo a few miles away. On the
public lands remaining there, this second wave of migrants began to plant
small fields of potatoes as they had done in the uplands of Boyacá before
their wanderings began.[18] The municipality of El Líbano, then, took form
through a series of step migrations that were conditioned by the expansions
and contractions of the export economy.

The settler migrations of the late nineteenth and early twentieth centuries
thus reflected the economic, social, and institutional movements of Colombian life. In some areas settlement was conditioned by push factors—the
slaves' abhorrence of slavery, the Indians' loss of communal lands, economic depression, population pressure, political strife. And so, the frontier
became a kind of refuge where families forced out of their home communities could provide for their subsistence needs with a certain measure of in-

dependence. In many of the migrations that began after 1850 pull factors were also at work. These migrations acquired momentum from the expansion of export agriculture and the extension of the transport network that accompanied it. The peasants themselves responded to the incentives of free land and of new markets that emerged in regions of export agriculture.

Economic Activities

In many areas, in the initial occupation of the land each settler cleared several small parcels some distance from one another.[19] The reasons for this behavior are not fully understood. In the highland or Andean areas some cultivators perhaps sought to minimize the risk factor inherent in agricultural production by maintaining gardens in more than one ecological zone. The scarcity of available land in other regions may have compelled colonos there to adopt a similar practice. Explained an inhabitant of Lorica (Bolívar) on the Caribbean coast:

> Here small colonos are restricted in their productive activity . . . to those intermediate areas left . . . by the rich who monopolize the land voraciously. As a result the settlers usually possess two or more cultivated parcels some distance apart which, added together, total no more than twenty hectares.[20]

Another motive may have been speculation. By clearing several areas, settlers were attempting to establish property claims to the intervening land which could then be sold off to later arrivals.[21]

Clearing was accomplished using slash and burn techniques: the trees and brush were hacked down with axes and machetes, left to dry for a time, and then set afire. Clearing by fire not only saved human labor, but produced soil rich in vegetal matter. The next step was to sow a crop of maize, a productive staple that could be expected to provide for a family's subsistence within a few months and also yield a marketable surplus. All planting was done with digging sticks: ploughs have always been impracticable in a mountain setting.[22]

The initial period of homesteading was a difficult time for most colonos in that it required investments in tools, seed, and food before the land came into production. Settlers tried to meet such expenses in a variety of ways. They hunted and fished to sustain their families. Some also made charcoal or cut wood, which they sold in town or to river boats for fuel. Others panned the streams for gold. In Caldas, which was dotted with pre-Columbian Indian graves, a number of settlers became *guaqueros* who looted funerary caches for the gold jewelry and implements for which the original inhabitants of Colombia were noted. Settlers who lived near larger populations sometimes hired themselves out as day laborers on haciendas in the vicinity. Many also had to borrow money from local merchants.[23]

In the more isolated areas along the Pacific coast and the Gulf of Urabá, colonos made their living from the collection of tropical wood products, especially rubber and vegetable ivory *(tagua)*, which they sold to export companies. So long as export prices remained high, the colonos devoted most of their energy to collecting, planting only a few subsistence crops on the side. When the market plunged, most turned to agriculture full time.[24] An essential part of the initial stages of colonization, these various activities continued to provide colono families with supplementary income even after they had established themselves on the land.

Those who lived in remote areas, generally the poorest of the colonos, practiced shifting agriculture. After several harvests of corn, beans and sweet manioc *(yuca)* in one place, they moved a short distance away to prepare new fields, leaving the forest to grow back over the previous clearing.[25] As commercial crops increased in value and competition over public lands grew, settlers, particularly those in more centrally located areas, tended to remain in one spot. They enlarged their fields by a hectare or two each year, resulting in small farms of about ten to twenty hectares in size.

Once they had become rooted in one place, settlers planted a greater variety of produce, including both basic foods for local consumption and a selection of commercial crops. Maize, beans, sweet manioc, potatoes, plantains, *arracacha*, and fruits figured among the staples of colono agriculture, depending on the climatic zone. Squatters also produced significant quantities of sugar cane, wheat, rice, cotton, tobacco, cacao, and coffee, all of which had a wider market. Although many settlers kept hogs, chickens, and a milk cow or two on the side, they did not devote their claims to extensive grazing. Only along the Caribbean coast did colonos sometimes own small herds of cattle that fed on the grasses growing wild in that part of the country.[26]

Like most Latin American peasants, Colombian colonos farmed by interplanting their crops. Instead of maintaining separate fields for each product, tubors, vegetables, and productive trees were planted together. As many as seventy species of plants often were crowded into plots no more than two to three hectares in size. What appeared a tangled mass of vegetation was in fact a highly productive and efficient agricultural system that fed the settlers' families and supplied their basic needs. From these plots they also took building materials for the thatched huts of bamboo and adobe in which they lived and extracted wood for fuel, gourds for cooking, and medicinal plants for home cures.[27]

Though often limited to subsistence production in the first years of settlement, most colonos were not content just to eke a living from the soil. Rather, they sought to improve their economic situation through production for commercial markets. In choosing where to settle, colonos throughout Colombia showed a decided preference for sites with access to markets. Many clustered along the waterways—on the banks of streams and rivers and on fertile river islands—where produce could be transported to town in dugout canoes. Colonos also squatted along roads and railways in those areas where the land had not already been monopolized by speculators.[28] In such regions as the central cordillera and the Cauca Valley where lucrative cash crops like coffee or cacao could be grown, colono smallholders accounted for much of their production. In other less advantageously situated areas, colonos were eager to increase their incomes by creating market contacts. Groups of squatters living in particularly isolated regions frequently cut mule paths to the nearest river or town. Occasionally they sent impassioned pleas to the central government asking for penetration roads that would allow them to break out of subsistence into the market economy.[29]

Social Relations Among Settlers

The economic circumstances of colono life profoundly influenced social relations. Evidence of cooperation is particularly notable on the Caribbean coast where ecological conditions gave rise to close-knit communities with common lands. In the coastal lowlands, the rhythm of peasant life revolved around the alternation of wet and dry seasons. As the water in rivers and marshes receded in dry periods, settlers moved onto the fertile river banks where they planted crops and grazed their livestock. With the return of the rains that brought flooding, they moved cattle to higher ground and hunted and fished the swollen streams. Making optimal use of the riverine environment required a flexible approach to landholding. In this ever-changing landscape, fixed individual claims made no sense, and so peasant communities continued to regard the marshy lowlands and brush-covered hills as common lands—territory that could be used by all members of the community— well into the twentieth century. For years after municipal ejidos had been abolished in Colombia, they maintained these communal lands which they similarly called "ejidos".[30]

If the coastal environment fostered a strongly communal orientation, in the Andean region settlers also provided one another with mutual aid, particularly in the early stages of colonization. Generally settlers opened a new area either in extended family groups or *en companía*, meaning that several friends promised to farm together and divide the product among them for a few years. The initial back-breaking work of clearing and sowing virgin land often involved the whole neighborhood through labor exchanges called *convites*.[31] In contrast to the coast, however, settlers in the Andean region were more likely to stake individual claims, and it was in the interior that the individualistic, competitive side of colono life most clearly manifested itself.

Students of the Brazilian frontier have identified two distinct types of pioneers—the petty speculator *(grilheiro)* who cleared land to sell it and the farmer who followed behind.[32] No such distinction is possible for Colombia where many farmers of public lands, seeking to get ahead, also indulged in small scale speculation. Often the first settlers to enter a given region simply claimed large areas of unimproved land around their fields. They either tried to keep other settlers out or else charged them for the right to settle there.[33] By Colombian law, public lands could not be bought and sold, but the improvements or *mejoras* on such land—clearings, sown crops, fences, and buildings—were negotiable. There was much buying and selling of mejoras among colonos, and in many places colonos tried to use such negotiations to assert illegal claims to the land. For example, it was common for a settler who sold usufruct rights to a field of one or two hectares to include in the sale some fifty to one hundred hectares of unimproved land nearby. If a latecomer tried to settle there, the new "owner" complained to local authorities, presenting the bill of sale as proof of property. Where the authorities were responsive to such de facto claims, the first settlers assumed a privileged position in local society.[34] In other places, where local officials were not so compliant and where later settlers refused to recognize the claims, chronic friction resulted.

The efforts of colono families to improve their economic position at the expense of their neighbors precipitated numerous conflicts between first occupants and later arrivals. A report written in 1919 by the commissioner of Caquetá in southwestern Colombia described problems there which characterized many zones of colono settlement:

> It often happens that new colonos arrive who think that they have the right to clear land that never has been occupied or granted to anyone, and they extend their clearings right up to where the cultivated fields of another colono begin. The first settler thus is deprived of the possibility of enlarging his holding and of his legal right to an unimproved portion of land in the event that he seek a

government grant. These practices give rise to many disputes. . . . Usually
the stronger of the two contenders wins, and either the original settler is compelled to sell his crops to the newcomer, or the latter sells his clearing to the
former.[35]

Thus, in rapidly developing areas, competition over land generated many
controversies. These tensions were symptomatic of incipient socioeconomic
differentiation within the colono group itself. They were also indicative of a
strongly individualistic, competitive streak within colono society. To an un-
determinable degree, such endemic frictions probably reduced the settlers'
capacity to organize in their own defense when their claims to the land were
challenged by outsiders in later years.

Despite these circumstances, colonos sought to create a social life by living in close proximity to other settler families. Once a nucleus of colonos
established themselves in an especially fertile region, others usually joined
them, settling nearby. They formed small groups of families related by blood,
marriage, and godparenthood. In the more isolated areas up to ten or twenty
families usually congregated in one place.

The tendency of colono families to stake claims along transport routes
gave rise to the particular settlement pattern that rural sociologists call
the line village. Common in Colombian frontier areas both on the coasts and
in the interior, these settlements consisted of many separate homesteads
strung out along a river or dirt road stretching back into the forest in long,
narrow strips.

Where an expanse of public lands provided adequate marketing opportunities and the population grew rapidly, colonos often grouped together to
form nucleated villages, known as *caseríos*. On the coast peasant settlers
usually lived in such hamlets from which they went out each day to work
their fields. In the interior Andean area, dispersed settlement patterns were
more common: each family built its hut on its own claim some distance away
from its neighbors; caseríos, then, emerged primarily as marketing and reli-
gious centers. Many later took on administrative functions as well.[36]

The first step in founding a caserío was the construction of the chapel, a
collective task. Then came the market place, the Catholic cemetery, and the
jail. Later, perhaps, a school would be built and an office for the justice of
the peace *(inspector de policía)* assigned there by departmental authorities.
At the same time shopkeepers and artisans appeared on the scene, eager to
supply the commodities like machetes, cloth, salt, and matches that the
colonos could not themselves produce. Gradually these frontier settlements
became complex, thriving little communities like those in older regions.[37]

With continued in-migration, some caseríos won official recognition with designation as a *corregimiento* or a municipal subdivision. Eventually, the most important were raised to municipal status. Indeed, many new municipalities were carved out of old ones in Colombian frontier regions in the late nineteenth and twentieth centuries.[38]

Some spontaneous colono settlements grew to considerable size. The caserío of Guayaconero, located on public lands twenty-two miles from the municipal seat of Cunday (Tolima), had in 1933 over 500 dwellings and 3,000 residents, the majority colonos. At the same time the coastal corregimiento of San Juan in Turbo (Antioquia) claimed around 2,000 people, mainly settlers from Bolívar.[39] And there were hundreds of other colono settlements scattered throughout the frontier regions of Colombia.

The settler movements of the late nineteenth and early twentieth centuries opened many wilderness areas to production. Their contribution to the Colombian rural economy was an important one. Frontier settlers did more than feed themselves: they also fed the country. Together with other peasants—small proprietors from the highlands, service tenants, and sharecroppers—frontier settlers produced almost all of the foodstuffs sold in local and regional markets. Contemporary observers were well aware of the economic role played by the settlers. "Most staple food crops are cultivated by the needy people of this country on public lands," wrote a congressman in 1859.[40] The next half-century brought little change. "Agriculture, as a rule is confined to small producers," noted another legislator in 1917. "It is the domain of the poor classes, of the colonos of our cordilleras."[41] This productive orientation answered a need to which the great estates, owned by the upper classes, did not respond, for haciendas in Colombia, as in other parts of Latin America, tended to specialize in pastoral activities or in one or another export crop. By providing foodstuffs for domestic consumption, then, colono families filled a vital economic function within Colombian society as well as producing significant quantities of coffee, cacao, and other crops for export markets.[42]

Legal Relation of the Settlers to the Land

To the casual observer, peasant settlers in frontier regions would have appeared identical to small proprietors throughout the country. It is for this reason, perhaps, that historians have overlooked the importance of the colonos as a distinct subgroup within the Colombian peasantry. In reality, settlers of public lands differed significantly from their highland counterparts in that they had no legal title to the land they farmed.

It is not surprising that in the first part of the nineteenth century few settlers of public lands managed to obtain titles. Public debt certificates could be bought only in the major cities where peasants rarely, if ever, went. Furthermore, few poor settlers had the money or the bureaucratic know-how to use the certificates to acquire land. Thus independent colonos outside of the Antioqueño poblaciones were excluded from the possibility of titling their fields. After 1874, this generalization no longer held true. As we have seen, the Colombian land policy reforms of the 1870s and 1880s apparently opened to all colonos the opportunity to obtain land grants free of charge. Given these laws, it is puzzling that most Colombian settlers never established property rights in frontier areas.

One might assume that the pioneers themselves were at fault, that they simply did not know enough to seek the grants to which they were entitled. This assumption is, however, unfounded. Although most colonos could neither read nor write, they showed a surprising awareness of the national directives that bore on their lives. It was not the ignorance of the colonos, but that of the legislators that rendered the law inoperative. Whether deliberately or not, the men who framed the land policy of the 1870s and 1880s demonstrated a profound insensitivity to the material conditions of colono life that, in the end, made it virtually impossible for settlers to title their land.

Although the law promised free grants to cultivators, there were many hidden costs. The most onerous was the surveyor's fee. By law, every applicant for a public land grant had to hire a surveyor to measure and map the territory. For the rural poor, this expense was prohibitive: indeed, for a parcel less than fifty hectares in size, the surveying costs generally exceeded the market value of the land itself.[43] And there were many more payments to be made—for a lawyer to write the petition, for official paper and postage stamps, and for the registry of the property. The settler also had to pay travel costs of witnesses and local authorities from the municipal seat to the site of the claim and back. For the poor colono whose holding often lay ten to twenty miles from town by rutted mule path, the costs were impossibly high.[44]

Yet another discouraging factor was the prospect of interminable delays in the processing of applications. Such delays stemmed both from the incompetence of country lawyers, who often produced defective petitions, and from the centralization of the grant procedure which, in an age of inefficiency and poor communications, required that multiple messages be sent between the ministries and departmental and local officials.[45] The impor-

tance of using bribes to lubricate the bureaucratic machinery added yet another financial burden. One lawyer from Tolima complained:

> My experience in these matters has taught me that to acquire a public land
> grant, however small in size, one needs influence in the government minis-
> tries which costs a pretty penny. Only by making great sacrifices does a settler
> manage to scrape together fifty or sixty pesos to cover the paperwork and court
> hearings required by law. He is not able to pay this other, much greater
> expense.[46]

In practice, the promise of free grants to cultivators was a grand illusion.

The official statistics give rise to the following conclusions concerning
grants to settlers in the period from 1827 through 1917. Most settlers who
received title to their holdings belonged to the Antioqueño poblaciones. Between 1840 and 1914, the Colombian government donated public lands totalling 250,760 hectares to twenty-one Antioqueño settlements in southern
Antioquia, northern Tolima, and Caldas.[47] Assuming that this territory was
divided into the 32 hectare family farms required by law, as many as 7,600
settlers gained property rights. Because these small proprietors kept their
farms and because the new municipalities that took form around them became major coffee centers after 1900, they have attracted all the attention.
These are the visible colonos of Colombian history whose existence promoted the ideal of a democratic frontier.

Most frontier settlers in Colombia, and even most settlers of Antioqueño
origin, were not so fortunate. According to the official grant lists, in the
period from 1827 through 1917, only 1,256 small farmers outside of the
Antioqueño poblaciones successfully obtained government land grants *a tí-
tulo de cultivador*. These grants ranged in size from 1 to 100 hectares for a
total of 65,000 hectares. Nearly half of these grants were awarded in the
department of Caldas where the expansion of coffee after 1900 gave colonos
active in its production both the motivation and the means to pay off the
surveyors. In all other parts of the country combined, only 628 frontier households managed to title their claims and so become proprietors.[48] These represented but a fraction of the many thousands of peasant settlers who farmed
public lands in late nineteenth and early twentieth century Colombia.

During the period of export growth, the Colombian countryside was a countryside in movement. As the lure of the frontier regions took hold, Indians,
ex-slaves, tenant farmers, artisans, and small proprietors migrated out of
the older settled areas toward the public lands. Spontaneous colonization of
the public domain contributed significantly to the economic and demographic

shift which occurred between 1850 and 1930 from the eastern cordillera toward western Colombia and, to a lesser extent, toward the Caribbean coast.

The economic behavior of the colonos corresponded not at all to the image of the immobile, tradition-bound peasant prevalent in the literature on Latin America.[49] The concern of frontier peasants to improve their economic situation emerges clearly in their settlement patterns and economic activities. Although many families were limited in the early years to subsistence production, they made every effort to tie into the market economy by planting cash crops, seeking outside sources of income, and building access routes. In the buying and selling of improvements and squatters rights, Colombian frontier settlers also manifested a concern for economic gain.

The life of the colono was not an easy one. Soil exhaustion, pests, and natural catastrophes sometimes destroyed the crops, while yellow fever, malaria, anemia, and parasites afflicted the people. And the isolation was hard to bear. But this first difficult stage of frontier expansion ultimately gave rise to many new communities of people who produced a large surplus of food crops supplying local and regional markets and augmented the volume of Colombian coffee exports. Although the law stated that for their efforts the colonos should be recompensed with property rights, most never got them. The insecurity of their land claims left settler families particularly vulnerable to the opposing claims of people of higher social status who were more adept at acquiring property rights. In fact, most colonos remained in any one place for no more than ten to thirty years before their claims to the land were challenged by more powerful and wealthy individuals—people usefully termed land entrepreneurs.

3

The Land Entrepreneurs

Peasants were not the only people attracted to frontier regions in late nineteenth and early twentieth century Colombia. In the same years, individuals from the upper and the middle strata of Colombian society also turned their sights to the public lands. In any given area, the arrival of these land entrepreneurs heralded the onset of the second stage of frontier expansion. Energetic people with money and political connections, they sought to establish private property rights to large tracts of frontier land and to turn the peasants living there into dependent workers.

Motivations

The land entrepreneurs who attempted to establish new haciendas in frontier regions included a broad cross-section of the upper and middle sectors of Colombian society. Some were merchants, lawyers, landowners, or politicians from families prominent in Colombian life since the colonial period. Others were individuals on the rise—ambitious youths from the provinces who came to Bogotá or Medellín for a university education and stayed on to make their fortunes. Still others were political bosses, shopkeepers, and money-lenders known only to the frontier towns in which they made their homes. Despite the diversity in background, land entrepreneurs shared certain characteristics: all had economic resources and political connections, and all aimed to profit from the new opportunities created by the growth of the export economy.

Just as peasants are often said to be traditional, so too the label traditional has been used to describe the rural upper classes of Latin America—the great landowners or hacendados. The word *traditional*, as applied to both groups, means simply *non-economic*, that is that their prime motivation was not the maximization of profit. According to this viewpoint, the sixteenth century Hispanic ethos reproduced in Spanish America a system of values that associated landholding primarily with social prestige rather than economic production or accumulation. For this reason, landlords were content to monopolize great tracts of land that they neither sold nor put to economic use. These entrenched values, it is said, contributed to the persistence of the great estate from colonial times into the nineteenth and twentieth centuries. And because the great landowners were not fully responsive to economic incentives, they themselves were in part responsible for the backwardness of the rural areas.[1]

This image of the traditional landlord, which runs through the development literature of the 1950s and 1960s, does not apply to those Colombians who sought to consolidate new haciendas in frontier regions. Beneath their aristocratic veneer, Colombian elites had always been concerned with money-making.[2] Wealth and social status went hand in hand and, although people of upper class origin would not deign to hard manual labor, there were many more honorable and remunerative occupations. Landowning was one, and so were commerce and mining. Some of the largest and most respectable Colombian fortunes were forged in the gold mines of Antioquia and in the import-export trade.

In the years following Independence, individuals concerned with profit-making faced an uncertain economic environment. Transportation and communications were in an abominable state, markets fragmented, prices unpredictable, capital and credit in short supply, and labor often hard to come by. The constant civil wars added yet another dimension of risk: political strife almost invariably brought in its train the disruption of trade, destruction of property, forced loans, and confiscations. Under such conditions, only extended family networks provided a measure of economic security. And so the extended family became an organizational underpinning for most economic enterprise.

To cushion the very real possibility of failure in any one area, families tended to spread their investments among many different economic activities. Even in the colonial period, it was not unusual to find great landowners also involved in mining and trade. This tendency toward diversification became more pronounced in the nineteenth century. The same family clans— and often the same individuals—engaged in the import-export business, retail sales, finance, mining, and transport contracting, and they owned both urban and rural properties.

The diversification of assets, so typical of nineteenth century Colombian economic life, not only minimized risk in a highly unpredictable environment, but also allowed for flexibility in investment priorities. Members of the Colombian elite were responsive to shifting opportunities and, at any point in time, tended to concentrate in those areas that promised the best returns. During the first half of the nineteenth century when the rural economy was stagnating, agriculture and even ranching had little appeal. Landowners held onto their rural estates, but their major interests centered on commerce and, in the case of the Antioqueños, gold mining. In the 1830s and 1840s, a number of Bogotanos also made some brief, unsuccessful forays into manufacturing.

After 1850, with the growth of the agricultural export economy, a decided shift in emphasis occurred. As markets, both foreign and domestic, expanded, as transport improved, and as the settler movements began in earnest, so land in the middle and lower altitudes became increasingly attractive. Many public lands which lay worthless and abandoned, beyond the reach of the national economy, now began to take on market value. Investment in frontier land, it seemed, made good economic sense.

Many urban merchants, either individually or in companies formed for the purpose, set out to develop agricultural land and market the produce. Although merchants led the way, others too were drawn to invest in frontier areas by the promise of profits to be made. The lists of applicants for large grants of public lands include politicians and generals from the Liberal and Conservative parties, doctors, lawyers, importers, exporters, landowners, miners, bankers, engineers, and transport entrepreneurs.[3] On these lists are names like Tomás Mosquera, a president of Colombia who invested in the cinchona bark boom of the 1860s; Indalecio Liévano, an engineer and public works contractor; Gabriel Echeverrí, merchant, gold miner, and colonization entrepreneur; Andrés Rocha Castillo, the Liberal politician; and Manuel Dávila Pumarejo, prominent *costeño* landowner and progenitor of Alfonso López Pumarejo, president of Colombia in the 1930s.

Land entrepreneurs were attracted to frontier regions for several reasons. Some aimed to establish commercial enterprises producing for export markets. The collection of cinchona bark was the first of the major Colombian exports to attract entrepreneurs to remote frontiers. Coffee also motivated large-scale entrepreneurs to seek out public lands in temperate zones. Most of the coffee exported from Colombia in the late nineteenth and early twentieth centuries was produced on large estates. Some of these estates dated from the colonial period; others, however, were new properties consolidated from public lands. The dynamic growth of the banana economy after 1910 also sent many Colombian entrepreneurs to the frontier. Although, as with coffee, the first bananas were planted on private estates, the extraordinary profits to be made in the banana business led Colombians who contracted with the United Fruit Company to open new plantations on the more than 50,000 hectares of public lands that blanketed the area around Santa Marta.

While some entrepreneurs aimed to establish export enterprises in frontier regions, others founded cattle ranches. As will be recalled, the Colombian ranching economy was transformed after 1850 with the introduction of sown pasture grasses, new breeds of cattle, and barbed wire fencing. Ranching that made use of these innovations required substantial investment, but it also promised high returns: as early as 1860, steers fattened on guinea pastures brought two to three times the price of those fed on native grasses.[4] The profits to be made in ranching attracted a new kind of rancher— merchants or progressive landowners with merchant ties. Because of their efforts and the extraordinary adaptability of the new grasses, pastures began to spread into wilderness areas previously unsuitable for livestock grazing. In the early twentieth century, cattle ranches multiplied along the rivers of the interior and particularly along the Caribbean coast.

An equally important reason for entrepreneurial interest in the frontier was speculation in land. As roads improved and railways were built, as settlers opened wilderness areas, and as new territory came into production, land prices began to rise. They grew all over the country, but most notably in export areas in the middle and lower altitudes.[5] There rising land values affected not only cultivated fields but undeveloped territory, and public lands as well as private properties. As land values moved upwards, individuals naturally sought to monopolize an increasingly valuable resource in anticipation of future gains. Not surprisingly, then, inflation fuelled speculation. Many members of the upper groups speculated at the same time in rural properties, urban real estate, and government debt paper. While contemporaries and later analysts deplored such activities as a waste of productive energy that contributed little to national development[6], speculation was a rational economic activity like any other from the perspective of the individual. It constituted an important means of capital accumulation for the Colombian upper classes.

Although petty speculation ran rampant through colono society, it was land entrepreneurs who had the means and the connections to monopolize much larger areas. While some well-to-do Colombians attracted to public land regions were primarily speculators, many coffee planters, cattle ranchers, banana growers, and others also sought to form large holdings, the larger the better. No matter if they could not put much of the land into production; it might be sold later to someone who would. Thus, the possibility of long-term profits motivated many land entrepreneurs to accumulate as much territory as possible, more than any one person could possibly put to use.

Speculative activity was most intense in areas where a quick turn-over and high returns could be expected—in areas, for example, where new railroads were to pass or foreign companies showed an interest in purchasing land.[7] Such conditions were, however, unusual. Generally in Colombia capital was scarce and the land market sluggish. In contrast to the United States where speculators sold out to pioneers moving west[8], the Colombian rural population was too poor and the credit system too rudimentary to create a mass market for land. In most regions of Colombia, a landowner could wait for years before an advantageous sale might be transacted. Individuals who carved large estates from public lands tended to hold onto their properties in the meantime. There was always the hope that a railroad would pass nearby or a new export crop be discovered, precipitating a sudden upsurge in real estate values.

Meanwhile, the possession of unimproved land was no liability. Since land taxes were low, the tax burden did not pressure landlords to sell off their territory or put it to productive use. At the same time, investment in landed property acted as a hedge against inflation, and rural holdings could be used as collateral to obtain loans for other undertakings.[9] Given these conditions, it was in the economic interest of people of means to acquire as much land as possible in developing frontier regions.

The Labor Problem

Colombian policy-makers assumed there was enough land for large and small farmers alike in frontier zones. However, land entrepreneurs bent on forming new estates showed an interest not in vacant frontier land, but specifically in that land already occupied by peasant settlers. That is, they sought to enclose the peasants' fields.

A clear economic reasoning lay behind such behavior. The territory the peasants chose was generally fertile, with some access to markets. More importantly, the colonos' land was already cleared and ready for production. To form a coffee hacienda or plant new pastures, the forest had first to be cleared and a couple of corn crops sown to turn the soil. For the entrepreneur who depended on hired workers, such tasks could be expensive.[10] To appropriate the peasants' fields, then, meant a significant savings of time and money. Moreover, the work the colonos incorporated in the land increased its market value. According to a survey carried out by the Ministry of Agriculture in 1916, public lands improved by colonos brought two to three times the price of unimproved baldíos in most areas.[11]

What further increased the value of the land was the physical presence of the colonos themselves. Land without people to work it has no intrinsic worth. Without labor, a coffee hacienda, a banana plantation, or even a cattle ranch is not a viable undertaking.[12] The attraction the settlers held for the land entrepreneurs can only be understood in terms of a serious problem the entrepreneurs faced: the problem of labor supply.

Until the 1930s, labor was relatively scarce in the Colombian countryside and particularly so in frontier regions which are, by definition, sparsely inhabited.[13] The fact that the population of Colombia was much smaller in those times accounts in part for the difficulties large proprietors had in acquiring labor.[14] The social organization of the countryside was also a contributing factor. In the nineteenth century and first decades of the twentieth, a mobile pool of wage-earning laborers had not yet come into existence. Much of the rural population was tied to the soil, either as small proprietors or as service tenants and sharecroppers in the densely populated highlands. These roots, combined with problems of transport and communications, inhibited to some extent the free movement of people toward the middle and lower altitudes. But, most important, peasants who did migrate into developing frontier regions had no intention of subordinating themselves to new employers. They jealously guarded their economic independence, producing for themselves and reaping the benefits. The Colombian situation clearly illustrates anthropologist Sidney Mintz's observation that "free men do not willingly work for agricultural entrepreneurs when land is almost a free good."[15]

During the late nineteenth and early twentieth centuries, Colombian landowners manifested a constant preoccupation with securing an adequate supply of workers.[16] The large landowners themselves took various initiatives intended to ease the problem. Hacendados from western Cundinamarca and Tolima imported workers from the eastern highlands through a system of labor contracting called *enganche*.[17] Other landlords pleaded with the government for an effective immigration policy. Colombia, however, as noted above, held little attraction for foreigners. The result was that Colombian entrepreneurs were forced to rely on domestic resources to meet the ever-growing demand for labor generated by the primary export economy.

Colonos comprised a major part of the population in many areas that emerged as centers of commercial agriculture and ranching in the latter part of the nineteenth century. Colombians who aimed to form new properties in frontier regions naturally focused on these settlers as the most readily available potential source of labor. In order to compel them to work the estates, it was necessary to deprive them of their economic independence. For this reason, land entrepreneurs generally sought to establish rights of private property to large tracts of public lands occupied by colonos. If peasants could no longer work the land for themselves, they would, of necessity, be more willing to sell their labor power.[18]

This solution to the problem of labor scarcity helps to explain why entrepreneurs tried to monopolize tracts of public lands much larger than they could possibly put to use. Only by restricting the free access of peasants to the most advantageously located public lands, thus depriving them of an alternative economic base, could the landowning classes hope to tie them to the estates. Thus, entrepreneurs formed vast holdings in economically dynamic areas not only for speculative reasons, but also to generate a supply of cheap labor to work the limited area under production.[19]

The Public Land Archives repeatedly allude to the labor motive for the creation of latifundia in frontier regions. Reported a congressional investigative committee in 1882:

> It is generally through the dispossession of the poor settlers that rich people acquire large landholdings. . . . Many obtain immense extensions of territory that they hoard with the sole purpose of excluding colonos from those areas or else reducing them to serf-like conditions.[20]

The municipal council of Espejuelo (Cauca) was even more explicit in 1907:

> Here the majority of the hacendados have taken over vast zones of public lands and even parts of the Indian resguardos that they neither work themselves nor allow others to work. By monopolizing the land they aim only to undermine the position of the independent cultivators so as to form from their ranks groups of dependent laborers.[21]

Land entrepreneurs, then, followed on the heels of the peasant settlers who were the first to open new frontier regions. The timing of the juncture by which large entrepreneurs began to take action against the colonos varied from place to place. It typically occurred when the value of the land rose significantly, whether because of an influx of settlers, the construction of transport routes, the introduction of new crops, or the opening of markets. At this point, generally some ten to thirty years after the first colonos had arrived, the large investors made their appearance.

The methods land entrepreneurs used to appropriate the peasants' land and labor involved two successive steps. First, they sought to establish rights of private property to large tracts of public lands already occupied in part by colonos. Then, titles in hand, they pressured the colonos to sign labor contracts, threatening them with eviction if they refused. Such contracts permitted the settlers to continue farming the parcels they had cleared only on the condition that they surrender all claims to the land and become tenants of the haciendas.

Privatization of the Land: The Public Land Grants

In order to generate a labor force, to protect fixed investments, and to capitalize on rising land values, entrepreneurs logically sought to turn the public lands into private properties. Whereas peasant settlers had found this impossible, the land entrepreneurs had no such problems.

The legal way to title public lands was to apply to the national government for a grant. Many entrepreneurs who took this route purchased the territory with debt certificates. Debt certificates were a valid way to obtain public land grants throughout the nineteenth and early twentieth centuries. Once on the market, the certificates tended to depreciate rapidly to but a fraction of their face value. In 1873 they were selling for between twenty-five and thirty-five centavos per hectare, and fifty years later the price remained the same.[22] Such certificates could easily be acquired by anyone with some savings and contacts in Bogotá. Getting the actual grant application through the bureaucracy was a more formidable task. The result was that many entrepreneurs relied on a few financial firms in Bogotá known to specialize in the acquisition of land grants for a fee. In the latter part of the nineteenth century, such firms included the very reputable houses of Francisco Pereira Gamba, Camacho Roldán Hermanos, and Koppel and Schloss.[23] Despite the extra charges involved and, of course, the surveyor's fee, land certificates provided a relatively inexpensive way for those with some resources to acquire large tracts of public lands.

The reform laws of the 1870s and 1880s opened a second way for entrepreneurs to acquire grants—by putting the land into production. In the years after 1874, increasing numbers of land entrepreneurs chose this path.[24] Indeed, it was people of means, not peasant settlers, who benefitted most from the new legislation permitting free grants of land to those who made it productive. Most large entrepreneurs did not work the land themselves. Some sent groups of wage laborers *(peones)* or sharecroppers *(aparceros, agregados)* from the highlands to clear and plant the land under the direction of an overseer. Others went into regions already opened by settlers, bought up several peasants' improvements, and then petitioned for grants as owners of the crops. Most large grants awarded under the reform laws went to ranchers who established "cultivators' rights" by planting improved pasture grasses and fencing their grazing lands. Some also went to coffee planters.

The lists of public land grants published by the Colombian government provide detailed information on the formation of private properties during this second stage of frontier expansion.[25] Between 1827 and 1931, certificate-holders and large-scale cultivators obtained some 1,782 grants from the Colombian government totalling 2,657,000 hectares.[26] Figure 1 shows the cumulative number of hectares of public land granted each year. Maps 4-6, which follow, pinpoint the location of public land grants in successive time periods, and map 7 indicates the economic areas to which reference is made. This figure and the maps illustrate the major areas of frontier expansion over time and the relation of frontier development to the growth of the export economy.

Before 1865 when the export economy began to affect the Colombian countryside, few entrepreneurs sought land grants and relatively few public lands were allotted. Most of the land privatized in this period was in Antioquia where the expansion of the mining industry made agricultural endeavors remunerative and where elites became involved early in profit-oriented land investments and colonization schemes. The largest concession, 102,700 hectares in 1835, went to three wealthy Antioqueños in Caramanta who built a road connecting the region to the Marmato-Supía mining district and fostered settlement of the territory as a profit-making venture.[27] This grant aside, the allocation of public lands to private individuals averaged only 7,855 hectares a year from 1827 through 1869.

Growing foreign demand for Colombian forest and agricultural products led to a significant increase in the quantity of public lands solicited after 1869. In his 1870 report, the minister of finance made the connection clear:

> Baldíos that yield cinchona bark, rubber, vanilla, vegetable fibers for rope and cloth, valuable lumber for construction, and a variety of medicinal substances, and public lands suitable for the cultivation of indigo, tobacco, coffee, and cacao have begun to interest enterprising men, for they point the way to economic progress.[28]

The dramatic upsurge in land grants in 1872 and 1873, when concessions totalled 394,843 hectares, related directly to the cinchona bark boom, which reached its apogee at precisely that time, and to speculation along the path of a railroad projected to run through the coastal department of Bolívar.[29] Grants to several Antioqueño poblaciones in Caldas and Tolima also elevated the figures for these years. After this exceptional time, the alienation of baldíos continued at a lower rate, but significantly higher than in the

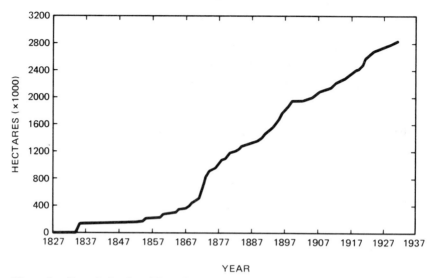

Figure 1   Cumulative Land Distributed in Public Land Grants, 1827–1931
Source: *Memoria de Industrias*, 1931, vol. 5, pp. 249–410.

early nineteenth century. Between 1874 and 1900, allocations of public lands averaged 41,644 hectares annually.

Grants were intended for various kinds of economic ventures. In these years several merchants from Bogotá, including Emiliano Restrepo, José Bonnet, and Sergio Convers, obtained multiple grants for thousands of hectares in the Llanos at the foot of the eastern cordillera. It seems likely that they intended to exploit the forest products and establish large-scale cattle and farming operations along the Meta River on which there were attempts to open steam navigation at the time.[30] Other entrepreneurs sought grants in developing coffee regions in the Santanders, Cundinamarca, and southern Tolima, and in northern Tolima and Caldas where the influx of Antioqueño settlers and road construction made large-scale undertakings feasible. In these areas the grant figures also reflect an expansion of ranching. Along the Caribbean coast most grants were directly linked to the growth of the livestock industry. In those places, the years after 1870 saw the rapid expansion of cattle ranching owing in part to the opening of the Antioqueño market, which previously had been supplied from the south. From the 1880s through 1930, public land grants on the Caribbean coast centered in the Sinú valley around Montería where Antioqueño entrepreneurs founded immense cattle ranches. Livestock produced there was driven overland or shipped down the Magdalena River to the eastern lowlands of Antioquia where other grants formed the basis for ranches specializing in the fattening of cattle for the highland market.[31] Still other grants on the Caribbean coast clustered along the Magdalena River (the principal transport route to the markets of Antioquia and Tolima) and near the border with the Santanders where significant quantities of coastal cattle were also consumed.

When the War of a Thousand Days erupted in 1899, the Colombian government virtually suspended the processing of grant applications. Once peace returned in 1902, the number of hectares distributed quickly rebounded to an average of 31,375 hectares a year. These allocations responded primarily to the steady expansion of cattle and coffee production and to the ongoing construction of railroads. In the early years of the twentieth century, land grants in the interior followed the movement of coffee out of the eastern cordillera into the central mountains, that is, into the departments of Tolima, Caldas, and Valle. Many large entrepreneurs sought to found coffee haciendas and cattle ranches near the Antioqueño settlements.[32]

The last of the coffee areas to feel the stimulus was the department of Valle del Cauca in southwestern Colombia. An isolated area, Valle had fallen into depression in the latter part of the nineteenth century.[33] The construction of a railroad network that linked Valle both to the interior and to the Pacific port of Buenaventura, and the completion of the Panama Canal in 1914 did much to revitalize the region. These transport developments set off a land boom accompanied by large numbers of petitions for public lands. After 1915, many land entrepreneurs sought large concessions both in the northern areas into which Antioqueño settlers were moving and in the mountains bordering the Cauca River further south.

Around the same time, several new factors were encouraging land entrepreneurs to seek government grants along the Caribbean coast. The advent of the United Fruit Company set off a wild rush for land that reached its peak around Santa Marta in the 1920s.[34] Foreign investment in ranching, forest products, and oil exploration also drew the interest of Colombian nationals who sought grants elsewhere on the coast to sell to the foreigners.[35] In conjunction with the ongoing expansion of the cattle industry, such incentives made the Caribbean coast a major center of investment in public lands in the first decades of the twentieth century.

Distinct patterns of landownership, meaning the relative proportion of large, medium, and small properties, emerged in different frontier regions.[36] Between 1827 and 1931 individuals, land companies, and settlements received 5,914 grants in all, totalling 2.9 million hectares. Figures 2 and 3 show the size distribution of these grants. Over time the mean size of grants perceptibly decreased as a consequence of legal restrictions on maximum area and the growing numbers of grants to middle-sized cultivators, particularly in the

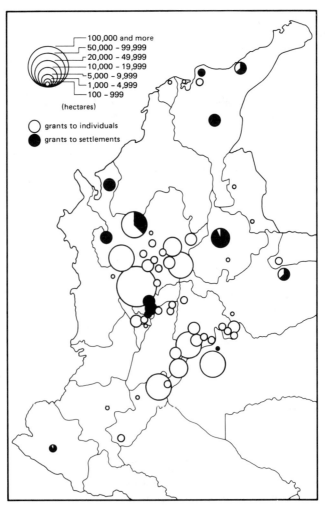

Map 4   Public Land Grants by Municipality, 1827–1869

Each symbol represents a municipality where one or more public land grants were awarded. The size of circle indicates total quantity of public lands in that municipality granted by the national government. See appendix D for names of municipalities, number of grants, and number of hectares allocated.

Source: *Memoria de Industrias*, 1931, vol. 5, pp. 249–410.

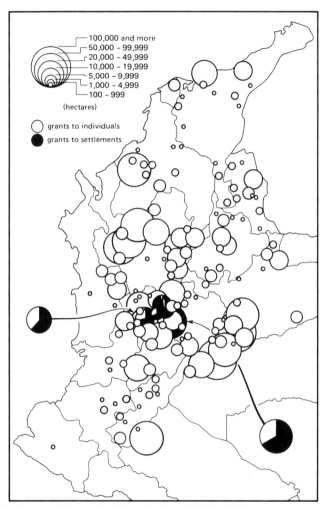

Map 5 Public Land Grants by Municipality, 1870–1900
Each symbol represents a municipality where one or more public land grants were
awarded. The size of circle indicates total quantity of public lands in that municipality granted by the national government. See appendix D for names of municipalities, number of grants, and number of hectares allocated.
Source: *Memoria de Industrias,* 1931, vol. 5, pp. 249–410.

45

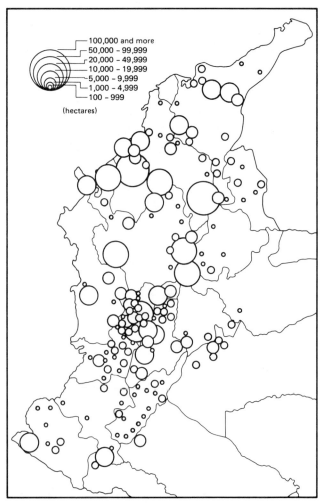

Map 6   Public Land Grants by Municipality, 1901–1931
Each symbol represents a municipality where one or more public land grants were
awarded. The size of circle indicates total quantity of public lands in that municipality granted by the national government. See appendix D for names of municipalities, number of grants, and number of hectares allocated.
Source: *Memoria de Industrias*, 1931, vol. 5, pp. 249–410

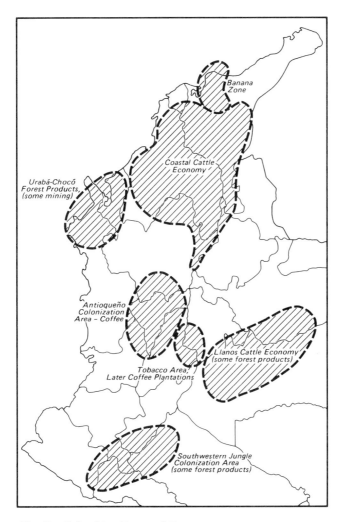

Banana
Zone

Coastal Cattle
Economy

Urabá-Chocó
Forest Products,
(some mining)

Antioqueño
Colonization
Area – Coffee

Llanos Cattle Economy
(some forest products)

Tobacco Area,
Later Coffee Plantations

Southwestern Jungle
Colonization Area
(some forest products)

Map 7   Colombian Regional Economies

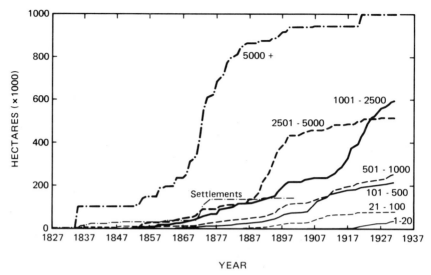

Figure 2 Cumulative Amount of Public Land Allocated to Individuals, Companies, and Settlements by Size of Grant, 1827–1931

If an applicant received more than one grant in one year, the sum of those grants has been used to determine size of allocation.

Source: *Memoria de Industrias*, 1931, vol. 5, pp.249–410.

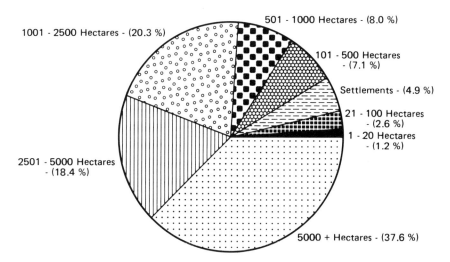

Figure 3 Distribution of Public Land by Size of Grant, 1827-1931
If an applicant received more than one grant, the sum of those grants has been used to determine size of allocation.
Source: *Memoria de Industrias*, 1931, vol. 5, pp. 249-410.

western coffee zone. What stands out most clearly, though, is the concentration of landownership. More than three-quarters of all territory granted to individuals, companies, and settlements from 1827 through 1931 was distributed in grants 1,001 hectares in size or larger. These figures support the notion that the privatization of public lands reinforced the predominance of the great estate in the Colombian countryside. Just 5 percent of the land went to the Antioqueño settlements, of which so much has been written, and only another 4 percent consisted of parcels smaller than 100 hectares. Certainly large grants were more common in cattle ranching areas than in coffee regions, but even in the department of Caldas, the heart of the so-called democratic coffee frontier, nearly 30 percent of the land granted comprised properties larger than 1,000 hectares.

The actual concentration of landed property in grants was even greater than the preceding figures suggest. Some entrepreneurs received more than one large grant, which was quite legal so long as the concessions did not border on one another. In the years 1875 through 1895, ten merchants from Bogotá obtained thirty-three grants covering more than 200,000 hectares in western Cundinamarca, southern Tolima, and the Llanos.[37] Other people, seeking to consolidate single properties that surpassed the legal limit, engaged front men *(hombres de paja)* who applied for land grants with certificates provided by their employers. Once the grants came through, the recipients immediately transferred the land to the promoters through trumped-up bills of sale. Such transactions contributed to the formation of enormous properties in Antioquia, Caldas, and Bolívar in the early years of the twentieth century.[38]

Privatization of the Land: Illegal Usurpations

Revealing as they are, the grant lists tell only one part of the story. To understand fully the formation of private property on the Colombian frontier, the de facto appropriation of public lands must also be taken into account. Outside of the official grant system and in violation of the public land laws, land entrepreneurs successfully incorporated several million more hectares of public lands into private properties. The widespread usurpation of public lands contributed significantly to the consolidation of new latifundia in developing regions.

Entrepreneurs who usurped public lands instead of filing for grants did so for various reasons. Appropriation of the land was usually less expensive than working through official channels. Those who usurped public lands may not have had access to debt certificates or may have been unwilling to make the investment in the land necessary to qualify for cultivators' rights. Bureaucratic delays inherent in the processing of grants also discouraged applications.[39] Provided that the instigator was a person of some resources and influence, appropriation of the land generally proved less costly, more efficient, and not significantly less secure than proceeding lawfully.

Review of the means land entrepreneurs used to accumulate territory illicitly or quasi-illicitly sheds light on the magnitude of the process and on regional variations within it. In all areas where public land grants were distributed, entrepreneurs often masked large-scale appropriations within the grants themselves. It was the responsibility of each grantee to engage a surveyor to measure and map the territory for which he or she applied. Because of the use of metes and bounds surveys, which designated boundaries by natural phenomena such as trees, rivers, and stones, no one could tell from the boundaries how much territory was enclosed therein. Frequently the grantee and the surveyor colluded to ensure that the property limits designated actually took in much more land than the government intended to award.[40] In 1888 Ruperto Ferreira, who had been commissioned by the government to recommend changes in land policy, elaborated on this aspect of the land problem:

The measurement of public lands presents many difficulties for those who undertake it. These lands usually are located in isolated forest regions far from town, without roads, etc. Because of this experienced engineers, who make precise measurements and, of course, charge higher fees, rarely take on the work. Less scrupulous surveyors are preferred. Also, individuals seeking grants are interested only in complying with the formalities by submitting any map drawn up by whoever demands the lowest price. The larger the area of land included, the better, for the grantees stand to lose nothing by such maneuvers. In the few cases in which the government has rectified the maps of land grants, every time it has found that enormous extensions of land have been incorporated without authorization. Let me cite the following examples: in 1849 the Nation granted a lot which should have contained 7,680 hectares, but when recently reviewed was found to include an extra 13,459 hectares. Later, in 1878, several grants were approved which, according to the surveyor's calculations, totalled 2,396 hectares. A check revealed 2,964 hectares more enclosed within the boundaries indicated on the map.[41]

The amount of public lands aggregated to grants varied from concession to concession. It tended, however, to be larger in sparsely populated regions with extensive public lands. Thus entrepreneurs in the Llanos and Panama easily inflated grants of 5,000 hectares into holdings two, three, even five times that size.[42] Similar appropriations on a smaller scale occurred in allocations to certificate-holders and to cultivators throughout the country. Another practice grantees used was to extend de facto control over adjacent public lands by monopolizing water resources and road access. Officials took note of this practice in the introduction to Law 48 of 1882, which deplored the "common abuse" of individuals seeking long, very narrow grants, often along the base of mountains, in order to appropriate the uplands as well.[43]

Other usurpations occurred that lacked even the legal guise of land grants. In many places entrepreneurs simply claimed and later sold public lands with no lawful grounds whatsoever. Such practices were particularly common in remote areas where public officials with legal training were few and land values low. At the end of the nineteenth century, in the Llanos and Chocó, on the slopes of Santander, and in northern Valle individuals with local influence found it quite simple to sustain de facto claims to extensive public lands. Near Ocaña (Norte de Santander), for example, in 1906, speculators delimited several huge tracts of baldíos containing up to 100,000 hectares each and then spread the word that they were the rightful proprietors to justify future land deals.[44]

The expansion of the cattle industry and growing foreign investment motivated many similar usurpations along the Caribbean coast after 1900. There wealthy entrepreneurs used barbed wire to encircle large tracts of public lands, sometimes inhabited by whole villages of colonos, which they alleged to be private property.[45] At times small grants or purchases provided the basis for subsequent enclosures. In Río de Oro (Bolívar), for example, one man granted 100 hectares in 1907 proceeded to fence in an additional 4,900 hectares of public lands.[46] The situation in Magangué (Bolívar) typified that in many coastal communities in the early years of the twentieth century. Reported one citizen in 1907:

> The use of barbed wire is creating many problems for the future. Here the expansion of private property is in direct proportion to the ability of each person to acquire more and more barbed wire. Individuals are enclosing great quantities of land. . . .[47]

If a buyer could be found, the entrepreneurs did not hesitate to sell such claims; if not, they passed the "property" through wills to their children.

Although such usurpations were illegal, many received, with time, the sanction of the Colombian judicial system. Until 1926, the government never specified the legal criteria by which public lands were to be distinguished from private properties. During the nineteenth century, local judges had customarily accepted bills of sale or wills as legal proof of property, so long as such documents showed possession for at least thirty years.[48] Thus much land that never officially left the public domain was incorporated into private properties through de facto claims and later sales or inheritances.

Yet another means used to monopolize public lands involved the presentation of mining claims. According to Colombian law, individuals who filed claims to mines also won the right to exclusive use of 500 to 1,000 hectares of land on the surface. To stake a mining claim, any interested person had merely to declare that a mineral deposit existed and pay an annual tax of one peso. If forty pesos were paid at once, the supposed mine and adjoining territory passed under the concessionaire's authority in perpetuity.[49] In large areas of the Chocó, northeastern Antioquia, and the mountainous parts of Huila, Caldas, and Valle, entrepreneurs took advantage of these regulations to claim often imaginary mines so as to secure control over public lands and forests.[50]

In parts of the interior where much land already was titled, the usurpation of public lands took a variant form. There landowners enlarged old haciendas to encompass adjacent public lands.[51] Deficiencies in traditional surveying practices considerably facilitated such maneuvers. Colonial deeds rarely fixed clear property boundaries. Given this imprecision, hacendados whose land bordered on baldíos found it possible in later years to "clarify" their boundaries to their own advantage. With each sale and each inheritance, the owners gradually extended their property limits. The name of one river was attributed to another river a kilometer or two further on, one mountain ridge was said to be another ridge and one marker stone, another stone. Barring an on-the-spot inspection, these changes could not be detected in the property deeds. The quantities of public lands involved in these subterfuges were significant. It was said, for example, that Dr. Lisandro Caicedo of Salento (Caldas) had appended more than 100,000 hectares of baldíos to his estate "La Paila" in this way.[52] Striking as it is, this case was by no means unique. Large proprietors situated in the Cauca and Magdalena river valleys were prone to assert without proof that their domain extended to the top of the adjacent mountain ranges.[53]

Beyond the modification of boundaries in wills and bills of sale, hacendados used two kinds of legal actions—partition suits (*juicios de partición*) and boundary actions *(juicios de deslinde)*—for similar ends. Partition suits were initiated by a number of joint tenants *(comuneros)* who owned a tract of land in common (an *indiviso*) as the consequence of a land grant, inheritance, or the purchase of shares. The object of the suit was to divide the property legally and to mark the individual portions of each part-owner. Boundary actions, in contrast, aimed to determine the borders between two or more privately owned properties or between one individual's property and adjoining public lands. They were generally filed by an interested landowner. Many proprietors purposely used such court cases to fix new boundaries which, on occasion, took in thousands of hectares of public lands. Because property titles were unclear, because surveyors were often inept and sometimes partial, and because judges rarely took time to study the old deeds seriously, the landowners usually succeeded in manipulating the evidence to their advantage.[54]

The case of the Iriarte family of Chaparral (Tolima) provides an instructive example of how legal processes could be used for such purposes.[55] Around 1875, at an auction of disentailed church properties, Marco Aurelio Iriarte purchased a large estate known as "Ambeíma" for 300 pesos or about one-tenth of its true market value. Iriarte then claimed that his property extended all the way to the department of Cauca, thus appropriating to himself between 50,000 and 100,000 hectares of public domain. In a boundary action subsequently brought in a neighboring municipality, the Cauca border limit was accepted by the judge without the on-site inspection required by law. Iriarte had the Supreme Court in Bogotá confirm this decision and by 1881 was charging rent to people who moved into the region to farm or to collect rubber and cinchona bark. Despite protests from some local citizens as well as from the treasurer of the department, the land was never reclaimed for the nation.

The expansion of old haciendas by encroachment on public lands was particularly common in Antioquia, Tolima, Huila, Caldas, and Valle. In these departments the rising price of land was the most important consideration motivating landowners to extend their boundaries. At times, merely the anticipation of future gains sufficed. The rumor of a new road or railroad often gave rise to a rush of applications for public land grants as well as to boundary and partition suits and sales by which haciendas were enlarged. Most public lands incorporated into old haciendas were hoarded for speculative purposes; they were rarely put into production.[56] Thus, in the Andean region, new titles were continuously being fabricated from old ones, and relatively small haciendas dating from the colonial period continued to expand in the nineteenth and twentieth centuries.

Along the Caribbean coast a variation on this theme occurred. In the colonial period, vast expanses of land around the ports of Santa Marta and Cartagena and along the Magdalena River had been distributed on paper among the most powerful families of the region. These families ran cattle and produced some tobacco and cacao on a small part of the land, but with the trauma of Independence and the abolition of slavery these enterprises failed. In the nineteenth century, the titles were not registered, nor were property taxes paid. The land itself fell into disuse. Small hamlets of peasant cultivators settled unchallenged and an occasional rancher ran livestock on these holdings which locally were reputed to be public lands.[57]

The advent of American, French, British, and German companies at the turn of the century precipitated the sudden resurrection of old property claims. Coastal elites ransacked family trunks for antiquated titles to land they had never seen; they then sold these titles to the foreigners for an easy profit.[58] Such real estate deals were particularly common in the Santa Marta banana zone where the United Fruit Company accumulated 60,000 hectares of property between 1899 and 1929. They were also evident in the Mompós area where around 1910 the American Colombian Corporation purchased the great "Terrenos de Loba," an area of more than 100,000 hectares covering five municipalities. Foreign firms also bought land in Tenerife, Plato, Chiriguaná, and El Banco (Magdalena) and in Majagual and Magangué (Bolívar) in the early years of the twentieth century.[59] Here we see the reassertion of property rights that had never been clearly defined and had been allowed to lapse for decades, if not centuries.

The appropriation of public lands occurred in many areas of Colombia in the late nineteenth and early twentieth centuries. The illicit conversion of public lands into private property was most prevalent in areas undergoing intense economic growth. Like public land grants, usurpations concentrated in western Colombia and along the Caribbean coast. Given the covert nature of such activities, it is impossible to say exactly how much land was lost to the public domain. Qualitative sources, however, suggest that the amount of land illegally transferred to private use equalled and probably surpassed that allotted in government grants.

It is clear that the instigators of the process were generally people of means. To petition for land grants, stake mining claims, file boundary and partition suits, or purchase barbed wire required capital far beyond the reach of the rural poor. In fact the prime beneficiaries of public land usurpations were large landowners, merchants, and financiers, most of whom saw in the accumulation of public lands a relatively low cost and potentially profitable investment.

In this second stage of frontier expansion, then, enterprising individuals carved great expanses of public domain into private properties. The parallel processes of alienation and appropriation transformed the Colombian countryside. In the Andean region, immense zones of public domain in the middle and lower altitudes passed into private hands. Meanwhile, an equally far-reaching change took place on the Caribbean coast: after 1870 many baldíos, as well as municipal common lands, were absorbed into private holdings or grants and, outside of the banana zone, converted into extensive grazing ranges. The formation of private property in the Colombian countryside was an ongoing process: many great estates either came into existence or were significantly enlarged in recent times.

The consolidation of new latifundia in public land regions attracted little attention from the ministries in Bogotá. Legislators occasionally deplored the usurpation of public lands but never set any criminal penalties. The government did establish some procedures to reclaim land stolen from the national domain, but the land entrepreneurs used these procedures instead to sanction their appropriations.[60] The records suggest that the Colombian government was either unaware of or indifferent to the widespread usurpation of public lands.

The Colono to Tenant Transition

Those most aware of what was going on were, of course, the peasant settlers inhabiting frontier regions. The privatization of the land had a tremendous impact on their lives. It signified, in effect, the loss of their land claims. To understand how the colonos were despoiled of their farms necessarily implies an understanding of how entrepreneurs circumvented the laws meant to protect the settlers. The legislative reforms of 1874 and 1882, as will be recalled, aimed in part to prevent the concession to large-scale investors of public lands already occupied by settlers. According to these statutes, individuals who petitioned for public land grants could be awarded only unimproved baldíos or territory which they themselves had put into production. If colonos were found to be settled within the desired area, their possessions were to be excluded from the larger grant.

The reform laws established several concrete procedures to safeguard peasant interests. For example, anyone who applied for a land grant had to call upon three local witnesses to testify whether or not any settlers lived in the area. The surveyor of the grant was then required to note the location of the colonos' plots on the maps submitted to Bogotá. Settlers whose parcels were marked thereby secured title to their fields. Broadsides describing the grant also had to be posted for a month to give colonos who had been overlooked the chance to voice their opposition. And finally, just before the mayor formally transferred ownership to the grantee, local authorities were charged once again to notify all settlers whose rights might be adversely affected and to postpone the grant if they protested against it.[61]

Clearly, the effectiveness of these laws depended on the compliance of local authorities, witnesses, and surveyors, and on the ability of the colonos to make their presence known. The problem, of course, was that the national government wielded little effective power in the rural localities, while many land entrepreneurs were influential indeed. Most entrepreneurs simply bribed needy witnesses to swear that the land they wanted was uninhabited when in fact it had been farmed by peasant settlers for years.[62] Responsive to the grantees who paid their salaries, surveyors almost never noted the colonos' existence on their maps, while mayors often posted descriptions of pending grants for only a few days, if at all.[63] Even when broadsides were posted, they were not always accurate. As one citizen of a small town in the eastern lowlands of Antioquia wrote to President Rafael Reyes in 1906:

> They apply for a tract of land which they say is baldío specifying boundaries that are not the real boundaries . . . and they are very careful not to mention the names of the real owners or of the neighboring proprietors. . . . They take these precautions so that no one will realize that the interests of other people are at stake. . . . Only when full title to the land is bestowed on the petitioner is the immoral sham revealed, for then the new owner takes it upon himself to dispossess the cultivator of the land. If the latter is financially unable to bring the issue to court (and this is most often the case), he falls victim to the *influential speculator* who always has at hand more than enough witnesses to prove that the land of a poor man is baldío. In this way, many defenseless souls have been dispossessed, reducing them to dire poverty.[64]

Even when, against all odds, settlers did take cognizance of a pending grant that enclosed their fields, local authorities sometimes simply refused to admit their objections.[65] The result was that in flagrant violation of the new laws, land entrepreneurs after 1874 regularly continued to apply for and obtain grants of public lands occupied by colonos.[66]

Such enclosures commonly occurred in concessions to large-scale cultivators as well as those to certificate-holders. In some enclosures, but a few settlers were affected, while other grants took in the fields of hundreds of colonos. The inhabitants of the caserío of Pedral (Santander), for example, were unpleasantly surprised one morning in 1880 to find that the whole village had been granted to one man.[67] Generally the central government never realized the land was inhabited, and the colonos did not know that someone else had petitioned for the land they cultivated until it was too late.

Territory opened by colonos was the primary focus of large-scale usurpations as well.[68] Hacendados often allowed settlers to occupy public lands adjacent to their properties only to claim the territory years later when the land had taken on value. If the colonos attempted to title their claims, hacendados quickly moved to preempt them by initiating boundary actions or partition suits. In many areas colonos who had been settled for as long as forty years on land they believed baldío were startled to find their petitions for grants blocked by local hacendados who swore that the territory formed part of their properties.[69] Uncertainty over whether the land they had occupied was truly baldío, together with fear of precipitating the aggression of large landowners, probably inhibited many settlers from applying for government land grants.

Where colonos had in fact occupied abandoned properties, the owners generally reactivated their titles once the land values increased.[70] A letter from Santa Marta sent to the minister of agriculture in 1919 described yet another variant on these tactics:

> After obtaining public land grants, some individuals draw up deeds proving that they are the owners of tracts of land much larger than that to which they have a legal claim. They allow colonos to settle there, and then, using the false titles, they assert their claims over the entire area as if it were their property, depriving the poor peasants of their rights.[71]

The covert appropriation of baldíos through fabricated deeds, illicit sales, mining claims, and court suits allowed no possibility for colonos to raise legal opposition. This consideration helps to explain why land entrepreneurs often preferred covert methods for the titling of public lands.[72]

Once entrepreneurs had established property rights over the land, whether through grants or by illegal means, they then took action to deprive the settlers living there of their independence. Accompanied by the local mayor or a police patrol, they informed the settlers who had opened the land that they had mistakenly occupied private property. The entrepreneurs then presented the peasants with two alternatives: either they could vacate the property at once or else sign tenancy contracts. If the peasants agreed to become tenants, they abandoned their claims to the land and also relinquished control over their own labor. As rent for the continued use of their parcels, they were obliged to provide part-time labor for the alleged landowners.

The installation of tenants on a property benefited land entrepreneurs in various ways. For those intent on usurping public lands, the establishment of tenancy relationships with colonos already settled on the land provided another means to legitimize their claims. In Colombian tenancy contracts, the tenant explicitly recognized his employer's legal right to the land. Because courts accepted such contracts as evidence of rightful possession equivalent to planting crops, grazing livestock, or constructing fences and buildings, tenancy contracts could be used to buttress questionable property claims.[73]

For hacendados engaged in the production of cash crops, tenancy arrangements also permitted the satisfaction of labor requirements with a minimal expenditure on wages. The use of tenant labor reflected the abundance of land and the scarcity of liquid capital typical of rural Colombia in this period. Even in areas where commercial production was only minimally profitable, to have tenants on a property was desirable. The settlement of tenants along the periphery of a hacienda served to discourage encroachments by neighboring landowners and squatters. But more than this, tenants provided the owner with a basic income from rents, while at the same time, by working their fields and maintaining mule paths and fences, they increased the value of the property. In addition, for the speculator interested in convincing a buyer of the commercial viability of his holding, the presence of a labor force on the land comprised in and of itself a decided attraction. Usually, then, land entrepreneurs first established property rights and then pressured peasant settlers to sign tenancy agreements.

A few variations on the general pattern deserve mention. In very remote regions, individuals who sought to monopolize public lands without any legal grounds typically refused to allow colonos to settle there at all. The exclusion of the colonos constituted in itself an assertion of ownership, while, given the lack of markets, economic activities requiring a resident labor force were not feasible.[74]

In other areas where land values shot up very suddenly, as, for example, along the paths of projected railroads, previously vacant territory attracted both large-scale speculators and small settlers simultaneously. In such areas, land entrepreneurs directed their principal efforts toward acquiring rights over the land per se from which, owing to its advantageous location, an immediate profit through sales could be expected. Under these conditions, entrepreneurs were generally unconcerned to generate tenant labor. Like claimants in very remote regions, they tried to exclude settlers altogether so as to avoid difficulties with them. Just such a situation occurred in Yolombó

(Antioquia) in the 1890s when a number of large-scale grant petitioners clashed with hundreds of colonos seeking to open land along the tracks of a railroad from Medellín to Puerto Berrío then under construction.[75]

In the department of Caldas, several prominent families and land companies who held colonial titles to vast tracts of land adopted a different policy in relation to settlers. They founded towns, built roads, and promoted the settlement of their holdings with the aim of subdividing the land and selling it off to the peasants.[76] The momentum of the colonization movement to the south of Antioquia, the relative prosperity of the settlers, and the opportunities for alternative investments provided by the unusual dynamism of the Antioqueño regional economy may account for the form that land entrepreneur-colono interactions assumed in those parts of Caldas. Whatever the motivation, such transactions were exceptional in the Colombian context. A similar pattern of real estate development, however, also characterized parts of Brazil and many areas of the United States' frontier where speculators and land companies inserted themselves between the government and the actual settlers.[77]

Still another variation in entrepreneur-colono interactions evolved in the tropical rainforests along the Pacific coast and the Gulf of Urabá, which were designated inalienable national woodlands after 1900. Private entrepreneurs who leased the forests from the central government monopolized the export of wood products from the areas they controlled. Against their volition, settlers already established within the boundaries of the concessions became in effect workers for the lease-holders. The lease-holders obliged the settlers to sell them all the rubber or vegetable ivory they collected at a fixed price significantly below its true market value. Thus, in acquiring a forest concession, the contractors also secured a captive labor force. Because the territory on which they squatted was not technically public land, settlers in the national forests did not qualify for the protection due colonos before the law.[78]

The above-mentioned variations aside, frontier areas generally were opened in Colombia by settler families who put the land to productive use. The gradual integration of the public domain into wider markets led to a second stage of economic activity in which large-scale entrepreneurs asserted claims to vast areas of baldíos with the aim of appropriating the land and labor of the independent settlers.

Both the settlers, who dominated the first stage of frontier development, and the entrepreneurs, who dominated the second, were economic actors. The economic logic of the entrepreneurs, however, was fundamentally contradictory to that of the peasant pioneers. In moving to frontier regions, the settlers sought economic independence, that is, control over productive processes; they sought as well to feed their families and to improve their economic situation by producing surplus foodstuffs for market. The peasant vision of frontier development was that of a smallholding economy with widespread distribution of the land among those who farmed it. Although some tried to monopolize large tracts (and a few succeeded), peasant settlers generally were unable to establish private property in land. Therefore, among them the major criterion for access to land remained its effective cultivation. The entrepreneurs, in contrast, were after profits that, given their dependence on hired labor, could only be had in the production of export crops, in cattle ranching, and in speculation. To make such large-scale undertakings a success, they urgently needed labor, which they sought to generate by depriving the peasants of their economic independence and incorporating them into the new haciendas. The entrepreneurs' vision was of a rural economy of large estates worked by a variety of tenant laborers and often supplemented by wage workers. Thus, their economic logic required the projection of the latifundia system of land tenure into new areas.

4

The Struggle for Land and Labor

To complete the consolidation of their new estates, the entrepreneurs needed to win not only the acquiescence of the authorities, but also that of the colonos. The crucial juncture occurred in each area when an entrepreneur's representative informed a group of settlers that the land they farmed was private property and that they must either sign tenancy contracts or move away. If the peasants accepted these terms, the shift from an independent smallholder economy to a hacienda system was complete. Many colonos did not, however, passively acquiesce in the loss of their claims. The settlers' determination to maintain their independence gave rise to hundreds of localized conflicts throughout the middle altitudes and lowlands of Colombia in the years 1874 through 1920. The precise forms the struggles assumed reflected the legal-institutional context in which they emerged.

Forms of Colono Resistance

Before 1874, the options of independent colonos threatened by large entrepreneurs were few. Either the settlers entered into tenancy agreements, which allowed them to continue working the land they had opened, albeit under prejudicial conditions, or they refused the contracts and moved on. The decision to emigrate or to stay, taken by each family individually, implied no collective organization. Only within the Antioqueño poblaciones did settlers openly oppose great landowners who reasserted claims to the territory where the settlements had been founded. Led by educated and resourceful local elites, a number of Antioqueño poblaciones in the mid-nineteenth century fought such claims in court. The economic importance of the areas involved caused the national government to intervene in several of these disputes, resulting in compromise agreements beneficial both to the colonos and their adversaries.[1] The relative isolation, poverty, and illiteracy of the independent colonos deprived them of similar possibilities for resistance. Although the documentary record is sparse, it appears that in this early period the transition from a smallholder to an estate economy was generally a peaceful one.[2]

In the years after 1874, however, a significant change occurred: independent colonos began to organize themselves to oppose the encroachments of land entrepreneurs. In many parts of the country, small groups of peasants, threatened by a single entrepreneur or land company, put up a stiff fight against expropriation. These struggles provide evidence that the colonos possessed a strong sense of their own interests, separate from those of the large landowners and political bosses, and that they endeavored to defend those interests as best they could.

The decisive factor that persuaded the settlers to resist expropriation was the passage of national legislation supportive of settlers' rights.[3] Although the reform laws of the 1870s and 1880s were ineffectual, their passage profoundly influenced the settlers' perception of their situation. These statutes, as will be recalled, not only allowed peasants to homestead on the national domain, but also stated that the land they occupied was legally theirs and should not be taken from them. This legislation gave colonos the sense that the national government was on their side; it imbued their interests with legitimacy; and it provided a focal point around which they began to organize in their own defense. Squatter resistance to the incursions of land entrepreneurs grew out of a profound sense of legal wrong, out of the conviction that the propertied had obtained their wealth by illegitimate means. As will be seen, the entrepreneurs tried to implement their goals and the colonos to resist them through the use of judicial and administrative channels, through appeals to bureaucrats, congressmen, and the executive in Bogotá, and last but not least through the selective use of violence.

From 1874 on, settlers threatened with dispossession did their best to alert the government to the violation of their legal rights. In the years 1874 to 1920, colonos sent hundreds of petitions to authorities in Bogotá describing their problems with landgrabbers and asking the government to protect them. The drafting of such petitions required a concerted group effort. Because most colonos were illiterate and ignorant of legal formalities, they had to engage a lawyer to write their appeals.[4] A number of families from the same area, all of whom were menaced by one land claimant, generally pooled their resources to hire an attorney who would argue their position collectively. More than four hundred such petitions, each signed by between five and two hundred colono families, are deposited in the Colombian Public Land Archives.[5] In their pleas, the settlers expressed but one aim—to be left in peace to farm their land independently.

Written from the colonos' viewpoint, the petitions provide insight into the settlers' perception of their situation. Many of the petitions indicate a consciousness of the opposing interests of rich and poor, combined with a bitterness that the rights of the poor could be so easily violated. A petition from twenty-five colono families in Frías-Guayabal (Tolima) whose parcels had been granted to English mining entrepreneur William Welton noted,

> Incidents like the one we describe have occurred here on other occasions for which reason it would appear that we live in a state of anarchy and not under a government whose republican institutions guarantee the security of our persons and property. . . . [The] rights of a poor man, won through hard work and affliction, are worth nothing when countered by the interests . . . of influential people.[6]

Many colonos, from previous experiences, were well aware of the patterns of interaction between land entrepreneurs and settlers that affected their lives. Settlers in Sucre and Majagual (Bolívar) in 1917, for example, showed a lucid understanding of their own vulnerability to the tactics employed by land claimants:

> We inform you opportunely of the fact that our land is to be granted to a large entrepreneur because it has and may well happen again that individuals who acquire enormous grants of land, so large they could not possibly cultivate them in a lifetime, not only deprive the poor cultivators of the natural use of the mother earth, but also deceive the government in their grant applications, making it appear that the land is vacant when, in fact, it is completely populated and exploited; and afterwards come the violent evictions, the abuses, and the subsequent dispossessions and disregard of all rights in accordance with that Law by which the powerful always impose their will over the weak. The consequences, if our observations are neither heard nor attended, will not escape your Excellency. For these reasons, we implore justice.[7]

Despite consciousness of wrong-doing, most colonos saw little possibility of effective resistance against land claimants if the government were unwilling to defend them. A communication from a group of settlers in Margarita (Bolívar) clearly expressed this outlook:

> If the law will not protect our property rights, if because we are poor and weak we cannot defend ourselves, if honorable labor is not to be respected, we know which roads we must follow: either the path of crime or that of migration.[8]

In its curious melding of legalism and outrage, the argument put forth by a group of colonos from Villahermosa (Tolima) typified many settler petitions in the years before 1920. The colonos of "Palocabildo," whose land was claimed by the family of Anselmo Pineda, ex-governor of Panama, wrote,

> In determining the true possessor of this territory, neither equity nor justice have been consulted, nor have the acquired rights of we, who have farmed the land for so many years, been respected. . . . We do not deny the written titles of the Pineda family, nor do we repudiate the ruling of the authorities on this question. But we do protest that they are usurping the rights that we have acquired, and we call to your attention the fact that, by taking an extension of land larger than that to which they have a legal claim, the Pineda family is defrauding the Nation as well. It is not lawful that they should dispossess us, robbing us of the bread of our children that we have won at the cost of so many privations and in accordance with the public land laws, particularly Law 48 of 1882. The spirit of justice is offended and all philanthropic and humanitarian principles cry out before the honorable conscience of reason which attends us in our petition to the supreme government in the hope that in accordance with its highest duty, it will bestow on us a favorable solution and protect our downtrodden rights.[9]

Beyond appealing to the national government, colonos also used other institutional channels to assert their position. Some, situated on land claimed to be private property, continued to submit grant applications, seeking institutional support for their contention that the territory was baldío. Uldarico Leiva and his wife Lucía Caicedo, for example, reported in 1917 that, despite an executive resolution confirming the legitimacy of their property titles in Prado (Tolima), settlers persisted in applying to the departmental governments of both Tolima and Cundinamarca for public land grants of their parcels. After several rebuffs, an official finally admitted the colonos' petitions, thus inadvertently providing them the administrative sanction they needed to counter the Leivas' ownership claims.[10]

Another means to which settlers resorted was to inscribe themselves on municipal tax lists. Cultivators of public lands were not required to pay property taxes and in regions where settlers faced no immediate threat to their holdings, they complained vociferously against the occasional functionary who tried to force them. Confronted by land entrepreneurs, however, settlers in several areas begged municipal authorities to inscribe their names on tax lists, hoping in this way to reinforce their claims to the land. The governor of Boyacá, referring to the colonos of Territorio Vásquez, noted, "They are happy to pay property taxes, believing that this gives them legal ownership of the land, in which belief they are sadly mistaken."[11]

Although many did not realize the danger until too late, colonos menaced with dispossession through judicial suits occasionally took steps to protect themselves. Some pooled their resources to hire a lawyer, while several too poor to engage legal counsel endeavored to defend themselves in court.[12] In a few instances settlers even brought criminal charges against land entrepreneurs who had used violence against them.[13] Some settlers also resorted to broadsides, pamphlets, and newspapers to give their viewpoint a wider hearing. A petition of colonos from Magangué (Bolívar) in 1907 asserted, "We are prepared to defend our rights before the Law and in the Press."[14]

The legalistic orientation of colono protest made sense in Colombia. Given the existence of protective legislation, the colonos could logically suppose that the central government would support them if only it were informed of their situation. Throughout Latin American history, Indians faced with threats to their communal lands have adopted similar protest strategies for similar reasons.[15]

Conflicts between colonos and land entrepreneurs were not only played out on paper but also generally involved direct and sometimes violent confrontations. In order to assert colono status before the law, the peasants had to remain on the land without signing tenancy contracts. As settlers became familiar with the legislation, they frequently refused either to sign tenancy agreements or to vacate their parcels. Faced with opposition, proprietors called on local authorities to evict them. The colonos, however, typically hid to elude official notification. When evictions actually occurred, settlers often defied local authorities, returning surreptitiously to farm their fields once the police patrols had withdrawn.[16]

In some areas, groups of squatters openly and persistently defied the attempts of landlords and local authorities to expel them. In Garzón (Huila) in 1906, colonos occupying part of the Hacienda Laboyos refused to acknowledge the property rights of the alleged owners which had been confirmed several times in court. The mayor found it necessary to effect successive evictions.[17] A year later, one Ricardo Vejarano from Cajibío and El Tambo (Cauca) requested protection against more than fifty Indian families who, he claimed, were usurping his property "Dinde" in the guise of colonos, soliciting grants of their clearings, and inciting his tenants against him. Even by destroying their shacks and making them post bonds, he could not wrest from them an admission of his legal right to the land.[18]

Clearly, when their holdings were threatened, colonos manifested little of the deference often attributed to Latin American peasants in relation to people of higher social standing. The Public Land Correspondence provides ample evidence of the thinly veiled anger and frustration that informed the colonos' side of such interactions. The following report on the eviction of a colono in Calarcá (Caldas) is particularly revealing of one individual's response to dispossession:

> And soon [the cultivator] Antonio Hernández arrived and upon seeing the policemen, . . . he became enraged. . . . The mayor spoke to him, but Hernández would not listen. He entered his hut with a shotgun he had with him and a machete on his belt in a menacing fashion. Seeing this, to avoid any misfortune, the mayor ordered the policemen to capture him and tie him up, which they did. In the rumpus Hernández was hurt, but not because the police had meant to injure him.[19]

Similar outbursts of colono hostility occasionally took collective form. Vindicated by an official resolution in 1911 that thousands of hectares along the Sogomoso river were in fact baldío, the settlers of Pedral (Santander) stoned the offices of the Ogliastri and Martínez Lumber Company which had claimed the whole area. Later the same night a mob more than one hundred strong tried to assassinate the company manager.[20] This response appears to have been a spontaneous act of popular retribution.

In several other cases groups of colonos, thwarted by an obvious miscarriage of justice, purposefully determined to oppose force with force. In 1907 in Magangué (Bolívar), for example, cultivators who were settled on territory the government had years before designated baldío found their grant applications blocked by an alleged proprietor and the municipal judge. A cultivator warned President Rafael Reyes, "The inhabitants, who are angry, intend to take justice into their own hands."[21] An official from Tolima reported on a similar situation in the municipality of Prado eleven years later:

> The mayor had to use the police to stop the settlers who threaten retaliation against proceedings they call illegal assaults perpetrated by the Sres. Leiva. Some have been made to post bonds; others refuse to do so, for which reason they have been jailed until they comply.[22]

The forms of settler resistance described above grew out of a socioeconomic process of land concentration, an institutional framework, and a context of power relations, the combination of which was historically specific to Colombia. Given the circumstances in which they found themselves, Colombian settlers made effective use of available options within the constraints imposed by their poverty and isolation.

The Middle Sector Allies

The preceding analysis of forms of colono resistance draws a composite picture. In reality settlers' responses to landlord pressures varied over time and space. In some places, settlers showed almost no recalcitrance in signing tenancy contracts, while, in others, open struggles between entrepreneurs and settlers continued for decades.

To explain the differential duration and intensity of colono resistance, it is essential to consider the role played by individuals of middle sector origin in providing settlers with rudimentary leadership. Such individuals played an important role in some disputes by informing illiterate settlers of their rights, drafting petitions on their behalf, and occasionally furnishing monetary support. The people who performed these functions were most often country lawyers, large cultivators, and local officials.

Familiar figures in rural localities, the country lawyers, known as *tinterillos* (ink-spillers), were reputed to engender the disputes from which they made a living. Liberal statesman and merchant Salvador Camacho Roldán aptly expressed the irritation of the urban educated classes with these self-taught legal experts when he called them "ignorant pettifoggers who defend unjust causes and complicate the controversies."[23] Some tinterillos, it would seem, hoped to generate an income by informing colonos of their rights and then writing their petitions for them. Acting from economic self-interest, such individuals nevertheless played an important role in disseminating knowledge of the land laws in frontier regions.

Having once informed a group of settlers menaced by a land entrepreneur of their legal situation, the tinterillo would offer to appeal to Bogotá and, if the settlers' land rights were vindicated, to see their grant applications through the bureaucracy for a price.[24] Although individually poor, colono families together were capable of contributing a sizeable sum toward their own defense. Represented by a magistrate in Popayán, the Indian colonos of "Dinde," numbering 130 households in all, paid 14,000 pesos in legal costs over the fifteen years of their dispute with the Vejarano family.[25] Some lawyers who acted as brokers for the colonos honestly met their promises; others, however, unscrupulously cheated the settlers and may have tried to set colonos against rightful property owners. Tinterillos in El Carmen (Norte de Santander), for example, were said to have extorted some 20,000 pesos from settlers there anxious to title their holdings.[26] In regions with a large colono population, it is likely that some lawyers also supported

settlers so as to win their electoral following. Colonos represented mobilizable political capital, particularly in areas where, as in Belalcázar (Caldas),
the majority of the colonos were of one party affiliation (Liberal) and the
majority of the landowners the other (Conservative).[27]

Whatever their motives, country lawyers in some places were instrumen-
tal in convincing settlers that the land they occupied was not privately
owned, as local notables insisted, but rather public domain. They also
called usurpations and title irregularities to the attention of national authorities.[28]

In addition to the tinterillos, large cultivators sometimes played a role in
mobilizing and focusing colono discontent. Usually these cultivators were
local storekeepers, artisans, or administrators who had hired a few workers
to plant crops or run livestock on nearby public lands. If outside entrepreneurs tried to appropriate their claims, these cultivators made common cause
with small colonos similarly threatened. One such colono leader was Tobías
Enciso, a printer and former public market manager from Honda (Tolima).
When Enciso's claim to public lands in the neighboring municipality of Victoria (Caldas) was challenged by the Isaacs Brothers in 1917, he resisted in
the name of the many small colonos living in the region. Enciso not only
took his case and that of the colonos to court, but also published a pamphlet
presenting an eloquent picture of the struggle from the colonos' point of view.[29]

In general, land entrepreneurs who sought to expand their properties
avoided direct confrontations with large-scale ranchers or cultivators of
public lands. They focused their attention instead on the clusters of settler families who represented a potential labor supply. Furthermore, some entrepreneurs purposefully employed divisive tactics in dealing with different strata
of colonos. One claimant in Antioquia, for example, who evicted the poorest settlers without compensation, agreed to buy out some well-to-do colonos who threatened him with a judicial suit.[30] For these reasons, pragmatic
alliances among the various socioeconomic strata of colonos were less common than might have been expected. Most cultivators who supported peasant settlers in land disputes claimed relatively small areas of public land
themselves, generally under 250 hectares, and lived in the area, often in the
municipal seat.

To clarify the various conditions under which large cultivators assumed a
leadership role in organizing poor settlers, it is necessary briefly to examine
the related issue of rent disputes, in which wealthy cultivators clearly did
take the initiative. Rent disputes, of which there were various kinds, pitted
colonos accustomed to free use of the public domain against government
authorities charged with enforcing new laws that required settlers to pay

rent on their farms. An early example of such a conflict occurred near the abandoned mines of Santana (Tolima) in 1883. Scores of settler families squatting on national territory around the mines denied the government's right to charge them rent. Urged on by a local tinterillo who farmed a large tract of land with hired labor, the settlers "refuse(d) to acknowledge the government's authority over this property, saying that this is public land, and that they have acquired title to it by the mere act of planting corn, rice, and vegetables."[31]

A rash of similar disputes grew out of a law passed in 1905 that permitted rural municipalities to charge rent on public lands to raise money for building schools and roads.[32] In Ataco (Tolima) enforcement of the new policy generated serious frictions. Hundreds of colonos settled on a vast expanse of public lands in the southern part of the municipality refused to comply; in response, local authorities pushed some colonos off their holdings and allotted the land to whoever agreed to pay the levies. By 1921 the situation had become extremely tense.[33] Replying to colono complaints of excessively high rents, the municipal advocate submitted a report to the national government that illuminates both the intensity of the settlers' reaction and the particularly strong resistance of the more prosperous cultivators:

> pernicious and scheming individuals . . . have influenced the colonos, who are very ignorant, to resist paying rent, even though occupants of public lands have been subject to rental assessments here since 1910. . . . The persuasions of the instigators . . . have had such an effect that the colonos of Sur de Atá have paid no rent whatsoever and refuse to do so; with a few exceptions, the settlers of Norte de Atá and Pole follow suit. The colonos of Atá, who have the most fertile land, are relatively well-off. These people show hostility against all authority, so much so that they will not respond when ordered to appear before the mayor or the judge. The area least apt for agriculture, where the poorer colonos live, is Chilircó, and yet most of the families there sign rental agreements with the municipality and meet their obligations willingly. The injustice of the complaints of the petitioners, who pay the instigators to write letters and newspaper articles arguing their position, is evident. It would be no hardship for them to pay rent on a few hectares of public land.[34]

A related conflict in Bodega Central (Bolívar) illustrates how large-scale cultivators could successfully mobilize peasant settlers in support of their mutual interests.[35] The problem in Bodega Central originated in 1920 in a law that allowed the government to impose rents on settlers of river banks and islands. When the mayor of Bodega Central set out to enforce the ruling, the colonos of the islands Morales and Popayal in the Magdalena River resisted. While most of the 125 families involved were poor people with small farms, several local notables, including municipal councilman Laureano Arce and the Zurek brothers, also claimed tracts of public lands of 1,000 to 2,000 hectares where they grazed cattle. Faced with the prospect of rent payments, these ranchers began to spread the word that the island people owned not only their improvements but also the land itself, a notion to which the settlers were, of course, receptive. The Zureks, who lived in another municipality, simply ignored the rent, while Laureano Arce convinced his fellow councilmen to declare the law unconstitutional. Meanwhile, the peasants "refuse(d) to pay the assessments on their holdings, saying that they consider(ed) themselves to be the rightful owners, for which reason none of them showed up to sign the rental contracts."[36] The mayor was stymied.

At this point Bogotá designated an inspector to negotiate with the cultivators. The inspector, however, found his mission increasingly impracticable as the mayor and the municipal treasurer, through whom he had to work, decided to support the powerful cultivators. When the inspector ventured into the "rebellious village" of Morales in order to collect the rents himself, his efforts were countered by

> Sr. Antonio A. Cruz E., who has made himself owner and master over a large area of the islands of Morales and El Toblar, preventing others from using the land on the pretext that it belongs to him. . . . He declared himself vehemently opposed to the rents to the point of threatening me and denying my authority. . . . The next day he called together some of the inhabitants and gave them liquor to intoxicate them. Then he counselled them to resist, saying that if they were notified to pay the rent, they should take up arms against the undersigned.[37]

The inspector beat a hasty retreat.

Ataco and Bodega Central provide examples of large cultivators who quite logically sought to mobilize settlers in opposing levies inimical to their common interests. The interests of the various socioeconomic strata of occupants of public lands, however, proved to be more cohesive in rent controversies than in struggles over land. Although in situations where their holdings were claimed by a third party affluent cultivators sometimes united with poor settlers, this tendency was relatively weak because land entrepreneurs took precautions to avoid precipitating such alliances. At any particular juncture, the mutually supportive or antagonistic relations of prominent cultivators and small colonos obviously depended on the issue at stake. Generally speaking, large cultivators more often played the role of despoilers in their interactions with settlers than that of benefactors.[38]

In areas where the activities of land entrepreneurs were especially pronounced, a few colono leaders emerged who showed an exceptionally strong commitment to the settlers' cause. Bonifacio Torres Peña, a self-identified "artisan and trader," represented the settlers of Belalcázar (Caldas) for several years after 1904, during which time he was shot at and jailed for six months by local authorities who sided with the landlords he opposed.[39] Arrested along with a number of squatters in 1919, cultivator Gregorio Garzón from Ciénaga (Magdalena) became an adamant champion of colono interests in the United Fruit Company's banana zone. He carried out detailed studies of fraudulent property titles and threatened to encourage direct forms of resistance if local officials denied the legal rights of squatters settled on the land.[40]

In general, individuals of higher social standing who supported colonos in the years before 1920 acted neither from ideological nor from altruistic motives: rather, as we have seen, most sought to promote their own economic interests. Country lawyers and large cultivators in certain areas did, however, provide settlers with information and skills in their struggles against outsiders seeking to appropriate their land and labor. The issue such individuals raised was a valid one, and the process of agitation served to strengthen the colonos' consciousness of the violation of their rights and to instruct them in the possibilities for resistance.

The role of country lawyers and large cultivators in organizing colono resistance highlights the importance of intermediaries in facilitating communications between the rural poor and authorities in Bogotá. Local officials, too, could fulfill such a function. By their compliance with or disregard of legal prescriptions, municipal authorities shaped the expression and resolution of the public land conflicts. Given their strategic position in the bureaucratic hierarchy, they also played a significant role in interpreting the issues involved in any given dispute to authorities at higher levels.

Large landowners, for the most part, declined to occupy local political posts.[41] Many, in fact, resided not in the rural towns, but in larger cities which provided a better vantage point to oversee their diverse economic interests. Local mayors, judges, councilmen, and municipal advocates (personeros), therefore, came from less prominent social backgrounds. They were poorly educated and often ignorant of the law. Explained the minister of agriculture in 1920,

Laws and decrees concerning the national domain are rarely found in the public offices of our municipalities, and since most of the functionaries are individuals without higher learning, they are always committing errors.[42]

In fact, local authorities most often erred on the side of land entrepreneurs who were expanding their properties at the expense of the colonos.
Municipal officials naturally tended to comply with the persuasions of powerful and influential persons, particularly those with well-established roots
in the region. Given the overriding importance of patronage in Colombian
political life, petty bureaucrats depended on connections with such individuals for their appointments and career advancement. In some instances,
friendship, *compadrazgo*, or kinship ties also inclined officials, most of whom
were born in the region in which they served, to favor certain land claimants.[43] Thus where large estates were already in existence and the landlords took an active role in municipal affairs, local officials were mainly
responsive to the landlords' concerns.

By their failure to comply with the stipulated grant procedures or to ad-
here to the channels by which disputes should be settled, mayors in particular could easily shift the advantage to an entrepreneur. Appointed by
departmental governors who were themselves named by the executive in Bogotá, the mayors were supposed to represent the central government in the
rural areas. However, because they depended on the municipal councils for
their salaries, mayors frequently allied with the local elites who controlled
the councils.[44] The Public Land Correspondence indicates that mayors in
most areas showed themselves either indifferent or actively hostile to settlers of public lands. The fact that colonos found it necessary to appeal to
Bogotá at all provides an indication that opportunities for redress at the local level were often closed to them.

Interestingly enough, however, in some cases one or all of the authorities
of a certain locality sided with the settlers. Full explanation of such align-
ments would require insight into the labyrinthine complexities of local politics. Apart from idiosyncratic and political party motives, however, the
decision of some local officials to support the colonos seems to have issued
from a concern to stimulate local economic growth.[45]

The formation of large properties tended to constrict population growth and
commercial activity in rural areas. Medardo Rivas, writing in 1899, described
the stullifying effects of the concentration of landholding on rural life:

In Colombia villages in the countryside languish and die, extinguished by the
great haciendas which encircle them. The villages usually subsist on a narrow

strip of land, with no common lands (ejidos), pastures, or even a little forested area where wood can be cut. The commercial activities of the townspeople are limited to opening a few groceries or to supplying the travellers who pass through.[46]

In contrast, an increase in the settler population generated business for village storekeepers and artisans. And, in some municipalities, particularly those where large haciendas had not yet taken form, it was the traders and artisans who wielded political influence.[47]

Local officials were particularly responsive to colono concerns in areas made up almost entirely of public lands where the majority of inhabitants were settlers. From time to time, a sudden shift in international prices or rumors of a new railroad would stimulate a rapid rise in land values in one or another of these frontier municipalities. When this happened, local officials tried to fend off the land entrepreneurs whose arrival, they knew from experience, heralded a rapid concentration of landholding. Such was the situation in Pandi (Cundinamarca) in 1908 when the priest, the mayor, and the municipal council petitioned the national government to prohibit all large grants within municipal limits on the grounds that hundreds of smallholders faced imminent dispossession.[48] The authorities of Victoria (Caldas) presented a similar case in emphatic terms:

> We desire assurance from the government that the petitions of numerous certificate holders who are seeking public land grants here will be rejected. . . . The grants would make it impossible for Victoria to develop economically and to acquire through colonization the population base necessary for this county to survive as an administrative entity in accordance with the Political and Municipal Code. . . . If such individuals obtain the concessions they want, this municipality will surely be annihilated. We implore your aide in the worthy defense of this pueblo.[49]

Municipalities along the Caribbean coast sometimes also protested the alienation of common lands used by the poor for agriculture and by most people for the seasonal grazing of livestock.[50] In Aguachica (Magdalena) in 1919, for example, the local government ruled that several men with colonial titles to a vast area that they had never put to use, and that the inhabitants believed to be public domain, should not be permitted to sell them. The mayor ordered the notary to refuse to register the transaction.[51] In a variation on the same theme, municipalities in the tropical rainforests of northeastern Antioquia and western Nariño often petitioned Bogotá not to award forest concessions to export companies because of the potential damage to settler interests. They sometimes raised the threat of massive emigration to Panama or Ecuador if such concessions were approved.[52]

In general, only when the massive alienation of public lands portended an exceedingly rapid and profound transformation of regional life did municipal authorities take concerted action against land entrepreneurs. In other places, where some estates already existed and where entrepreneurs had local political connections, the authorities either supported the entrepreneurs or divided their allegiances. In 1907 the municipal advocate joined with the inhabitants of Sucre (Bolívar) in opposing the grant of a tract of public lands to the mayor of that municipality.[53] Five years later, the municipal council of Prado (Tolima) protested on behalf of the colonos against an eviction order initiated by the Leiva family and sustained by the mayor and the governor.[54]

Whether or not certain municipal authorities chose to side with the colonos reflected complex political, social, and occupational tensions and alliances at the local level extending upwards into the departmental and national arenas. This configuration differed greatly from municipality to municipality and, to a certain extent, from time to time in the historical evolution of any locality. Speaking generally, however, the municipal advocates and councilmen who were most tied into local affairs tended to be more sympathetic to the colonos, while the judges and mayors, through whom the crucial judicial and administrative decisions were made, backed large land claimants.[55] The role played by local officials in the public land conflicts was therefore an ambivalent one.

In some areas, middle class allies helped groups of settlers to articulate their interests. The middle sector allies also inadvertently shaped the character of colono resistance in subtle ways. The influence of sympathetic tinterillos, cultivators, and officials may well have served to direct the settlers toward legalistic solutions.[56] By opening channels of communication from the settlers to national authorities and by encouraging the settlers to seek favorable action from above, such individuals injected the colonos' resistance with a vertical orientation.

In this period, which preceded the spread of mass politics and of leftist ideologies in rural Latin America, the colonos' supporters, like the colonos themselves, took a limited and particularistic view of the conflicts in which they took part. They made no attempt to help the settlers understand their plight in generalized terms or to foster horizontal coordination among the various colono groups. So, the colonos' reaction to the encroachment of land entrepreneurs remained narrowly and immediately defensive in character.

In the years after 1874, the concentration of landholding gave rise to hundreds of localized, structurally similar struggles over public lands, each of which ran its course independently. The Public Land Correspondence documents more than five hundred such conflicts that pitted colonos against land entrepreneurs. Maps 8 and 9 below and Map 10 (p. 95) show the location of these conflicts in successive time periods. Each dot represents one conflict in which at least twenty-five colonos were involved. In many, fifty or more families took part. The conflicts clearly follow the geographical pattern of public land grants and usurpations described in Chapter 3. These maps suggest that localized struggles gradually increased in number in the decades after 1870 as the public lands took on value with the growth of exports, the construction of railroads, and the expansion of the internal market. The growing number of colono petitions may also indicate that peasants were becoming more aware of the national government and felt themselves more able to communicate with it.

Some of the land disputes involved only a few people and lasted a short time. Where the colono population was sufficiently numerous and where middle class allies were present, conflicts between colonos and land entrepreneurs sometimes lasted for decades. In Pandi and San Bernardo (Cundinamarca) and Prado (Tolima), for example, hundreds of colonos fought the land claims of the Pardo Roche, Torres Otero, and Leiva families for thirty years.[57] Another important conflict centered in Belalcázar (Caldas) where merchant companies from Medellín disputed 10,000 hectares of land with some 2,000 Antioqueño colonos who had migrated south into the area in the 1890s.[58] Conflicts over public lands also were frequent on the Caribbean coast along the Magdalena River, on the Sinú plain, and in the United Fruit Company banana zone in the early twentieth century. One particularly notable and protracted dispute pitted the American Colombian Corporation, an American cattle company, against five municipalities in the department of Bolívar. The company claimed it had purchased the great "Terrenos de Loba," while the local people maintained the territory was public land. The controversy, which began around 1910, was still being played out in the 1930s.[59]

The Land Entrepreneurs' Response

As we have seen, the intensity and duration of the settlers' resistance in any one place depended on several interrelated factors: the socioeconomic and political conformation of the locality, the role played by municipal authorities, and the involvement of large cultivators or tinterillos. The efficacy of the colonos' resistance still remains to be discussed. The Public Land Correspondence provides no definitive answers about the resolution of individual struggles over land. In some places, it seems, settlers managed to stay on the land, the legal status of which remained undefined. In other instances, landlords surely bought up the colonos' improvements. A few colonos probably made a business of opening frontier lands, selling the clearings either to entrepreneurs or other settlers, and moving on.

In the majority of cases, however, available evidence suggests that the colonos lost out. The formation of large properties through the dispossession of frontier squatters was the dominant tendency in the 1870 - 1920 period. To understand why, we must consider the tactics land entrepreneurs used to counter peasant protests and the reaction of the national government.

According to the reform laws of 1874 and 1882, rural landlords who had problems with peasant squatters were supposed to bring a court suit (a *juicio plenario de propiedad*) against them. To win the suit, the plaintiff had to present written titles proving ownership of the land. Even if the titles were valid, he or she could not lawfully expell squatters without first paying them for their improvements.[60] These statutes were meant to ensure that colonos on public lands did not lose their claims to encroaching landlords and that settlers who unwittingly occupied private properties would receive compensation for developing the land. Because the titles of many land entrepreneurs were defective or non-existent, they consistently refused to take disputes with colonos to court. Instead, in connivance with local officials, they used intimidation, force, and administrative loopholes to get their way.

Land claimants often threatened settlers with immediate eviction if they did not sign tenancy agreements on the spot. The presence of the mayor and local police sometimes reinforced these threats. In San Cayetano (Santander), for example, Ramón González Valencia, backed by the mayor and several policemen, in 1893 forced colonos on public lands next to his hacienda to negotiate sale and mortgage documents with him.[61] Four years later, colonos from Junín (Cundinamarca) complained that Liberal merchant and coffee grower Sixto Durán pressured them to sign labor contracts in similar ways. More than 100 of the 400 settler families in the region had already given in.[62]

Map 8   Conflicts Over Public Lands, 1870–1900
Each symbol represents one conflict reported to governmental ministries in Bogotá. See appendix D for list of municipalities where conflicts occurred.
Source: ANCB volumes 1–78.

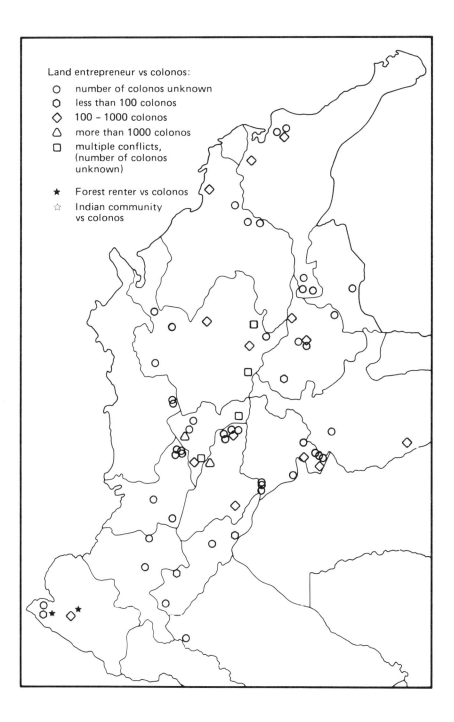

Land entrepreneur vs colonos:

○ number of colonos unknown
⬡ less than 100 colonos
◇ 100 – 1000 colonos
△ more than 1000 colonos
□ multiple conflicts,
  (number of colonos
  unknown)

★ Forest renter vs colonos
☆ Indian community
  vs colonos

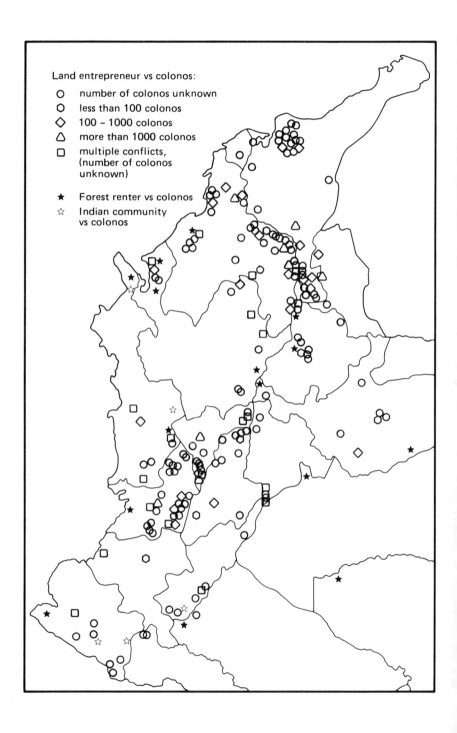

Land entrepreneur vs colonos:

- ○ number of colonos unknown
- ○ less than 100 colonos
- ◇ 100 – 1000 colonos
- △ more than 1000 colonos
- □ multiple conflicts, (number of colonos unknown)

- ★ Forest renter vs colonos
- ☆ Indian community vs colonos

If verbal intimidation proved ineffective, the land entrepreneurs generally responded with force. Some threw pasture seed into the peasants' crops
and turned cattle into their fields, destroyed their fences, confiscated their
work tools, and burned down their huts. Others, working through local officials, fined recalcitrant colonos and arrested those who went to town on market day.[63] A report submitted by colonos from Villahermosa (Tolima) in 1889
sheds light on the effects:

> At least twenty settler families here have been forced to flee the enormous
> fines, the threats, the odious treatment, and the excessive rents with which
> Sr. Pineda D. tries to oppress them; they have been compelled to abandon
> their possessions without any recompense and to take to the roads with no
> comfort except their tears and their faith in God to begin work anew. . . .
> Some of us, hoping to escape the fines, have ceded our rights to the above-
> mentioned Sr. Pineda D., remaining as tenants and in even worse conditions
> than before, because the obligations he imposes strangle the productive im-
> pulses of the cultivators.[64]

In some instances land entrepreneurs made use of an administrative procedure called a possessory action *(juicio de posesión)* to put pressure on colonos. Colombian law specified that in disputes between rural proprietors
and individuals claiming to be settlers of public lands, administrative solutions were inadmissable.[65] Municipal officials were, however, ignorant of such
technicalities. Often an entrepreneur seeking to appropriate some colonos'
land accused them before the mayor of disturbing him in the peaceful en-
joyment of his property rights. The purpose of a possessory action was to
provide immediate protection to an injured party, not to decide who really
owned the land. Therefore, rather than showing written titles, plaintiffs were
required only to prove they had "possessed" the territory for a year or more.
The testimony of three witnesses sufficed. Land entrepreneurs usually had
no trouble producing compliant witnesses: as one contemporary observer
noted, "The latifundista's economic resources and political connections put
all the probatory means on his side, making him appear 'the better posses-
sor.' "[66] If the mayor supported the large landowners, as generally occurred,

Map 9   Conflicts Over Public Lands, 1901–1917
Each symbol represents one conflict reported to governmental ministries in Bogotá.
See appendix D for list of municipalities where conflicts occurred.
Source: ANCB volumes 1–78.

colonos who refused to sign tenancy agreements faced eviction without compensation.[67]

A law passed in 1905 provided land claimants involved in expropriating settlers with an additional tool for their purposes. Article 15 of Law 57 of that year specified eviction procedures to be used against peasants who occupied private properties with full knowledge that the land was titled. In its entirety, the article read:

> When a landed estate has been occupied de facto without the intervention of a rental or tenancy contract and without the consent of the owner, the chief of police before whom the complaint is made will go to the said estate within forty-eight hours after the written presentation of the complaint; and if the occupants cannot show tenancy contracts or if they conceal themselves, he will proceed to evict them, admitting no appeals or formalities which might delay their removal from the property.[68]

Grantees and proprietors with fabricated titles turned this article against settlers of public lands. The National Labor Office reported in 1930:

> Municipal authorities are in the habit of constantly abusing Law 57 of 1905. . . . Colonos and their families very often are despoiled by the misapplication of this statute which, in truth, has become a legal betrayal of our poor citizens.[69]

The Public Land Correspondence amply confirms the truth of this statement.[70] Two detailed accounts of evictions effected under Law 57, one in Calarcá (Caldas) in 1911 and the other in Victoria (Caldas) in 1917, are particularly revealing of the concrete processes involved.[71] Ignacio Londoño and Francisco Mejía, alleged owners of the land and salt mines of "Playarica" in Calarcá, swore to the mayor that peasant invaders had occupied their property a scant three months earlier. In fact, these were settlers who had been peacefully cultivating public land for a decade. Without warning, the mayor, accompanied by a representative of the owners, local police, and witnesses, confronted the settlers, demanding written evidence that they were the plaintiffs' tenants. When they could not produce such evidence, the police threw their belongings into the road and pulled down their dwellings. The colonos, thus evicted, were warned that if they tried again to farm their fields without signing labor agreements with Londoño and Mejía, they would be prosecuted. Confronted in a similar way with eviction, five of the approximately twenty colono families in Victoria "declared before the chief of police that they were ready to recognize the Isaacs Broth-

ers as the rightful owners of the land, and they promised to present themselves at the main house of the hacienda to sign their tenancy contracts."[72]

In areas where local officials refused for whatever reason to comply with
the land entrepreneurs, some tried to impose their will directly by forming
terrorist bands *(cuadrillas)*. A letter from a large proprietor in Belalcázar
(Caldas) in 1907 complained bitterly that investors received inadequate "protection" against squatters. "Here," he warned, "where the authorities are
unreliable, the landowners soon may find it necessary to organize cuadrillas
to make the population respect what the owners so legitimately have acquired."[73] A petition from some colonos in Prado (Tolima) presents a vivid
picture of the activities of such bands in pushing colonos off their claims.
Fifty settler families in Prado on public lands adjacent to the Hacienda de
Saldaña owned by Uldarico Leiva M. were threatened by Sr. Leiva's henchmen when they sought to title their fields. According to the settlers, a mounted
band of twenty of Leiva's tenants *(arrendatarios)*, led by the administrator
of his coffee hacienda "Balcanes," systematically harrassed them. Between
April and August of 1899, this band selectively destroyed the huts, crops,
fences, and sugar mills *(trapiches)* of the seven most prosperous colono families and imprisoned several of their members on another of the Leivas' haciendas. Fearing an analagous fate, the remaining colonos felt they had no
alternative but to recognize the Leivas' claims to their land or abandon their
farms.[74]

Using administrative procedures, intimidation, and force, land entrepreneurs effectively circumvented the reform laws of 1874 and 1882. A petition from settlers in San Antonio (Tolima), sent to the Ministry of Agriculture
in 1924, epitomized the general pattern:

> In the face of an apocryphal title, the poor colono . . . , full of fear, cedes to
> the false proprietor the fruit of his toil and vigils or else is converted into a
> tenant-renter on the land that rightfully belongs to him more than to anyone
> else.[75]

The National Government and the Public Land Conflicts

Our knowledge of the landlords' tactics comes mainly from colono appeals to the central government. Settlers pressured by land entrepreneurs
saw in the national government their last resort against the entrepreneurs
and their local supporters. In writing their petitions, settlers expressed the
hope that if national authorities knew the law were being violated, they would

rectify the situation. To understand the outcome of the conflicts, it is necessary to consider not only the landlords' tactics but also the government's
response to the hundreds of settler petitions that flowed into the ministries
in Bogotá.

The Colombian government espoused a pro-settler policy throughout the
1874 - 1920 period. Several circulars sent to regional authorities in the 1880s
clearly laid out the government's position:

> The State aims to safeguard the rights of the colonos on all occasions. . . .
> The Governors are enjoined to prevent arbitrary dispossession of cultivators of
> public lands by all means at their disposal. [76]

In instructions to local authorities, Bogotá repeatedly stressed that land occupied by settlers should not be granted to other people. Furthermore, Bogotá ordered that the statutes on settlers' rights be posted in all municipal
plazas for ten consecutive market days and remain thereafter on permanent
display in the public offices. The government also asked local authorities to
enumerate the settlers in their jurisdictions so that the government could
protect them. And it urged the settlers to title their parcels in self-defense. [77]

In accordance with this procolono policy, national ministries generally
responded positively to the appeals of settlers threatened by land entrepreneurs. Occasionally the government refused to approve grants that took in
settlers' claims. In reaction to several petitions from Yolombó (Antioquia),
for example, the Ministry of Finance decreed in 1893 that land along the
railroad there be reserved for colonization even though applications for large
grants totalling 30,000 hectares had already been approved. [78] In other instances, the government granted colonos the stay against eviction *(amparo
de posesión)* they requested. This ruling was intended to forestall the dispossession of squatters through administrative channels or by force. In a
stay against eviction, the government instructed local authorities to maintain the status quo until the dispute could be taken to court, as dictated by
law. Thus, the national government tried to enforce the legal procedures
that strengthened the colonos' position. [79]

Despite the government's ostensibly good intentions, these supportive measures had little practical effect. The fact that the state was completely dependent on local reports for its perception of the controversies interfered
with its attempts to influence their outcome. In their appeals, settlers generally depicted themselves as true colonos whose holdings were menaced by
ambitious usurpers of public lands. Petitions from the land entrepreneurs
portrayed the situation in reverse, arguing that the problems stemmed from

the efforts of squatters to encroach on legitimate properties. The divergent interpretations presented by the landlords on the one hand and the colonos on the other made it difficult for authorities in Bogotá to comprehend and act on the single, underlying reality they described. The lawmakers' failure to recognize that land entrepreneurs purposefully accused colonos of illegal occupations under Law 57 of 1905 to dispossess them of their claims probably stemmed in part from this communication problem. At any rate, government authorities took no action to interfere with the practice until 1930. Bogotá tended to respond to whatever appeal it received on an ad hoc basis, depending on the information contained therein. This led the government to vacillate in its response to some controversies as its perception of the issues at stake shifted in accordance with the viewpoint expressed by each petitioner.[80]

Even when, in response to colono appeals, the ministries ordered regional and local officials to safeguard the rights of certain settlers, the execution of such directives depended entirely on local authorities. If those authorities were hostile to the colonos, the government had little means of enforcing a protective ruling or even of knowing whether or not it had been implemented.

The Public Land Correspondence contains numerous reports of cases in which underlings, in their dealings with colonos, purposefully contradicted national authorities. The most blatant example, perhaps, comes from Potosí, Obando (Valle). In the 1880s, two well-to-do cultivators of public lands, threatened by a neighboring hacendado, resisted expulsion by taking judicial action. Defeated in district court, they appealed to a superior court in Bogotá that revoked the earlier sentence. The local judge, however, nullified the favorable decision by flatly refusing to acknowledge it and clipping news of the ruling out of official publications as they arrived in the locality. Disheartened, the cultivators abandoned their possessions which passed into the hands of the hacendado.[81] In another case, departmental officials in Cundinamarca who had been instructed to defend the colonos of "Palenquero" in Caparrapí instead ordered local authorities to support the alleged proprietor.[82] And settlers in Bodega Central (Bolívar) in 1919 charged that the mayor, reneging on instructions from Bogotá that some colonos be left in peace, instead had ordered them to vacate disputed land within ninety days.[83] Thus decisions taken in Bogotá often were undermined at the departmental or local levels.

The reluctance of national authorities to challenge measures adopted by lower officials also weakened the government's procolono stance. Once concrete measures had been taken—once a large grant was approved or a group of colonos evicted—the central government often refused to consider the matter further. This was so even when the procedures used did not accord with the law. Informed that the mayor and judge of Turbo (Antioquia) had committed a series of errors resulting in the wrongful eviction of a number of settlers, the Ministry of Agriculture in 1918 responded that nothing more could be done: administrative and judicial rulings had already been handed down.[84] Furthermore, in some apparently ad hoc decisions, authorities in Bogotá arbitrarily refused to grant settlers who requested protection stays against eviction. They delegated such decisions instead to departmental officials who tended to identify with the land entrepreneurs, many of whom exercised influence at the regional level. In still other cases, colonos' appeals for help were rejected with replies similar to that appended to a petition from Pandi (Cundinamarca) in 1919: "Whosoever believes himself prejudiced by the acts of others should seek redress through the established administrative and judicial channels."[85]

Ultimately, it was left to the judiciary to decide public land disputes. The Colombian court system, however, did not provide colonos with an effective means of resistance. Court suits were expensive, prohibitively so for most settlers who had to hire their own lawyers. Circuit court judges were overworked and often corrupt, which generally meant partial to the landlords. The fact that court cases dragged on for years put the settlers at a further disadvantage. Land claimants frequently made use of the intervening period to increase pressure on the settlers, hoping to win de facto compliance with their demands before a ruling could be handed down. In the municipality of San Antonio (Tolima), for example, a state's attorney was instructed in 1920 to take action against the usurpers of 40,000 hectares of public lands. Four years later, hundreds of colonos settled on the land complained that the as-yet-untried defendants harried them mercilessly, destroying their huts and their crops. It appears that the defendants hoped to pressure the settlers into tenancy contracts, thus strengthening their tenuous claims to ownership of the land.[86] Land entrepreneurs also tried to obstruct the court suits colonos filed with countervailing charges. The mayor of Yotocó (Valle) informed the Ministry of Government in 1915 that "in several instances the provincial prefect of Buga has ordered the eviction of colonos who have suits pending against alleged proprietors."[87]

In general, then, the colonos' hope of eliciting effective support from the national government in their resistance to the encroachments of land claimants was disappointed. Despite its procolono pronouncements, the central authority in Bogotá was too weak to intervene purposefully and effectively in municipal affairs, while administrative and judicial institutions primarily served the more privileged sectors of Colombian society.[88] Clearly power lay not in any far-sighted pronouncements emanating from Bogotá, but in the labyrinthine networks of patronage, influence, and interest that textured daily life and turned the laws to their own purposes. Government in this period existed mainly to satisfy the political and economic interests of a relatively small group of powerful families, who, though they were often violently divided against each other, were still the only people with political leverage.

The result was that the formation of large properties and of a dependent labor force to work those properties proceeded concurrently. Untold thousands of colonos were deprived of their independent status and transformed into tenants, while others were evicted, thus losing the work of years. Large landowners created a supply of workers on the new estates by restricting access to public lands for the rural poor. In a report in 1935, the treasurer of Cauca correctly stressed the element of extra-economic coercion involved:

> Under the illusion of a freely celebrated labor contract, an economic struggle is concealed in which the stronger party exercises power over the weak and the destitute.[89]

The fate of those who were pushed off their holdings is unclear. Some perhaps remained in the vicinity as day laborers (*jornaleros, peones*) or signed on as tenants or sharecroppers (*aparceros*) elsewhere.[90] Other colonos, expelled from their parcels, moved as settlers toward more remote areas of the public domain where the paucity of markets limited them to subsistence production. If, after a few years, a substantial number of colono families joined them and a road went through, they usually were pushed off the land once again.[91]

Economic Consequences

As we have seen, between 1850 and 1920 thousands of settlers opened new areas to agricultural production only to be deprived of their land claims and turned into tenant farmers. The Colombian rural experience was not unique. The cumulative dispossession of peasant smallholders that marked Colombian rural life was also an integral feature of the expansion of commercial agriculture in other Latin American countries during the nineteenth and early twentieth centuries. On the Brazilian coffee frontier, the emergence of large estates was accompanied, as in Colombia, by the expropriation of settlers (*posseiros*) who were expelled onto public lands further toward the interior. The growth of agricultural exports in Peru and Mexico occasioned a similar pattern of hacienda aggrandizement. However, because economic growth in those countries centered in populated areas where land had been partitioned since the colonial period, the expansion of the estates for the most part deprived Indian communities and small proprietors, not settlers, of their holdings.[92]

In Colombia, the continuing formation of latifundia effectively limited the economic possibilities of colonos in frontier areas. Fertile land close to transport facilities and to markets passed under the control of hacendados. The opportunities for economic advancement of colonos who, as rent-paying tenants, continued to cultivate their parcels were severely restricted.

There were three major types of tenants in Colombia: arrendatarios (sometimes also known as *agregados, terrazgueros,* or *concertados);* aparceros; and *colonos a partido.*[93] Arrendatarios were service tenants who, as rent for a small plot of land on which to raise foodcrops, were expected to provide labor for the landlord's fields. Such arrangements were common both in areas of traditional agriculture in the highlands and in some coffee regions, for example western Cundinamarca and southern Tolima. In other coffee regions, like Santander, Antioquia, and Caldas, arrendatarios were few, and aparcería or sharecropping was the dominant form of tenancy. Sharecroppers paid for the use of the land with a percentage of their crops. On the cattle ranches, yet a third form prevailed. Tenants known as colonos a partido were allowed to clear a parcel of land for their own use on the undeveloped outskirts of the property on the condition that they turn it over to the landlords planted in pasture grasses after two or three years. On ranches and on some coffee estates, colonos a partido were used to expand the productive area of the haciendas. Almost all large rural enterprises also employed some wage laborers for specific tasks: they were used on coffee estates at harvest time, on cattle ranches as cowboys, and on the United Fruit Company banana plantations.

Historical variations in rural labor arrangements in Colombia have yet to be studied with the thoroughness devoted to Mexico and Peru.[94] Nevertheless, it is known that in Colombia tenants were not permitted to expand their family plots, and many were forbidden to devote their parcels to perennial cash crops like coffee that might compete with the hacienda's production. Thus, with the aim of assuring that a pool of reserve labor was always available, landlords inhibited peasant production within the haciendas. Furthermore, they appropriated most of the surpluses generated by their workers' efforts. In addition to labor obligations in the proprietors' fields, tenants and wage laborers frequently were required to do road work and police duty for free; yet they had to pay to use paths across the haciendas. Owing to these regulations, resident laborers on the large haciendas remained near the poverty level with little hope for significant improvement in living conditions.[95]

In the Antioqueño colonization area a large number of small farmers emerged with the spread of coffee cultivation in the early years of the twentieth century. Beyond this central coffee region, latifundia devoted primarily to pastoral activities came to monopolize the fertile valleys and lowlands, while the mass of peasant agriculturalists (colonos, tenants, and small proprietors) had to struggle for a meager existence on marginal land on hillsides and in the coastal hinterlands. This pattern of land use has drawn repeated criticism from Colombian and foreign observers alike who view it as an impediment to increasing agricultural productivity and to raising living standards in the rural sector.[96] In discussions by development experts, the skewed distribution of landholding and social benefits is variously interpreted as a direct legacy of the Spanish colonial past, a reflection of the noneconomic values of traditional elites, or an outgrowth of the conservatism of peasant producers. Fundamentally, however, it is regarded as a given, static phenomenon that is in itself a root cause of underdevelopment.

The present investigation advances a different perspective. It indicates that in many regions of Colombia such patterns of land use were of relatively recent origin. They constituted the logical outcome of an on-going historical process by which preexistent inequalities were projected into newly developing areas. In the Colombian context the primary motor of economic growth, the agrarian export economy, prompted the large-scale appropriation of land and labor on the part of the entrepreneurial elite during the late nineteenth and early twentieth centuries. Structural problems, including high transport costs, the lack of credit, and labor shortages, prevented the new landowners from putting their properties to full productive use. At the same time the economic activities of the elites deprived the rural poor of the control of productive resources and, consequently, of direct participation in the benefits of economic growth. The particular form of frontier development that took place under the impulse of the agricultural export economy fostered economic growth without a more equitable distribution of that wealth. The Colombian experience epitomizes the cruel dilemma of Latin American development: production rises but poverty remains.[97]

The prevalence of social conflict on the Colombian frontier graphically attests to the frustration of peasant aspirations. But because public land conflicts were localized, because both sides expressed limited goals, and because the articulation of local, regional, and national spheres was as yet tenuous, the impact of such frictions remained sharply circumscribed. Struggles over public lands surely contributed to the turbulent character of local politics in Colombia. Yet newspaper articles, scholarly essays, and government reports of the time contain almost no mention of these struggles, which were overshadowed by political issues. In the years before 1920 no one, not even the policymakers themselves, seemed to have perceived the magnitude of the land concentration that had such far-reaching effects on Colombian rural society.

5

Transformation of the Conflicts

Although, in most cases, Colombia's land entrepreneurs overcame the colonos' resistance and integrated them into their newly formed estates, they could not obliterate the settlers' memory of the injustices they had undergone. The experience of dispossession, which touched so many peasant families, imbued them with a personal conviction of the illegitimacy of the properties on which they worked and an underlying resentment against the landlords who had expropriated them. This consciousness lay dormant, however, until economic and political changes in the 1920s and early 1930s provided colonos with the leverage to renew their struggles against the predominance of the latifundia.

Following World War I, the Colombian economy expanded at heretofore unheard-of rates only to contract sharply in 1929 with the world depression. Meanwhile, the national government considerably extended its radius of influence, and the laboring classes began for the first time to take an active role in politics. These kinds of changes precipitated a shift in the relative balance of power between landlords and settlers in the old frontier regions.

Whereas before settlers had resisted the encroachments of land entrepreneurs, now they passed to the offensive. In the years after 1928 thousands of peasants invaded unproductive haciendas which, they argued, were really public lands, while at the same time resident workers on those properties threw off their tenant status, claiming to be colonos. The squatter movements, which spread rapidly to envelop whole regions where the process of land concentration had been most relentless, challenged the illegal claims on which the system of landed property was based. By the early 1930s, the new conflicts and, by extension, the property issue itself had become problems of national concern.

The origins of the transformation of the public land controversies can be traced to the economic developments of the years following World War I. The expansion and subsequent contraction of the Colombian economy affected the magnitude of entrepreneurial activity in rural areas, the agricul-

tural policies of the Colombian government, and the experiences and expectations of an important part of the rural population. All of these factors
influenced the interaction of peasants and proprietors in public land areas.

Economic Growth in the Countryside

Remembered by those who lived through it as a time of unmitigated prosperity, the decade of the 1920s marked an important transition in Colombian economic history. One investigator has described it as the passage from
a relatively closed and fragmented economic structure to a modern one, fully
integrated into the world market and possessed of the bases for industrial
expansion.[1] Viewed from a slightly different perspective, the decade witnessed the beginnings of the shift from an export-oriented economy to one
in which primary and industrial production for internal consumption would
play an increasingly salient role.[2]

The extraordinarily rapid economic growth of the 1920s stemmed from
two principal sources—the inflow of foreign capital and the expansion of
coffee exports. Whereas foreign investment had played a relatively insignif-
icant part in the Colombian economy previously, capital from the United
States began to pour into Colombia in the years after World War I. The
interest of the United States in Colombia was an outgrowth of the more general expansion of the American industrial economy, which accelerated markedly in the post-war period. During the boom years of the 1920s, North
American capital sought productive outlets overseas. Loans and investments
to Colombia climbed quickly from 4 million dollars in 1913 to 30 million in
1920, and thence to 80 million in 1925. In the years immediately preceding the depression, United States financial operations in Colombia spiralled
vertiginously to a peak of 280 million dollars.[3]

American petroleum companies, seeking to lessen their reliance on Mexican sources, invested heavily in the search for oil deposits in Colombia
during the 1920s.[4] The banana business of the United Fruit Company and
various mining endeavors counted among other important activities of U.S.
firms in these years.[5] Most of the foreign capital that flowed into the Colombian economy, however, took the form not of direct investments but rather
of loans. Between 1923 and 1929 the national, departmental, and municipal governments and Colombian banks borrowed nearly 200 million dollars
from North American agents.

While some of this capital was used to develop industrial, communications, and energy resources and municipal public services, the major part

of the foreign loans received in these years was directed toward improvement of the transport system. Convinced of the primary utility of railroads, the national government concentrated its efforts on the construction of state-owned lines. The Colombian rail system expanded by 80 percent between 1920 and 1929, from 1,320 kilometers to 2,385 kilometers.[6] Highway and arterial highway mileage also increased significantly. Undertaken with the aim of facilitating the export of coffee and other primary products, the rapid extension of the transport network had an unforeseen impact on the domestic economy. It served to break down the isolation of many local markets, especially in the western coffee zone, and thus set the bases for the unification and expansion of the internal market, for the "consolidation of a national economic space."[7]

In addition to the influx of foreign capital, the expansion of international demand for coffee, Colombia's primary export, also contributed to the economic growth of the post-war period. Coffee prices on the world exchange rose rapidly after 1920, and the volume of coffee exports increased apace. Whereas in 1915 Colombia shipped abroad approximately 130 million pounds of coffee annually, that figure had doubled by 1921 and nearly trebled by 1929. The value of Colombian coffee exports increased over 400 percent in the same period.[8] Not only did the producers themselves profit from this sudden windfall, but the associated marketing and transport sectors expanded, as did the government bureaucracy. Consequently, the coffee bonanza resulted in a notable growth in the internal market for consumer goods, both agricultural and manufactured.[9]

The search for petroleum deposits, the extension of the transport network, and the heightened demand for coffee and other foodstuffs together precipitated a marked appreciation in rural land values in Colombia during the course of the 1920s.[10] Vast tracts of hitherto worthless public lands began to attract the attention of large entrepreneurs who, as in the past, acted to enlarge their private holdings. The integration of new land into the rural economy was particularly evident in the western coffee zone, including parts of Cundinamarca, Tolima, Caldas, and Valle, and on the Caribbean coast where the banana and cattle industries were in full expansion and where petroleum speculators focused their activities. In those areas, as the Public Land Correspondence clearly indicates, elite entrepreneurs stepped up pressure on the baldíos and on colonos already settled there. Whereas the archives provide evidence for only 177 encroachments between 1901 and 1917, in the years between 1918 and 1931 the number of incidents grew dramatically. Map 10 illustrates the geographical distribution of the 307 incursions mentioned in the Public Land Correspondence for those years. The very rapid valorization of large areas of the public domain during the 1920s may also account for an increasing number of conflicts between landlords and colonos of the type described in the last chapter. Significantly, it was precisely in regions where such encroachments had been most intense that the colonos initiated their counteroffensive after 1928.

The mere intensification of pressure exerted by the landlords on settler families does not in itself, however, provide an adequate explanation for the colonos' initiative in reoccupying the land from which they had been dispossessed. Equal, if not greater, consequence must be attributed to a shift in the articulation of power between landlords and settlers. This shift stemmed from political changes at the national level associated with an increasing concentration of power in the central government and with the concurrent determination of national authorities to enforce a strongly procolono policy. To understand these tendencies, the influence of the economic transformation of the twenties on political structures and policy must be considered.

State Centralization and Agricultural Policy

The economic growth of the early twentieth century and particularly of the 1920s set Colombia on the path toward industrialization. Taking advantage of the availability of credit and the expansion of the internal market, many small textile and food processing plants appeared in the years after 1915. Although the background to this activity remains to be studied, it appears that some capital accumulated in coffee production and in the import-export trade was transferred into industry at this time.[11] Thus the birth of an industrial sector did not signify a sudden break with the past, nor did it entail the abrupt substitution of one elite group for another. Rather, economically prominent families previously involved in commerce and land speculation gradually enlarged their interests to include industrial concerns.

In conjunction with these developments, both the Liberal and the Conservative parties took the position that industrialization was beneficial and should be promoted by the state.[12] Meanwhile, the expansion of coffee ex-

Map 10   Conflicts Over Public Lands, 1918–1931
Each symbol represents one conflict reported to governmental ministries in Bogotá.
See appendix D for list of municipalities where conflicts occurred.
Source: ANCB volumes 1–78.

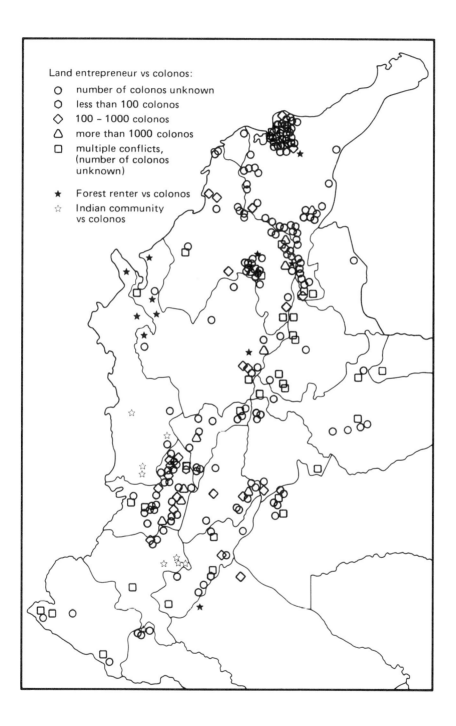

Land entrepreneur vs colonos:

○ number of colonos unknown
○ less than 100 colonos
◇ 100 – 1000 colonos
△ more than 1000 colonos
□ multiple conflicts,
(number of colonos
unknown)

★ Forest renter vs colonos
☆ Indian community
vs colonos

ports significantly increased government revenues: between 1919 and 1929 annual government income more than quadrupled. The new revenues enhanced the power of the central government, enabling it to extend its sphere of activity. [13]

A tendency toward the strengthening of state structures, culminating in the full-blown corporativism of the 1930s, has been remarked throughout Latin America in this period. [14] The 1920s were for many Latin countries a difficult time of transition during which the thrust of economic change seemed to clash with outmoded legal and institutional structures. In Colombia this incongruence was keenly felt. The government's tentative efforts to take a more energetic role in stimulating economic activity and in providing an institutional framework for economic development contributed directly to the emergence of the so-called "agrarian problem" of the late 1920s and early 1930s.

The Colombian government's concern with promoting industrialization logically led to a shift in agricultural policy. During the 1920s Colombian authorities began to redirect their attention from export agriculture to the internal market. They stressed the need to increase the production of foodstuffs for domestic consumption in order to sustain the accelerating pace of national economic development. This objective was to be attained through the reform of public land policy. Specifically, Congress took concrete measures to recover from the great latifundistas those public lands that had been usurped and left unproductive, in order to reallocate them to settler families who would farm them.

Colombian agrarian policy in the 1920s, then, was marked by a tendency to assert national economic priorities over the speculative interests of individual landowners. While the administration took steps to extend more effective control over the public domain, Congress acted to close the loopholes that had permitted land entrepreneurs to flout the laws. Simultaneously the government began to take a more active role in supporting small cultivators of public lands. The ultimate consequence of these changes was to deprive the latifundistas of certain legal-institutional support structures on which they had relied to assert their power over the colonos. The implications of the reorientation of public land policy for landlord-colono relations become evident through examination of the emergence of the new agrarian philosophy and its implementation.

The adoption of a particularly vigorous procolono policy was in part a response to inflationary problems stemming from the economic boom. During the 1920s domestic food prices in Colombia soared: between 1923 and 1929 the prices of agricultural produce more than doubled. [15] Such inflation resulted from a growing demand for foodstuffs in Colombia that, it seemed, the rural sector was unable to satisfy. Policy-makers expressed deep concern that such deficiencies in agricultural supply might well interfere with overall economic growth and particularly with industrial development. If food prices remained high, manufacturers would have to pay their workers more; as a result both investment incentives and capital accumulation would suffer.[16]

The government's immediate response to spiralling inflation was to allow the duty-free importation of food from abroad. This stop-gap measure, embodied in "Emergency" Law 3 of 1926, did in fact slow inflation rates.[17] But, as the politicians were well aware, because competition tended to depress domestic production and because food imports drained valuable foreign exchange, this solution was clearly unsatisfactory in the long run.

Within Colombia, the long-range implications of the inflation problem prompted serious discussion of factors responsible for the apparent inelasticity of agricultural supply. Interpretations advanced by Liberals and Conservatives revealed a significant measure of agreement. Most observers identified the monopoly of land by the great latifundia as the root cause of agricultural backwardness. Ministerial reports and independent economic studies alike argued that the great estates, which encompassed the most fertile and accessible territory, were chronically underutilized, inefficient, and resistant to innovation.[18] This analysis led to the conclusion that it was imperative "to have done with the noxious and antiquated latifundia system, the cause of the ruin of our agriculture," a viewpoint repeatedly voiced by Colombian statesmen in the decade 1925–1935.[19]

Policy-makers in this period stressed the need to reform the structure of landholding in order to stimulate economic growth. Specifically, they advocated the spread of family farms in the well-founded belief that small producers work the soil more intensively than large landowners. Conservative Minister of Industries Antonio Montalvo forcefully expressed the dominant attitude when in his report to Congress in 1929 he wrote,

> As the foundation of social organization, of the valorization of rural property, of collective enrichment, of domestic production, and therefore of national autonomy, it is imperative that the proprietorship of the land be distributed widely among the inhabitants of our country.[20]

Thus, there occurred a resurgence of the liberal concern to foster the formation of a rural middle class that had marked the reforms of the mid-nineteenth century. A recurrent theme in Colombian political thought, this orientation found new popularity in the 1920s and early 1930s because it responded to the exigencies posed by an economy in the initial stages of industrial development. Industrial growth required not only an adequate supply of primary materials but an expanding domestic market for its products. The Liberal party newspaper *El Tiempo* explained the implications for agricultural policy as follows:

> The agrarian question in Colombia is, or should be understood to mean, the orientation of the State in all its vigor toward a more economic concept of production that encourages the expansion of agricultural output and, at the same time, leaves the peasants with a greater margin of profit. In this way the rural population may become both more active consumers of national products and more skillful producers of collective wealth. [21]

By advocating the transformation of poor tenants, sharecroppers, and colonos into hardworking and prosperous peasant proprietors, policy-makers proposed to integrate the rural population into the national economy both as producers and as consumers.

In practice, the government attempted to foster the emergence of a rural middle class by vigorously supporting the efforts of cultivators of public lands. If the latifundistas were deemed villains, then the colonos became the protagonists of national development. "Surely it is the agriculturalist who deserves to be called 'the first citizen of our country,'" wrote the minister of industries in 1930. "There exists no more legitimate and admirable aspiration than that of the Colombian peasant to acquire a plot of land he can call his own."[22]

Colombian authorities took steps to implement the new agrarian philosophy through a two-pronged initiative. They endeavored to promote the rapid settlement of frontier areas by peasant families, while at the same time seeking to recover for the purpose of colonization territory usurped from the national domain in previous years. Although the Colombian government did not directly attack the haciendas in this period, it attempted to free some of the land hoarded by the great proprietors through rigorous enforcement of the public land legislation.

The new land policy evolved gradually during the 1920s and early 1930s. Soon after World War I the Colombian government began to show serious interest in promoting colonization of the public lands. For the first time Colombian legislators admitted the difficulties colonos faced in titling their claims and tried to remedy the situation. Law 71 of 1917 exempted settlers with holdings of twenty hectares or less from the requirements that had made grants so costly. No longer were small settlers required to hire a surveyor, buy official paper, or pay postage in applying to Bogotá for titles. Thus it became somewhat easier for settler families to obtain land grants. A further law in 1926 simplified grant procedures for colonos even more and promised that the government would provide them with credit, tools, and seed.[23]

Meanwhile, Congress, in association with the Ministry of Industries initiated the first planned colonization program, the purpose of which was to found government-financed colonies in selected areas of the country. Such colonies, it was hoped, would become poles of attraction for hundreds of other settler families, leading to the rapid development of many frontier areas. Congress agreed to aid people accepted into the new colonies with transportation, loans for food and tools, and free surveys of the land.[24] Several landed penal colonies were set up in the early 1920s, while concrete plans for purely agricultural communities in the Sumapaz region of Tolima, western Valle, Huila, Chocó, and Caquetá were disclosed in 1928.[25]

The government's efforts to encourage the growth of a rural middle class through settlement initiatives soon encountered a serious stumbling block. Because it lacked accurate information pinpointing the location of public lands, Bogotá could not guarantee that cultivators who settled land that appeared baldío would not later be evicted by some unknown titleholder. This fundamental uncertainty concerning the location and extent of the public domain tended to undermine the settlement effort. As the minister of industries observed in 1930, "Where the property issue is not defined, colonization can not prosper."[26]

Although immense, the practical difficulties of surveying the national domain might have been overcome had it not been for a fundamental juridical confusion between public lands and private property. In Colombia the public domain was defined to be all territory not privately owned. But the criteria for proof of property remained unspecified in Colombian jurisprudence. This imprecision worked to the advantage of the land entrepreneurs whose fraudulent deeds the courts generally accepted. Existing legislation gave the state no countervailing grounds on which to assert public ownership against the trumped-up claims of individuals bent on speculative gain. This situation, which frustrated the government's efforts to survey the public domain and to protect settlers against further encroachments, drew much criticism in the early 1920s.[27]

Responding to the new priorities, the Colombian Supreme Court in 1926 handed down a landmark decision intended to facilitate official colonization efforts by strengthening the position of the government in its relations with private individuals. The justices ruled that henceforth all land in Colombia would be presumed public land unless proven differently. Only by showing the original title by which the state had alienated a given tract of land from the national domain could a landowner sustain his or her legal right to that property. Wills, bills of sale, or court decisions indicating possession of the land for thirty years were no longer sufficient to prove private property.[28]

Designed primarily to protect the remaining public lands, the Supreme Court ruling of 1926 inadvertently withdrew legal sanction from many of the great estates consolidated in frontier regions in earlier years. As was to become clear, the majority of landlords in Colombia did not have the first titles the court required. Some deeds dating from the colonial period had been lost or destroyed in the civil wars that ravaged the country in the nineteenth century. In many cases, however, such titles had never existed because the land had been illegally appropriated from the national domain. Given the magnitude of land usurpation and title fraud in rural areas, the Supreme Court decision threatened to undermine the extant system of private landholding. Reported the attorney general in 1931: "There exists [in Colombia today] an almost absolute insecurity of private property stemming from the dearth of original titles."[29]

Intended to clarify the distinction between public and private land, the immediate effect of the Supreme Court ruling was to confuse matters further. In the meantime landlords with deficient titles retained control of the properties they claimed to own. Settlers who chose to squat on such properties could, however, rightfully argue that the land was public land. Many of the colonos who invaded the great estates in the early 1930s used the new ruling to justify their action.

Meanwhile, on the basis of the Supreme Court decision, the Colombian government for the first time took concrete steps to recover public lands illegally appropriated from the national domain. In 1927 Congress instructed the owners of all estates larger than 2,500 hectares to submit their original titles to the Ministry of Industries for review. If said titles were found defective or nonexistent, Congress declared its intention to reclaim the territory.[30] National authorities also endeavored to recover public lands through judicial channels: between 1918 and 1935, Bogotá authorized forty-eight law suits against large landowners who lacked titles or who were charged with inflating their boundaries.[31]

Despite the government's obvious commitment to land reform, the practical results were disappointing. A group of prominent landowners and petroleum entrepreneurs bitterly contested the title review on the grounds that it set undue limits on the exercise of private property and was therefore unconstitutional. They took their case to court, thus stalling further government action.[32] Meanwhile, most of the land suits bogged down in legal technicalities that were never resolved. Thus, the government's efforts were largely frustrated by opposition from landowning interests both inside and outside the administration and by impediments inherent to the legal-institutional system.

In the end the Colombian government did succeed in recovering a relatively small amount of territory from private owners through enforcement of the cultivation clause, which had been part of public land legislation since 1882. This clause stipulated that recipients of grants who did not make productive use of their concessions within one decade forfeited their rights to the land. Nothing, however, had ever been done to implement it. During the 1920s Colombian authorities showed a growing interest in using the cultivation provision to reassert public ownership over grants that had been left abandoned for years. When in 1931 Congress gave the administration new powers of enforcement, the recovery of unexploited land grants began in earnest. Between June 1931 and June 1936, the Ministry of Industries annulled 132 grants that had not met the cultivation requirement. This land, some 320,000 hectares in all, returned to the public domain and was made available for colonization by settler families.[33]

In the same years that the government questioned the property rights of the great landowners in frontier regions, it passed several reforms providing settlers with increased protection against land entrepreneurs. Modification of the land grant and eviction procedures, in particular, deprived landlords of the legal mechanisms they had so effectively used before to dispossess colonos.

Until 1926 anyone could contest a settler's grant application, saying that the land was private property. Land entrepreneurs often used the ruse to appropriate settlers' holdings. After 1926, this was no longer possible. Law 47 of that year, which detailed special grant procedures for plots smaller than twenty-one hectares, made no provision for objections to be raised. Thereafter, so long as a small cultivator filed the correct paperwork, he or she was assured of legal title to the land.[34] Whether or not the legislators consciously intended by this omission to favor settlers against land pretendents is unclear. In any case, the new ruling countered the tendency of hacendados to assert dominion over the fields of neighboring colonos whenever the latter petitioned for titles.

More important, national authorities revised the procedure for the eviction of squatters from rural properties. This procedure, based on Law 57 of 1905, had been abused by predatory landlords to deprive thousands of colonos of their land. In 1930, the Ministry of Industries ruled that landlords who intended to eject squatters from their properties had to present written titles proving ownership: the testimony of three witnesses no longer sufficed. Furthermore, peasants accused of trespassing were now encouraged to voice their side of the story. If the accused testified that they were not invaders of private property but instead settlers of public land, use of the administrative eviction procedure against them was prohibited. Thus hacendados and friendly local mayors who had relied on the eviction procedure to extend ownership over public lands found the ploy closed to them.[35] Such reforms provided colonos in frontier areas with new leverage against encroaching land entrepreneurs. They also weakened the defenses of latifundistas with defective titles against the occupation of their properties by peasants claiming to be settlers.

In sum, in the 1920s and early 1930s several juridical changes were instituted that increased the power of the state over the public domain and strengthened the position of the colonos. "The fields must remain unproductive no longer. . . . Alongside the right of the proprietors, a new right has been born which is that of the cultivators of the soil," observed a Colombian congressman in 1926.[36]

In the years after 1928 the cultivators themselves set out to vindicate that right by recovering from the hacendados the land of which they had been dispossessed. Peasants in some rural areas took advantage of their newly strengthened legal position to assert or reassert claims to the land. Thus the land struggles of the early 1930s, in which the colonos took the offensive, were in one sense a logical outgrowth of the agrarian policy espoused by national authorities.

It has been suggested that control of the central government by socialist or reformist parties is a necessary condition for peasant revolt.[37] Certainly, in many countries peasant mobilization has been closely associated with the rise of a sympathetic government to power. Often, it is the promise of land reform that precipitates conflict between peasants and landlords, each group seeking to assert its advantage within an altered legal framework. Such conditions contributed to the eruption of agrarian unrest in Mexico in the 1920s, in Guatemala and Bolivia in the early 1950s, and in Peru and Brazil in the early 1960s.[38]

Similarly the prospect of a change in landholding structures advocated by national authorities played an important role in the outbreak of the Colombian squatter movements of the late 1920s and early 1930s. The reforms that precipitated such activity in Colombia were not, however, the work of a reformist party, much less of socialists, but rather of establishment politicians. Begun by the Conservative party, which had held power for forty years, the elaboration of the new agrarian policy continued after 1930 under a coalition government headed by a Liberal president. The reforms reflected the efforts of a newly strengthened government to facilitate the transition from an export to an industrial economy using elements specific to the Colombian historical experience.

Although the new agrarian program surely influenced the transformation of the public land conflicts, it does not completely explain the land hunger manifested by a broad spectrum of the Colombian rural population in those years. To understand the motives that led thousands of rural people, calling themselves colonos, to occupy the great estates, it is necessary to examine the impact of the economic expansion of the 1920s and the subsequent depression on the Colombian peasantry.

The Peasant Experience: Rising Standards of Living, Rural Out-Migration, and Labor Organization, 1920-1928

In the decade after World War I, the prosperity that marked Colombian society touched the country people as well. Some got land in frontier regions under the new legislation: the number of small land grants rose dramatically in these years, particularly in the departments of Caldas, Huila, and Valle.[39] At the same time, just as many or perhaps even more colonos lost their claims to rapidly expanding estates in other frontier areas. The situation of those expelled was not, however, as grim as before: in the 1920s, members of the rural lower classes found new economic opportunities as wage laborers in the towns.

The creation of jobs and the promise of higher salaries in urban areas induced a significant number of peasants in the 1920s to leave rural life behind. The government-sponsored public works program, financed by foreign loans, particularly increased the demand for salaried labor. By 1928 aproximately 36,000 people, comprising more than 8 percent of the active rural labor force, were employed on railroad, road, and other construction projects.[40] Census material provides additional evidence of demographic movement from rural areas toward urban centers concurrent with the economic boom of the twenties. Towns with more than 1,000 inhabitants, which included only 21 percent of the total population in 1918, absorbed 38 percent of the population growth between 1918 and 1925 and 53 percent in the 1925-1930 period.[41]

At the same time, the spread of coffee cultivation gave rise to a demand for more workers on the coffee estates. Given the steady stream of cityward migration, the planters found labor in short supply. In the years after 1924, large coffee growers complained with growing insistence of a labor shortage *(escasez de brazos)* in the countryside.[42] The Assembly of Boyacá, a rural department near Bogotá, went so far as to prohibit by legislative fiat the movement of the rural population beyond departmental boundaries. The national government, however, overruled the restriction. Thus, there developed a tension between urban labor requirements and those of commercial agriculture during the 1920s. Landlords were notably unsuccessful in their efforts to elicit the support of the state in directing labor towards their estates.

The acute labor scarcity in rural Colombia contributed to an improvement in living standards during the 1920s for those workers who elected to remain on the haciendas. Rural wages for day laborers and tenant farmers doubled in some areas, rising to as high as 1.20 pesos a day.[43] Meanwhile, service tenants on the coffee estates of western Cundinamarca and eastern Tolima took advantage of their strengthened bargaining position to seek concessions from the landowners. They pressured landlords to reduce their work obligations and to allow them to plant coffee trees on their subsistence plots, seeking in this way to maximize family earnings by entering into commercial production. The proprietors generally opposed their tenants' demands, resulting in controversies on haciendas throughout the region in the years after 1926.[44]

Together with the new opportunities afforded by the economic boom, contact with the nascent Colombian labor movement also impressed both urban and rural workers with new attitudes and expectations. Before World War I, artisans comprised the bulk of the so-called laboring "class" in Colombia. Organization was limited to mutual aid societies, generally formed under the paternal auspices of the Catholic church. The economic growth of the post-war period, which gave rise to a larger concentration of wage workers, also stimulated the emergence of more combative organizations claiming to represent the interests of that sector.[45] Railroad, port, and river transport workers, together with laborers in the foreign petroleum and banana enclaves, provided the prime constituency for the developing labor movement. The years 1918–1923 saw the formation of the first Colombian trade unions and the first strikes for better working conditions. Strike activity became especially widespread after 1924, culminating in the great strike against the United Fruit Company in 1928 portrayed in the Nobel-prize-winning novel *One Hundred Years of Solitude*.[46]

The Colombian labor movement of the 1920s consisted of a diverse admixture of groups, the majority of which expressed in vaguely socialist, sometimes revolutionary language the general aims of bettering the workers' lives and spreading social justice. The leaders of this movement were themselves a heterogeneous lot, including "Liberal party generals from civil war days, politically neutral syndicalists, artisans the sons of colonos and of coffee farmers . . . , radical *caudillos* (bosses), agrarianist lawyers, and school teachers."[47] In contrast to Argentina and Brazil, European immigrants played a negligible role.

The National Workers' Congress instituted loose nation-wide coordination among the various labor groups in 1924. Two years later the Workers' Congress was supplanted by the newly formed Revolutionary Socialist Party *(Partido Socialista Revolucionaria* — PSR). A political party representing workers' interests, the PSR had little well-defined ideology. In general terms, however, it advocated improvement of the situation of the working class, agrarian reform with land for the peasants, and anti-imperialism, and its members expressed admiration for both the Russian and the Mexican models. A handful of party activists, of whom Ignacio Torres Giraldo, María Cano, Raúl Eduardo Mahecha, and Tomás Uribe Márquez were the most prominent, dedicated themselves to the tasks of lecturing and agitation. They toured cities and rural villages throughout the country, giving public speeches, encouraging the formation of regional coordination committees, and participating in the organization of local strikes. Owing in part to such activity, workers' newspapers sprang up in most departmental capitals during the 1920s.[48]

Although the PSR exercised its greatest influence among urban workers and those on public construction projects, the party sought a rural base as well. It invited rural delegates to national conventions, set up a committee for peasant and Indian affairs, and supported colonos and arrendatarios in several disputes with landowners in the late 1920s.[49] The banana strike of 1928 and the so-called "Bolshevik Rebellion" that occurred a year later in El Líbano (Tolima) furnish dramatic examples of PSR organization in some areas of commercial agriculture.[50] Given the widespread, albeit unfocused, impact of the Colombian labor movement in the 1920s, it is clear that many recent migrants from the countryside and rural people in some districts were exposed to the new currents reminding workers of their rights and calling for social change.

For the lower sectors of Colombian society, most of whom had strong roots in the countryside, the boom years of the 1920s were a time of new opportunities and experiences and of rising expectations. According to Minister of Industries Francisco José Chaux, the aspirations of many Colombian peasants who sought to better their lot focused on one ultimate objective:

The general development of the country between 1922 and 1930 awakened among the *campesinos* the intense desire to work for their own benefit and to acquire, as the fruit of their labor, rights to the land.[51]

The Depression

The onset of the world depression brought the era of prosperity in Colombia to an abrupt halt. Responding to world-wide overproduction, coffee prices began to fall early in 1928. The collapse of the international economy in 1929 made the situation much worse. Along with coffee prices on the international market, rural salaries declined precipitously by 50 to 60 percent. Meanwhile, with the suspension of foreign credit in 1929, public construction projects closed down and thousands of workers lost their jobs.[52]

Widespread unemployment raised the prospect of social disorder. Vagrants loitered on street corners, and petty robberies soared. Labor unions and the newly formed Communist party organized mass hunger marches in the larger cities. Meanwhile authorities from the departments of Caldas and Valle reported that roving bands of workers dismissed from railroad projects exacted food and supplies from fearful hacendados.[53] The government's response to what it perceived as an alarming situation was a logical one: it encouraged those without jobs to return to the countryside from whence they had come.

Intended to defuse the social problem in the cities, the reintegration of the unemployed into the rural sector, it was hoped, would also help alleviate the economic crisis. The coalition government that assumed power in 1930 stressed the importance of producing more foodstuffs for domestic consumption in order to replace food imports and keep prices down. It saw an increase in agricultural output as one essential prerequisite for economic recovery. The return of the jobless to agricultural pursuits was viewed to be a first step toward that goal.[54]

Although the government, headed by Liberal President Enrique Olaya Herrera, made no attempt to regulate the process through which the jobless reentered the rural economy, it strongly advocated the acceleration of colonization efforts.[55] Liberal party ideologues and newspapers took up the cause, while the minister of industries proclaimed, "Colonization represents without a doubt the source of our economic redemption."[56] Meanwhile, Congress, as already described, adopted several measures intended to protect settlers and hasten the reclamation of public lands.

To facilitate the movement of people back to the countryside, national and departmental officials offered free railroad tickets to whoever avowed their intention to take up a hoe. Many of the unemployed acted on the government's offer. In Bogotá alone in the first year of the depression, 1,700 laborers solicited rail passes enabling them to depart for the countryside.[57] While some of those who left the towns returned to the rural neighborhoods where they were born, others sought better economic opportunities in areas of commercial production. Thus, people in the interior gravitated toward the coffee regions in western Cundinamarca, Tolima, Caldas, and Valle.[58] The banana enclave and the Sinú Valley around Montería on the Caribbean coast drew numerous families as well.

Ironically, the government's policy to pacify social unrest in the cities inadvertently heightened tensions in the countryside. As the minister of industries reported a few years later, the urban migrants returned, "carriers of a new form of discontent that spread rapidly among the rural population."[59] Many former construction workers refused to accept contracts on the haciendas which, afflicted by falling profits and capital shortages, attempted to reimpose the low wages and arduous work obligations of the pre-boom years.[60] In the tenant farmers who stayed on the estates, the migrants encountered an affinitive dissatisfaction with the suddenly worsening work conditions.

As in times of economic recession in the past, the Colombian rural population manifested a defensive tendency to seek economic security as independent cultivators.[61] Many of the returning migrants as well as rural laborers and dispossessed colonos struck out in search of vacant land on which to raise food to sustain their families and produce a marketable surplus on the side. In the years after 1928, however, these people refused to be relegated to marginal lands in remote frontier areas where they would be limited to subsistence. Rather, they sought to realize their aspirations for economic mobility by occupying not only well-situated public lands, but also unused parts of large properties that had been usurped from the national domain.

Thus, distressed by the prospect of sudden impoverishment after a time of great prosperity, various elements of the rural population sought to ameliorate their economic position in a movement that reflected their own desire for landownership and, at the same time, mirrored the state's agricultural philosophy. In effect, they acted to implement the government's as yet unrealized policy of putting land immobilized by speculators to productive use. The peasants who took part in the land struggles of the early 1930s appear to have believed that their activities were not only legal, but also in harmony with national interests. They fully expected the government to support them in their efforts to carve from the underexploited latifundia thousands of intensively cultivated smallholdings.

In sum, in Colombia the transformation of conflicts over public lands resulted from a particular confluence of circumstances. During the 1920s land entrepreneurs stepped up pressure against colonos in economically dynamic areas. At the same time legal reforms, which weakened the repressive capacity of the landlords, altered the balance of power between the contending parties and gave the colonos a legal justification for reclaiming land. Meanwhile, migration to the public works encampments provided some peasants with new economic opportunities and with exposure to labor organizations calling for social justice. The advent of the world depression in 1929 aggravated the discontent of the rural populace and concurrently heightened the colonization impulse that, in accordance with the government's agrarian philosophy, came to focus on those public lands wrongly claimed by latifundistas. Thus a number of factors frequently mentioned as causes of peasant movements—including increased exploitation, closer ties between city and countryside, political centralization, and the frustration of rising expectations—were all present in the Colombian case.[62]

Most students of rural history would admit the importance of studying structural changes in the larger society in order to explain the emergence of peasant movements. Some disagreement exists, however, concerning whether peasants are capable of mobilizing themselves or whether the initial impulse must necessarily come from individuals with urban experience, often of middle class origin. Some analysts argue that only when enlightened by outside organizers do peasants become capable of accurately perceiving their own interests and acting upon them.[63] Otherwise, it is said, rural folk remain deferential, fatalistic, and suspicious of one another, the victims of a "feudal-religious" world view or, alternatively, of a "culture of repression." In accordance with this viewpoint, many Colombians believe that the agrarian conflicts of the 1930s originated in the organizational efforts of leftist sympathizers who became involved with peasants at that time.

Such an interpretation, which disregards the historical evolution of the land problem in Colombia, is not only simplistic but largely erroneous. The root cause of the public land conflicts of the 1930s must be sought in the fundamental and enduring conflict of interest between landlords and colonos over control of the land, of which the colonos were acutely conscious. Colombian peasants had not taken concerted action to reclaim the land in earlier years because of a realistic appraisal of the circumstances, that is, because they lacked the means and the support structures to do so. By 1928, the situation had changed.

6

The Peasants Take The Initiative

The late 1920s and early 1930s was a time of agrarian unrest in Colombia. Tenant farmers agitated for better work contracts and the right to plant coffee on their plots, while Indians clamored for the return of their communal lands.[1] At the same time, thousands of peasants in frontier regions invaded newly formed haciendas, seeking to reclaim the public lands they had lost. Although the means and justifications each group used were different, underlying these movements was one common theme. Indians, tenants, and colonos all sought to liberate themselves from the great estates and to become independent producers once again.

This was an important period in Colombian agrarian history. In the early 1930s, non-Indian peasants first made use of the land invasion tactic, the first Colombian peasant leagues took form, and peasants first began to identify with left-wing political parties. The purpose of this chapter is to explore the forms the struggles took in frontier regions. Just as the new public land conflicts reflected the larger changes affecting Colombian society, so they were also to shape the economic and political evolution of Colombia in the years to come.

The Squatter Movements: A Regionalization

After 1928 the peasants in regions of recent frontier development passed to the offensive. Many tenant farmers suddenly declared that they were settlers, not tenants, and that the land was public, not private property. They refused to pay their obligations and began to till their family plots independently of the haciendas in which they were embedded.[2]

Meanwhile groups of settlers, rural wage laborers, and construction workers laid off in the first years of the depression invaded idle portions of the same properties. Like the tenants, the newcomers called themselves colonos. And, as colonos had always done, they built huts, cleared small fields, and petitioned the government to protect them against the attacks of the landlords who, they said, had robbed the nation of its patrimony.

In their initial incursions, these squatters often escaped detection by working collectively at night. Thus, in less than a week, cleared and planted fields and improvised shelters appeared where only forests stood previously. Many such occupations took place on holdings where tenants had already denied the proprietors' claims to ownership. They occurred, as well, on cattle ranches, banana plantations, and abandoned properties where no tenant population existed.[3]

Once they established themselves on the haciendas or, in the tenants' case, ceased to pay obligations, the squatters sent petitions to Bogotá asserting that the land they farmed was public land. They argued either that the territory had been usurped from the public domain or that it should have reverted to the public domain for lack of cultivation. On these grounds, squatters requested that the government take judicial action to reclaim the land for the nation. In the meantime, they asked to be accorded the full protection due colonos of public lands under Colombian law.[4]

The land occupations described above occurred in seven different areas of Colombia in the early 1930s.[5] Organizationally unconnected, the various squatter movements were shaped by similar factors. They all emerged in regions of large latifundia with a recent history of land concentration and colono-land entrepreneur tensions. Moreover, the focal regions tended to be commercially important areas in which the impact of the world depression was felt with particular severity. As shown in map 11, the major regions included the coffee zones of Sumapaz, Quindío, Huila, and northern Valle, the Sinú cattle ranching area, and the United Fruit Company banana zone. A brief overview of the origins of these movements sheds light both on similarities among them and on their regional variations.

The department of Cundinamarca was "the nerve center of the agrarian problem"[6] in Colombia in the late 1920s and early 1930s. The squatters' movement there centered in the province of Sumapaz, which extends southwest from Bogotá down the mountains into the department of Tolima.[7] An isolated frontier zone, the province first attracted commercial investors at the time of the cinchona bark boom in the mid-nineteenth century. Several merchants based in Bogotá acquired large grants, while others bought land from a speculator, one Ignacio Umaña, who is said to have sold great tracts

Map 11   Areas of Squatter Occupations, 1928–1936

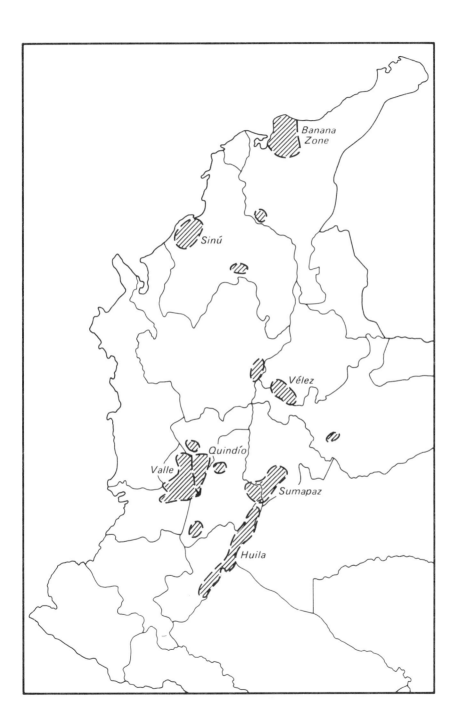

of baldíos to which he held no legal title. Only with the spread of coffee cultivation after 1860 and particularly after 1900 were these properties put into production.

The expansion of the coffee economy drew migrants from the crowded eastern highlands and from Antioquia into the Sumapaz region. Contracted for the coffee harvest, many stayed to try their fortunes as colonos on the huge expanses of public land remaining in the area. In the years after 1909 national authorities were inundated with complaints from settlers that hacendados, particularly the Leiva, Torres Otero, and Pardo Roche families, were extending their boundaries to enclose the colonos' fields.[8] Many settlers in Sumapaz, it appears, were turned into tenants, while those who maintained their independence were pushed onto marginal lands above the coffee line. Among colonos and tenants alike, new encroachments kept memories of the illegal expansion of the great estates alive.

From 1920 on, there were references to growing tenant dissatisfaction in the Sumapaz region. Many tenants in the area were colonos a partido who cleared new land on the outskirts of the haciendas and left it planted in coffee trees. These people, who often lived ten to thirty kilometers from the manor house, rarely came into contact with the landlord. They controlled their own work processes, and what they wanted most was to sever all ties with the hacienda, to work for themselves.[9]

In 1928 the Colombian government provided them with the justification they sought. Intending to launch a government-sponsored colonization program, the Ministry of Industries set aside several thousand hectares for a colony in the municipalities of Iconozco and Cunday. In the decree establishing the colony, the ministry ruled that all territory within the colony's designated boundaries should be considered public land, with the exception of those estates whose owners could show first titles in accordance with the Supreme Court ruling of 1926.[10] This decree had unforeseen consequences.

Immediately the tenants on several coffee estates within the area declared themselves colonos, arguing that the land they tilled had been usurped from the public domain. Massive invasions of the unexploited uplands of those estates followed.[11] Some of the squatter invaders were wage laborers previously employed by the tenants to perform their labor obligations; others were tenants from adjacent properties; and still others probably were unemployed laborers from the nearby port of Girardot on the Magdalena River or from Bogotá.

The squatter movement promptly spread to properties outside of the official colonization reserve. In May 1930, 800 families of arrendatarios ceased to pay their obligations on the immense Hacienda de Sumapaz, which covered parts of the municipalities of Bogotá, San Bernardo, Pandi, Usme, and Gutiérrez (Cundinamarca) and San Martín and Uribe (Meta).[12] Ten additional estates, including those of the Leiva and Torres Otero families, were also affected by tenant rebellions and squatter invasions.[13] By 1931 approximately 2,500 colono families or more than 10,000 individuals were established on 500,000 hectares of disputed land throughout the Sumapaz region. And the movement was spreading to the north and the east.[14]

When national authorities reviewed the titles of the disputed properties, they found the squatters were correct in questioning the legality of the landlords' claims. The Hacienda de Sumapaz, with what was at best a questionable legal right to 9,300 hectares, had appropriated 290,000 hectares of public lands over the years. The Torres Otero estate had expanded even more, from 426 hectares in 1823 to 300,000 hectares by 1930.[15] Moreover, the owners of these vast properties had left them virtually unexploited: when the squatter invasions began, less than 5 percent of the land they claimed to own was being used in cattle pastures, coffee plantations, or cane fields.[16]

On the Caribbean coast, a squatters' movement also emerged in the early 1930s in the Sinú region of the department of Bolívar.[17] In the nineteenth century, this region, which centered on the municipality of Montería, had a few slave haciendas and a mass of poor cultivators on public lands. The settlers raised foodcrops in small fields called *rozas*, which they cleared from the grass-covered plains, and made some money on the side collecting *raicilla* and various woods for sale. With the development of the cattle economy after 1870 and an influx of French and North American investors in the 1880s and 1890s, the area underwent a dramatic change. Some speculators resurrected titles to long forgotten concessions, while others applied to the government for public land grants covering thousands of hectares. In the years after 1910, the onset of petroleum exploration further heightened the speculative impulse. Usurpations of public lands were legion, resulting in the consolidation of numerous latifundia, some more than 25,000 hectares in size. Many of these properties were put to no use whatsoever.[18]

The rapid privatization of public lands in the Sinú stripped many squatters of their claims.[19] Some became tenant-colonos on the cattle estates, obliged to move to a different part of the property each year leaving newly sown pastures behind. Others fell into a particularly harsh form of indebted wage labor, known as *matrícula*. And still others were forced off the land altogether: in the 1920s hundreds of peasant families left for the jungles of northeastern Antioquia because, one official remarked, landlords were monopolizing the whole of the Sinú.[20]

Settlers organized against predatory latifundistas relatively early in this region owing to the catalytic role played by Vicente Adamo, an Italian immigrant with socialist convictions who arrived in Montería in 1915. During his first years in Colombia, Adamo formed workers' societies in the municipal seats of Montería and Cereté. Then in 1919 he organized a group of several hundred colonos from Lomagrande to defend themselves with arms against the constant encroachments of neighboring landlords. The murder of a police lieutenant who tried to dislodge the colonos in 1921 led to increased repression. Pressures on settlers in the region intensified; many colonos only marginally associated with the conflict received long prison terms, and, finally, in 1927 Adamo himself was deported from Colombia. Lomagrande, however, remained in colono hands, the occupied territory known far and wide as the "Red Bastion" *(Baluarte Roja)*.[21] This early history of struggle profoundly influenced the rural poor of the Sinú.

As land pressures escalated during the 1920s, so did the level of social tension. This tension expressed itself in various forms. In 1927 a wandering prophet proclaimed the end of the world and thousands of peasants converged on the municipality of San Marcos in what appears to have been an incipient millenarian movement.[22] Four years later on election day Montería was wracked by violence, leaving sixty-nine dead and 146 houses burned to the ground. Local authorities blamed the violence not on political passions, but on the underlying social problem.[23]

In the months following the elections of 1931, the squatters' movement began in earnest. Organized groups of 100 to 300 peasants invaded latifundia in several municipalities. Early in 1932 the mayor of Montería reported to the governor: "Serious, nay alarming conflicts over the ownership and possession of land are now in progress throughout the Sinú."[24] Land invasions occurred at this time in other parts of Bolívar as well, most notably in the municipality of Majagual where hundreds of colonos occupied cattle ranches claimed by a British firm, the Lancashire General Investment Company.[25]

Several hundred kilometers to the east, conflicts over land also erupted in the United Fruit Company banana zone, which covered five municipalities around the port of Santa Marta. Although Colombian entrepreneurs early on had expressed an interest in exporting bananas, the endeavor required large capital investments that only the Boston-based company was able to provide. During the first decades of the twentieth century, the United Fruit Company built the wharves, rail lines, and irrigation canals that permitted Colombia to produce bananas for world markets.[26]

The North American firm's eagerness to purchase great quantities of land, together with the high profits to be made from bananas, produced a sudden

upsurge in land values after 1915. Public lands, which had been plentiful
in the area, were avidly sought after both by the United Fruit Company and
by nationals with investment capital. "The desire for territory and the conflicts over land which have been aroused in this region are unbelievable,"
wrote the state's attorney in 1923. "Everyone wants to start up a banana
farm in two months or less."[27]

Those who suffered most from the real estate boom were, of course, the
settlers who farmed public lands.[28] As in Sinú and Sumapaz, colonos comprised a significant part of the rural population of Santa Marta. Settler families squatted in the interstices of the great plantations on unirrigated land
unfit for bananas. They provided the local market with foodstuffs and the
United Fruit Company with a supplementary work force at harvest time.

In the 1920s, as plantations expanded through the frenetic appropriation
of public lands, many settlers found themselves involved in a hopeless struggle against dispossession. In those years more conflicts between colonos
and encroaching landlords occurred in the banana enclave than in any other
part of Colombia.[29] Pushed off the land, many colonos had no alternative
but to become full time wage laborers on the banana plantations.

During the depression, many plantation workers who had become unemployed reasserted colono status. In response to the contraction of world markets, the United Fruit Company cut back production in Colombia: between
1928 and 1934, the Company reduced the acerage it cultivated in bananas
by 75 percent. At the same time it restricted the use of export facilities and
advances of credit to national producers, thereby causing many Colombians
to abandon their plantations as well. As a result, several thousand plantation workers lost their jobs.

At this juncture, the unemployed, some of whom had been settlers in
earlier years, turned their sights towards the land. In June of 1930, the
public lands commissioner discerned among the laboring classes of the area
"a vehement, collective desire . . . to make themselves landowners."[30] During that summer and fall, thousands of unemployed wage workers, calling
themselves colonos, moved onto idle United Fruit Company properties, cleared
small fields, and planted foodcrops. Some 10,000 hectares formerly controlled by the company were repatriated by squatters between 1930 and
1935.[31] The new settlers' outlook, which combined strict legalism with an
increasing assertiveness, was clearly expressed in a petition directed to Bogotá in 1930. The petition demanded an immediate grant of land

> because we are colonos . . . and therefore are, according to the Sr. Minister,
> 'the first citizens of Colombia'; and also because we believe that now is the

time the public land laws must be put into effect so that they no longer constitute ornamental illusions for the poor and for the North American imperialist
capitalists real and effective means for the easy accumulation of property.[32]

In the Andean mountains of central Colombia, a squatters' movement
emerged in southwestern Caldas, today the department of Quindío. One of
the last frontiers of the Antioqueño colonization, Quindío is generally thought
to have been an area of small coffee farmers. In reality, members of the
Caldense commercial elite had carved several large cattle ranches from public lands as settlers were opening the region. In the years after 1890, the
landlords actively sought to attract more colonos from neighboring departments to settle on or near the territory they claimed.[33] By the early 1930s,
according to a contemporary observer, the concentration of landed property
and accompanying colono-landlord tensions posed as much of a problem in
Quindío as in the Sinú.[34]

The squatters' movement, which began slightly later in Quindío than elsewhere, found its motive in Law 52 of 1931 which stipulated that all unexploited land grants should revert to the public domain. In November and
December of 1931, hundreds of colono families invaded eleven estates in
the municipalities of Armenia, Quimbaya, and Montenegro.[35] They claimed
that, for lack of cultivation, the land they occupied had returned to the national domain. Despite emergency eviction measures taken against them,
650 squatters in Montenegro managed, with the support of the municipal
council, to remain on four haciendas through 1936. In that year the Hacienda Nápoles was invaded once again, as were previously unaffected properties in the municipalities of Pijao and Belalcázar.[36]

The department of Valle del Cauca, to the southwest of Caldas, was yet
another focal point of confrontation. Valle experienced rapid growth after
1915 when the completion of the Panama Canal and of a railroad linking
Cali to the port of Buenaventura opened international trade from the Pacific
coast of Colombia.[37] Responding to new economic incentives, many hacendados with colonial titles to valley flatlands began to enclose public lands
higher up the mountains. These encroachments led to a growing number of
conflicts between the proprietors of cattle, sugar, and coffee estates and the
hundreds of Antioqueño settlers who had recently moved south into the
area.[38]

Around 1930, a time when unemployment was severe in Cali and in the
surrounding coffee municipalities, colono resistance to landgrabbers began
to assume new forms. In 1932, the governor explained the situation as follows:

The basic principle of our agrarian reform is summed up in the phrase, 'The right of property must be founded in the productive expoitation of the land.' In the belief that agrarian reform can be implemented outside of lawful and orderly channels, recently there have occurred in this department many acts of violence against private property. . . . Very frequently, daily in fact, settlers of public lands . . . organize themselves in groups and refuse to leave when they are notified that the land on which they have squatted is private property. In other cases, which are equally common, groups of people born in a given region and sometimes even the very tenants of a hacienda seize it, knowing full well that it is privately owned. They pretend to justify such actions on the grounds that the owner cannot or will not exploit the territory to its full productive capacity, and they begin to work the land, in effect usurping it.[39]

Such land occupations occurred in many municipalities throughout Valle, including Ansermanuevo, Toro, Obando, Cartago, Caicedonia, Riofrío, and Pavas.[40]

Centers of colono-proprietor antagonism developed, too, in the eastern part of the department of Huila in the early 1930s. Although the aggravating influence of rapid economic growth was somewhat less pronounced there, conditions in Huila east of the central cordillera resembled those in Valle. Large cattle haciendas on the plains had never been delimited from public lands higher up the mountains. As the uplands were gradually cleared and settled through the years, hacendados tended to extend their boundaries.[41]

With the onset of the depression, more and more people moved onto the mountain slopes seeking to wrest a living from the soil. As early as 1931 national authorities noted that tensions between the settlers and the alleged proprietors of the land were escalating.[42] In June of 1936 the governor of Huila reported:

In this department we have a series of conflicts between landlords, on the one hand, and colonos and arrendatarios, on the other, all along the eastern mountains from the municipality of Colombia [in the north] to that of Guadalupe [in southeastern Huila]. In many cases the agriculturalists, who penetrate virgin forests to till the land, have reason on their side. The squatters are opposed by proprietors who claim great extensions of territory that they neither exploit themselves, nor permit others to farm.[43]

The province of Vélez in southwestern Santander also witnessed the intensification of squatter activity in the late 1920s and early 1930s. Colonos were drawn to the municipalities of Sucre and Jesús María in part because of the welcome given them by local authorities. Seeking to promote eco-

nomic growth, in 1925 the municipal council of Sucre asked Bogotá to revoke unexploited grants in the region so that the land could be opened for
settlement.[44] The request went unanswered. The first indication that the
cultivators themselves intended to claim unproductive properties came in
1929 when tenants on the Hacienda La Peña refused to pay their obligations and squatter invasions followed.[45] Meanwhile, as the depression deep-
ened, colonization increased: by 1935 more than 3,000 cultivator families
had settled in Sucre and Jesús María. The absence of legally established
property limits in the region aggravated disputes between landlords and squatters, both within private holdings and in zones generally considered baldío.
The departmental secretary linked the intensification of such conflicts in
1936 to the government's agrarian reform policy:

> Because of the discussion and passage of the agrarian reform bill by the pres-
> ent Congress, the social problem, previously dormant, has risen to a crisis
> point. The law has stimulated a three-pronged campaign of agitation on the
> part of settlers who demand their legitimate rights, invaders and usurpers who
> aim to give a demagogic interpretation to the new statute, and some landlords
> who still regard the right of property with the same superstitious reverence
> with which the ancient Egyptians venerated the sacred crocodile.[46]

The regions described above were, then, the principal areas of Colombia
that gave birth to colono movements in the 1920s and early 1930s.[47] The
Colombian squatter initiative consisted of numerous spontaneous movements
that emerged independently of one another. What was evident in these movements was the emergence of a new form of peasant protest. Those who, calling themselves colonos, took part in the hacienda invasions of the early 1930s
were not necessarily the same settlers who had been involved in the earlier
struggles. Rather, adoption of the colono role and the claims of public land
rights inherent to it comprised one strategy embraced by many segments of
the rural and even urban population to ameliorate their economic condition.
Tenants, rural day laborers, construction workers, and plantation hands all
turned their sights toward the land because other options were few and because the government's agrarian policy made the reclamation of public lands
a distinct possibility.

The squatters' initiative consisted, essentially, in a spontaneous, mass
assertion of legal rights. In this period legalism proved to be "a potent, if
limited social force"[48] contributing to the mobilization of the Colombian peasantry. Beyond the letter of the law, squatters in all areas also invoked the
general principle of cultivators' rights: "Whether or not they actually be-

lieve it," one observer noted in 1933, "the peasants commonly claim that they are the true owners of the land because they have worked it."[49] Advanced by Spanish jurists in the colonial period and later incorporated into Colombian public land legislation, this principle naturally held great appeal for the rural poor. As the concept of the social function of property became popular among Colombian policy-makers in the late 1920s, it provided the squatters with a rallying cry. In opposition to the landlords' assertion of written titles, the colonos argued that effective exploitation of the land should be the true criterion for landownership. In accordance with this conviction, wrote the minister of industries in 1931,

> The peasants have begun to believe that land not utilized at present by its proprietor can be freely settled by colonos. In the peasant mind, the notions of uncultivated land and public land have become increasingly confused.[50]

Thus, the new agrarian policy discussed in the preceding chapter informed that rudimentary ideology expressed through the colono movements. Significantly, the squatters consistently avowed that by reclaiming unexploited baldíos and putting the land to use, they were acting in the national interest.[51]

Despite their legalistic orientation, the colonos' initiative presaged a major change in landholding patterns in the Colombian countryside. In the wake of massive land invasions, many landlords in these regions retained effective control over only the relatively small areas that they had planted with export crops. Meanwhile, as dependent laborers declared themselves settlers once again, the haciendas dissolved into their constituent parts. The tendency toward the concentration of rural property, so marked in the period of export growth, reversed itself in the early years of the depression. A popular agrarian reform was in the making.

The Landlords' Response

Hacendados all over Colombia responded to the squatters' initiative in similar ways: they sought to reassert their claims to the land by expelling the squatters. However, given the new juridical framework, the landlords dared not bring lawsuits against colonos for fear that the courts would find their titles invalid. Instead, most hacendados whose estates were invaded instituted administrative evictions through municipal authorities.[52]

This action brought landlords and squatters into direct confrontation. The squatters, protesting that they were colonos on public lands, refused to be expelled under laws applicable to tenants or illegal occupants *(ocupantes de hecho)*. If, as often occurred, the local mayors evicted them anyway, the colonos invariably reoccupied disputed territory within a few days.[53] And so continuing conflicts were born.

In their efforts to dislodge the squatters, landlords depended on the support of local and regional authorities. Most municipal officials saw the land invasions as crimes to be punished immediately, rather than passed on to the judiciary as required by law. At the landlords' behest, they carried out many evictions and arrested scores of colonos.[54] The departmental authorities, many of whom were landowners themselves, also vehemently opposed the squatter invasions. Until the courts actually ruled that a tract of disputed land was baldío, departmental officials nearly always defended the alleged proprietors. The governor of Cundinamarca, for example, ordered local authorities in Sumapaz to proceed on the assumption that all land there was private property. Meanwhile, the Assembly of Cundinamarca, as well as those of Bolívar, Caldas, and Valle, passed emergency ordinances denying squatters the right to contest eviction by claiming to be settlers of public lands.[55]

Beyond molding the legal context in the hacendados' favor, two departments also provided them with police reinforcements. Members of the Civil Guard of Cundinamarca, composed of 350 army reservists, aided local officials in the eviction of numerous squatters from 1930 through 1936. These troups were fed and lodged by the landlords of Sumapaz in their great country houses.[56] In Valle, too, a rural police corps was created in 1930 by the departmental government to protect private estates from colonos and bandits. The hacendados showed their enthusiasm by supplying the 400 policemen with horses and uniforms.[57]

Even with the backing of regional authorities, the hacendados found it difficult to clear their estates of squatters. The large numbers of colonos involved undermined the efficacy of traditional eviction procedures. Therefore, many landlords resorted to more direct methods, methods used in earlier years to force settlers off public lands. The landlords threw grass seed and loosed cattle in the squatters' fields, confiscated their produce on the way to market, cut bridges, and blocked water sources and market roads. In the course of evictions, they burned the colonos' huts, pulled down their fences, and destroyed their crops. Squatters who refused to swear on the spot that they would not return received stiff fines or jail sentences. And colono leaders were often falsely accused of wanton property damage, electoral fraud, or vagrancy to remove them from the area.[58]

In Sumapaz, where the review of property titles revealed immense usur-

pations of public lands, the landlords' offensive against the squatters assumed a particular intensity. Civil guards living on the Pardo Roche and
Torres Otero estates daily evicted squatters whose fields were then turned
over to obedient tenants. The landlords organized these tenants, known as
fieles or loyal ones, into bands to attack the squatters. The latter responded
in kind by destroying the crops and fences of the fieles at first opportunity
and reoccupying their parcels. Tensions escalated rapidly; in 1932-33 several peasants and civil guards were killed or wounded in separate
confrontations.[59]

In earlier times land entrepreneurs had found it a relatively simple matter to push settlers off the land. Despite their continuing control of local
power resources, landlords in the early 1930s discovered this was no longer
so easy. Many squatters managed to keep possession of the land they occupied throughout the period of agrarian unrest from 1928 through 1936, thus
effectively challenging the latifundista structure of landholding.

The increased capacity of the squatters to resist the landlords' pressures
is attributable to new forms of colono leadership and organization and to
new institutional support structures. These changes in the context of colono
protest activity reflected important transformations in Colombian political
and social life. Specifically, they stemmed from the growing incorporation
of popular elements into the political system and the increasing intervention of the national government in social and economic affairs.

Colono Leadership: The New Political Allies

Landlords often attributed the colono movements of the 1930s to the ne-
farious instigation of outside agitators. Minister of Industries Francisco José
Chaux came nearer the truth when in 1933 he wrote, "The agitators should
be considered not a cause, but a product of our current problems. They are
the flies that feed on our social tumors."[60]

As in the past, disputes over land attracted a variety of profit-minded
individuals eager to assume leadership roles. Peasants welcomed educated
people who could assure them that the titles of local haciendas were defective, and they willingly paid them to petition Bogotá for protection and grants
of the land. Some such country lawyers and artisans honestly served small
groups of colonos as intermediaries, while others unscrupulously exploited
their clients.[61] While they played a positive role in some conflicts, these
petty entrepreneurs were in the 1930s no longer the only outsiders to es-
pouse the colonos' cause.

The most important developments affecting the colonos were being determined in the national political arena. For the first time in the 1920s and early 1930s, new political groups began to build electoral constituencies by appealing to the interests of the laboring classes. In contrast to most other Latin American countries (for example, Peru, Chile, and Argentina) where populism was primarily an urban phenomenon, opposition groups seeking mass support in Colombia focused on the rural areas.[62] The depression had seriously weakened the labor movement in the cities. Meanwhile, the ongoing struggles over public lands provided fertile ground for organizational efforts in the countryside. The fact that thousands of peasants were already involved in the conflicts naturally attracted various competing political groups, each seeking to consolidate a popular base.

Radical political organizers with urban experience provided a new kind of leadership for colonos in the early 1930s. They proved particularly adept at uncovering usurpations in old property titles, publicizing the colonos' grievances, and fostering coordination among squatter groups. The organizers' presence also imbued the land conflicts with political significance: they threatened the traditional authority exercised by Conservative and Liberal elites over the lower classes. Study of the precise role the rural organizers played helps explain why the new public land conflicts had a heightened impact on government thinking. It also sheds light on why, despite this impact, the colonos proved unable to exert continued pressure on the government in their own interests.

Leftist groups that became active among the squatters included the Revolutionary Leftist National Union *(Unión Nacional Izquierdista Revolucionaria* — UNIR); the Communist party of Colombia *(Partido Comunista de Colombia* — PCC); and the National Agrarian party *(partido Agrarista Nacional* — PAN). These parties represented three divergent approaches to rural mobilization.

The Revolutionary Leftist National Union, founded by Jorge Eliécer Gaitán, was essentially a populist organization.[63] A charismatic politician whose murder was later to set off La Violencia, Gaitán first built a personal following by supporting popular causes in the late 1920s. By 1930 he had already spoken out on the colono problem. In a series of passionate addresses to Congress, the young Liberal urged his fellow congressmen to side with the squatters in their fight for the soil.

In 1933 the fiery young Gaitán split off from the Liberal party to form his own political organization, UNIR. For three years this party organized peasants and, to a lesser extent, urban workers and members of the middle sectors into a coalition supportive of Gaitán and his vision of social change.

The vision espoused by Gaitán at this point was fundamentally populist, nationalist, and developmentalist in nature. Despite the revolutionary rhetoric in which his statements were couched, Gaitán advocated a program of gradual reforms leading to a kind of state-directed capitalism, a program not dissimilar to that implemented by President Alfonso López Pumarejo after 1934. In harmony with the progressive thinkers of his time, Gaitán supported agrarian reform as a way to increase rural production. At the same time he opposed too rapid a breakdown of the latifundia, arguing that peasants were incapable of productively working the land without improved education, technology, and credit facilities.[64]

Nevertheless, seeking to garner votes, the Uniristas pragmatically defended peasant squatters in their struggles with landowners. In a gesture that considerably bolstered his prestige among them, Gaitán agreed to represent squatters in the official studies of titles to several haciendas in Cundinamarca and Tolima where disputes had reached crisis proportions. Meanwhile, in well-publicized speeches to Congress, Gaitán and other Unirista sympathizers railed against the "violent and unjust" methods latifundistas used to throw squatters off the land.[65] Gaitán's attention to the squatter problem in Sumapaz paid off in strong support throughout the region in the years 1933–35. Groups of squatters from other parts of the country also actively sought to affiliate with the Unirista movement in those years.

The Colombian Communist party, which supplanted the old Revolutionary Socialist party in 1930, competed with Gaitán for the disaffected peasants of Cundinamarca and Tolima. A member of the Communist International, the PCC saw itself as a revolutionary Marxist-Leninist organization. In these early years, the party platform gave top priority to the transformation of the countryside: "The substance of the Revolution," it stated, "consists primarily in solving the agrarian problem. All remnants of feudalism must be abolished, and the land distributed to those who work it."[66] By involving itself directly in the agrarian conflicts of the time, the PCC sought to politicize the peasants and to build an electoral constituency as well.[67]

Relations between the PCC and UNIR were acrimonious and their rivalry fierce in the rural areas. The two parties ultimately established bases of support in different regions and among different sectors of the rural population. In contrast to the Uniristas who appealed to the squatters, the PCC paid primary attention to tenants engaged in contract disputes and to Indians seeking to recover communal lands. In the province of Tequendama (Cundinamarca) to the north of Sumapaz, PCC organizers encouraged tenants to defy landlords by planting coffee trees on their subsistence plots and by refusing to supply labor for the patrons' fields. Although the Communists called such actions "revolutionary land occupations," the party never questioned the legality of the hacendados' property claims. The PCC's neglect of the public land issue derived partly from objective conditions in the areas it organized: the Tequendama, for example, was not a frontier area; it had had no public lands since the colonial period. Beyond this, the Communists were put off by the legalistic orientation of the squatters, which implied complicated entanglements with national ministries and courts. Such an approach was not consistent with their more autonomous strategy.[68]

Nevertheless, the Central Committee encouraged Communist groups that sprang up in the provinces to involve themselves in local struggles. In areas of Communist influence where colono invasions did occur, such as the banana zone and southern Tolima, local party members helped squatters form self-defense groups to resist eviction.[69] Additionally, the PCC newspaper, *El Bolshevique*, provided squatters and other peasants with detailed news of agrarian conflicts in many parts of the country.[70]

Despite their differences, the PCC and UNIR both tried to incorporate peasants into larger political organizations with goals that transcended immediate issues of peasant concern. In contrast, the third group to support squatters in the early 1930s, the National Agrarian party, had but one purpose—to articulate and to defend the interests of the colonos of Sumapaz.

PAN was the creation of Erasmo Valencia, an independent lawyer and leftist organizer from Bogotá who was expelled from the Revolutionary Socialist party in 1925.[71] Following his ouster, Valencia became increasingly absorbed in the problems of colonos in the Sumapaz region. It was he who came closest to forming a grass-roots political organization focused on the public lands issue with a support base comprised entirely of colonos.

In the years after 1928, Valencia worked closely with colono leaders in the Sumapaz. Together with lawyer David A. Forrero, he undertook detailed studies of property titles that showed public land usurpations, informed squatters of their legal rights, and wrote petitions on their behalf to national authorities. Furthermore, for nearly a decade, Valencia published a weekly journal with news of the squatter movement. This newspaper, called *Claridad*, reported on conflicts on various estates, described defects in hacienda titles, pointed to the abuses of specific landlords and officials, and urged squatters to coordinate their efforts. As literate peasants eagerly related its contents to their unschooled neighbors, *Claridad* circulated widely throughout rural Sumapaz.[72]

Erasmo Valencia did not move to form a political party until early in 1935. This was the moment when Jorge Eliécer Gaitán, with whom Valencia was on friendly terms, announced his return to the Liberal fold. Valencia imme-

diately founded the National Agrarian party, the stated purpose of which
was to represent the peasants' interests. Although its constituency consisted
solely of squatters and a few middle sector sympathizers in Sumapaz, Valencia hoped eventually to appeal to a broader segment of the rural population.

During the spring of 1935, PAN representatives took an active part in
elections in Sumapaz. They called for the triumph of justice and moral government against the "feudal landlords" of the Liberal and Conservative parties.[73] The campaign was a success: PAN won seats on the municipal councils
of Fusugasugá, Pasca, San Bernardo, and Pandi, while Valencia himself
was elected to the Departmental Assembly. Bills he presented to unionize
peasants, construct a rural road, build sanitary housing, and create mobile
country schools were, however, defeated by the hostile assembly. Valencia
soon became disillusioned with political action as a means of improving the
peasants' condition. Similarly frustrated, the three PAN councilmen of Fusugasugá resigned in March of 1936.[74]

Although PAN, PCC, and UNIR had the most influence, they were not
the only political groups to avail themselves of a mass of squatters no longer
subservient to the hacendados. Once the colono movements got underway,
the squatters became mobilizable political capital and the reclamation of
public lands the idiom. In areas where land disputes erupted, some Liberal
and Conservative office-seekers also attempted to build electoral followings
by responding to squatter concerns.

In the early years of the depression, local politics in Colombia were particularly unstable, reflecting a national shift in power in the elections of
1930. Following years of subordination, the return of the Liberals to political prominence engendered a fierce jockeying for the control of municipal
power structures between Liberals and Conservatives all over the country.[75]
Under these circumstances, some ambitious people, seeking to advance their
careers, openly appealed to the land hunger of the rural populace. The secretary of Cundinamarca reported on this practice:

> It sometimes happens that a lawyer passes by a hacienda and exhorts the work-
> ers to deny the owner's property rights and to invade his fields. Two months
> later the lawyer runs for political office and, as might be expected, wins two
> hundred votes from the squatters who have acted on his advice. In the parts of
> this department where the first peasant organizations were formed in 1933,
> the politicians fell avidly upon them in search of an electoral clientele.[76]

In addition to leftist groups and some Liberal and Conservative local politicians, the national Liberal party also expressed an interest in the squat-

ters. In contrast to the Conservative regime of the 1920s, which had outlawed
worker protests, the bipartisan administration of Enrique Olaya Herrera in
1931 permitted urban and rural laborers to unionize.[77] With this legislation, the Liberal party tried to counter Communist influence in rural areas
by appealing directly to the peasants. Some Liberal politicians stressed the
importance of providing the peasantry with greater economic benefits and
with more direct access to political authorities. Meanwhile, the party's left
wing established a rural syndical committee, the purpose of which was to
form peasant unions affiliated to the Liberal party. Thus, leftist Liberals
sought to incorporate the peasants into the party in functional interest groups
rather than through the traditional multitude of vertical patronage networks.
Beyond political support, the Liberal unions were meant to provide an instrument for a peaceful and gradual transformation of the countryside directed by national agencies.[78] In the same period the Ministry of Industries,
controlled by Liberals, also created a number of government-sponsored peasant unions and cooperatives.[79]

The position the Liberal unions took on the public land question is unclear. In any case, owing to intraparty discord over the issue of mass political mobilization, Liberal efforts to channel peasant unrest were, at best,
halfhearted. Leftist Liberals did not succeed in their objective of winning
most tenants and squatters away from the opposition parties. Indeed, in the
early years of the depression the Liberal initiative merely added to the pro-
fusion of competing groups that sought to make use of the squatter movement for conflicting ends.

Thus despite the fact that Colombian peasants had begun to challenge
the latifundistas, their protests remained fragmented. The squatters identified not at all with Indians who sought to recover their communal lands or
with tenants who aimed to amend their work contracts. Even among the squatters, geographical barriers made communication, much less cooperation,
among the different centers of unrest extremely difficult. The political fac-
tionalization induced by the various groups that sought to organize the squatters divided them still further. This lack of cohesion diluted the pressure
that colonos could bring to bear on the government and weakened the colono movement in the long run.

Viewed from a slightly different perspective, the involvement of leftist
groups in the squatter movement served to project the public land conflicts
into the national consciousness. Through their public advocacy of the colono cause, Erasmo Valencia, Jorge Eliécer Gaitán, and others informed the
nation of the squatters' circumstances and concerns. More significantly perhaps, by their efforts to integrate the squatters into upstart political move-

ments independent of the traditional parties, leftist organizers imbued the social problem with a political dimension. National authorities and the press began to express anxiety over the growing influence of left-wing groups in rural areas.

Beyond impressing the government with the urgency of the public land issue, leftist organizers also strengthened the squatters' ability to resist the landlords' attacks. In some areas the electoral defection of the colonos threatened to deprive the landlords of their allies in the municipal power structure. The colonos' affiliation with leftist groups also supplied them with external support structures, with legal information, and with a sense of participation in a wave of public land reclamation that transcended local boundaries. Most important, the squatters' new political allies provided them with fresh strategies and forms of resistance.

The Coordination of Colono Resistance

To understand how the peasants managed to stay on the haciendas, one more factor must be considered—cooperation among colonos and the organizational forms it assumed. Many squatters who participated in the land seizures of the early 1930s spontaneously assisted and protected one another. When any of their companions was threatened with eviction, for example, all of the settlers on a given estate protested that they were colonos settled on public lands. Even if the invasions were very recent, all swore that they had been peacefully tilling the soil for months, if not years. Also, when individual squatters were hounded by the police, their neighbors harbored them, and when they were burned out, others provided them food and shelter.[80]

Given their well-founded distrust of local authorities, colonos refused to have anything to do with them: most would not answer summonses and, if presented with bonds to sign, literally took to their heels. When inspection or eviction parties approached, the squatters together faded into the mountains, returning later to reoccupy their parcels or, if the fields had been destroyed, to clear new land nearby.[81]

At the same time that settler groups did everything possible to remain on the land, they appealed directly for help to departmental and national authorities. In petitions signed by scores of families, colonos accused landlords, hacienda administrators, local officials, and sometimes even departmental officials of criminal acts against them. In addition to writing the

government, some groups of colonos posted letters to newspapers or distributed broadsides publicizing their viewpoint. The squatters of Sumapaz even
sent delegations to Bogotá to argue their cause. Invited to present their problems to Congress in 1929, 200 peasants from the Hacienda El Chocho left
the legislators with an emphatic warning: "If we are not listened to and if
the wrongs of which we speak are not righted, we will be back in two weeks
in still greater numbers."[82]

These various kinds of spontaneous cooperation helped many colonos maintain themselves on the land. The emergence of more formal organizations
called unions, leagues, or colonies also played a major role in squatter resistance efforts. The earliest colono league of which record exists in Colombia had been founded in Puerto Berrío (Antioquia) in 1921 by a large group
of settlers, including some wealthy ranchers, whose claims were menaced
by the reactivation of a 200,000 hectare grant to a land company. The league
hired a team of lawyers who defended the settlers in court and won the case.[83]
Meanwhile on the Caribbean coast six villages, threatened by the American
Colombian Corporation's purchase of the "Terrenos de Loba," organized *jun-
tas de defensa territorial* that gave rise in 1922 to colono leagues. By the
mid-twenties, settlers in the banana zone had begun to join local unions
representing their interests as well as those of plantation, port, and railroad
workers. Rural unions also sprang up in the same period among the discontented arrendatarios of western Cundinamarca.[84]

In the early 1930s, the number of peasant leagues multiplied, reflecting
in large part the organizational efforts of the Communist party and the National Leftist Revolutionary Union. The leagues formed by these parties helped
colonos present a united front in their dealings with both the landlords and
the government. Although detailed information on affiliation and internal
organization is lacking, it is clear that squatter leagues took form when land
invasions occurred in some parts of the departments of Cundinamarca, Tolima, Caldas, Valle, Bolívar, and Magdalena. As might have been expected,
the Communist and Unirista groups differed in outlook. The Unirista leagues
collected dues to cover the costs of petitions, lawyers, and broadsides to
defend the squatters' interests within the legal system. The Communist party,
in contrast, cautioned its peasant affiliates against appeals to the national
government, which was viewed as cooptive; instead it encouraged the peasants to form armed self-defense groups to confront the landlords directly.[85]

Most peasant leagues in the early 1930s, it seems, grouped together the
squatters of one estate who viewed their struggle against the same hacendado as a common one. In some areas, however, such peasant bodies took
on greater dimensions. The General League of Colonos of Magdalena, which

coordinated squatter groups in the banana zone, claimed more than 3,000 members in 1930.[86]

The largest squatter organization of the period was not, however, a peasant league, but a "colony," the *Colonia Agrícola de Sumapaz* founded by Erasmo Valencia, Juan de la Cruz Varela, and other peasant leaders of that region around 1930. The most important and least known of the squatter associations, the Sumapaz Colony gave expression to the colonos' vision of their cause on a heretofore unprecedented scale.[87] In many ways this colony prefigured the "Independent Peasant Republics" that emerged in Sumapaz and other parts of central Colombia during La Violencia some twenty years later.[88]

The agrarian colony, which covered the whole of the Sumapaz, included more than 6,000 squatters. A fascinating picture of the colony is found in the writings of government officials who passed through the region in the early 1930s. The chief of justice of Cundinamarca described it succinctly as "a special agrarian government . . . or an agrarian party sui generis".[89] The secretary of Cundinamarca elaborated on this remark in 1931:

> The situation in Sumapaz is abnormal and dangerous from all points of view. In that area the so-called colonos maintain a kind of state within the state with their own administrative and judicial authorities. There exists among them, for example, an institution called the "court judges" *(jueces de cortes)* that makes all decisions on the distribution of land among the squatters. Departmental officials dare not enter the area except when accompanied by an armed escort.[90]

The colony made its own laws and flew its own flag, a green banner symbolizing its rural origins.

Responsibility for the colony as a whole lay with a junta of directors. Each rural neighborhood, however, had its own coordinating committee of squatters chosen by the local population. There were also six larger geographical sub-sections, each with its own president. The colonos of each section met frequently in groups of 100 or more to coordinate their resistance to the landlords.[91] According to the secretary of Tolima, who visited the region in 1932,

> The squatters are forever holding meetings in different places. They roam through the mountains in bands dedicated solely to the defense of their community and to collective resistance against whoever claims to own the territory that they consider public lands.[92]

Aiming to win the land for the squatters, the colony posted constant appeals to Bogotá: it called on the authorities to enforce the public land laws and give all colonos in the region property titles. Large groups of squatters from Iconozco and Cunday also applied for several 1,000 hectare land grants, which they planned to farm together. To defray the costs of such appeals, each peasant family, according to its means, contributed from twenty centavos to one peso each month to the treasury of the colony. These funds paid for lawyers, surveyors, travel, and postage. They also paid for printing the newspaper *Claridad,* which facilitated communications among the various sections of squatters and presented the colony's views to the outside world.

Not only did the colony send appeals to Bogotá, but it also helped the squatters coordinate their opposition to the landlords who were constantly trying to evict them. Moving beyond the evasive tactics used elsewhere, the colonos of Sumapaz adopted more forcible methods. In 1932 a band of squatters boldly attacked a patrol of civil guards and freed several colonos who had been taken prisoner. Thereafter, guards sent to evict squatters more often than not found themselves confronted by scores of angry peasants with hunting rifles who had come from other haciendas to defend their own people. Outnumbered, the guards often withdrew, their mission unaccomplished. Occasionally, skirmishes broke out between squatters and police. Such violent encounters gave rise to commemorative observances: in June of 1936, more than 1,000 squatters gathered at the spot called La Georgina in Iconozco to honor the memory of several colonos murdered there by guardsmen three years before.[93] In addition to direct confrontations with the civil guard, the colony also tried to divide the upper classes of the region by calling for an economic boycott of landlords and merchants antagonistic to the colonos' cause.

Although the colony existed only in Sumapaz, it expressed its goals in more general terms, applicable to Colombia as a whole. According to *Claridad,* the colony aimed essentially "to recover the territory that has been violently usurped by the latifundistas and to put into the hands of each peasant . . . a plot of land."[94] It sought to distribute the great, unproductive estates among the colonos who would till the land in individually owned family farms. Furthermore, the colony claimed to stand for justice, law, and peace against the "criminal" attacks initiated by latifundistas and their local henchmen.

Despite the colony's tactical defiance of the landlords, it did not advocate the abolition of private property, nor did it ever question the authority of the national government. In fact, like the colonos of earlier times, the squatters of Sumapaz sought to strengthen their position by securing the patronage of higher authorities. Thus, although it remarked on the suffering of peasants under Conservative and Liberal regimes alike, *Claridad* in 1935 assured President Alfonso López Pumarejo of the colony's support and requested his protection. Symptomatic of the times, however, the colony also formed horizontal alliances with other labor groups: it affiliated with the Workers' Directorate of Cundinamarca and sent representatives to the second National Congress of Labor Unions, which met in Medellín in August of 1936.

The politicization of the public land conflicts thus gave rise to Colombian peasant organizations in the 1920s and early 1930s. Building upon the squatters' spontaneous inclination to support one another, peasant leagues and colonies helped squatters coordinate their efforts and, in so doing, contributed to their successful resistance to eviction.

Government Intervention

The colonos' determination to remain on the land came partly from their conviction that the national government would back them in their reclamation of illegally appropriated public lands. They were not wrong. In contrast to El Salvador where a peasant uprising was brutally repressed in 1932, the Colombian government never turned the army against the squatters.[95] Instead, Colombian authorities sought to make use of the squatters' initiative to further the productive transformation of the countryside proposed in the 1920s. The direct intervention of the government in the new land conflicts provided the squatters with an additional source of support in their struggles against the landlords.

Charged with responsibility for labor and for the public domain, the Ministry of Industries was the governmental agency to involve itself most directly in the new land conflicts. At first, the ministry reacted negatively to the squatter invasions: during the initial wave, Minister Francisco José Chaux argued that peasants had no right to settle land claimed to be private before the government had determined its legal status. And in November of 1931, Chaux authorized emergency evictions following the massive land invasions in Quindío.[96]

Once the colonos actually occupied thousands of hectares of land, however, the Ministry of Industries changed its attitude. Faced with a complex and potentially explosive situation, the ministry acted forcefully to protect the legal rights of both landlords and squatters and to prevent escalation of

the conflicts. The ministry stressed that because the squatters asserted colono status, by law all disputes had to be submitted to the courts for resolution. While judges were reviewing the property titles, official policy was "to
maintain the status quo [on the affected haciendas] and to restrain all disor-
derly or violent activity."[97]

Efforts to enforce this policy led the Colombian government to intervene
directly in the new land conflicts. The primary instrument of such intervention was the National Labor Bureau. Created in 1923 as a division of the
Ministry of Industries, the bureau was originally mandated to compile information on labor conditions in the urban and rural areas. In response to the
burgeoning labor problem, the bureau began to take on new functions. In
1927 Congress instructed the agency to mediate strikes and other labor disputes. In that year the bureau also established regional labor inspectors
throughout the country, thus extending its radius of influence.[98]

State intervention in the land conflicts of the 1930s began with a change
in the government's information-collecting procedures: Congress and the Ministry of Industries sent fact-finding missions to some of the affected regions.
These missions were instructed to decipher the reality that lay behind the
vituperous countercharges levelled by hacendados and squatters. Thus, for
the first time the national government established channels of information
from the rural zones independent of local and departmental authorities.[99]

Acting on the reports thus obtained, the National Labor Bureau sent agents
to negotiate provisional pacts between landlords and squatters in Cundinamarca, Tolima, Valle, and elsewhere. In such agreements, the landlords
consented to leave the squatters in peace, and the colonos promised not to
enlarge their clearings until the courts reviewed the property titles. The effectiveness of such pacts depended on the good will of the participants: the
Labor Bureau had no power to enforce them, and many broke down after a
few weeks or months. Nonetheless, government agents continued to inter-
cede in areas of chronic unrest.[100] Beyond its efforts at mediation, the National Labor Bureau also sent lawyers to inform squatters of their legal rights
and of the government's position on the land question. The government aimed
in this way to counter the influence among the colonos of rumors spread by
the landlords, on the one hand, and by leftist organizers, on the other.[101]

The Ministry of Industries maintained that it was acting impartially and
in strict compliance with the law. In fact, the presence of national agents
worked to the colonos' advantage by preventing the landlords from employ-
ing their usual tactics. Like the new allies and organizations, government
intervention in the land conflicts of the 1930s reinforced the squatters' ability to remain on the land they occupied.

The national government's responsiveness to the plight of the colonos had complex and unanticipated consequences. By contributing to the peasants' sense of government support, it may well have stimulated more squatters to invade uncultivated estates. It also enhanced the prestige among peasants of political organizers who elicited responses from the Ministry of Industries.[102] The government's refusal to repress the colonos, not surprisingly, incensed the landowners. Some labelled the Ministry of Industries "Communist" and accused it of fostering the destruction of private property. As the squatters became more and more defiant, the landlords began to direct their hostility not only against the peasants but against the Liberal government as well.[103]

In sum, the public land conflicts took on national significance in the early 1930s because they dramatized the fundamental issues and interests at stake in the administration's attempts to intensify rural production through support for the small farmer. The colono movement presaged a fundamental, indeed, a revolutionary change in landholding patterns. Despite the regional fragmentation of the movement, its limited aims, and its profoundly legalistic overtones, the squatters' initiative directly challenged the predominance of the latifundia in the Colombian countryside.

The squatters' ability to remain on the territory they invaded signified an obvious strengthening of the peasants' position in their ongoing struggles with the landlords. Lacking political or military power, the squatters could not, however, force the hacendados to give up the land they claimed to own. The result was chronic conflict between landlords and squatters in many parts of the country.

The continuing confrontations between landlords and colonos presented the Colombian government with a clearly untenable situation. Even though the peasants affirmed their loyalty to the national government, squatters in widespread areas had begun to behave in a disturbing fashion. They denied and vigorously resisted the authority of local landowners, mayors, and policemen. Meanwhile, landlords were becoming increasingly disaffected. And the vertical coordination of government activity seemed to be breaking down as officials at different levels responded to the conflicts in contradictory ways.

Here and there fears of class conflict began to be openly expressed. Some observers argued that the influence of leftist organizers and continual confrontations might well radicalize the peasantry, leading them to repudiate the notion of private property altogether. By 1936 expressions of alarm emerged from within the government itself. In that year several governors joined the minister of state in warning that social revolution was not an impossibility. They wrote:

The peasants are often exposed to propaganda asserting that the government
protects assaults on private property. The laboring classes . . . hear it widely
said that now is the time for revolution and that the government will do nothing to stop it, whether because national authorities are in agreement with the
revolt or because they no longer have the courage to repress the peasants with
the barbarous procedures of earlier times.[104]

Beyond the social problem, the ongoing disturbances appeared to be undermining efforts to stimulate rural production. Given the intensity of the
conflicts, neither the hacendados nor the squatters could devote themselves
full time to economic activities. National officials remarked that production
was falling in the affected zones, and they noted with concern that declining
confidence in the security of property might well cause a drop in land values and rural investments.[105]

Ironically, the growing penetration of urban political agents and national
institutions into the countryside exacerbated the conflicts by reinforcing the
squatters' position. The influence of these external elements was most clearly
visible in Sumapaz, located near Bogotá. In that region where squatters were
most exposed to urban influences, where leftist organizing was most intense,
and where the presence of the national government was most strongly felt,
conflicts between squatters and landlords took the most virulent forms. Con-
versely, the proximity of Sumapaz impressed the people of the capital with
the magnitude and gravity of the public land problem.

Clearly, the land disputes could not be left to run their course. To resolve
these conflicts, the Colombian government had to take more decisive action. Resolution of the conflicts required new kinds of state intervention,
the precise thrust of which reflected the interaction of economic development considerations and the realities of political power.

7

The State and The Agrarian Problem

By 1934 the public land disputes had become a national problem. In his report to Congress that year, Minister of Industries Francisco José Chaux expressed the concern that many educated people were feeling. "For several years now, the Colombian countryside has been marked by serious social conflicts," he wrote.

> Independent in origin, the various disputes have begun to assume a common dynamic, signalling the emergence of a collective consciousness of the land problem among the rural population. The persistence of the conflicts, which involve great masses of peasants in activities detrimental to the economy and to public tranquility, has generated intense concern among the Colombian people. The land question now is considered one of the most important and pressing of national issues. In Congress and the administration, as well as in the press and in political and social life, a healthy agitation is stirring that anxiously seeks a solution to the land struggles in progress.[1]

In its diagnosis of the conflicts, the government in Bogotá disagreed with the landowners who attributed peasant unrest to outside agitators. The administration, instead, saw in the rural disturbances the social expression of the agrarian problem first formulated in the 1920s. Thus, the Ministry of Industries pinpointed the origins of the conflicts in the existence of large, unexploited, and often illegally consolidated estates. It interpreted the hacienda invasions as a logical, if unforeseen, extension of the official policy of reclaiming public lands and putting them to use. "The administration resolved that uncultivated territory accessible to markets should be put into production," explained the National Labor Bureau. "It so happened that the social movement toward this end rapidly bypassed our halting steps to implement the policy through judicial channels, resulting in the occupation of great expanses of previously unused property by peasant cultivators."[2]

As the conflicts dragged on, the logical problem they posed came into focus. The fundamental issue at stake was the structure of land tenure in frontier areas. In the public land disputes of the early 1930s, the two trends in Colombian land law—support of written titles and support of cultivators of the soil—had come into direct confrontation. A decision between the landlords' and colonos' claims meant, in essence, a decision on whether the development of Colombian agriculture should be based on the existing system of large landed estates or on an alternative one of family farms.

The Colombian government's attempts to resolve the conflicts, thus understood, centered on three successive initiatives. Bogotá tried to settle the controversies first through the courts, then through subdivision of the affected estates, and finally through an agrarian reform law that incorporated the new concern with economic production into the definition of private property. In the problems debated and the proposals advanced, the early 1930s was a particularly fecund period. Pragmatic responses to a conflictual situation, the solutions put forth in the years 1930-36 continue to inform Colombian thought on the aims and methods of state-directed reform in the rural sector.

The Judicial Solution

The first official efforts to settle the colono conflicts occurred within established channels. The titles of disputed properties were to be reviewed first by experts in the Ministry of Industries and then, if found defective, by the courts. Using the criteria set down by the Supreme Court in 1926, the judges were to rule on the validity of the landowners' claims. By applying the rigorous standards of 1926, then, the Colombian government aimed to reclaim illegally usurped land for the nation so that it might later be distributed to colono families.[3] Obviously favorable to the squatters, judicial review in most cases would have deprived the landlords of the territory they claimed to own.

The inability of the Colombian judicial system to respond quickly and efficiently to the social crisis, however, frustrated the effort to clarify property rights through the courts. The titles to each disputed property had to be investigated separately. Given the great number of documents involved, the first step, the ministerial review, generally took several months. Even if the Ministry of Industries found that a tract of land invaded by squatters was actually public land, it could do nothing: by Colombian law, only the judiciary could rule on the validity of property titles. So when irregularities were found, the ministry passed the case to the courts.

The judicial process, in turn, proved to be extraordinarily slow and cumbersome. The fact that a significant proportion of the disputed properties were owned in common as indivisos contributed to the duration of many suits. Indivisos were large properties belonging to more than one individual, whether because of inheritance, collective land grants, or the purchase of shares. Sometimes there were scores of part-owners: notification of all these people was a long and tedious, if not impossible, task.[4] The several surveys and on-site inspections required by law also contributed to delays and, furthermore, drained the public purse. The demarcation of one large property from public lands in Cundinamarca, for example, cost the government 1,600 pesos ($900 U.S.) in 1934.[5] Whatever the complexities of each case, by 1935 only four of a total of forty-eight land reclamation suits authorized by the government had been decided. Many of these cases had been in court for at least five years, and some for as long as ten.[6]

The unwieldy judicial machinery of an earlier time thus proved inadequate to the social problems of a new age. Instead of clarifying the legitimate property rights involved in each dispute, working through the courts merely produced a permanent state of litigation. Meanwhile, confrontations between landlords and squatters were spreading and intensifying. Reports from the Ministry of Industries in the early 1930s indicated growing dissatisfaction with the high costs and meager results of the land reclamation suits. In 1934 the secretary of Cundinamarca voiced official disillusionment with this piecemeal approach to the resolution of social conflict. "The complexity of the judicial process," he wrote, "implies the postponement for years, and probably for decades, of a definitive solution to the land problem."[7]

Despite their impracticability, the title reviews had one important effect: they enhanced the administration's understanding of the historical process that underlay the agrarian conflicts. The reviews revealed time and again the importance of the usurpation of public lands to the consolidation of private property in Colombia. In this period, government publications began to refer for the first time to the prevalence of defective titles and to the chaotic state of land rights in many areas of the country.[8] Thus, through title reviews, officials in Bogotá became increasingly aware of the significance of the issues raised by the land conflicts and the magnitude of the interests at stake.

The Parcelization Program

Frustrated with the inefficacy of the land reclamation suits, the Colombian government soon began to take a supplementary approach to the land problem. Bogotá proposed to purchase estates affected by work contract or property disputes and subdivide them among the tenants and squatters who actually farmed the land. This new approach was called parcelization *(parcelación)*.[9]

Viewed as a practical alternative to protracted judicial proceedings, the parcelization program was well received in the Colombian press and official circles. The secretary of Cundinamarca optimistically called it "the policy of amicable compromise that unravels the gordian knot posed by our public land legislation."[10] By subdividing the disputed estates, Bogotá hoped to bring the conflicts to an immediate end and, at the same time, satisfy all parties involved.[11]

The interests at stake included those of the landowners, the banks to which many estates were mortgaged, the squatters and tenants, and the government in its concern to encourage economic development. Landlords who had bought properties believing their titles legitimate and banks that had advanced credit on the land, it was argued, should not be penalized if the titles were later found defective. The stability of the banks was a particularly serious consideration at this time. During the 1920s, many landowners had mortgaged their estates to obtain capital for agriculture or urban investments.[12] Already in difficulty because of the depression, the banks faced further losses if the courts found disputed properties to be public lands. Because it permitted full compensation of the landlords and through them the banks, parcelization offered a way out of this dilemma.

Furthermore, parcelization would satisfy squatters and tenants by permitting them to acquire title to the land they tilled. Subdivision of the great estates, it was anticipated, would reinforce the concept of private property among the rural poor and at the same time stimulate them to work the land more intensively, since they would now reap the benefits. By contributing to the formation of a rural middle class, parcelization would resolve the economic and social aspects of the agrarian problem: the dual goals of social peace and economic prosperity might thus be achieved. So, parcelization provided a mechanism to pacify the conflicting groups that, it was hoped, would promote the kind of rural transformation advocated in the 1920s and early 1930s.[13]

The parcelization program represented a hybrid approach to the solution of agrarian unrest. In one sense, it signified a weakening in the government's committment to reclaim illegally usurped public lands for the national domain. In another sense, the parcelization policy was a logical outgrowth of the new agrarian philosophy that stressed the importance of dividing the great estates among those who worked the land.

Initial attempts to apply parcelization to the solution of the land conflicts involved the Haciendas de Sumapaz and Doa in Cundinamarca and the Hacienda de Dinde y Ortega in Cauca. Ministerial reviews showed that these estates contained primarily usurped public lands. However, the court suits to recover the land for the nation had bogged down, and the conflicts between landlords and squatters were becoming violent. The landlords indicated to Bogotá that they were eager to sell off their properties.

Late in 1933 the Ministry of Industries agreed to purchase "Dinde y Ortega" in its entirety and the parts of "Sumapaz" and "Doa" not directly exploited by their owners, a total of 200,000 hectares. The urgency of ending the disturbances in those regions provided the justification. The 1,700 colono families who had occupied parts of this territory in the late 1920s and early 1930s received free title to the land they farmed.[14]

Although these subdivisions succeeded in calming social unrest on the three haciendas, they represented a considerable financial outlay for the Treasury.[15] Bearing costs in mind, the Colombian government decided that henceforth peasants who received grants through state-mediated parcelizations would be charged the full market value of the land. This provision was incorporated into plans for a national parcelization program, to be administered by the Agricultural Mortgage Bank, set forth in 1933.[16] Following Bogotá's example, most departments passed ordinances intended to facilitate similar transactions.

Apparently so promising, the parcelization program was a disappointment in the end. The reason was that many colonos refused to pay for land they believed to be public land. The history of the first subdivisions where the government required squatters to pay illustrates the problems of applying parcelization to properties affected by disputes over land.[17]

Tenants on the Hacienda El Chocho in Fusagusagá (Cundinamarca) and on the Hacienda El Soche near Bogotá began to pressure their landlords for better working conditions around 1925. In the first years of the depression, they challenged the landlords' rights to the land itself and claimed colono status. Following its usual procedure, the Ministry of Industries reviewed the property titles: in these cases, it found that original titles did exist and so refused to initiate judicial action. On the basis of this administrative review, the department of Cundinamarca decided to subdivide the properties to bring the conflicts to an end.

In late 1933 and early 1934, Cundinamarca purchased 7,000 hectares for 620,000 pesos ($384,400 U.S.) using bonds issued expressly for the purpose. It offered then to divide the land among the nearly one thousand peasant families already living there in properties of 3 to 10 hectares in size. The price charged the peasants ranged from 75 to 110 pesos ($46.50

to $68.20 U.S.) per hectare, this at a time when rural laborers generally made less than 1 peso ($0.62) for a day's work.[18] The government, however, was not profit-hungry: this amount barely covered the price paid the landlords, surveying costs, and interest. The colonos were allowed ten to thirty years to pay off their debts; only when the full amount was cancelled would they receive title to the land.

To the department's dismay, the colono organizations active in Cundinamarca reacted vociferously against the parcelization. The Agrarian Colony of Sumapaz labelled it a "destructive, deceptive, and scandalous policy,"[19] and Communists and Uniristas opposed it as well. All three groups maintained that the price paid the owners was outrageously high, that the terms extended the colonos were oppressive, and that the distribution of the land was influenced by political considerations.[20]

The most serious critique the colonos raised, however, centered on the legal status of the land. Many squatters from "El Soche" and "El Chocho" correctly asserted that, by Colombian law, the proprietorship of the land remained in doubt. Without a judicial review of the titles, no one could be sure that the land was not public land. Given this legal confusion, how, then, could the government reward the landlords by buying them out, while at the same time requiring peasants to pay for land that by right was theirs? Furthermore, the colonos complained, they were being asked to pay for the land not once, but twice over: first they had invested in the land to make it productive and now they were being penalized by having to pay high prices for land that had taken on value only because of the work they had put into it. Thus the colonos and their representatives rejected the government's contention that parcelization responded to the interests of landlords and peasants alike. Rather, they said, by circumventing judicial procedures that would have given colonos free land rights, parcelization was a tactic that favored only the hacendados who had criminally appropriated the public domain.[21]

Even after the department finalized its purchase, the colonos of "El Soche" and "El Chocho" continued to argue that the territory on which they lived was public land. The squatters refused to pay for it; instead they called for a new study of the titles, to which the Ministry of Industries consented.[22]

The colonos' denial of the department's rights to the land and their subsequent refusal to sign purchase agreements placed the officialdom of Cundinamarca in an awkward position. Not only did the department become the focus of the colonos' discontent, but it was unable to recoup the payments it had made to the landlords. Fearing similar budgetary fiascos, departments elsewhere in the country suspended their parcelization programs, leaving the continuation of such projects to the Ministry of Industries and the Agricultural Mortgage Bank.[23]

The national government continued to support parcelization projects: by December of 1936, sixty-two properties had been purchased for subdivision. But after the hapless experience of "El Chocho" and "El Soche," the Agricultural Mortgage Bank was careful to negotiate only with hacendados who could present legitimate first titles. Most of the properties purchased in these years were estates affected by bankruptcy or by contract disputes with tenants, the owners of which requested the government to extricate them from their difficulties. In this way the parcelization program facilitated the transfer of capital out of agriculture into the more dynamic industrial sector.[24]

The problem of the haciendas afflicted by land controversies persisted. By 1934–35, the Ministry of Industries began to express disappointment with parcelization as a response to the colono issue. "The attempt made by the government to buy and subdivide land," wrote the director of the National Labor Bureau, "has served only transitorily . . . to remedy the situation in a few areas. This system in no way provides a general solution to the larger agrarian question."[25]

The Legislative Response

The colonos' rejection of parcelization focused attention on the fundamental juridical problem of the confusion between private properties and public lands. "How can we justify . . . the transfer of landed property," asked the minister of industries, "when the legal question of who owns the land remains undefined?"[26] As the years passed, it became increasingly obvious that only by establishing clearly the distinction between private property and public domain would the land struggles be decided once and for all.

Debates concerning the legal foundations of property rights preoccupied the Colombian government for an entire decade, from 1926 through 1936. Intended to specify the conditions for proof of property, the Supreme Court decision of 1926 merely worsened the confusion. According to Colombian jurisprudence, to acquire the force of law the Supreme Court decision had to be confirmed by Congress. But for ten years no related legislation was forthcoming. Instead, a bitter debate broke out between reformers, who applauded the high court's decision as a step toward the breakdown of the latifundia, and their opponents, supporters of the landowning classes. Mean-

while, the Supreme Court justices themselves vacillated: in 1927 the Court
seemed to reverse its stance, but seven years later it reaffirmed the original
judgement.[27]

This state of legal uncertainty, which obstructed the reclamation of public lands, might have continued indefinitely had it not been for the squatters' initiative. The colono movement, as has been seen, was essentially a
popular uprising to implement the Supreme Court decision and to assert the
primacy of cultivators' rights. In violently resisting the peasant incursions,
the landlords advanced an opposing concept of proprietary right based on
their titles. "When, intending to cement the economic bases of their lives,
some peasants began to agitate a little," the minister of industries wrote in
1933, "it was found that we lack the juridical norms by which to extend
effective guarantees, whether to the private proprietor, to the nation for its
public lands, or to the colono who puts vacant land into production."[28] The
land disputes made urgent the need for new legislation to decide the conflicting claims of landlord and colono.

Beyond this primary motive of resolving the land controversies, economic
considerations also influenced Colombian policy-makers to develop a new
legal definition of property. As manufacturing picked up momentum after
1933, government officials frequently expressed the need to stimulate rural
production.[29] By supplying domestic food requirements cheaply and providing the foreign exchange to import machinery, agricultural growth was
essential to fuel the national economy. The outbreak of the agrarian conflicts in the early 1930s focused attention on certain impediments to realiz-
ing this goal. They revealed an embarrassing disjunction between the professed
aim of encouraging economic use of the land and legislation allowing those
who hoarded unproductive land to expel squatters intent on cultivation.

To bring the law into harmony with the new economic priorities, it was
suggested, the concept of the social function of property should be incorporated into the definition of property rights. In other words, the government
should revise the terms of private property in a way that would compel land
claimants to make productive use of their holdings.[30] Minister of Industries
Francisco José Chaux was a particularly strong advocate of this viewpoint in
the early 1930s. He justified his position in the following manner:

> private property is a legal fiction meant to support material possession (that is
> to say, human labor) and to give security to work that is incorporated in the
> land. Recognition of the right of property does not in any sense rule out social
> regulation of the use of that property. . . . The law guarantees landed prop-

erty for it to be made productive and not for it to be wasted or plundered or abandoned.[31]

In the years after 1929, then, government officials expressed a growing awareness that the present laws were inadequate to deal with new social and economic problems.[32] Through legislative reform, the government sought a definitive solution to the land question. It aimed both to mediate the social relations between landlords and squatters and to make of the law an instrument for state-directed economic growth in the rural sector.

In accordance with the preceding considerations, two policy alternatives were envisaged. Wrote the minister of agriculture:

> There were two paths we might have followed. On the one hand, the State, protected by an advantageous juridical structure which relieved it of the necessity of proving its ownership of the public lands and which made it difficult for alleged proprietors to prove their claims, might have promoted lawsuits to reclaim thousands of hectares of land that had been held as private property for many years. This territory then could have been redistributed among the landless rural population. On the other hand, the State could accept the extant structure of landholding by legalizing defective titles and at the same time impose upon those who benefited from such legislation obligations intended to encourage economic production.[33]

Thus, the fundamental choice was either to legalize extant landholdings or to confirm the Supreme Court decision of 1926 and follow through with a review of all property claims, returning to the national domain those that lacked original titles. The large landowners supported the first approach, which promised to legitimize their claims. Favorable to the colonos, the second approach would have opened possibilities for a wide-ranging reform of land tenure in the Colombian countryside.

The legislation of a new regime of property in land preoccupied the administrations of Enrique Olaya Herrera (1930–34) and Alfonso López Pumarejo (1934–38). They presented two important bills on the subject to Congress. The first bill, submitted in 1933 by President Olaya Herrera, was defeated later that year. Developed by the Liberal government of Alfonso López Pumarejo, the second proposal became Law 200 of 1936, also known as the first modern agrarian reform law in Colombia.

The two bills expressed different approaches to the issue at hand. The defeated Olaya Herrera proposal took the side of the colonos in the effort to encourage agricultural production through the proliferation of intensively-

worked smallholdings. In contrast, Law 200 signified a reorientation of Colombian agrarian policy away from the peasant cultivator toward support for
large agricultural enterprise. A closer examination of these land policy initiatives against the backdrop of political controversy from which they emerged
should help to clarify the significance of Law 200.

In May of 1933 the Olaya Herrera government set up a special commission to study the agrarian problem. Members of this commission, called the
Junta de Cuestiones Sociales y Agrarias, included the minister of industries,
the minister of finance, and representatives of the Agricultural Mortgage
Bank, the Syndicate of Rural Proprietors, the National Labor Bureau, the
National Land Office, and the president's legal staff.[34] The commission drew
up a bill which the administration presented to Congress in August 1933 as
its solution to the colono problem.

This bill represented the culmination of the thrust toward agrarian reform
that had originated in the 1920s. Its principal concerns were to reclaim for
the nation those baldíos that had been usurped through the years, to encourage a wider distribution of landholding, and to compel the economic
use of private property.[35]

The first and most important issue to which the bill addressed itself was
that of establishing the criteria for private property. Following the Supreme
Court decision of 1926, its authors concluded that most landholdings in Colombia were, in fact, baldío: "Since the great majority of those who today
consider themselves landowners are unable to trace their titles back to the
original grant of land," they explained, ". . . it can be said that in this country, generally speaking, private property in land does not exist."[36] On these
grounds, the proposal left the issue of written titles aside.

Instead, the bill designated a new criterion for property rights: use of the
land. The legitimacy of titles to land that was fenced and farmed or devoted
to livestock would be confirmed by the government. All unused land, however, would be presumed public land. Landowners with written titles who
did not put their territory to productive use within ten years after the bill
became law would lose their holdings to the public domain. In the meantime, anyone who cleared and farmed unfenced land for five years merited
title to it, whether or not someone else claimed to be the proprietor. This, of
course, applied to the colonos. By these provisions, the bill of 1933 aimed
to accomplish "the incorporation of work into the legal definition of property rights in land."[37]

With reference to the conflicting claims of landlords and colonos, the
most important aspect of the bill lay in its presumption that all land was
public land. The introduction to the bill acknowledged the insecurity of colo-

no life. The authors of the proposal explained their intentions as follows:

> we have meant to attack [the inequality between landowners and colonos] at
> its legal foundation, by linking the peasant's interests with those of the State
> which should represent and protect him. For this reason, we have established
> a presumption of rightful domain in favor of the squatters.[38]

In accordance, then, with the aim of encouraging economic use of the land,
the bill of 1933 took the colonos' side against that of the landlords who had
left their properties abandoned. This broad definition of public lands would
have legitimized most squatters' claims, providing them the legal support to
petition the government for titles.

The land bill of 1933 also aimed to prevent the reconcentration of landholding in later years. To this end, it reduced the maximum size of land
grants. The bill prohibited anyone from conveying by sale or inheritance
more than 2,000 hectares in a single block. Within twenty kilometers of
urban centers, the limit for sales was set still lower at 250 to 1,000 hectares, depending on the size of the city and the nature of the terrain. These
articles responded to the oft-repeated idea that rural property should be more
widely distributed and agricultural production encouraged in commercially
viable areas.[39]

The last section of the bill established new procedures to settle land conflicts. It gave the Ministry of Industries the power to review property titles
and instituted a special court suit to separate public from private land without delay. By accelerating the judicial process, these provisions were intended to facilitate resolution of the conflicts in accordance with the general
principles on property rights laid down earlier in the bill. The final chapter
of the proposal, dealing with eviction procedures, protected colonos against
arbitrary dispossession and assured them compensation for their improvements if eviction were warranted.

As should be obvious, the bill of 1933 was a direct outgrowth of the thought
of the 1920s and 1930s on the agrarian problem, which, beginning as an
economic and legal issue, took on social dimensions with the land invasions
of the early 1930s. Given the new concern with rural economic development and the predisposition toward small, intensively worked holdings,
this bill followed one thread in Colombian legislation to its logical conclusion. In doing so, it challenged the tenuous bases on which much private
property had been consolidated and tended toward a radical reform of Colombian agrarian structures. According to one contemporary, had the 1933
bill been put into effect, more than three quarters of all privately held prop-

erty in Colombia would have reverted to the nation.[40] It is not so surprising that the bill failed to become law as it is that the bill was proposed in the first place by a high ranking committee from within the coalition government of Enrique Olaya Herrera. Not only was the state taking an increasingly interventionist role, but it was also beginning to formulate development policies that directly clashed with the interests of certain elite groups.

Over the next two years, during which time Alfonso López Pumarejo assumed the presidency, the government's perspective on the agrarian problem altered. The change reflected shifts in the political organization of the interests at stake: specifically, the colono groups lost influence, while the landlords gained more effective control over national policy. To understand the López solution, which became Law 200 of 1936, this shift in political forces must be explored in greater detail.[41]

In the years 1933–36 the colono movement began to lose its political influence due to the cooptation of the movement's political leaders, internal dissension generated by the parcelization program, and the resurgence of the industrial working class as a power base for urban politicians. Although struggles over land continued unabated in the rural areas of Colombia, the leftist threat they embodied gradually receded. This change resulted from the efforts of the colonos' representatives to seek accomodation with the party in power. In the spring of 1935, UNIR disbanded and its founder, Jorge Eliécer Gaitán, ran for reelection to Congress on the Liberal ticket. The reasons for Gaitán's decision to rejoin the party from which he had broken only two years previously are not entirely clear. It has been suggested that because President López's reformist platform closely resembled the Unirista program, Gaitán found working with the Liberal party once again appealing.[42] A short time later, the Colombian Communist party also announced its support for the López administration. The conciliatory stance adopted by the PCC was a direct outgrowth of the antifascist popular front policy dictated by the Communist International to its affiliates in the mid-1930s.[43] And so the leftist opposition ebbed in Colombia as an avowedly reformist president came to power. This assimilation of new political forces into the prevailing party structure, a recurrent tendency in Colombian history, deprived the squatters of autonomous channels of political influence.

The political marginalization of colono interests also reflected the disorientation of the squatter movement near Bogotá. The decline of the Agrarian Colony of Sumapaz stemmed from the government's parcelization program which affected some of the most important haciendas of that region. Noting that the number of small coffee farms in the departments of Tolima and Cundinamarca, which included Sumapaz, almost doubled in the years 1932 to

1939, some observers have suggested that peasant agitation in those regions receded because the peasants won their struggle for the land.[44] Through parcelization, government-sponsored colonization, and the purchase of plots directly from landlords, many squatters and rural laborers managed to acquire small properties. As they entered into production for themselves, their interest in political organization diminished. Meanwhile frictions broke out among the peasants as each family sought to maximize its access to resources, often at the expense of its neighbors. Whether or not most squatters in Sumapaz acquired land (a question that remains to be investigated), parcelization certainly eroded the solidarity of the Sumapaz squatter movement.[45] It lessened the perceived immediacy of the "colono problem" in Bogotá and diminished the influence that might have been brought to bear by the Valencia group, the only independent organization representative of colono interests.

In these same years, as industrial growth gained momentum, the focus of political mobilization in Colombia moved back to the cities. From his new post as mayor of Bogotá, Jorge Eliécer Gaitán directed his attention away from peasants toward the urban middle and working classes. Meanwhile, President Alfonso López Pumarejo built a power base in urban labor through government-sponsored unionization and strike mediation. It was he who first demonstrated the potential of this sector of Colombian society as an organized political force.[46] In contrast to Lázaro Cárdenas of Mexico, however, President López never appealed to the rural population for political support, nor did he integrate them into his system of governance. In large measure abandoned, the colonos were left without direct means of exerting political pressure on the government either from within or from without.

At the same time that colono organization weakened, landlords from the Liberal and Conservative parties began to respond together to the threat posed by the 1933 bill. The Society of Colombian Agriculturalists (*Sociedad de Agricultores Colombianos* — SAC) and the Colombian Federation of Coffee Growers (*Federación de Cafeteros de Colombia* — FEDECAFE) took up the landowners' cause in publications and petitions to the government.[47] The SAC then gave rise to the Syndicate of Rural Owners and Entrepreneurs (*Sindicato de Propietarios y Empresarios Agrícolas*), which brought together hacendados embroiled in disputes in Cundinamarca and Tolima. Formed in 1933, this syndicate pressured the government to take the landlords' side. It founded chapters in cities all over the country and hired lawyers to defend embattled property owners. In Medellín and probably elsewhere, the syndicate won the patronage of high Catholic Church officials.[48]

In March of 1935 FEDECAFE sponsored the formation of an even more powerful organization, the Employers' National Economic Association *(Aso-ciación Patronal Económica Nacional —* APEN). Through APEN the proprietors mounted a sophisticated campaign against the López regime by focusing elite hostility toward any extension of state power on the land issue. In most of the larger countries of Latin America, reformist executives sought in the 1930s to endow the state with the financial and legal tools necessary to promote import-substitution industrialization.[49] Colombia was no exception. In 1936 President Alfonso López Pumarejo convinced Congress to amend the constitution to sanction state intervention in the economy and in labor disputes. Sweeping changes in tax and educational policy were not far behind.[50] These reforms elicited vehement opposition not only from the more traditional elites, but also from certain commercial and manufacturing sectors who resented the government's intrusion into the private sphere and its increased economic demands. APEN sought to articulate this opposition and ultimately to sabotage the López initiative by exerting bipartisan pressure on the regime.[51]

Not surprisingly perhaps, given the high incidence of landownership among Colombian elites, APEN's campaign to influence the López administration centered on the land question. APEN's publications imbued the land issue with a new interpretive slant. The motive of fostering the breakdown of the great estates to provide peasants with family farms never surfaced. Rather, the Apenistas openly charged the government with seeking to destroy private property in Colombia. They maintained that in recovering public lands, the government aimed to assert state ownership over the rural sector. Labelling López a "bolshevik," APEN proclaimed its own dedication to "the defense of private property, threatened today by the infiltration of socialist theories into the highest spheres of the governing party."[52] Should the government continue to side with the "rebellious" squatters, it warned, revolution was imminent.

Such inflamatory statements stirred the fears of a broad cross-section of the Colombian upper and middle classes. They facilitated the coalescence in APEN of a united front of landowners, merchants, professionals, and some financial and industrial interests, all of whom objected to the López program. As President López was painfully aware, APEN sympathizers included not only Conservatives but many moderate Liberals, members of his own party. In 1935 APEN announced its decision to confront López in local elections. The formation of APEN alerted the president to a serious erosion of his support among the upper levels of Colombian society. As the organization made clear, López could hope to regain his ground only by resolving the property issue in the landlords' favor.

In public statements the López administration, like the Olaya regime, asserted that its primary objective was to foster the spread of independent peasant properties.[53] To this end, it continued to revoke unused land grants and to support colonization and parcelization projects. Despite these ostensible continuities, the López administration took a different perspective on the land question. It stressed above all the need to reassure the large estate owners.[54] This change of emphasis clearly reflected the decline of squatter influence in the political arena and the concurrent formation of a united pressure group of landowners.

The López government's response to the land struggles was embodied in a bill presented to Congress on 22 July 1935. The committee responsible for elaborating the proposal included the minister of government, the minister of industries, two Supreme Court justices, the director of the Department of Public Lands, and the president's son, Alfonso López Michelsen, who would himself become president in the 1970s.[55] After long debates and some small but significant modifications, this bill was approved as Law 200 of 1936.[56]

The Land Act of 1936 is widely regarded as one of the most important reform initiatives of the López administration. Generally it is thought to have been a socially progressive measure that aimed to give the peasants land.[57] This interpretation is fundamentally inaccurate. Because the problems to which the statute responded have not been well understood, the significance of Law 200 has remained unclear.

In fact, the Land Act of 1936 signalled the government's assumption of an expanded role in fostering rural development and in defining the legal rights of social groups in relation to one another. Within this framework, however, the influence of the landed elites was strong. Law 200 proposed a compromise between the interests of the colonos and those of the landlords that favored the latter in the long run.

In areas of ongoing struggles where colonos were firmly established on the land, the legislators sought to end the conflicts by legitimizing the status quo. This part of the law was particularly responsive to squatters who had participated in the hacienda occupations of the late 1920s and early 1930s. It required the owners of estates invaded before 1935 to present either the original title or a deed dating from colonial times as proof of property. If the documents were non-existent, the haciendas would be presumed baldío; squatters settled there could then apply to Bogotá for free grants. Landlords who could prove legal ownership had to reimburse squatters for their improvements before evicting them. If a landowner refused to do so, the colonos thereby acquired the right to buy the land they tilled from him.[58]

The articles on adverse possession also favored some colonos. Law 200 reduced the period of adverse possession in Colombian jurisprudence from thirty to five years. This meant that if squatters farmed territory owned by someone else for five years, they gained rights to the land. To claim such rights, a squatter had to prove that he or she had acted in "good faith," that is without prior knowledge that the land was private property. These provisions together constituted a practical admission that squatters who had already farmed their fields for several years neither could nor should be dislodged. Thus, to groups of squatters who had developed the organizational strength to remain on the land, Law 200 opened the opportunity to acquire legal titles. These provisions, however, applied only to regions where squatter movements began before 1935.

The most important section of Law 200 was that which distinguished private properties from public lands. On this fundamental issue, the statute took the landlords' side. The López administration admitted that its major concern was to quiet upper class fears of land redistribution by providing estate owners with a legal foundation for their claims. President López explained this point in his message to Congress in 1935:

> Because the great majority of private landholdings in Colombia lack perfect titles, in the light of abstract jurisprudence they should return to the public domain. Technically, then, we find ourselves faced with the juridical alternative of directing this country toward a socialist orientation, or of revalidating such property titles, purifying them of imperfections. My government has chosen the second path. Accused of doing away with individual property, this administration instead presents to you, honorable members of Congress, the bases that it considers adequate to defend the extant system of private property in the rural areas.[59]

To this end, Law 200 established a presumption of right in favor not of the nation, as the bill of 1933 had done, but rather of individual proprietors. Thus the law nullified the Supreme Court decision of 1926. The original title requirement now applied only to hacendados whose property claims were disputed by colonos before 1935. For everyone else, it was no longer necessary to present the original title to prove property rights. Instead a chain of deeds showing possession for at least thirty years sufficed. Thus Law 200 sanctioned what had been customary judicial practice before 1926. This provision closed the debate that arose out of the confusion between public and private lands. By once again accepting sales, wills, and court documents as proof of property, Law 200 effectively legitimized the usurpations of public lands that had occurred over the preceding century. Despite the government's avowed interest in creating family farms, the law rejected the goal of breaking up the latifundia that lay at the heart of the agrarian reform initiative. In the same vein, the law omitted altogether the notion incorporated into the 1933 bill of limiting the size of properties conveyed through sale or inheritance.

Intended to reassure the landowners, the general confirmation of property titles also aimed to stop the squatter movement. Law 200 of 1936 disallowed all claims from squatters who participated in land invasions after 1934. More importantly, by reversing the decision of the Supreme Court, the statute undermined the colonos' argument that the land they tilled was public land. Henceforth settlers who occupied private properties could not claim colono status; instead they became illegal intruders (ocupantes de hecho or *detentadores de propiedad ajena*) and, as such, subject to eviction. New squatters who refused to be ejected faced sixty days imprisonment.

Thus Law 200 of 1936 marked a shift in Colombian agrarian policy toward acceptance of a system of landholding based on large properties. This policy reorientation signified an admission of the continuing vitality of elite interests in the Colombian political system and the effectiveness of their resistance to redistributive reform. The state's aim of encouraging rural productivity was not, however, abandoned. The Land Act of 1936 incorporated into Colombian law the concept of the social function of property. It stipulated that land titles should be confirmed only if the land were used for agriculture or the grazing of livestock. To compel hacendados to intensify their economic activities, Law 200 provided that any property not exploited within ten years after the law was approved would revert to the public domain. The statute also clearly defined the concept of possession in Colombian jurisprudence to mean economic use of a property, not merely the possession of written titles.

By transforming the concept of possession and by setting certain limits to the exercise of private property, Law 200 introduced important modifications into the Colombian legal system. In practical terms, however, these modifications had little impact. During the ten years after the law's passage, the political climate in Colombia shifted further to the right. The impulse toward social reform receded as national associations representative of large commercial landholding interests took a more prominent role in setting rural development priorities.[60] In 1944 the Federation of Coffee Growers and the Society of Colombian Agriculturalists prevailed on Congress to add five years to the ten year grace period allowed proprietors to initiate production.[61] Finally, the land use provision was suspended indefinitely.

Only in the 1960s, some twenty-five years after Law 200, did the Colombian Agrarian Reform Institute make a feeble attempt to reclaim some abandoned latifundia using the Land Act of 1936 as a precedent.[62]

In the end, then, the Colombian government sought a final solution to the land disputes through legislative reform. Law 200 of 1936 grew out of the new agrarian policy of the 1920s and the controversies it precipitated between landlords and self-designated colonos. The Land Act did respond to the legal confusion between public and private lands in which the conflicts originated. It signified, however, not the realization of the new agrarian policy, but rather its reversal. Certainly, by espousing the concept of the social function of property, Law 200 intended to foster exploitation of the land. But the law contradicted the aim of breaking down the latifundia, which constituted the keystone of agrarian reform. It did not address the problem of inequality in the distribution of landed property in Colombia.

Nor did Law 200 impede the continuing appropriation of public lands in frontier regions. Although aware of the historical fact of public land usurpation, the policy-makers seem to have been blind to the ongoing process. The legislation of 1936 did not confront the tension between settlers and large entrepreneurs over public lands that was to remain a root cause of social conflict in the Colombian countryside.

Viewed from a long range perspective, the significance of Law 200 to Colombian rural development lay in its legitimation of the extant agrarian structure. It provided a legal basis for many large properties consolidated through the appropriation of public lands during the period of agricultural export growth. By reinforcing the economic and political position of the landholding elites, the Land Act of 1936 set the stage for the future development of the Colombian countryside in large private estates.

What role, then, had the squatter movement played in influencing official policy on the rural sector? Indubitably, the land invasions brought the property question to national attention. The outbreak of rural unrest required a direct response from the Colombian government: it made state intervention necessary to clarify the fundamental legal and socioeconomic issues at stake. The peasant land occupations, however, were not sufficient to elicit from the government a decision favorable to the colonos as a social class. Lacking enduring structures of political influence, the squatters were unable to counteract the strong pressures exerted on the government by the landed elites.

It is true, of course, that Law 200 of 1936 gave some squatters who occupied idle properties before 1935 the opportunity to title their fields. Confusions inherent in the law itself, however, rendered the actual implementation of such provisions doubtful.[63] In the light of other official initiatives such as the parcelization program and the formation of rural unions, the purpose of such procolono gestures becomes clear. They were intended to defuse and, to an extent, coopt the squatter movement. Through concessions to some colono groups, Colombian politicians sought to forestall greater peasant radicalization, to pacify the major centers of unrest, and to reinforce the positive image of the government in rural areas. In Law 200 of 1936, the Colombian government set the terms by which access to land henceforth would be determined. Favorable to the landlords, this law denied the possibility of transforming the rural poor into commercial farmers. For years thereafter, the policy of increasing rural production would remain devoid of redistributive content.

In the 1930s the modern Colombian state was taking form. This study of the government's response to the agrarian problem adds a dimension to the analysis of the Colombian political system set forth by Robert H. Dix and others.[64] The kind of institutional responses advanced during the depression were indicative of the alignment of social forces that would prevail in subsequent years. In the rural sector, private elite groups succeeded in undermining the reform policy that posited an alliance between an increasingly autonomous state concerned with national development and the peasant cultivators.

Epilogue

Law 200 of 1936 brought to a close an era of Colombian agrarian history that had begun around 1870. This was the period of externally oriented export growth that witnessed the tremendous expansion of coffee cultivation, the spread of cattle ranching, and the construction of the railroads. In terms of land policy, Law 200 signified the end of the perspective that sought, unsuccessfully, to stimulate agricultural production through the promotion of smallholdings and the support of colonos against land speculators. In the years after 1936, and particularly after World War II, rapid industrialization and urbanization profoundly influenced the rural sector. Large-scale, mechanized agriculture supplanted extensive cattle grazing in the Cauca Valley, the plains of Tolima, the Llanos at the foot of the eastern cordillera, and the Caribbean coast. At the same time a significant rural wage labor pool came into existence.[1] Such developments were, of course, accompanied by a revised assessment of the "agrarian problem" and of ways to deal with it.[2]

Despite the enactment of Law 200 of 1936 and these subsequent changes, the public land issue has remained alive in the Colombian countryside. The ongoing appropriation of baldíos and the evolution of colono-landlord tensions has continued to shape the course of Colombian rural history. The importance of these processes in recent years has not, however, been fully recognized. This chapter sketches in the outlines of the story.

Results of the Land Conflicts for the Colonos

In the social history of the Colombian countryside, the decade 1937-47 remains an enigma. Eager to leap ahead to La Violencia (1948-65), most authors rely on a few standard interpretations based on little empirical research. Generally it is assumed that the Land Act resolved the agrarian conflicts of the 1930s. It is thought, then, that rural Colombia remained peaceful until 1946 when electoral in-fighting sparked political violence in some municipalities.[3]

Contemporary writings suggest that the land disputes of the early 1930s did in fact diminish in intensity after 1936. Contributing factors included the improved state of the economy, the political cooptation of the squatter movement, the guidelines provided by Law 200, and the continuing influence of the parcelization program. Gradual recovery from the depression, which produced rural salary increases after 1934, lessened economic distress among the Colombian rural population. This economic upswing may have been partly responsible for a levelling off of agrarian agitation.[4] Additionally, the reintegration of Gaitanista forces into the Liberal party and the Popular Front policy of the Communist party had predictably debilitating effects on the colono struggle. In the late 1930s, as independent colono organizations declined, the Liberal government intensified its efforts to channel and institutionalize peasant unrest. More than seventy-five new rural leagues and syndicates received juridical status in the decade after 1936, many with the express intention of promoting improvements the national government deigned desirable.[5]

Although economic recovery and the decline of the independent organizations had some effect, the Land Act and the parcelization program were more important in bringing the land disputes to a close. Law 200 established procedures for settling the conflicts within the judicial system. The responsibility for arbitration fell to the land judges (jueces de tierras), a new class of functionaries created by the law. From 1937 through 1943, the land judges dealt with all suits related to enforcement, that is, cases concerning public lands, title disagreements, and conflicts of interest between squatters and proprietors.[6] The judges acted expeditiously: according to the Ministry of Industries, more than 80 percent of existing disputes had been decided by the end of 1938.[7]

Unfortunately, the records of the Land Courts have yet to be located; therefore no concrete information is available on the resolution of specific conflicts. From scattered evidence, however, it appears that land judges in their interpretation of the law tended to side with the large proprietors. Many of the problems that had made it hard for colonos to get a fair hearing in the past still applied. In some areas influential landowners used their connections to appoint compliant justices, often members of their own political cliques. The fact that the land judges covered a large geographical area and sat in the cities meant that even those who were impartial rarely had the on-the-spot knowledge necessary to sort out the complexities of local controversies. Meanwhile, the poverty and illiteracy of the colonos put them, as always, at a disadvantage.[8]

In the years after 1936, land judges in various regions of the country called for the eviction of colonos from occupied haciendas.[9] Because they were not protected by the law, settlers who had participated in invasions after 1934 were particularly vulnerable. Others evicted included squatters on land the government intended for subdivision who were unable or unwilling to purchase their shares. Thus, buttressed by Law 200, some landlords succeeded in reclaiming land from colonos in the years after 1936.[10]

Other squatters managed to stay on the land they tilled. The terms under which such colonos prevailed are not entirely clear. In some places, it appears that the proprietors simply desisted in their efforts to remove the squatters, whose legal status remained undefined.[11] In other instances, colonos may have secured titles through the special provisions of Law 200 favoring peasants who occupied haciendas before 1935. Such was the case in Chaparral (Tolima) where a sympathetic land judge awarded 1,500 parcels to peasant families. His decision, however, was adamantly opposed by the mayor, the local judge, and the landlords who refused to acknowledge the peasants' landrights.[12] In the end official parcelization projects provided the most important mechanism by which squatters acquired rights to the land.

The parcelization policy contributed significantly to quieting the public land conflicts that had begun in the early 1930s. By legitimizing most haciendas, Law 200 undercut the colonos' argument that the land was baldío. Thus, Law 200 facilitated the application of parcelization to areas affected by disputes over land. Although they continued to criticize the terms of the government projects, the Valencia group and the Communist party supported the idea of parcelization after 1936.[13]

In the years from 1933 to 1940, the Colombian government purchased a total of 240 estates for subdivision. Through this program more than 11,000 peasants, including many colonos who had participated in the conflicts of the early 1930s, obtained legal rights to their fields.[14] The subdivision of haciendas affected by work contract or land controversies was particularly widespread in the western part of the department of Cundinamarca and in eastern Tolima. In these areas small coffee farms gradually supplanted the great estates of earlier years.[15] This transformation resulted in part from the squatter movement and in part from economic considerations, of which the rising cost of labor was most important.[16] Afflicted by high production costs, low returns, and problems with tenants and squatters, many hacendados sought through parcelization to transfer capital out of agriculture into more profitable investments in the urban sector.

Although peasants did get the land in this region, descriptions of the parcelization process cast grave doubt on its efficacy in assuring cultivators the true product of their labor. Financial and political manipulations played a large part in early subdivisions. Some outsiders who were able to pay the price received plots, while cultivators who had been there for years were expelled without compensation. Also, colonos who sympathized with Gaitán sometimes were supplanted by *parcelarios* who voted for APEN.[17]

The tactics of distribution aside, it soon became clear that subdivision of the haciendas would not automatically lead to quantum increases in production. The landlords generally sold off their least fertile territory. Squatters who bought this land often found themselves burdened with long term debts on small and unproductive parcels. To meet the first payment, reported *Claridad*, many colonos had to sell their chickens, a milk cow, or the family shotgun; to meet subsequent quotas, the crops had to be mortgaged. If peasants fell too far behind, the bank might well repossess the land they had farmed for many years as squatters or tenants. Furthermore, parcelarios could not get credit to make improvements: banks accepted land as security only if the owner showed valid titles, but the beneficiaries of parcelization could not obtain titles until they paid off the land.[18]

The subdivision of haciendas in many cases also raised the spector of minifundismo, if not immediately, then for later generations. In the parcelization of "Rastrojos" in Ambalema (Tolima), each family received only one fourth of a hectare. Even the more typical allocations of five to twenty hectares spelled excessive fragmentation once the land was split through inheritance among the sons and daughters of the first parcelarios. Such small holdings prevented the efficient use of family labor.[19]

In addition to these basic problems, the peasant farmers could not step up production without improved support structures. Government publications occasionally admitted that the new proprietors needed credit, tools, irrigation, and better transport, but such help was not forthcoming.[20] Furthermore, within the parcelization projects, surveyors neglected to compensate for variations in soil fertility and to provide for equitable access to water and roads. As a result, the parcelization process accentuated socioeconomic differences within the colono group. The wealthier peasants, storekeepers, and local moneylenders soon began to accumulate large amounts of land as others sold out in frustration.[21] Thus the distribution of the land did not generally lead to significant increases in the peasants' standard of living.

Meanwhile, the struggle for resources in parcelization zones generated frictions among the peasants themselves.

Parcelization continued to form part of official policy throughout the 1940s and 1950s, and it was incorporated in a modified form into Agrarian Reform Law 135 of 1961. In later as in earlier years, the government used this alternative mainly to intervene where peasants protested on unproductive, debt-ridden haciendas.[22]

In addition to the official parcelization projects, some landowners privately subdivided part or all of their holdings during the 1930s and 1940s. Responding to social agitation and the problem of obtaining sufficient labor, proprietors sold plots on the outskirts of their estates to their own tenants or squatters. In a few areas, professional and commercial people invested in parcelization companies that purchased idle estates to sell them off in smaller parcels. The new smallholders could be counted on to provide part-time labor for neighboring haciendas. Such a reserve labor pool was particularly essential in coffee areas at harvest time.[23]

In some regions, then, the conflicts of the early 1930s resulted in land for colonos and tenants. Most obtained this land not through their own action directly, but instead through government intervention. Those who became independent proprietors suffered from the lack of credit, marketing facilities, and technical aid. Some few became prosperous coffee producers. Many, however, came to resemble poor minifundistas in other parts of Colombia, indebted to storekeepers and the banks. In the areas they were implemented, the parcelization projects failed to give rise to the productive and independent rural middle class that had been envisaged.[24]

The Impact of Law 200: Social Conflict and the Formation of a Rural Wage Labor Force

As has been noted, the effect of Law 200 of 1936 on the resolution of existing land disputes is unclear. While it appears that the parcelization program had a more direct impact, the agrarian reform law did influence the evolution of rural labor relations.

In the decades after 1930, a tendency away from service tenure toward wage labor occurred throughout rural Latin America.[25] Colombia was no exception. In some areas of Colombia, parcelization provided a mechanism by which estate owners obtained a dependable seasonal supply of labor by shifting peasant families from the status of tenants to that of independent proprietors. All over the country the essential day-to-day work on coffee farms, on rice, sugar, and cotton plantations, and on the cattle ranches eventually came to be performed by hired wage laborers, some of whom owned small plots of land on the side. While theoretical explanations for this gradual shift in labor systems are best left to the economists, the concrete, historical motivations that led many hacendados in Colombia to employ salaried day laborers in place of tenant farmers can be discerned through investigation of the effects of Law 200 on the ongoing struggle between large proprietors and landless peasants.

Scattered references to this process of rural proletarianization suggest that the decade after 1936 was not as tranquil as has been believed. Although the Land Act settled many of the earlier conflicts, it inadvertently gave rise to a new wave of disputes. The effects of Law 200 on the evolution of rural labor relations stemmed from the peasants' efforts to turn the law to their own advantage and from the landlords' reaction to tenant agitation in a time of economic recession.

News of the agrarian reform law spread rapidly through the countryside. The peasants frequently seemed to confuse Law 200 with the bill of 1933. Oblivious to the legislators' real intent, many clung to the belief that the Land Act would give title to the land to those who cultivated it. Ironically, the interpretation adopted by the rural population coincided with that propagated by elite opponents of the statute who stressed the provisions relating to the social function of property and the protection of colonos.[26]

In response to the passage of Law 200, service tenants and sharecroppers in areas hitherto unaffected by squatter activity tried to assert property claims to the subsistence plots they tilled inside the estates. Some swore to own their fields by the right of adverse possession, while others, denying they had ever been tenants, claimed the rights of colonos who had occupied haciendas before 1934. If landlords moved to dislodge rebellious tenants, they resisted by hotly disputing the valuation of their improvements.[27] Thus service tenants and sharecroppers, whose rights remained undefined in Colombian jurisprudence, sought to reinforce their position by alleging to be settlers of public lands. Information on the distribution and frequency of such conflicts is scanty. The National Federation of Coffee Growers and the Ministry of the Economy, however, refer to a generalized antagonism between landlords and tenants in these years.[28] Land occupations continued to occur, and the land judges were inundated by new property suits.[29] In contrast to the preceding decade, however, the land conflicts after 1936 found no overt political expression. For this reason they drew little comment in the press or in official publications and have been neglected by historians until recently.

In response to continuing problems with tenant labor, many hacendados determined to dispense with the system once and for all. Gradually the proprietors bought their tenants out and turned them off the land. If the tenants disputed their property rights or refused to leave, landlords initiated eviction proceedings. In the end then, Law 200 left the system of large estates intact, but hastened the transformation of service tenants and sharecroppers into rural wage laborers.[30]

The results of continuing colono agitation were manifold. Fearful of labor problems, many hacendados turned land previously used for agriculture into pastures, which required only a handful of workers. For similar reasons, cattle ranchers were reluctant to exploit their fields more intensively. Consequently estate production did not increase notably in the late 1930s and early 1940s.[31] The decline in service tenure and sharecropping arrangements particularly affected the availability of food for internal consumption. As large numbers of subsistence farmers were expelled from the haciendas, the supply of foodstuffs they produced for local markets decreased precipitously. In coffee and other areas, the tendency toward monoculture was accentuated, with an attendant rise in domestic food prices.[32] Thus, Law 200 did not succeed in stimulating the intensification of land use in the Colombian countryside.

The transition away from tenancy toward wage labor produced severe dislocations. For the peasants, insecurity in landholding and in living conditions increased. The fate of those tenants who were evicted is unclear. Many, it would appear, joined the burgeoning ranks of salaried laborers in the rural areas, while others migrated to the cities or on to more remote frontiers. In some depressed regions, central Cauca for example, the curtailment of tenancy resulted in a surplus of unattached workers and a decline in rural salaries. Vagrancy and squatting along the roadways became more frequent.[33] In more prosperous areas the expulsion of the tenants had the opposite effect: landowners in Santander, Caldas, and Valle complained constantly of the scarcity and high cost of labor. The coffee producers, in particular, had trouble securing pickers for their semiannual harvests.[34]

By 1944 the problems of low production and labor shortages became so acute that the government deemed corrective measures necessary. The second important agrarian statute to be passed in eight years, Law 100 of 1944, provides corroborative evidence for the processes described above. The law endeavored to defend landlords against tenants who tried to assume colono status, to solve the problems of food and labor shortages, and to stimulate more intensive use of the estates legitimized in 1936. Law 100 defined the rights and obligations of tenant labor in a way that would guarantee the land-lords control of the land. It also sought to reverse the trend toward wage labor by reviving the sharecropper as an important element of the rural la-bor force.[35]

Law 100 of 1944 signified the culmination of the modern alliance be-tween the government and the large landowners that began in 1936. It gen-erated little opposition, for the economic interests of the great proprietors were no longer at stake. The aim of dissolving the latifundia system by turn-ing tenants and colonos into independent smallholders had been completely abandoned.

In the long run, Law 100 of 1944 had little practical effect. The trend toward wage labor continued, as did peasant agitation.[36] According to soci-ologist T. Lynn Smith, until the outbreak of widespread rural violence in 1948, "The colono problem was generally considered to be the country's primary social problem."[37]

Agrarian Unrest in Recent Years: The Continuing Transformation of Colono-Landlord Tensions

In the two decades after 1948, the colono conflicts became part of the larger upheaval known simply as La Violencia. This ostensibly anarchic civil war, which lasted from 1948 until 1965, is of central importance to the modern history of Colombia. In part a political clash between Liberals and Conservatives, in part a social upheaval, the Violence left 200,000 Colom-bians dead and 800,000 homeless.[38]

Initially most observers saw La Violencia in political terms, as a revival of traditional party hatreds. Those few who looked for socioeconomic moti-vations tended to interpret the killing either as a manifestation of peasant resistance to modernization or as an incipient social revolution.[39] In the past two decades, the complexity of the conflicts and regional differences have come into focus. A new generation of Colombian scholars emphasize that this was not just a peasant war, but one in which political bosses, land-lords, estate managers, muleteers, moneylenders, the military, and the state played major parts. In at least some areas, La Violencia signalled a new offensive of estate owners against peasants who had made some inroads in the 1930s and 1940s.[40] Such observations raise the obvious question of the connection between the agrarian changes set in motion in the 1920s and

1930s and the eruption of La Violencia in the 1940s and 1950s. This is an important question, one that has yet to receive a satisfactory answer.

What is certain is that continuing struggles between landlords and colonos contributed to the intensity of La Violencia in some parts of the country. Significantly, with the exception of the Caribbean coast, the areas of concentrated land disputes in the 1930s became foci of violence in the 1950s. In these zones, left-wing political groups established a particularly strong base among the peasantry. The Sumapaz, southern Tolima, and the eastern cordillera of Huila emerged as Communist strongholds, called "Independent Republics." In Huila and southern Tolima, Communist and Liberal peasants, persecuted by the Conservative government, formed guerrilla self-defense groups. They then withdrew into isolated frontier regions where they put aside their guns and turned to agriculture once again. These independent settler movements (Marquetalia, Riochiquito, El Pato, and Guayabero) drew devastating attack from the Colombian army in the early 1960s. Beyond its antagonism to the Communists, the army was pressured to act, it has been suggested, by local landlords eager to monopolize the newly opened land.[41] In Sumapaz and southern Tolima, the rural self-defense efforts of the Violencia years were led by people who had been active in the struggles of the 1930s. The head of the Communist movement in Sumapaz, Juan de la Cruz Varela, was a peasant of Boyacense origin who had collaborated with Erasmo Valencia in the 1920s and 1930s.[42]

In other areas, northern Tolima, Quindío, and Valle, for example, La Violencia in part masked a renewal of the agrarian struggle, the nature of which is not yet clear. Given the breakdown of national authority structures, some rural laborers and tenants may have tried to take over the land they worked. A much more common pattern during this epoch, however, was that of violence directed by land entrepreneurs against small proprietors and colonos. Death threats and burn outs compelled many peasants to sell their fields cheaply or simply abandon them, leaving the land consolidated in the hands of those who initiated such tactics.[43]

In newly opened frontier areas, the large-scale usurpation of public lands intensified at this time, along with the accompanying conflicts.[44] Two recent studies illustrate this process in different areas of the country. In the department of Valle, La Violencia centered not in the river valleys where haciendas were already solidly established, but rather in the mountains, on the edge of the agricultural frontier. In the municipalities of Tuluá, Sevilla, and Caicedonia, thousands of colonos were massacred or burnt out, leaving their homesteads to urban speculators who took up dairy ranching.[44] At the same time, La Violencia pitted predatory latifundistas against colonos in the coastal department of Córdoba (a subdivision of Bolívar). In northern Córdoba the landlords, who were mostly Conservatives, succeeded in pushing the colonos, who identified with the Liberal party, off the land; in the south where colonos formed armed self-defense bands (cuadrillas), many succeeded in maintaining their independence.[46]

The Violence itself induced important migrations of peasants out of the most conflictual regions. While some sought refuge in the towns and cities, others moved toward the remaining areas of public lands. In this way, the populations of Sumapaz and of southern Tolima were swollen by an influx of rural people of various political persuasions who sought security within the Communist-controlled zones. Other migratory currents headed into the Llanos, Caquetá and Putumayo, the Carare-Opón region in lowland Santander, the upper Sinú, and Urabá in northwestern Antioquia, all relatively undeveloped frontier areas.[47]

In these regions, spontaneous colonization goes on today as it has in Colombia for the past one hundred years. So does the privatization of public lands: between 1931 and 1971, the Colombian government distributed more than 11 million hectares of baldíos in grants to individuals and land companies.[48] The encroachment of land entrepreneurs onto peasant holdings continues with predictably contentious results. As political scientist Paul Oquist has noted, "In twentieth century Colombia, 'colonization area' is synonomous with chronic conflicts and high degrees of violence."[49]

Since the experience of the 1930s, colonos pressured by land entrepreneurs have tended to identify with left-wing political groups. In an insightful analysis of peasant radicalization in Cimitarra (Santander) in the mid-1970s, the Colombian Communist party stressed the primacy of the public land problem. The colonos of Cimitarra identified with the Communist party because it helped them resist the incursions of land entrepreneurs, while the government did nothing to protect them.[50] Significantly, the areas in which rural guerrillas have found a solid base of support in the Colombian countryside in the past fifteen years are all pioneer zones: southern Tolima, Urabá, Magdalena Medio, the Macarena, Caquetá, and Chocó.[51] Regions of ongoing colonization also provided the Liberal Revolutionary Movement (Movimiento Revolucionario Liberal), a short-lived leftist Liberal faction that emerged in the early sixties, with its principal electoral backing.[52] Colonos comprise a major group, too, within the independent Colombian peasant organization, the National Association of Peasant Usuaries (Asociación Nacional de Usuarios Campesinos, linea Sincelejo—ANUC).[53]

Beyond the element of political identification, the tactics of agrarian agitation in Colombia still resemble those developed during the 1930s. Countless invasions of haciendas—called land recuperations *(recuperaciones)* by the rural population—have occurred in the twenty years since La Violencia.[54] Generally factors similar to those that provoked the squatter occupations of the 1930s are present. In western Cundinamarca, the presence of abandoned estates motivated numerous invasions in the municipalities of Ospina Pérez, San Bernardo, Cunday, and Iconozco in the first years after La Violencia.[55] Serious unemployment, caused by the United Fruit Company's withdrawal from Colombia, led to similar activity around Santa Marta in the early 1960s. Hundreds of former banana laborers, now jobless, initiated colonization efforts both on public lands and on unused estates in the region. The landlords responded in classic fashion by burning down the squatters' huts and turning cattle into their crops.[56] Along the Caribbean coast, peasant land invasions were particularly frequent in regions where the formation of mechanized rice and cotton plantations displaced thousands of smallholders after 1960. Colonos pushed off their claims and tenants and day laborers thrown out of work by tractors occupied outlying sections of the great properties in squatter groups.[57] Although the accelerated development of capitalist agriculture that motivated such occupations was recent, the squatters' understanding of their situation had been forged through more than a century of conflict. A group of day laborers who established a squatter community on "recuperated" hacienda land in the Sinú in 1972 baptized themselves *El Baluarte Vicente Adamo* in memory of the feisty Italian who had initiated the agrarian movement there fifty years previously.[58] Meanwhile, employees of the Agrarian Reform Institute, sent to investigate one major confrontation in the municipality of Valledupar (Magdalena), reported, "The squatters maintain that these lands are public lands; they argue that in the old days this whole region was public land and that there have always been . . . colonos living on it."[59]

In the early 1960s, in the wake of La Violencia and the land invasions, the issue of land reform revived briefly in Colombia. In 1961 a new agrarian reform law was passed as Law 135. This statute expressed many of the same objectives as its predecessor twenty-five years before: the stated aims were first, to increase rural production and, secondly, to quiet peasant unrest by redistributing estate land.[60] The Colombian reform initiative was one of several similar proposals advanced by various Latin American countries during the 1960s—a period in which development experts pushed the idea that only by breaking down the latifundia might the rural sector reach higher levels of production.

The new Colombian reform law was a disappointment for the peasants. The concerted opposition of major sectors of the Liberal and Conservative parties and agricultural pressure groups representing the interests of the estate owners undermined the redistributive aspects of the reform. Meanwhile, credit, pricing, irrigation, and mechanization policies contributed to the modernization and expansion of the great estates, which began producing for both export and domestic markets. Even in the more traditional coffee sector, characterized for a time by a relatively wide distribution of landholding, observers have noted a tendency toward the reconcentration of landholding. This is in large part the result of the introduction of new coffee varieties and green revolution cultivation techniques.

At the same time many peasants have sold out or been turned off the land. Some have joined the growing migratory wage labor force in the countryside that works a few months a year harvesting coffee, rice, and cotton. Others swell the stream of country people who move to the cities, to the sprawling urban slums.[61]

The Colombian rural population has not been successful in pressuring the government for reforms in its favor. The first national peasant organization which made its appearance in the late 1960s —the National Association of Peasant Usuaries (ANUC)—today is badly fragmented and ineffectual. Meanwhile the Colombian government has abandoned all pretense of redistributive reform. Agrarian policy remains the province of a small group of industrial and landowning interests, while peasants have virtually no channels to express their concerns.

Given this situation, it is no surprise that guerrilla organizations have found some support in the Colombian countryside. There are at present at least five active groups with a total of more than 5,000 militants in arms.[62] They are, as noted earlier, concentrated in frontier regions. Such areas, which are to an extent outside the radius of state authority, provide a natural setting for guerrilla activity. Beyond geography, however, some Colombian researchers suggest another reason that the guerrillas, who are mostly young people of urban, middle class origin, have been able to put down roots in frontier zones. This reason has to do with the conflict there between colonos and land entrepreneurs, which inclines at least some peasants to receive the guerrillas sympathetically. Peasant pioneers, threatened by land entrepreneurs, many well turn to guerrilla forces willing to defend them and to assure them control of the land.[63]

As this final chapter suggests, our understanding of the development of capitalist agriculture in Colombia and its effects on peasant life and social movements has only just begun. One finding, however, is clear: colono-proprietor tensions arising out of an underlying conflict of interest over land constitute a fundamental continuity in Colombian rural history.

*   *   *   *   *

The purpose of this study has been to describe the patterns of landholding and social relations that took form in Colombian frontier areas and to
examine how and why such patterns emerged. A basic explanation has been
sought in the interaction of two fundamentally opposed social groups—the
land entrepreneurs and the colonos—within an evolving socioeconomic and
political context.

There are several conclusions to be drawn. First, it is important to emphasize that the large estates existing in contemporary Colombia are not a
colonial heritage. In the Spanish period there were haciendas, but most were
located in highland areas that at present are regions of minifundia. Today
the larger properties are situated not in the colonial highlands, but in the
middle altitudes and lowlands, in areas that as late as 1850 were frontier
zones.

The privatization of public lands provides a key to the consolidation of
latifundia in Colombia in the late nineteenth and early twentieth centuries.
The conversion of squatter families already settled on such land into tenant
farmers was an important element in the creation of a rural labor force at the
disposal of the new haciendas. Colombian entrepreneurs who asserted private domain over public lands deprived many peasants of free access to
land, thus relegating them to a subordinate position within the expanding
export economy. The image of a democratic frontier was illusory: the existence of an abundance of cheap land did not produce a more equitable distribution of landholding or a more fluid social structure in most frontier zones.
As in many other parts of Latin America, the development of commercial
agriculture and stock grazing strengthened the hacienda enterprise at the
expense of the peasant economy.

Study of the process of frontier expansion helps to explain the persistence of poverty in the Colombian countryside. Specialists in rural problems frequently assume that peasants remain poor because of their inherent
"traditionalism," their adherence to non-economic values, and their reluctance to adopt modern farming practices. This study supports an alternative
perspective, one that places primary responsibility on differential access to
productive resources.

Clearly in Colombia both peasants and land entrepreneurs were economic
actors. Their interests, however, clashed. An opposition between settlers,
determined to keep their independence, and land entrepreneurs, who depended on the peasants' land and labor for their own accumulation, was

intrinsic to the Colombian frontier experience. The failure of most settlers
to improve their situation in the long run should not be attributed to any
lack of determination on their part. The failure stemmed, rather, from the
superior authority of elite groups whose economic interests were directly
opposed to those of the colonos and from the colonos' relative lack of economic and political power.

While the conflict between colonos and land entrepreneurs was fundamentally over access to economic resources, laws and government institutions influenced the forms in which the conflict was expressed and the tactics
adopted by each side in its struggle for the land. In the late nineteenth and
early twentieth centuries, colonos were the only Colombian peasants with
rights defined by law. This juridical status comprised an integral aspect of
the colonos' identity, motivating them to take collective action against hacendados who denied them their land rights. Despite the landlords' effective
use of the law to reinforce their property claims, estate owners found it impossible to persuade many colonos of the validity of their titles. In opposition to the landlords' assertion of written titles, colonos consistently argued
the priority of use rights, that is, the right of cultivators to the land they
tilled. Thus the contradictory proprietary norms embodied in Colombian jurisprudence provided both the landed elites and the colonos with ideological justifications—opposing justifications. The law became "the medium
through which social conflict [found] expression."[64]

If the motivations of Colombian public land protests are to be found in a
specific process of property formation together with a particular legal-
institutional structure, what of their outcome? At the beginning of this study
reference was made to the great social movements of modern times— revolu-
tions with agrarian roots such as the Chinese revolution. Clearly nothing
like this has occurred in Colombia. There has been no social revolution:
through the conflicts of the 1930s and through La Violencia, the Liberal
and Conservative parties have continued to govern the country. In terms of
political institutions and policy, many observers agree, Colombia shows greater
continuity than most other Latin American nations.

This does not mean that the frontier struggles had no effect. The outcome
of peasant movements must be judged in relation to their original goals.
Throughout the 1850-1936 period and after, the aim of the colono struggles
focused on the land: each settler sought to win rights to a plot of land adequate to his or her family needs. The colonos did not mean to start a revolution:
they did not intend to overthrow the government, but rather to elicit its
support.

The demand for land is characteristic of many peasant uprisings the world over. Whether or not such movements become part of larger social movements with more radical political goals depends not only on the peasants themselves but on two external factors —the aims of those who ally with them and the government's response to peasants' initiatives. Just as rural unrest originates in the interaction of peasants and landlords, so the outcome of the conflicts depends on the response of opposition groups and of the government.

In Colombia the government has not been rigid. In its dealings both with peasants and with opposition political groups, the government has played a cooptive role. Through the public land reforms of the 1870s, 1880s and 1920s, the parcelization program of the 1930s and 1940s, and officially sponsored colonization projects, the government extended to peasants the promise of land. The ideology of the democratic frontier is still alive in Colombia, and it is actively promoted by official organizations.

In some times and places, settlers have gotten what they wanted. In the Antioqueño settlements, in some frontier regions (particularly after 1917), and in the hacienda parcelizations of the 1930s, peasants obtained title to the land. This was particularly true in coffee areas in the years 1930-1950. One observer has concluded from this that Colombian peasants were victorious in their struggles; for this reason, no greater radicalization has occurred.[65] But did the peasants win the land? Statistics indicate that, even taking these coffee areas into account, landholding is as concentrated in Colombia as in other Latin American countries, and the concentration of rural property has been increasing in recent years.[66] As a result, while some peasants get land and drop out of the struggle, others are being pushed off their fields.

A number of factors may have inhibited the emergence of a wider agrarian-based opposition: the turn-over of land seekers, the legalistic orientation of the conflicts, the government's occasional responsive gestures, and the lack of enduring opposition movements sensitive to settler concerns. Some believe that the current guerrilla struggle in this respect signals a new departure; the guerrillas, however, are divided among themselves. Meanwhile the present government led by Conservative President Belisario Betancur has instituted an amnesty, perhaps to coopt its violent opponents back as participants into the system.[67]

Despite their lack of enduring political influence, the settler movements have had an impact on national life. The public land conflicts compelled the government to define the meaning of private property as it applies to landownership and to become directly involved in structuring rural social relations. The settler movements also impelled the landlords to take a more active role in national politics by forming pressure groups representative of their interests. Although the colonos lost out in most instances, they emerged from the conflicts with a consciousness of their own rights. Colombian frontier expansion gave rise to an ideology of peasant protest centered on the reclamation of public lands that remains a vital tradition in the rural areas today. This tradition is as important in Colombia as the Indian struggles to reconstitute communal lands in Mexico and Peru.

Through consideration of the Colombian experience, this study, it is hoped, paves the way for comparative work on Latin American frontiers in the nineteenth and twentieth centuries. Of the various kinds of Latin American peasants, frontier settlers are particularly prone to mobilize in defense of their interests. Posseiros on the Brazilian frontier have taken up arms against speculators, while in Cuba the *precaristas* of the Sierra Maestre supported Fidel Castro's guerrillas during the war against Batista.[68] In Honduras, Costa Rica, and El Salvador, too, there have been major squatter movements in recent years.[69] Yet such conflicts have been little studied. Attention to such movements should provide much-needed comparative insight into the interests and issues at stake in frontier development and, at the same time, shed new light on the active role frontier settlers have played in shaping Latin American rural history.

A Note on Sources and Directions For Colombian Agrarian History of the Nineteenth and Twentieth Centuries

The past fifteen years have witnessed a surge of interest in the agrarian history of Latin America. In comparison to the other larger countries of the region, however, Colombian rural history has been neglected by North American and European researchers. This brief note indicates some sources and directions for research that may be of use to others.[1]

Sources

A good place to start is with the writings of early observers of the Colombian rural scene. For the nineteenth century, there exist a number of insightful essays and travel accounts by Colombian landowners, merchants, and statesmen that shed light on rural economy and society. The writings of Manuel Ancízar, Salvador Camacho Roldán, Aníbal Galindo, Medardo Rivas, José María Samper, and Miguel Samper—educated men involved in the new economic enterprises of the late nineteenth century—are particularly useful. In *Problemas colombianos* and *Idearium Liberal*, Liberal economist and engineer Alejandro López provides an excellent analysis of the problems of rural development as perceived in a somewhat later period—in the 1920s and 1930s. Diego Monsalve's treatise on coffee, which contains a survey of Colombian production in the 1920s, also makes a valuable contribution. The publications of the geographical commission headed by Agustin Codazzi and the later geographies of Francisco Vergara y Velasco, Felipe Pérez, Antonio García, and Ernesto Guhl are helpful too. Additional material is to be found in *El Agricultor*, published irregularly from 1869 through 1901, and in the *Revista Nacional de Agricultura*, the official organ of the Sociedad de Agricultores Colombianos (SAC), published from 1906 to the present. Since 1928, the SAC journal has been supplemented by the *Revista Cafetera de Colombia*, the mouthpiece of the Federación de Cafeteros de Colombia (FEDECAFE). The above-mentioned journals contain information on

economic conditions, agricultural practices, regional variations, and relations between large agricultural producers and the government. Other published sources of note include the *Boletín de la Oficina General de Trabajo*,
which provides detailed descriptions and in-depth analysis of the agrarian
conflicts of the 1920s and 1930s, and the annual reports of the various governmental ministries to Congress—particularly the Ministry of Finance for
the nineteenth century and the Ministries of Agriculture, Industries, and
National Economy for the twentieth century.

The archival sources for Colombian agrarian history are varied. For Colombia, as for the rest of Latin America, notarial, judicial, parish, and hacienda records may ultimately prove the most useful, though little in-depth
research using such material has as yet been done.[2] The major historical
collections in Bogotá, where I did my research, are to be found at the National Library and Archive and at the Biblioteca Luis Angel Arango. Let me
begin with the Public Land Correspondence, half of which is located in the
National Archive and half in the archive of the Colombian Agrarian Reform
Institute (INCORA). Although I used these records to explore the peasant
side of the frontier expansion process, they also shed light on patterns of
native and foreign elite investment in the rural sector. The collection contains much information on the Santa Marta banana zone in the form of reports from a public lands commission the government created there to protect
the national domain. The reports vividly portray the land boom of the 1920s
and give an inside picture of relations between Colombian authorities and
the United Fruit Company.

Beyond the public land papers, the library and archives of the Colombian Agrarian Reform Institute (INCORA) in Bogotá, though somewhat difficult of access, are of great potential value for twentieth century rural
historians. They contain extensive information on the areas designated agrarian reform projects in the 1960s, areas including Sumapaz, southern and
eastern Tolima, and the banana zone, which were generally marked by social unrest. Mimeographed studies of land tenure and socioeconomic conditions in these regions, which are deposited in the INCORA library, often
include sections on the history of the areas as well. The agrarian reform
project files are said to include detailed documentation on each estate effected and surveys of all property in the immediate area. The correspondence files, which contain all communications from the public to the institute,
may also be a rich source on rural problems. The Public Land Correspondence for the post-1930 period is probably to be found in the INCORA archives, for in the early 1960s the Institute inherited responsibility for the
public domain and official colonization projects. Finally, the internal min-

utes of INCORA meetings should provide insight into the formulation and implementation of agrarian policy over the past twenty-five years.[3]

The Colombian Congressional Archive also contains much material of interest—for example, letters from rural people to their congressmen detailing the problems of their localities, reports from fact-finding missions sent to investigate violations of public order, and, last but not least, the originals of all bills considered for adoption by Congress. In the prologues to the bills, called *antecedentes*, the person or persons proposing the bill state their justifications for the new legislation. Such statements, which are often several pages long, shed light on the socioeconomic conditions motivating governmental response. Through such prologues, the bills themselves, and the subsequent debates, the evolving conceptualizations of the agrarian problem can be traced.[4]

One additional official archive that has yet to be fully explored is that of the Caja de Crédito Agraria—the Agricultural Credit Bank. As Marco Palacios has amply demonstrated, it can be used to study the parcelization programs of the 1930s and 1940s. From 1945 on, each branch office of the Caja has complete records of applications for rural credit and of correspondence with its clients. Such files shed light on the patterns of rural credit distribution and the assets and productive organization of those farms receiving credit.

Other institutional sources include the Society of Colombian Agriculturalists (SAC) which has its own archive; the Colombian Federation of Coffee Growers; the Ministry of Public Works, which is reputed to have a rich archive; the Agustín Codazzi Geographical Institute, which has carried out the first cadastral survey of the entire country, as well as soil surveys; and the National Administrative Department of Statistics (DANE) which has a useful library and computerized information bases on many sectors of the national economy, including agriculture. The historian should also be aware of the independent Jesuit-run Centro de Investigaciones y Educación Popular (CINEP), which is a center for research on current urban and rural problems. CINEP's newspaper file, organized by subject for the past twenty years, supplements the excellent newspaper collection at the National Library.

The personal papers of leading Colombian statesmen constitute one final source for social and economic, as well as political history. Deposited in the Colombian Academy of History, the papers of Enrique Olaya Herrera, president of Colombia from 1930 to 1934, include local reports on the agrarian conflicts of the 1920s and 1930s. Of even greater potential value is the personal archive of Jorge Eliécer Gaitán, which is in the possession Gaitán's daughter and is presently located at the Centro Jorge Eliécer Gaitán in Bogotá. This immense collection covers the years from 1930 when Gaitán rose to national prominence through his death in 1948. It includes a voluminous correspondence, which should illuminate not only the evolution of Gaitán's thought and tactics but also what Gaitanism meant to the rural people of Colombia, a question fundamental to making sense of La Violencia.

The New Colombian History: Agrarian Themes

Despite the existence of abundant primary sources—some of which are described above—the formation of a cadre of Colombian researchers able to make use of such material to interpret the socioeconomic evolution of their country has been slow in coming.[5] Pioneers in this area were Luis Eduardo Nieto Arteta, whose writings on coffee shaped all subsequent interpretations; Luis Ospina Vásquez, whose *Industria y protección* remains the best economic history of Colombia; Juan Friede, a Russian immigrant who opened up the field of Colombian Indian history; Jaime Jaramillo Uribe, who laid the bases of colonial economic and social history and who has written the best intellectual history of Colombia; and Frank Safford, whose dissertation is a pathbreaking contribution to the economic history of the nineteenth century.[6]

Only in the past fifteen years have these early efforts born fruit in the emergence of *la nueva historia*, which centers on economic and social themes.[7] The new history is the work of Colombian historians, anthropologists, sociologists, political scientists, and economists, many of whom have acquired graduate training in England, France, or the United States.[8] These people agree that an understanding of Colombian history is essential to illuminate the present and, perhaps, to change it. Centers for the new work include the Universidad del Valle in Cali; the Universidad de Antioquia and the Universidad Nacional de Medellín in Medellín; and the Universidad Nacional and the Universidad de los Andes in Bogotá.

In Cali, a core of historians has formed around Germán Colmenares in collaboration with Jorge Orlando Melo, Jorge Escorcia, and others. They have produced fine work on the history of western Colombia during the colonial period and the early nineteenth century. This work focuses on the interrelations between plantation agriculture, slavery, and gold mining. American historian Richard Hyland, Australian anthropologist Michael Taussig, and Colombian anthropologist Nina S. de Friedemann have also contributed to our understanding of this area.

In Medellín, one also finds a strong regional focus, this time on the unique

trajectory of Antioqueño economic development that began with gold mining, then moved into coffee, and later into rapid industrialization. A wealth
of information is available in the innumerable municipal histories produced
by local historians in this most educated and self-reliant of Colombian departments. Professional geographers, historians, and economists who stimulated the Antioqueño school include James Parsons, Alvaro López Toro,
Jorge Villegas, Alvaro Tirado Mejía, Roger Brew, Ann Twinam, and researchers associated with the Centro de Investigaciones Económicas (CIE)
at the Universidad de Antioquia. Antioquia boasts a well-organized and accessible provincial archive and a newspaper collection at the Universidad
de Antioquia. Also important is a new scholarly center established by the
Ospina Vásquez family in memory of Don Luis Ospina Vásquez—the Fun-
dación Antioqueña Para Los Estudios Sociales (FAES). This foundation houses
the family archive as well as much other valuable archival material and a
fine library. Since 1978 FAES has become a major stimulus to historical
research and publishing in Medellín.

In Bogotá, the focus is on twentieth century history. The most active groups
are to be found at the Universidad Nacional in the History and Economics
departments and in the Political Science and Economics departments of the
Universidad de los Andes. A number of independent researchers associated with government agencies or independent research organizations are
also based in Bogotá. The work coming out of Bogotá addresses several interrelated themes.

One theme concerns the growth of commercial agriculture, with particular attention to the coffee economy.[9] Using the Antioqueño studies as a spring-
board, new works on coffee include those of Mariano Arango, Absalón
Machado, and Marco Palacios, who is the first Colombian historian to make
extensive use of local archives and hacienda records to do agrarian history.[10]
Economists who have extended our understanding of Colombian commercial agriculture include José Antonio OCampo, who has produced the most
thorough investigation of the export economy in the late nineteenth century,
and Jesús Antonio Bejarano and Salomón Kalmanowitz, who deal with twentieth century agrarian development and the social contradictions there involved. Foreign economists and economic historians who have done valuable
work include Albert Berry, Albert Hirschman, William Paul McGreevey[11],
and Rosemary Thorpe. Rural sociologists, too, have analyzed the development of commercial agriculture and ranching. T. Lynn Smith, who lived in
Colombia for several years in the 1940s, and Eugene Havens did much to
open the field.[12] The most innovative and prolific of the Colombian sociologists is Orlando Fals Borda who began his career with rather traditional stud-

ies of highland peasant life in Cundinamarca and Boyacá. Fals Borda has subsequently evolved toward a concern with Marxist theory and political action, and has spent the past ten years immersed in investigations of his native Caribbean coast. Recently, in *Historía doble de la costa*, he has produced a regional history of Mompós from colonial times to the present that is intended not only for the educated, but also for the peasants themselves.[13]

If one thread of research centers on the development of commercial agriculture, Colombian scholars also manifest a strong interest in the related issue of agrarian conflict. Such a focus is natural, given that many of the new historians came to maturity during La Violencia and that there was a resurgence of conflict over land and guerrilla activity in the 1970s. Most of the work on social struggle in the countryside has concentrated on the agrarian transformation of the 1920s and 1930s. The social histories of Ignacio Torres Giraldo, Gonzalo Sánchez G., Jesús Antonio Bejarano, Victor Negrete B., Charles Bergquist, and Michael Jiménez are particularly insightful on this period. Darío Fajardo, Gloria Gaitán de Valencia, and Hermes Tovar Pinzón's works are also worth consulting. Recently, the research on social conflict has been moving forward in time. Paul Oquist's book on La Violencia, published in Spanish in 1978, has had a major impact in stimulating regional studies of La Violencia. These studies are beginning to shed new light on the variety of regional dynamics involved. Gonzalo Sánchez and Donny Meerten's book on political banditry and Carlos Ortiz's dissertation on La Violencia in Quindío exemplify the most original of this work which draws on both written and oral sources. Useful contributions also are to be found in the undergraduate and masters theses coming out of the Universidad de Los Andes and the Universidad Nacional. Among the best are the theses by Darío Sánchez Reyes, Fabio Zambrano et al., Carlos Enrique Pardo, and Luis Bottía G. and Rodolfo Escobedo D.

One final theme addressed in Colombian historiography is that of the state and the agrarian problem. Whereas political historians have tended to emphasize party conflict and to neglect the state, this neglect is beginning to be remedied. The works of Darío Mesa, Pierre Gilhodes, Paul Oquist, Daniel Pécaut, Bruce Bagley, and Bernardo Tovar Zambrano together provide insight into the evolution of the Colombian state in the twentieth century and the approaches it has taken to economic development.[14]

*　*　*　*　*

As should be clear, agrarian history is beginning to come into its own in Colombia, mainly under the impulse of Colombian researchers concerned to make sense of their own reality. The people involved in such work are dispersed, as are the sources, and the major issues of debate are only now emerging. But, with time and energy, it should become possible to piece together a picture of Colombian rural life in its vast complexity and diversity.

Appendix A

Colombian Public Land Grants by
Type of Grantee, 1827–1931

Grantee	Number of Grants Awarded	Number of Hectares Granted
men	5,496	2,517,238
women[a]	309	31,327
1 person	5,386	1,945,188
more than 1 person[b]	423	605,395
companies		
railroad	11	54,571
mining	11	11,845
agricultural	4	6,165
ranching	1	1,710
type unknown	60	143,428
settlements (poblaciones)	18	141,819
municipalities[c]	13	64,120
departments[d]	6	251,417
provinces[d]	2	32,000
a school	1	640
churches	2	.2
Total	5,938	3,258,298

a. These include 28 grants to widows.
b. Often several people applied for a public land grant together. Such grantees usually are listed as "_____ and others." A few such grantees are referred to as "cultivators," but most seem to have been large scale investors. They probably applied for grants in groups of two to five persons in order to share surveying costs.

c. Grants to municipalities generally provided for the establishment of a county seat in frontier areas. Occasionally such grants were auctioned by the municipality to raise money for local public works.

d. Grants to departments and provinces could be rented or auctioned in order to raise money for regional coffers or pay for transport improvements.

Source: *Memoria de Industrias*, 1931, vol. 5, pp. 249–410

Appendix B

Distribution of Public Land by Size of Grant
for Periods Between 1827-1931[a]

Grant Size	1827–69	1870–1900	1901–17	1918–31	Total
1–20 h					
# grantees	17	63	156	1,935	2,171
# hectares	115	598	1,985	31,484	34,182
21–100 h					
# grantees	9	344	648	303	1,304
# hectares	568	23,444	38,416	13,118	75,546
settlements					
# grantees	10	8	0	0	18
# hectares	37,772	104,047	0	0	141,819
101–500 h					
# grantees	21	241	461	127	850
# hectares	6,223	61,459	103,196	35,068	205,946
501–1000 h					
# grantees	14	114	98	64	290
# hectares	11,259	87,760	84,146	54,091	231,256
1001–2500 h					
# grantees	16	107	64	129	316
# hectares	26,684	185,460	112,032	264,518	588,694
2501–5000 h					
# grantees	16	95	14	9	134
# hectares	57,810	395,163	53,070	30,797	536,840

Appendix B

Grant Size	1827–69	1870–1900	1901–17	1918–31	Total
5000 + h					
# grantees	19	56	1	2	78
# hectares	331,208	702,956	6,000	53,799	1,093,963

a. If an applicant received more than one grant, the sum of those grants has been used to determine size of allocation. Grants to provinces, departments, and municipalities are excluded from this table.

Source: *Memoria de Industrias*, 1931, vol. 5, pp. 249–410.

Appendix C

Colono Participation in Conflicts over Public Lands

Information on colono resistance to encroachments by land entrepreneurs in the late nineteenth and early twentieth centuries comes from the petitions received by national authorities compiled in ANCB vols. 1-78. Often several such petitions refer to a single conflict over a period of years. The following table illustrates the rise in number of petitions over time:

Petitions on Encroachments and Conflicts over Public Lands

Time Period	No. of Petitions From Colonos or Colonos' Representatives			No. of Petitions From Others: Municipal Authorities, Landlords, Private Individuals			Totals		
1870-79	2			3			5		
1880-89	23			18			41		
1890-99	37	+	1[a]	43			80	+	1[a]
1900-09	64	+	2[a]	95	+	3[a]	159	+	5[a]
1910-19	94	+	3[a]	98	+	3[a]	192	+	6[a]
					+	1[b]		+	1[b]
1920-29	210	+	8[a]	160	+	4[a]	370	+	12[a]
		+	3[b]		+	1[b]		+	4[b]
1930-31	24			39					
Total	454	+	14[a]	456	+	10[a]	910	+	24[a]
		+	3[b]		+	2[b]		+	5[b]

a. A conflict between a renter of national forests and the settlers and collectors of wood products living in the area.

b. A conflict between Indians claiming communal landrights and colonos encroaching on that land. Occasionally in such conflicts the colonos were also of Indian descent.

Many petitions do not mention the exact number of colonos involved in a conflict. Some indication of numbers, however, is provided by the signatures on petitions from colonos. Approximately 60 percent of petitions from colonos' representatives are signed, generally by male heads of household. Such signatures provide a rough minimum estimate of the number of settler families participating in any one conflict. There are no significant variations in the number of signatures over time.

Distribution of Signatures on Colono Petitions

Number of Signatures	Number of Petitions	% of Signed Petitions
5 to 24	150	56
25 to 49	70	25
50 to 74	19	7
75 to 99	16	6
100 to 149	8	3
150 to 200	6	2

A second indication is provided by the approximately 28 percent of colono petitions that directly state the number of settlers involved in a given conflict. The reader should be aware that just as counting signatures probably underestimates the number of families affected, so direct statements may inflate the numbers in order to encourage government intervention.

Distribution of Petitions Indicating Number of Colonos Involved in a Given Conflict

Number of Colonos/ Conflict	Number of Petitions	% of Signed Petitions
10-49	29	23
50-99	18	14
100-499	40	31
500-999	12	3
"hundreds"	4	3
1000-2999	20	15
3000 +	10	5

Appendix D

Public Land Grants and Conflicts by Municipality, 1827–1931

Municipality[a]	1827-1869		1870-1900			1901-1917			1918-1931		
	No. Grants	No. Hectares Granted	No. Grants	No. Hectares Granted	No. Conflicts Reported	No. Grants	No. Hectares Granted	No. Conflicts Reported	No. Grants	No. Hectares Granted	No. Conflicts Reported[b]
Department: Antioquia											
Amaga			1	10							
Amalfi			9	12,757		1	603		2	1,106	
Andes (San Agustín)			1	996							
Antioquia			1	50							
Cáceres			21	19,800		9	14,880	1	1	1,250	
Cañafistula								1			
Cañasgordas			1	80 (+50,000 to Dept. Antioquia)							
Caracolí											2
Caramanta	1	102,717									
Causasia (Margento)									2	2,575	1
Chigorodó									44 (+18 of 1h[c])	3,706	1 + 1 forest[d]
Cisneros									2	34	
Cocorná			2	4,400				1			
Concepción			3	463							
Copacabana (Canoas)	1	1,439									
Dabeiba			3	6,970	1						

185

Department: Antioquia

Municipality	1827-1869		1870-1900			1901-1917			1918-1931		
	No. Grants	No. Hectares Granted	No. Grants	No. Hectares Granted	No. Conflicts Reported	No. Grants	No. Hectares Granted	No. Conflicts Reported	No. Grants	No. Hectares Granted	No. Conflicts Reported
Frontino	2		1	800 (+50,000 to Dept. Antioquia)				1 forest			
Ituango (Pascuita)	113	19,212 (+5,760 población)	113	68,452		21	8,439		19	640	
Marinilla	1	3,840									
Medellín	2	5,798									
Montaño	1	7,680 (población)	1	181							
Murindó	1	7,680 (población)			1						1 +2 forest
Mutatá	5	33,347			1						1 forest
Nare				1					11	182	
Provincia del Centro			3	19						1	
Puerto Berrío	6	8,355	4	5,692	1	3	2,493	2	21	19,006	2
Río Mata	1	8,898	31	15,428		2	652		6	4,410	2
San Carlos (Muralla, Palmichal)	2	6,707	8	13,094							
San Luis			4	13,082		3	544				
San Pedro (San Martín)			2	624							
San Rafael			12	6,887							
Santo Domingo	1	3,850	1	3,850							

Location	n	ha	n	ha	n	n	ha	n	n	ha	n
Santa Rosa de Osos	1	2,560 (Excl. 64,000h grant to Tyrell Moore revoked within 10 years)	2	13		2	399	1			1
Santuario											
Segovia			5	2,428							
Singa			1	178							
Sonsón	1	2,177									
Sopetrán	1	5,760									
Turbo		5,120 (población)				11	12,744	3 +1 forest	24	25,477	2 +2 forest
Urrao (Arquía)	6	10,146 (+16,000 to Prov. Antioquia)	6	8,178	1	22	20,481		3 (+8 of 1h)	4,713	+2 forest
Valdivia						2	452				1
Yambo Bonito			1	40							
Yarumal (El Rosario)	1	274	31	31,996	1	1	32	1			
Yolombó	4	17,086	43	22,878	1	15	3,253	1	8	1,751	
Zaragoza						3	352		3	2	
Zea						1	4,505				
Unspecified	3	8,769	6	7,641					1	2,500	
Totals	44	283,175	317	346,988	8	96	69,829	13	146	67,659	20

Intendency: Arauca

Location	n	ha	n	ha	n			n			n
Arauca											
Tame	2	4,605	2	14,893	1			1			1

Department: Atlántico

Location											n
Baranoa											1

Municipality	1827-1869			1870-1900			1901-1917			1918-1931		
	No. Grants	Hectares Granted	No. Conflicts Reported	No. Grants	Hectares Granted	No. Conflicts Reported	No. Grants	Hectares Granted	No. Conflicts Reported	No. Grants	Hectares Granted	No. Conflicts Reported

Department: Atlántico

Municipality	No. Grants	Hectares Granted	No. Conflicts Reported	No. Grants	Hectares Granted	No. Conflicts Reported	No. Grants	Hectares Granted	No. Conflicts Reported	No. Grants	Hectares Granted	No. Conflicts Reported
Barranquilla				1	8,272							
Puerto Colombia (Sabanilla)	1	264										

Department: Old Bolívar (present-day departments of Bolívar, Córdoba, and Sucre)

Municipality	No. Grants	Hectares Granted	No. Conflicts Reported	No. Grants	Hectares Granted	No. Conflicts Reported	No. Grants	Hectares Granted	No. Conflicts Reported	No. Grants	Hectares Granted	No. Conflicts Reported
Achí												1
Ayapel				2	8,903		3	2,342	1	16	30,167	1
Barranco de Loba									2			3
Caimito				1	631				1			
El Carmen de Bolívar (Miraflores)									1	1	208	1
Cartagena									1 forest			
Cereté										4	8,074	
Ciénaga de Oro				1	4,986							
Coloso												1
Córdoba										2	3,058	2
Corozal									1			
Lorica				1	533		7	9,303	1 forest	20	9,269	1
Magangué				1	594	2	1	1,450	6	3	4,399	4
Majagual							1	881	1	19	17,288	13 +1 forest
Margarita				1	29							3
Mompós (Talaigua)				1	1,184	1	1	1,581	2			1
Montería				22	62,344		41	41,959	3	48	47,571	2
Morales (Bodega Central)								395	3			5 +1 forest

188

Pinillos (Palomino)									2	40	
Puerto Escondido			1			6	14,823	1	2	5,000	
Sahagún				2,754							
Sampués								1			
San Andrés de Sotavento (Codazzi)								1			
San Benito Abad			1	1,056							
San Carlos			2	2,627		1	3,176				
San Fernando								1			
San Jacinto								1			
San Martín de Loba					1			3	1	1,900	1
San Onofre			1	3,979		3	1,949	4			1
San Pelayo (Retiro)								1 forest	15	7,980	
San Sebastián de Madrid			2	1,691							
Santiago			1	1,327				1			
Simití						1	992		15	56,266	3
Sincelejo			2	6,199					1	875	
Sinú											
Soplaviento									1	920	
Sucre			1	3,979		2	847	1	7	136	
Tolú								1			
Zambrano								1	2	40	
Unspecified			2	369				1			
Totals	0	0	40	103,185	4	68	79,698	40	159	191,191	46

Department: Old Boyacá (present day Department of Boyacá and Intendency of Casanare)

Campohermosa			2	9,225							
Canipa									1	132	
Chameza					1						
Chíbor			1	765							
Chinavita			1	1,000							
Chita			1	923							1

Department: Old Boyacá

Municipality	1827-1869 No. Grants	1827-1869 Hectares Granted	1827-1869 No. Conflicts Reported	1870-1900 No. Grants	1870-1900 Hectares Granted	1870-1900 No. Conflicts Reported	1901-1917 No. Grants	1901-1917 Hectares Granted	1901-1917 No. Conflicts Reported	1918-1931 No. Grants	1918-1931 Hectares Granted	1918-1931 No. Conflicts Reported
El Cocuy				1	5,000							
Güicán				1	1,704							
Hato Corozal (Chire)	2	2,942 (+5,120 población)										
Macanal				1	900							
Naranjal	1	1,737										
Nunchia									2 +1 forest			2
Orocué	2			2	9,920							
Otanche												1
Pauna				1	4,531							1
La Salina												
Somondoco	1	256										
Sotaquirá				1	589							
Territorio Vásquez										1	42,890 to Dept. Boyacá	1
Tota				1	35							
Trinidad									2			
Yopal (El Morro, Marroquín)												
Unspecified	1	14,100		1	100,000							5
Totals	6	24,155		14	134,592	1	0	0	5	2	43,022	11

190

Department: Old Caldas (present-day departments of Caldas, Quindío, and Riseralda)

Municipality									
Anserma (Ansermaviejo)	5	20,694	1	22	3,418	1	1	555	
Apía				80	6,480	5	21	297	1
Armenia	18	9,667	1	186	24,980		23 (+12 of 1h)	295	2
Balboa							87	1,376	
Belalcázar	1	1,200	1	3	49	1	181	4,541	1
Belén				13	1,523		7	108	1
Calarcá	1	74		296	19,763	5	74 (+17 of 1h)	833	1
Circasia				41	3,761		25	376	
La Colonia	1	1,095				2			1
La Dorado									
Española	1	96				2			
Filadelfia									
Filandia	11	3,545	2	2	74	2	28	455	
	1			104	9,172				
Manzanares	1	12,000 (población)							
Marmato									1
Marulanda	2	822							
Montenegro				6	1,215		1	138	
Neira	1	7,680 (población)							
Nueva Caramanta	1	101							
Pereira (San Joaquín)	2	2,722	12	8	1,769	1	12	151	
		(+12,000 población)							
Pueblo Rico		4,942 (+12,000 población)		8	2,145		78	2,847 (+4,000 to Dept. Caldas)	
Quimbaya			2					14	
Quinchía (El Cedral)	1	603							
Riosucio	1	400		1	86		9	178	
Salamina	1	150							1

Municipality	1827-1869			1870-1900			1901-1917			1918-1931		
	No. Grants	No. Hectares Granted	No. Conflicts Reported	No. Grants	No. Hectares Granted	No. Conflicts Reported	No. Grants	No. Hectares Granted	No. Conflicts Reported	No. Grants	No. Hectares Granted	No. Conflicts Reported
Department: Old Caldas												
Salento	1	320		19	9,359 (+15,360 población)	4	10	1,766		2	1,111	
Santa Rosa de Cabal		2,710 (población)				1	1	287				
Department: Old Caldas												
Santuario							39	2,653	1	229	6,003	5
Victoria							29	4,264	2	4	4,680	
Villa María	23	7,680 (población)			22,228	1						
Totals	7	21,213		100	114,235	10	849	83,445	14	785	27,954	14
Intendencies: Caquetá and Putumayo												
Florencia (Sucre)									1	142	8,499	3 +1 forest
Mocoa							18	10,407		33	1,419	
Santa Rosa (Alto Caquetá)						1						
San Vicente de Caguán												1

Location								1	6	3 + 1 colonos vs Indians[e]
Sibundoy				1	18	10,407	2	176	9,924	
Unspecified	0	0	70,000							
Totals	0	0	70,000	1	18	10,407	2	176	9,924	8
Balboa										
Bolívar									20	1
Buenosaires								31	4,007	3
Cajia River				1						
Cajibío		2	221	1						
Guapi								8	160	
Inzá								7	128	1 + 1 colonos vs Indians
Jambaló										2 colonos vs Indians
Páez (Ricuarte)		1	1,275		5	239		1	1,050	1 colonos vs Indians
Patia (Bordo)		2		1						2
Popayán	492	2	2,707	1				13	206	
Puracé			2,702							
San Miguel								1	20	
Santa Rosa								25		
Silvia		1	330						473	1 colonos vs Indians
Totals	492	6	4,528	4	5	239	2	86	6,044	10
Intendency: Chocó										
Acandí				1 forest	3	7,000	2	9	10,086	1 forest / 1 colonos vs Indians
Alto Baudó (Baudó)		8	1,246		6	8,651		100	1,768	1 colonos vs Indians

Municipality	1827-1869		1870-1900			1901-1917			1918-1931		
	No. Grants	No. Hectares Granted	No. Grants	No. Hectares Granted	No. Conflicts Reported	No. Grants	No. Hectares Granted	No. Conflicts Reported	No. Grants	No. Hectares Granted	No. Conflicts Reported
Department: Chocó											
Atrato	1	2,000	2	46,400					1	20	
Bagadó			3	13,000							
Bajo Baudó (Pizarro)									1	20	
El Carmen			2	10,000							
Ensenada de Utria			1	1,571							
Istmina (San Pablo)						1	200	2	7	140	2 colonos vs Indians
Lloró			2	5,100					1	20	
Mugindó								2			
Novita			1	56							
Nuquí									8	160	
Quibdó			4	5,157	1	4	5,838	1	20	1,061	2 + 1 colonos vs Indians
Ríosucio									1	10	
Río Tutumendo								1			
San Juan									1	20	
Tadó			3	549		5	911	2	3	54	
Unspecified	2	422									
Totals	3	2,422	26	83,079	1	19	22,600	11	152	13,359	3
Department: Cundinamarca											
Bogotá	3	6,968									3
Caparrapí			1	3,332				1			
Chipaque	1	3,200									
Fómeque			1	1,700							

Fusagasugá				1,000						
Gachalá	2	4,758							1	500	1
Gachetá			1	529							
Guaduas (La Paz, Puerto Bogotá)	1	1,068	1	3,333	1						
Gutiérrez			1	2,101					2	3,018	
Jerusalén			1	7,000							
Junín	1	1,152	23	100,429							
Medina	2	3,901	1	1,057	1						1
Paime											
Pandi	5	32,388	4	11,678	3	14	3,226	5	28	3,029	2
Quetame	1	1,600		1,700	1						
San Bernardo									3	60	
Soacha	1										
Tibacuy		8,000 to Prov. Bogotá	1	180							
Ubalá (Mambita)		8,000 to Prov. Bogotá	7	13,703	4				2	4,357	2
Totals	**17**	**71,035**	**43**	**147,742**	**11**	**14**	**3,226**	**7**	**36**	**10,964**	**7**

Department: Huila

Acevedo (Concepción)											
Aipe			5	2,349		3	492		1	58	
Algeciras (San Juanito)								1	3	2,040	
Baraya								1			
Campoalegre	3	11,086	2	628					15	292	2
Colombia			1	60		1	30		24	345	1
Garzón									6	120	2
Gigante			1	140		2	104		3	46	1
Guadalupe	1	292	2	196		1	300		2	14	
Iquira											
Neiva (Caquán, Fortalecillas, Organos)	5	10,913	11	2,858		4	1,400		26	1,561	2

195

Table spanning periods 1827-1869, 1870-1900, 1901-1917, and 1918-1931.

Municipality	1827-1869 No. Grants	1827-1869 No. Hectares Granted	1870-1900 No. Grants	1870-1900 No. Hectares Granted	1870-1900 No. Conflicts Reported	1901-1917 No. Grants	1901-1917 No. Hectares Granted	1901-1917 No. Conflicts Reported	1918-1931 No. Grants	1918-1931 No. Hectares Granted	1918-1931 No. Conflicts Reported
Department: Huila											
Palermo (Guagua)	2	1,982	4	1,520		1	892		2	40	
Pitalito			6	9,933	1	1	258	1	6	120	1
La Plata											
(Platavieja)			4	2,101	1				109	1,908	1 colonos vs Indians
Rioblanco	1	2,260									
San Bartolo			2	167							
Suaza (Santa Librada)									13	142	
Sumapaz	1	10,240 to Prov. Neiva									
Tarqui (El Hato)			4	215				1	12	220	
Tello (La Unión)	1	1,632	1	79	1				3	571	
Teruel (El Retiro)			1	65					1	122	
Tesalia (Carniceras)			1	401							
Totals	14	38,405	45	20,712	4	13	3,476	7	226	7,599	10
Department: Old Magdalena (present-day departments of Magdalena, Cesar, and La Guajira)											
Aguachica (Loma Corredor)									3	5,631	5
Agustín Codazzi					2	4	1,367	2			2
Aracataca						9	10,791	2	6	6,016	5
Ariguaní	1	5,120 (población)	1	410							
El Banco											2
Barrancas			2	19		1	770				
Cerro de San Antonio			1	2,840					1	974	1

Settlement											
Chimichagua											5
Chiriguaná						2	75		2	1,366	4
Ciénaga (Manzanares, Riofrío, San Juan de Córdoba, Sevilla)	2		4	4,597	3	1	285	4	5	2,317	23
Fonseca		1,507							1	20	4
Fundación											3
Gamarra											
La Gloria (Simaña)			1	1,925		10	1,012	1			3
Guamal (Playablanca)			1	28							1
Islas Penates	1	18						2 +1 forest			
Pedraza			1	760							
El Piñón								1	1	20	2
Pivajay										20	2
Plato						7	7,440		5	10,767	3
Puebloviejo	1	341	1	271		3	1,153	1	2	2,853	2
Remolino			1	2	1						
Río de Oro (Los Angeles)	1		4	1,355							1
Ríohacha (Camarones)	5	2,714 (+4,598 población)	6	11,960		2	510		1	474	1
Robles-La Paz (Espíritu Santo, Medialuna)											
Salamina			1	673					3	5,020	
San Juan del César			3	240							1
Santa Ana						2	600		2	9,280	1
Santa Marta (Gaira, Mamatoco)	1	283 (+3,200 población)	34	25,776		1	3,000		1	15	12
San Zenón	1								2	2,793	
Sitionuevo		99				1	10	1			
Tamalameque			2	898		3	589	1	3	3,867	6
Tenerife											2
Tirosoca	1	128									

	1827-1869		1870-1900			1901-1917			1918-1931		
Municipality	No. Grants	No. Hectares Granted	No. Grants	No. Hectares Granted	No. Conflicts Reported	No. Grants	No. Hectares Granted	No. Conflicts Reported	No. Grants	No. Hectares Granted	No. Conflicts Reported
Department: Old Magdalena											
Valledupar (Padilla)			1	3,660		14	13,492		5	5,889	1
Villanueva	1	1,250	1	60							1
Unspecified			1	16							
Totals	16	19,158	66	55,490	6	60	41,094	16	44	57,322	92
Intendency: Meta (San Martín)											
Acacías			1	5,181							3
Bolívar			3	19,264							
Cabuyaro			2	9,912					8	4,236	
El Calvario			1	1,200							
Curumal											
Granada (Uribe)			15	20,487					4	4,606	1 / 1 colonos vs mission
Meta								1 + 1 forest			
Raicilla			1	12,915							
Restrepo									1	2,500	1
San Juan de Arama (Mesa de Fernando)											
San Martín	2	48,587	33	153,031		3	1,800		25	488	
Sucre									1	20	
Villavicencio	1	384 (población)	20	69,219		3	2,809	1 forest	4	4,780	2
Unspecified			5	31,034							
Totals	3	48,971	82	328,243	0	6	4,609	3	43	16,630	7

Department: Nariño

Los Andes	4	3,166 (+ 3,200)	7						2	40	
Barbacoas (población)			1	319					9	140	2
Cumbal									2	40	
Funes									1	18	
Ipiales											
Mosquera									10	200	4
Pasto								1 colonos vs Indians			
Ricuarte									2	38	
Roberto Payán (San José)			1	13				1	11	173	
Samaniego						7	2,154	1			
Santa Barbara (Iscuandé)									23	364	
Santa Cruz									3	1,927	
El Tablón									5	76	
Tumaco	2			27	3 +1 forest	13	9,882	1 +1 forest / 1 colonos vs Indians	195	4,231	3
Túquerres		6	1								
Totals	6	3,372	10	359	5	20	12,036	4	263	7,247	9

Department: Norte de Santander

Abrego (La Cruz)			3	3,504							
Buenavista			1	300							
Cáchira								1			
Carmen			1	1,596		3	2,995	3			
Chinácota			3	4,160							
Chitagá			1	506							
Cúcuta (San José de Cúcuta, San Faustino, San Pedro)			15	10,744		2	38				
Gramalote			106	7,627					11	3,599	1

Municipality	1827-1869			1870-1900			1901-1917			1918-1931		
	No. Grants	No. Hectares Granted	No. Conflicts Reported	No. Grants	No. Hectares Granted	No. Conflicts Reported	No. Grants	No. Hectares Granted	No. Conflicts Reported	No. Grants	No. Hectares Granted	No. Conflicts Reported
Department: Norte de Santander												
Guaranda	1	640					1	90				1
Naranjal	1	614										
Ocaña				3	1,554				1			
La Playa (Aspasica)							2	1,088				
Salazar	1	92		4	180					6	370	
San Cayetano						1				44	727	
San Calixto				3	179		1	929				
San José				1	461							
Santiago												
Teorama (Río de Oro)						1			2			
Toledo				1	70							
Totals	3	1,346		142	30,881	2	9	5,140	7	61	4,696	2
Department: Santander												
Barrancabermeja	2	850 (+ 11,520 población)							1 (+ 1 forest)	126 (+ 83 of 1h)	815	4
Betulia	2			3	13,090	1	5	608	1			
Bolívar				2	514							3
California (Vetas)				2	742					1	10	1
Carare												
Cerrito										1	12	
Chipatá				1	1,000							
Galán										1	20	
Girón				3	25,708							

Location											
Hato								5	497		
Jesús María			3	8,649							
Lebrija			6	7,616	1	68					
Puerto Wilches (Pedral)			1	981	2	43	5	1	20	1	
Rionegro								1	19		
San José de Miranda											
San Vicente de Chucurí			1	2,500	2			2	24		
Socorro	1	768									
Sucre					1	115		101	1,801	1	
Vélez (Chucurí)								1	904		
Zapatoca			6	16,555	3		2				
Unspecified	1	960									
Totals	5	14,098	28	77,355	9	834	10	240	4,122	11	

Department: Tolima

Location											
Alvarado (Caldas)			24	4,436	21	3,462					
Anzoátegui (Betulia, Briceño)								6	904		
Ataco			22	9,598	17	3,144		14	1,495 (+4,000 to Dept. Tolima)	1	
Cajamarca (Anaime, Quesada, San Miguel)			27; 1	13,870; 260 (+12,000 población)							
Casabianca (Sto. Domingo)			8; 3	28,920; 8,031	28	6,969		15; 1	6,649; 360	2	1
Chaparral			3	1,395							
Cunday	2	9,005	8	5,003				10	904	1	3
Falán (Frías, Guayabal, Sta. Ana)	1	1,139	10	6,278	1	35	2			2	3

Department: Tolima

Municipality	1827-1869 No. Grants	1827-1869 No. Hectares Granted	1870-1900 No. Grants	1870-1900 No. Hectares Granted	1870-1900 No. Conflicts Reported	1901-1917 No. Grants	1901-1917 No. Hectares Granted	1901-1917 No. Conflicts Reported	1918-1931 No. Grants	1918-1931 No. Hectares Granted	1918-1931 No. Conflicts Reported
Herveo (Soledad)	1	3,840	1	169 (+12,000 población)	1			1			
Honda			1	4,860	1			1			
Ibagué (Cocorná, Sta. Lucía)			56	26,265		44	11,175	1	38	7,510	1
Iconozco											
El Líbano (Murillo)			6	16,495 (+35,680 2 poblaciónes)		4	617		3	1,378	1
Margarita	1	1,280									
Mariquita						8	2,161				
Montecristo									1	937	
Ortega									31	460	3
Prado					1			1			
Rovira (Miraflores)			13	8,033		4	2,850		12	4,448	1
San Antonio									22	19,899	1
Santa Isabel						15	1,150				
Venadillo			51	12,685		29	2,623	1	12	373	1
Villahermosa			6	2,180 (+5,006 población)	1						
Viva			1	620							
Unspecified	3	979	10	331		1	311				
Totals	8	16,243	245	207,716	8	183	40,895	10	166	49,317	12

Department: Valle Del Cauca

Municipality									
Alcalá							2	39	2
Andalucía							2	40	2
Ansermanuevo		10,000	1				44	870	4
Bolívar	3			28	4,560	1	18	1,071	1
Buenaventura	31						10	727	2
Buga				5	797	1	11	1,675	1
Bugalagrande				1	180	1			
Cali		637	5				77	1,511	1
Calima (Darién)									
Candelaria						2			
Cartago		3,667	8	27	4,055		144	2,910	6
El Cerrito		52	2				9	252	2
La Cumbre (Pavas)		3,400	1	1	185	1			
Dagua			1				13	5,192	
El Edén				1	25	1	8	146	
Florida				1	58		2	531	
Guacarí				1	29		1	152	
Jamundí						2			
Palmira		1,590	3	3	1,056	1	3	46	1
Papaguayeros		598	1			1			
Pradera			1			1			
Los Remedios				1	115	1			
Restrepo							6	569	3
Riofrío		2,300	3			1	26	1,482	
Roldanillo		2,300	3				14	375	5
San Pedro							1	20	
Sevilla							3	739	
Toro				25	3,801	2	30	600	
Tuluá							10	2,568	3
Ulloa							5	56	
La Unión				19	2,215	1			
La Victoria				3	364		6	1,577	1

Department: Valle Del Cauca

Municipality	1827-1869			1870-1900			1901-1917			1918-1931		
	No. Grants	No. Hectares Granted	No. Conflicts Reported	No. Grants	No. Hectares Granted	No. Conflicts Reported	No. Grants	No. Hectares Granted	No. Conflicts Reported	No. Grants	No. Hectares Granted	No. Conflicts Reported
Vijes				1	60		1		1			1
Yotoco								80	2	25	2,929	2
Zarzal										1	20	2
Totals	3	31	3	25	22,304	3	149	23,168	20	489	27,064	42

a. Names in parentheses refer to older designations of a municipality or to municipal subdivisions which appear on the land grant lists.
b. Conflicts enumerated here refer to the resistance of at least five colono families against encroachments of land entrepreneurs, as described in Chapter 4. There may well have been many more conflicts of this type that never reached the attention of the ministries in Bogotá. Some conflicts erupted in response to usurpations of public lands, which do not appear on the grant lists. In the banana zone, for example, the national government put a moratorium on public land grants in 1923; as a result, the rapid privatization of public lands there after that date occured entirely through illegal appropriations.
c. Number of land grants of less than 1 hectare each. Such grants were usually of town lots in the municipal seat, not of agricultural land. These grants are excluded from the departmental totals.
d. "Forest" refers to a conflict between a renter of national forests and the settlers and collectors of wood products living in the area.
e. "Colonos vs Indians" refers to a conflict between Indians claiming communal land and colonos encroaching on that land.

Source: Number of grants and hectares: *Memoria de Industrias*, 1931, vols. 5, pp. 249-410. Conflicts: ANCB, vols. 1-78.

Notes

Abbreviations

AC   Archivo del Congreso Nacional de Colombia, Bogotá
AHOH   Academia Colombiana de Historia, Bogotá
        Archivo del Presidente Enrique Olaya Herrera
ANCB   Archivo Nacional de Colombia, Bogotá
        Ministerio de Industrias, Correspondencia de Baldíos
INBN   Archivo del Instituto Colombiano de la Reforma Agraria, Bogotá
        Bienes Nacionales

Introduction

1. For this perspective see, for example, Jacques Lambert, *Os dois Brasís* (Rio de Janeiro, 1959); Jacques Lambert, *Latin America: Social Structures and Political Institutions*, trans. Helen Katel (Berkeley, 1967); and Solon Barraclough and Arthur Domike, "Agrarian Structure in Seven Latin American Countries," in *Latin America: Problems in Economic Development*, ed. Charles T. Nisbet (New York, 1969), pp. 91–131. Elaborations of the argument that the latifundia constitute an impediment to development are found in Ernest Feder, *The Rape of the Peasantry: Latin America's Landholding System* (Garden City, N.Y., 1971); and Solon Barraclough, *Agrarian Structure in Latin America* (Lexington, Mass., 1973).

2. See Roberto Cortés Conde, *The First Stages of Modernization in Spanish America* (New York, 1974).

3. For this approach, see Robert Brenner, "Agrarian Class Structure and Economic Development in Pre-Industrial Europe," *Past and Present* 70 (February 1976), 30–75.

4. See John Womack, Jr., *Zapata and the Mexican Revolution* (New York, 1968); David Browning, *El Salvador: Landscape and Society* (Oxford, 1971), pp. 155–222; Gerrit Huizer and Rodolfo Stavenhagen, "Peasant Movements and Land

Reform in Latin America: Mexico and Bolivia," in *Rural Protest: Peasant Movements and Social Change*, ed. Henry A. Landsberger (New York, 1973), pp. 378–410; Eric J. Hobsbawm, "Peasant Land Occupations," *Past and Present* 62 (February 1974), 120–52; Robert Wasserstrom, "Revolution in Guatemala: Peasants and Politics Under the Arbenz Government," *Comparative Studies in Society and History* 17 (October 1975), 410–42; D.J. McCreery, "Coffee and Class: The Structure of Development in Liberal Guatemala," *Hispanic American Historical Review* 56 (August 1976), 438–60; and Arturo Warman, *"We Come to Object": The Peasants of Morelos and the National State*, transl. Stephen K. Ault (Baltimore, 1980).

5.   See Browning, *El Salvador: Landscape and Society;* and Andrew Pearse, *The Latin American Peasant* (London, 1975), pp. 120–40.

6.   See Frank Tannenbaum, *The Mexican Agrarian Revolution* (Washington, D.C., 1929), pp. 11–14; Carl C. Taylor, *Rural Life in Argentina* (Baton Rouge, 1948), pp. 177–86; Browning, pp. 222-70; Ciro F.S. Cardoso, "The Formation of the Coffee Estate in Nineteenth Century Costa Rica," in *Land and Labour in Latin America*, ed. Kenneth Duncan and Ian Rutledge (Cambridge, England, 1977), pp. 165–202; Manuel Chiriboga, "Conformación histórica del régimen agro-exportador de la costa ecuatoriana: la plantación cacaotera," *Estudios Rurales Latinoamericanos* 1 (January-April 1978), 111–43; and Olivier Delahaye, "Formación de la propiedad y renta de la tierra: un analysis regional en Venezuela," Serie Ciencias Sociales No. 3, Facultad de Agronomía, Universidad Central de Venezuela, Maracay (June 1980).

7.   It is generally accepted that in Brazil agricultural development has occurred through the extension of regional frontiers toward the interior. The present-day emphasis on developing the vast Amazon basin is but a logical outgrowth of the ongoing process of frontier expansion that gave rise to the Brazilian sugar economy of the 1600s, the cattle economy of the 1700s, and the coffee economy of the 1800s. See Preston James, *Latin America* (New York, 1942), pp. 401–559; Celso Furtado, *The Economic Growth of Brazil* (Berkeley, 1963); Stanley Stein, *Vassouras: A Brazilian Coffee County, 1850–1890*, 2nd ed. (New York, 1974); Warren Dean, *Rio Claro: A Brazilian Plantation System, 1820–1920* (Stanford, 1976); Martin Katzman, *Cities and Frontiers in Brazil: Regional Dimensions of Economic Development* (Cambridge, Mass., 1977); Malori Pompermayer, " The State and The Frontier in Brazil: A Case Study of the Amazon" (Ph.D. diss., Stanford University, 1979); and Joe Foweracker, *The Struggle for Land: A Political Economy of the Pioneer Frontier in Brazil from 1930 to the Present Day* (Cambridge, England, 1981). More general works on frontier expansion in Latin American history include Alvaro Jara et al., *Tierras nuevas: expansión territorial y ocupación del suelo en América (siglos xvi-xix)* (Mexico City, 1969); Alistair Hennessy, *The Frontier in Latin American History* (Albuquerque, 1978); and Silvio R. Duncan Baretta and John Markoff, "Civilization and Barbarism: Cattle Frontiers in Latin America," *Comparative Studies in Society and History* 20 (October 1978), 587–620.

8.   For this viewpoint, see James Parson's classic study, *Antioqueño Coloniza-*

tion in Western Colombia (Berkeley, 1949). See, too, Luis Eduardo Nieto Arteta, *El café en la sociedad colombiana*, 2nd ed. (Bogotá, 1971); Otto Morales Benítez, *Testimonio de un pueblo*, 2nd ed. (Bogotá, 1962); and William Paul McGreevey, *An Economic History of Colombia, 1845–1930* (Cambridge, England, 1971). This image of the Antioqueño movement also informs the publications of the Colombian National Federation of Coffee Growers (FEDECAFE) and numerous municipal histories of the Antioqueño area. A list of these histories can be found in the bibliographies of R.J. Brew, "The Economic Development of Antioquia, 1820–1920" (D. Phil. diss., Oxford University, 1975), and Keith H. Christie, "Oligarchy and Society in Caldas, Colombia" (D. Phil. diss., Oxford University, 1974).

9.   See Albert O. Hirschman, "Land Use and Land Reform in Colombia," *Journeys Towards Progress* (Garden City, N.Y., 1965), pp. 187-91; Camilo A. Domínguez, "Problemas generales de la colonización amazónica en Colombia," *Enfoques Colombianos* 5 (1975), 40; and Instituto Colombiano de la Reforma Agraria y Instituto Interamericano de Ciencias Agrícolas, *La colonización en Colombia: evaluación de un proceso*, 2 vols. (Bogotá, 1974).

10.   For this viewpoint, see Gustavo DeRoux, "The Social Basis of Peasant Unrest: A Theoretical Framework with Special Reference to the Colombian Case" (Ph. D. diss., University of Wisconsin, 1974), pp. 206–208; and Paul Oquist, *Violence, Conflict and Politics in Colombia* (New York, 1980), pp. 90–91.

11.   See Alvaro López Toro, *Migración y cambio social en Antioquia durante el siglo diez y nueve* (Bogotá, 1970); José Fernando Ocampo, *Dominio de clase en la ciudad colombiana* (Medellín, 1972); Brew; Absalón Machado C., *El café: de la aparcería al capitalismo* (Bogotá, 1977); and Keith H. Christie, "Antioqueño Colonization in Western Colombia: A Reappraisal," *Hispanic American Historical Review* 58 (May 1978), 260–83.

12.   See Mariano Arango, *Café e industría, 1850–1930* (Bogotá, 1977). This interpretation opposes that advanced by McGreevey and others, which stressed that the coffee economy contributed to industrialization primarily by providing a large internal market for domestically produced consumer goods. The revisionist studies portray Colombia in terms reminiscent of Costa Rica in the same period. In Costa Rica, where coffee also was produced by smallholders, elites maintained economic and political dominance through control of rural credit, and processing and marketing of the coffee harvest (see Cardoso).

13.   A much debated term, *peasant* in this study is used to designate small rural cultivators who rely on family labor to produce what they consume. Sharecroppers, service tenants, small proprietors, and frontier settlers would, by this definition, all be called peasants.

14.   See Archivo del Instituto Colombiano de la Reforma Agraria, Bienes Nacionales, 30 vols.; and Archivo Histórico Nacional de Colombia, Ministerio de Industrias: Correspondencia de Baldíos, 78 vols.

Chapter 1: The Setting

1. See "Informe del Sr. Vistador Fiscal de Ferrocarriles. . . , 12 Agosto 1915," reprinted in Colombia, Ministerio de Industrias, *Memoria del Ministerio de Industrias al Congreso Nacional de 1931* (Bogotá, 1931), vol. 5, pp. 444–45. Excluding Panama, which remained part of Colombia until 1903, Codazzi estimated that the public domain totalled around 98 million hectares in the 1850s. For other early estimates of the extension of public lands in Colombia, see José Maria Rivas Groot, *Asuntos económicos y fiscales*, 2nd ed. (Bogotá, 1952), p. 170; and Francisco Vergara y Velasco, *Nueva geografía de Colombia*, vol. 2 (Bogotá, 1901), pp. 795–800.

2. In 1873 it was estimated that these centrally located baldíos comprised approximately 24.3 million hectares. See Felipe Pérez, *Geografía física i política de los Estados Unidos de Colombia*, cited in Colombia, Ministerio de Hacienda, *Memoria del Ministerio de Hacienda al Congreso Nacional de 1873* (Bogotá, 1873), p. 65. Hereafter the annual reports of the Colombian Ministers of Finance to the national Congress will be cited as *Memoria de Hacienda*.

3. James, pp. 78–118 presents a useful description of Colombian geography. See also Ernesto Guhl, *Colombia: bosquejo de su geografía tropical*, vol. 1 (Bogotá, 1975).

4. On the prehistory of Colombia and the Spanish conquest, see Jorge Orlando Melo, *Historia de Colombia: el establecimiento de la dominación española* (Medellín, 1977).

5. Information on Colombian agrarian history for the colonial period can be found in Luis Ospina Vásquez, *Industria y protección en Colombia, 1810–1930* (Bogotá, 1955), pp. 32–48; Germán Colmenares, *Haciendas de los Jesuitas en el Nuevo Reino de Granada, siglo xviii* (Bogotá, 1969); Germán Colmenares, *Historia económica y social de Colombia, 1537–1719* (Cali, 1973); Orlando Fals Borda, *El hombre y la tierra en Boyacá* (Bogotá, 1973); Orlando Fals Borda, *Historia de la cuestión agraria en Colombia* (Bogotá, 1975); Juan A. Villamarín, "Haciendas en la sabana de Bogotá, Colombia en la época colonial: 1539–1810," in *Haciendas, latifundios y plantaciones en América Latina*, ed. Enrique Florescano (Mexico City, 1975), pp. 327–45; Orlando Fals Borda, *Capitalismo, hacienda, y poblamiento en la Costa Atlántica* (Bogotá, 1976); Salomón Kalmanowitz, "El régimen agrario durante la colonia," in *La nueva historia de Colombia*, ed. Darío Jaramillo Agudelo (Bogotá, 1976), pp. 367–454; Orlando Fals Borda, "Influencia del vecindario pobre colonial en las relaciones de producción de la costa atlántica colombiana," in *El agro en el desarrollo histórico colombiano* (Bogotá, 1977), pp. 129–60; Jaime Jaramillo Uribe, ed., *Manual de historia de Colombia*, vol. 1 (Bogotá, 1978); Margarita González, "La hacienda colonial y los orígenes de la propiedad territorial en Colombia," *Cuadernos Colombianos* 12 (March 1979), 567–90; Germán Colmenares, *Historia económica y social de Colombia*, vol. 2: *Popayán: una sociedad esclavista, 1680–1800* (Bogotá, 1979); Orlando Fals Borda, *Historia doble de la costa*, vol. 1: *Mompox y*

Loba (Bogotá, 1980); Hermes Tovar Pinzón, *Grandes empresas agrícolas y ganaderas, su desarrollo en el siglo xviii* (Bogotá, 1980); Ann Twinam, *Miners, Merchants, and Farmers in Colonial Colombia* (Austin, 1982); and Jane M. Rausch, *A Tropical Plains Frontier: The Llanos of Colombia, 1531–1831* (Albuquerque, 1984). For an overview of Colombian writing on the colonial period, see Bernardo Tovar Zambrano, *La colonia en la historiografía colombiana* (Bogotá, 1984).

6.   On land surveying in colonial times and the Colombian system of metes and bounds, see Luis E. Paez Courvel, *Historia de las medidas agrarias antiguas* (Bogotá, 1940); José María Ots Capdequí, *El régimen de la tierra en la América española durante el periodo colonial* (Ciudad Trujillo, 1946); T. Lynn Smith, *Colombia: Social Structure and the Process of Development* (Gainesville, 1967), pp. 147–57; Fals Borda, *El hombre y la tierra*, pp. 117–29; and Luis Arévalo Salazar, "The Legal Insecurity of Rural Property in Colombia: A Case Study of the Notarial and Registry Systems" (Ph.D. diss., University of Wisconsin, 1970).

7.   Colombia, Ministerio de Agricultura, *Memoria al Congreso Nacional de 1922* (Bogotá, 1923), p. 8.

8.   Colombia, Congreso Nacional, *Ley 110 de 1912 (Código Fiscal)* (Bogotá, 1913), p. 15 (article 47).

9.   See Frank Safford, "Commerce and Enterprise in Central Colombia, 1821–70" (Ph.D. diss., Columbia University, 1965); David C. Johnson, "Social and Economic Change in Nineteenth Century Santander, Colombia" (Ph.D. diss., University of California at Berkeley, 1965); Frank Safford, *The Ideal of the Practical: Colombia's Struggle to Form a Technical Elite* (Austin, 1976), pp. 21–27, 41–46; and María Teresa Uribe de H. and Jesús María Alvarez, "Regiones, economía, y espacio nacional en Colombia, 1820–1850," *Lecturas de Economía* 13 (January-April 1984), 155–222.

10.   The following account of Colombian economic growth in the late nineteenth and early twentieth centuries is drawn from Luis Fernando Sierra, *El tobaco en la economía colombiana del siglo xix* (Bogotá, 1961); Alvaro Tirado Mejía, *Introducción a la historia económica de Colombia*, 3rd ed. (Bogotá, 1974); Luis Eduardo Nieto Arteta, *Economía y cultura en la historia de Colombia*, 6th ed. (Bogotá, 1975); José Antonio Ocampo, "Desarrollo exportador y desarrollo capitalista colombiano en el siglo xix (una hipótesis)," *Desarrollo y Sociedad* 1 (January 1979), 135–44; Jorge Orlando Melo, "La economía colombiana en la cuarta década del siglo xix," in *Sobre historia y política* (Medellín, 1979), pp. 90–144; Marco Palacios, *Coffee in Colombia, 1850–1970* (Cambridge, England, 1980); José Antonio Ocampo, "Las exportaciones colombianas en el siglo xix," *Desarrollo y Sociedad* 4 (July 1980), 165–226; José Antonio Ocampo, "El mercado mundial del café y el surgimiento de Colombia como un país cafetero," *Desarrollo y Sociedad* 5 (January 1981), 127–56; and José Antonio Ocampo, "Desarrollo exportador y desarrollo capitalista colombiano en el siglo xix," *Desarrollo y Sociedad* 8 (May 1982), 37–75.

11.   Vegetable ivory *(tagua)* was a forest product used to manufacture buttons

in Europe in the nineteenth century. Dye woods exported from Colombia included *palo brazil, palo mora,* and *dividivi.*

12.   Robert Beyer, "The Colombian Coffee Industry: Origins and Major Trends, 1740–1940" (Ph.D. diss., University of Minnesota, 1947), pp. 362–67.

13.   Ibid., pp. 365–66. The history of the United Fruit Company in Colombia is recounted in Fernando Botero and Alvaro Guzmán Barney, "El enclave agrícola en la zona bananera de Santa Marta," *Cuadernos Colombianos* 11 (1977), 309–90.

14.   On Colombian transport and nineteenth century developments, see Beyer, "Colombian Coffee," pp. 17–28, 185–205; Robert C. Beyer, "Transportation and the Coffee Industry in Colombia," *Inter-American Economic Affairs* 2 (1948), 17–30; Robert L. Gilmore and John P. Harrison, "Juan Bernardo Elbers and the Introduction of Steam Navigation on the Magdalena River," *Hispanic American Historical Review* 28 (August 1948), 335–59; Safford, "Commerce," pp. 85–102; McGreevey, *An Economic History,* pp. 244–79; Fabio Zambrano, "La navegación a vapor por el río Magdalena," *Anuario Colombiano de Historia Social y de la Cultura* 9 (1979), 63–77; and Hernán Horna, "Transportation Modernization and Entrepreneurship in Nineteenth Century Colombia," *Journal of Latin American Studies* 14 (May 1982), 33–53.

15.   McGreevy, *An Economic History,* p. 255; and Joelle Diot, "Colombia económica 1923–1929: estadísticas históricas," *Boletín Mensual de Estadística* [DANE] 300 (July 1976), 169–71. See also Alfredo Ortega Díaz, *Ferrocarriles colombianos: resumen histórico* (Bogotá, 1923); and Alfredo Ortega Díaz, *Ferrocarriles colombianos: legislación ferroviaria* (Bogotá, 1949).

16.   See Parsons, pp. 132–36. The pasture grasses introduced into Colombia in the nineteenth century and early twentieth centuries included India or Guinea grass *(Panicum maximum)* from Africa and Pará *(Panicum barbinode)* from Brazil, both of which were particularly adaptable to the hot lowlands. Yaguará *(Melinis minutiflora)* and Micay *(Axonopus spp.)* pastures proved equally useful in the middle and higher altitudes.

17.   On innovations in the cattle industry, see Donaldo Bossa Herazo, *Cartagena independiente: tradición y desarrollo* (Bogotá, 1967), pp. 38–45, 83–85, 100–103, and 147–53; Brew, "Economic Development," Chapter 6; Alejandro Reyes Posada, *Latifundia y poder político: la hacienda ganadera en Sucre* (Bogotá, 1978); and Salomón Kalmanowitz, "El régimen agrario durante el siglo xix en Colombia," in *Manual de historia de Colombia,* vol. 2, ed. Jaime Jaramillo Uribe (Bogotá, 1979), pp. 274–84. Kalmanowitz (p. 280) estimates that cattle herds in Colombia increased from 1.4 million head in 1850 to 4.4 million head in 1898 and thence to 6.7 million head in 1925.

18.   Ocampo, "Exportaciones", 176–77, 179.

19.   See, for example, Germán Colmenares, *Partidos políticos y clases sociales en Colombia* (Bogotá, 1968); Frank Safford, "Social Aspects of Politics in Nineteenth Century Spanish America: New Granada, 1825–1850," *Journal of Social History* 5 (1972), 344–70; Charles Bergquist, *Coffee and Conflict in Colombia, 1886–*

1910 (Durham, N.C., 1980); and Marco Palacios, "La fragmentación regional de las clases dominantes en Colombia: una perspectiva histórica," *Revista Mexicana de Sociología* 42 (October-December 1980), 1663–89.

20.   Public land policy and the distribution of public lands in Colombia was always the responsibility of the central government. It should be noted, however, that during the period of Liberal administrative decentralization (1863–1885) Bogotá ceded thousands of hectares of baldíos to the sovereign states as a means of contributing to their revenues. When these concessions were nullified by the Conservative government in 1890, it was revealed that, of the relatively few public land vouchers actually distributed by regional authorities, most had been used to promote transport construction under state auspices. See Colombia, Ministerio de Industrias, *Memoria al Congreso Nacional de 1931*, vol. 3 (Bogotá, 1932), pp. 66, 97–98; and ANCB volume 10, folio 145, v. 11 f. 30, and v. 19 f. 156.

21.   See Ots Capdequí, pp. 41–52, 77; and Smith, pp. 81–82.

22.   See Ots Capdequí, pp. 53–78; David E. Vassberg, "The Sale of Baldíos in Sixteenth Century Castile," *Journal of Modern History* 47 (December 1975), 629–54; and David E. Vassberg, *La venta de tierras baldías: el comunitarismo agrario y la corona de Castilla durante el siglo xvi* (Madrid, 1983).

23.   This section draws heavily on Oficina Para Investigaciones Socio-económicas y Legales (OFISEL), "La acción del estado en Colombia y sus beneficiarios, 1820–1931," Bogotá, 1975 (mimeographed), pp. 82–144. See also Jorge Villegas, "Historia de la propiedad agraria en Colombia, 1819–1936," Chapters 5, 12, and 13, Bogotá, 1976 (typewritten); and Catherine LeGrand "From Public Lands into Private Properties: Landholding and Rural Conflict in Colombia, 1850–1936," (Ph.D. diss., Stanford University, 1980), Chapter 3.

24.   Malcolm Deas, "The Fiscal Problems of Nineteenth-Century Colombia," *Journal of Latin American Studies* 14 (November 1982), 287–328. See also David Bushnell, *The Santander Regime in Gran Colombia*, 2nd ed. (Westport, Conn., 1970), pp. 76–126; and Safford, *Ideal*, pp. 8–10, 21–27, 41–42 and 44–45.

25.   See Law of 20 April 1838 in Colombia, Consejo de Estado (Sala de Negocios Generales), *Codificación nacional de todas las leyes de Colombia desde el año de 1821 hecha conforme a la ley 13 de 1912* (Bogotá, 1926), vol. 8, pp. 31–42. A compilation of the most important laws, legislative enactments, and resolutions concerning public lands in Colombia for the years 1821–1931 is found in Colombia, Ministerio de Industrias, *Memoria al Congreso Nacional de 1931*, vol. 3 (Bogotá, 1931). Hereafter the annual reports of the Colombian Ministers of Industries to the national Congress will be cited as *Memoria de Industrias*.

26.   The limit on allocations to cultivator families before 1874 varied from 15 to 130 hectares, depending on the region settled. See LeGrand, "From Public Lands," pp. 44–48.

27.   For a compilation of Colombian laws on immigration from 1821 through 1931, see *Memoria de Industrias*, 1931, vol. 4, pp. 67–209.

28.   For information on this kind of immigrant, see Vicente Restrepo, *Estudio*

sobre las minas de oro y plata de Colombia (Bogotá, 1952); Bossa Herazo; and Horacio Rodríguez Plata, *La inmigración alemana al estado soberano de Santander en el siglo xix* (Bogotá, 1968). On the foundation of an unusual German farm colony in Colombia, see Juan Friede, "Colonos alemanes en la Sierra Nevada de Santa Marta," *Revista Colombiana de Antropología* 12 (1963), 401–11.

29.   For laws encouraging the settlement of border regions, see *Memoria de Industrias*, 1931, vol. 3, pp. 9, 27, 29, 35, 38–39.

30.   See Smith, pp. 269–70.

31.   *Memoria de Industrias*, 1931, vol. 3, p. 13, and Map 4, p. 44.

32.   See Parsons for the history of these municipalities. The main territorial divisions of Colombia are the departments (called states during the period of Liberal rule from 1863 to 1886) and the municipalities. The departments *(departamentos)*, of which there were thirteen in 1930, are administered by a governor, appointed by the president, and a departmental assembly of elected legislators. Each department is composed of a number of municipalities *(municipios)* which are comparable to rural counties in the United States. Each municipality has a town seat *(cabecera)* in which are located the offices of the mayor *(alcalde)*, municipal advocate *(personero)*, and municipal council *(consejo municipal)*, among other administrative posts. Municipalities may contain other smaller village administrative centers called *corregimientos*, in which the *corregidor* is the principal authority. Each municipality forms part of a judicial circuit. The sparsely populated, outlying areas of the country along the Pacific coast, in the eastern plains and in the Amazonian jungles to the south are called national territories *(intendencias* and *comisarias)* and directly administered by authorities appointed by the central government. See OFISEL, Chapter 2 for a history of the evolution of administrative units in Colombia.

33.   The laws determining how land in settlements should be allotted were Law of 5 May 1834, Law 14 of 1870, and Legislative Enactment 520 of 1878. (See Colombia, Consejo de Estado, *Codificación nacional de todas las leyes*, vol. 5, p. 178; vol. 25, pp. 18–21; and vol. 29, pp. 249–52.) Descriptions of the distribution of land in the poblaciones of El Líbano and Villahermosa (Tolima) in the 1870s and 1880s are found in INBN v. 10 fs. 659, 867, 884, and 895, v. 11 fs. 447, 473, 556, 581–82, v. 12 fs. 40–9; and ANCB v. 1 fs. 116–20, 135–38, and v. 12 fs. 33–38, 50–53.

34.   See OFISEL, pp. 113–14. Also *Memoria de Industrias*, 1931, vol. 3, pp. 90–91, 95–96, and vol. 5, pp. 232–33, 235.

35.   See Brew, "Economic Development," p. 204; Ospina Vásquez, pp. 300–10, and Safford, *Ideal*, pp. 197–200. José Manuel Restrepo, Mariano Ospina Rodríguez, Rafael Uribe Uribe, Nicolás Sáenz, Rafael Reyes, Salvador Camacho Roldán, Miguel Samper, and José María Samper count among the most important public figures committed to the development of commercial agriculture and ranching at this time.

36.   Safford, *Ideal*, pp. 185–200.

37. The text of these laws is to be found in *Memoria de Industrias*, 1931, vol. 3, pp. 121–24 and 149–51.

38. Specifically, Law 48 of 1882 stated that cultivators who planted improved pasture grasses or perennial crops such as coffee, cacao, or sugar cane should be granted the land they had under cultivation, plus an adjacent undeveloped portion equal in size. Colonos with annual crops were to receive the cultivated parcel and thirty hectares more, while those who built fences merited all of the territory enclosed, so long as it included no more than three times the area actually exploited. To apply for a free grant, a cultivator had to have been working and living on the land for a minimum of five years.

39. For discussions of Colombian Liberalism, see Gerardo Molina, *Las ideas liberales en Colombia, 1849–1914* (Bogotá, 1970); Bergquist, *Coffee and Conflict*; and Helen Delpar, *Red Against Blue: The Liberal Party in Colombian Politics* (Alabama, 1981). The best source on Colombian intellectual history is Jaime Jaramillo Uribe, *El pensamiento colombiano en el siglo xix* (Bogotá, 1964). Charles Hale analyzes the importance of the small rural property-holder in both the European and the Latin American liberal traditions in *Mexican Liberalism in the Age of Mora, 1821–1853* (New Haven, 1968), pp. 177–81.

40. See Nieto Arteta, *Economía y cultura*, pp. 118–35. The policy debates and legislative antecedents to the reform of public land policy are discussed in OFISEL, pp. 98–107.

41. See R. Albert Berry, "Land Distribution, Income Distribution, and the Productive Efficiency of Colombian Agriculture," *Food Research Institute Studies in Agricultural Economics, Trade, and Development* [Stanford Univeristy] 3 (1973), 199–231.

42. Colombia, Congreso Nacional, *Ley 110 de 1912 (Código Fiscal)*, p. 15. Law 85 of 1920 confirmed this restriction for certificate-holders and ranchers, adding that for land devoted to agriculture, grantees were limited to 1,000 hectares. (*Memoria de Industrias*, 1931, vol. 3, pp. 387–88.)

43. Law 48 of 1882, article 7. In establishing the proportion of a grant that had to be exploited, this statute set a sliding scale ranging from 40 percent for concessions of less than 200 hectares to 10 percent for grants of 3,000 to 5,000 hectares. Laws 56 of 1905, 110 of 1912, and 85 of 1920, which reiterated the reversion condition, set the land use requirement at between 20 and 50 percent of the area of the grant for farmers and between 50 and 67 percent of the total area for ranchers.

44. ANCB v. 40 f. 478. See also Alejandro López, *Problemas colombianos* (Paris, 1927), pp. 42, 50.

45. See, for example, Bergquist, *Coffee and Conflict*.

46. See Winstano Luis Orozco, *Legislación y jurisprudencia sobre terrenos baldíos*, 2 vols. (Mexico City, 1895); Carl F. Solberg, "A Discriminatory Frontier Land Policy: Chile, 1870–1914," *The Americas* 26 (October 1969), 115–33; and James Hamon and Stephen Niblo, *Precursores de la revolución agraria en México* (Mexico City, 1975), pp. 45–58.

47.   See Taylor, pp. 124–73; Solberg, pp. 123–25; Rollie Poppino, *Brazil: The Land and People* (New York, 1968), pp. 184–88; and Robert C. Eidt, *Pioneer Settlement in Northeastern Argentina* (Madison, 1971).

48.   See Warren Dean, "Latifundia and Land Policy in Nineteenth Century Brazil," *Hispanic American Historical Review* 51 (November 1971), 606–25; Angel Cárcano, *Evolución histórica del régimen de la tierra pública, 1810–1916*, 3rd ed. (Buenos Aires, 1972); and Dean, pp. 14–21.

49.   See *El Agricultor*, February 1883, pp. 392–95; Parsons, p. 83; and Jorge Villegas, *Colombia: colonización de vertiente en el siglo xix* (Medellín, 1977).

50.   Tobacco in Colombia generally was produced on a small scale. As result of the concentration of landed property in the tobacco zone in the 1840s, however, most tobacco cultivators *(cosecheros)* lost their position as independent producers, becoming renters of the great landowners instead. See Sierra; and René de la Pedraja Tomán, "Los cosecheros de Ambalema: un esbozo preliminar," *Anuario Colombiano de Historia Social y de la Cultura* 9 (1979), 39–62.

51.   On the Costa Rican experience, see Mitchell A. Seligson, "Agrarian Policies in Dependent Societies: Costa Rica," *Journal of Interamerican Studies and World Affairs* 19 (May 1977), 201–32; and Mitchell A. Seligson, *Peasants of Costa Rica and the Development of Agrarian Capitalism* (Madison, 1980). The mountainous terrain ruled out mechanization—and therefore economies of scale— in coffee production in both Colombia and Costa Rica; this may have also contributed to the parallel evolution of public land policies in the two countries. In Colombia, however, the crucial reforms of the 1870s and 1880s preceded by several decades the florescence of the coffee economy as a smallholder crop in the central cordillera.

Chapter 2: The Peasant Settlers

1.   In Colombia the term *colono* was loosely applied to a variety of rural people. Tenant farmers whose contracts required them to clear new land within the haciendas were typically called colonos. The same designation also applied to laborers in the sugar cane fields, to miners in some parts of the country, and to settlers of public lands. Cutting through the diversity of colloquial usages, Colombian jurisprudence provided a precise legal meaning for the term. Legally colonos were those, and only those, individuals who farmed or grazed livestock on public lands without written title to the territory. It is with the colonos of public lands that this chapter is concerned.

2.   ANCB v. 10 f. 32, v. 28 f. 240, v. 54 f. 587, v. 64 f. 504, and v. 68 f. 533. See also Fals Borda, "Vecindario" and *Mompox y Loba*.

3.   See Fals Borda, *Historia de la cuestión agraria*, pp. 57–61; and Oquist, pp. 26–28.

4.   See *El Agricultor* 14 (May 1898), 213–16; Robert West, *The Pacific Low-*

lands of Colombia (Baton Rouge, 1957), pp. 103–08; William F. Sharp, *Slavery on the Spanish Frontier: The Colombian Chocó, 1680–1810* (Norman, Oklahoma, 1976), pp. 153–70; Fals Borda, *Historia de la cuestión agraria*, pp. 61–63; Mateo Mina, *Esclavitud y libertad en el valle del río Cauca* (Bogotá, 1975), pp. 43–82; Michael Taussig, "The Evolution of Rural Wage Labor in the Cauca Valley of Colombia, 1700–1970," in *Land and Labour in Latin America*, ed. Kenneth Duncan and Ian Rutledge (Cambridge, England, 1977), pp. 409–21; and Jorge Escorcia, *Sociedad y economía en el Valle del Cauca* vol. 3: *Desarrollo político, social, y económico, 1800–1854* (Bogotá, 1983), pp. 74–75.

5.   Juan Friede, *La explotación indígena en Colombia bajo el gobierno de las misiones: el caso de los Aruacos de la Sierra Nevada de Santa Marta*, 2nd ed. (Bogotá, 1973), p. 96; and Juan Friede, *El indio en la lucha por la tierra: historia de los resguardos del macizo central colombiano*, 3rd ed. (Bogotá, 1976), pp. 143, 154.

6.   See Glenn Curry, "The Disappearance of the *Resguardos Indígenas* of Cundinamarca, Colombia, 1800–1863" (Ph.D. diss., Vanderbilt University, 1981). For a history of the legislation concerning resguardos in Colombia, see OFISEL, pp. 146–59.

7.   Friede, *Indio en la lucha*, pp. 89, 134, and 138; and Clara Inés Rodríguez Córdoba and Aydée Esmeralda Moreno Coronado, "Desintegración del resguardo y consolidación de la propiedad privada en Natagaima, siglo xix" (Tesis de grado, Universidad Nacional, 1983).

8.   ANCB v. 57 f. 448 and v. 65 f. 391. For other examples of Indian cultivators, see ANCB v. 53 fs. 355, 356 and v. 57 f. 315. Also AC, "Memoriales a la Cámara, sesiones extraordinarias de 1924 y 1925," vol. 13 folio 238; and *Boletín de la Oficina General de Trabajo* 5 (January–June 1934), 154. On the Indian movement in southwestern Colombia, see Diego Castrillón Arboleda, *El indio Quintín Lamé* (Bogotá, 1973); and Manuel Quintín Lamé, *Las luchas del indio que bajó de la montaña al valle de la 'civilización'* (Bogotá, 1973).

9.   It should be noted that some colono families were headed by single or widowed women. The censuses of Villahermosa and El Líbano (Tolima) indicate that such women received approximately 5 percent of the land grants awarded in those settlements (see Chapter 1, note 33 for reference). The proportion of women family heads among independent colonos outside of the Antioqueño settlements was probably similar. Women took an active part in agricultural activities: indeed coffee harvesting and sorting in the nineteenth century were primarily feminine occupations. For the history of women in Colombian agriculture see Magdalena León de Leal et al., *Mujer y capitalismo agrario* (Bogotá, 1980).

10.   The social and economic history of the Colombian highlands is an important subject on which little research has been done. Some information on the recession of the nineteenth century is found in McGreevey, pp. 132–46, 164–73; Ospina Vásquez, pp. 509–13, 539–40; and Johnson.

11.   ANCB v. 13 fs. 219 and 287.

12.   Tirado Mejía, *Introducción*, p. 150. For greater insight into the social im-

pact of the civil wars on nineteenth century Colombia, see Alvaro Tirado Mejía, *Aspectos sociales de las guerras civiles en Colombia* (Bogotá, 1976); and Bergquist, *Coffee and Conflict*.

13.   ANCB v. 25 f. 281.

14.   ANCB v. 71 f. 270; and Wolfgang Brucher, *La colonización de la selva pluvial en el piedemonte amazónico de Colombia*, trans. Gerda Westendorp de Núñez (Bogotá, 1974), pp. 31–32. For other examples of privately initiated colonization projects, see INBN v. 8 f. 184, and v. 21 fs. 609 and 985. Also ANCB v. 24 f. 415, v. 34 f. 302, v. 44 f. 289, v. 74 fs. 17 and 58, and AC, "Proyectos para el segundo debate, 1912 (Senado)," vol. 2 folio 442.

15.   See *Memoria de Hacienda*, 1883, anexos, p. 45; AC, "Proyectos, 1926 (Cámara)," vol. 8 folio 39; and AC, "Leyes autógrafas de 1917," vol. 4 folios 74–76.

16.   See ANCB v. 10 f. 94; Eduardo Santa, *Arrieros y fundadores: aspectos de la colonización antioqueña* (Bogotá, 1961); Luis F. Bottía and Rodolfo Escobedo D., "La Violencia en el sur del departamento de Córdoba" (Tesis de grado, Universidad de los Andes, 1979), p. 5; and Darío Betancourt, "Los Pájaros en el Valle del Cauca: colonización, café y violencia" (Tesis de grado, Universidad Santo Tomás, 1984), p. 20.

17.   See Roberto Velandia, *Encyclopedia histórica de Cundinamarca*, vol. 2 (Bogotá, 1979), pp. 680–81; and Gabriel Fonnegra, *Bananeras: testimonio vivo de una epopeya* (Bogotá, 1980), p. 18.

18.   Interview with Don Luis Eduardo Gómez, El Líbano, 26 September 1975. See also James D. Henderson, "Origins of the Violencia in Colombia" (Ph.D. diss., Texas Christian U., 1972), p. 248.

19.   INBN v. 19 fs. 10–11; and ANCB v. 33 f. 272, v. 38 f. 181, v. 42 f. 304, v. 43 fs. 34 and 379, v. 68 f. 283, and v. 76 f. 245. This pattern of small, dispersed holdings also is prevalent in the minifundista regions of highland Boyacá. See Fernando López G., *Evolución de la tenencia de la tierra en una zona minifundista* (Bogotá, 1975), pp. 28, 42.

20.   ANCB v. 43 f. 379.

21.   INBN v. 19 fs. 10–11; and ANCB v. 12 f. 193, v. 38 f. 181, v. 42 f. 304, and v. 76 f. 245. See also *Memoria de Industrias*, 1930, anexos, p. 117.

22.   See Antonio García, *Geografía económica de Colombia: Caldas* (Bogotá, 1937), pp. 238–40; Parsons, pp. 79–109; Raymond E. Crist, *The Cauca Valley: Land Tenure and Land Use* (Baltimore, 1952), p. 70; and Smith, p. 199.

23.   The Public Land Correspondence sheds little light on the issue of colono indebtedness. Studies of contemporary colonization in the southern jungles of Colombia, however, indicate that debt relations are an important mechanism by which settlers are deprived of their land. The land passes into the hands of the storekeeper who often becomes a large landowner, forcing the colonos to move on. See Camilo Domínguez Ossa, "El proceso de colonización en la Amazonia y su incidencia sobre el uso de los recursos naturales," *Revista Colombiana de Antropología* 18 (1975), 293–304; Alejandro Acosta Ayerbe, "Aspectos generales de los territorios

nacionales: perspectivas y requísitos para absorver un volumen grande de poblacion,"
Enfoques Colombianos 2 (1975), 44–80; and Jorge Vallejo Morillo, "Los colo-
onos del Putumayo," *Enfoques Colombianos* 5 (1975), 59–78. For some information
on colono indebtedness historically, see ANCB v. 75 f. 295, and v. 77 f. 210;
Colombia, Bolívar, *Informe del Secretario de Gobierno al Gobernador del departamento* (Cartagena, 1932), p. 4; and J.A. Osorio Lizarazo, *La cosecha* (Manizales,
1935).

   24.   See ANCB v. 44 f. 29, and v. 58 f. 374; AC, "Leyes autógrafas de 1913
(Senado)," vol. 3 folio 18; Brew, "Economic Development," p. 27; Colombia, Antioquia, *Informe del Secretario de Gobierno al Gobernador del departamento* (Mede-
ellín, 1932), p. 57; and Colombia, Antioquia, *Informe del Secretario de Hacienda
al Gobernador del departamento* (Medellín, 1934), anexos, p. 114. Hereafter the
annual reports of the secretary of government of a department to the governor of
that department will be cited as *Informe del Secretario de Gobierno*, preceded by
the name of the department and followed by the date. The annual reports of the
departmental treasurers to the governors likewise will be cited as *Informe del Secretario de Hacienda*.

   25.   Salvador Camacho Roldán, *Artículos escogidos* (Bogotá, n.d.), p. 25; and
Parsons, p. 109.

   26.   This kind of information is revealed by a survey of the extent and usage of
the public domain at the municipal level initiated by the Colombian Ministry of
Agriculture in 1916. The returns can be found in ANCB volumes 32, 39, 40, 43,
44, 46, 47, 48, and 67. Though interesting, the material is incomplete and of doubtful accuracy since, as local officials readily admitted, they often did not know what
territory in their jurisdictions was baldío.

   27.   For descriptions of contemporary smallholder production, which resemble
that of fifty years ago, see Michael Taussig, "Peasant Economics and the Development of Capitalist Agriculture in the Cauca Valley, Colombia," *Latin American Perspectives* 5 (Summer 1978), 62–91; and Nola Reinhardt, "The Independent Family
Farm Mode of Production: El Palmar, Colombia 1890–1978, A Study of Economic
Development and Agrarian Structure" (Ph.D. diss., University of California at Berkeley, 1981).

   28.   ANCB v. 6 f. 99, v. 13 fs. 219 and 287, v. 14 fs. 356, 365 and 367, v. 49
f. 202, v. 50 fs. 258, 411, 424 and 507, v. 54 fs. 203 and 553–54, v. 57 f. 146,
v. 58 f. 603, v. 70 f. 76, v. 71 f. 356, v. 72 f. 140, v. 75 f. 371, and v. 77 f. 33.

   29.   See ANCB v. 15 f. 375, v. 20 f. 21, v. 22 f. 349, and v. 77 f. 385.

   30.   See Fals Borda, *Mompox y Loba;* and ANCB v. 26 f. 715, v. 33 fs. 507–
15, v. 47 f. 317, and v. 49 fs. 202 and 213. Information on nineteenth century
settler movements on the Caribbean coast also can be found in Orlando Fals Borda,
Historia doble de la costa, vol. 2: *El Presidente Nieto* (Bogotá, 1981), pp. 77–87.

   31.   See García, *Caldas*, pp. 238–40; and Joel Darío Sánchez Reyes, "Colonización quindiana: proceso político-ideológico en la conformación del campesinado

cafetero, 1840–1920" (Tesis de masters, Facultad de Ciencia Política, Universidad de los Andes, 1982), pp. 79-88.

32. See Foweracker, pp. 110, 141.

33. See ANCB v. 22 f. 373, v. 23 f. 24, v. 24 f. 359, v. 33 f. 272, v. 38 f. 181, v. 39 f. 232, and v. 43 f. 254. Also, *Memoria de Industrias*, 1934, pp. 379–81.

34. See "Resolución del Ministerio de Hacienda de 23 Noviembre 1894," in Colombia, Congreso Nacional, *Leyes y disposiciones de terrenos baldíos* (Bogotá, n.d.), p. 81; *Memoria de Agricultura*, 1922, p. 7; and ANCB v. 26 f. 384, v. 33 fs. 48 and 246, v. 34 f. 366, v. 43 f. 273, v. 46 f. 166, v. 47 f. 302, v. 58 f. 364, v. 68 f. 36, v. 70 f. 75, v. 75 fs. 229 and 295, and v. 76 f. 113.

35. ANCB v. 44 f. 283. See also ANCB v. 41 f. 191.

36. See Smith, pp. 257–86 for a description of rural settlement patterns in Colombia.

37. For information on frontier caseríos and their formation, see Demetrio Daniel Henríquez, *Monografía completa de la zona bananera* (Santa Marta, 1939); Urbano Campo, *Urbanización y violencia en el Valle* (Bogotá, 1980), pp. 17–55; and Carlos Ortiz, "Fundadores y negociantes en la colonización del Quindío," *Lecturas de Economía* 13 (January-April 1984), 117–20.

38. Such municipalities include San Bernardo and Cabrera (Cundinamarca), Tierralta and Montelíbano (Córdoba), and Cimitarra (Santander). See ANCB v. 64 f. 508 and v. 77 f. 385.

39. Tolima, *Informe del Secretario de Gobierno*, 1933, p. 31; and Antioquia, *Informe del Secretario de Gobierno*, 1930, p. 264.

40. AC, "Proyectos pendientes de 1859 (Cámara)," vol. 3 folio 16.

41. AC, "Leyes autógrafas de 1917," vol. 6 folio 153. See also ANCB v. 43 f. 172.

42. This functional dualism, marked by the existence of a commercially oriented sector where the land is highly concentrated and a so-called subsistence sector of family producers that provides food for the internal market, has characterized agriculture in most Latin American countries historically. Studies of the origins and significance of this structure of production include Gervasio Castro de Rezende, "Plantation Systems, Land Tenure and Labor Supply: An Historical Analysis of the Brazilian Case With a Contemporary Study of the Cacao Regions of Bahia, Brazil" (Ph.D. diss., University of Wisconsin, 1976); José F. Graziano de Silva et al., *Estrutura agrária e produção de subsistência na agricultura brasileira* (São Paulo, 1977); Alain de Janvry and Carlos Garramon, "The Dynamics of Rural Poverty in Latin America," *Journal of Peasant Studies* 4 (April 1977), 206–16; Bernardo Sorj, "Estrutura agrária e dinâmica política no Brasil atual," London, 1977 (mimeographed); and Gervasio Castro de Rezende, "Estrutura agrária, produção e emprêgo no nordeste: uma visão geral," Rio de Janeiro, 1978 (mimeographed).

43. ANCB v. 4 f. 71 and v. 26 f. 713.

44. See AC, "Leyes autógrafas de 1917," vol. 6 folios 148–149; Antioquia, *Informe del Secretario de Hacienda*, 1935, p. 30; and ANCB v. 43 f. 253 and v. 74 f. 366.

45.   ANCB v. 44 f. 416, v. 69 f. 398, v. 70 f. 218, v. 71 fs. 1, 86 and 194, and v. 77 f. 173. See also AC, "Leyes autógrafas de 1917," vol. 6 folio 149.

46.   Samuel Silva R. to the Minister of Agriculture, 25 September 1919, in ANCB v. 45 f. 655.

47.   Parsons, p. 98. The grant list published by the Ministry of Industries (see footnote 48) presents a lower figure for the Antioqueño poblaciones. According to this list, only 141,819 hectares were allocated to settlements.

48.   These figures are calculated from the list of all public land grants awarded by the Colombian government between 1827 and 1931 published in *Memoria de Industrias*, 1931, vol. 5, pp. 249–410. They probably overestimate the number of grants obtained by peasant settlers, since most cultivators had no more than 5 to 10 hectares of land under cultivation. From 1827 through 1917, only 254 grants of 1–20 hectares were awarded for a total of 2,700 hectares.

49.   See, for example, Everett Hagen, "How Economic Growth Begins: A Theory of Social Change," *The Journal of Social Issues* 19 (January 1963), 20–34; and George M. Foster, "Peasant Society and the Image of Limited Good," in *Peasant Society: A Reader*, ed. Jack Potter, May Díaz, and George Foster (Boston, 1967), pp. 300–23.

Chapter 3: The Land Entrepreneurs

1.   See Frank Tannenbaum, *Ten Keys To Latin America* (New York, 1967), pp. 77–94; and Lambert, *Latin America*, pp. 59–105.

2.   The following interpretation of the composition and economic orientation of the Colombian upper classes is based on Safford, "Commerce and Enterprise"; López Toro; Safford, *Ideal*; Bergquist, *Coffee and Conflict*; Palacios, *Coffee in Colombia*; and Richard Hyland, "The Secularization of Credit in the Cauca Valley, Colombia, 1850–1880" (Ph.D. diss., University of California at Berkeley, 1979).

3.   See *Ministerio de Industrias*, 1931, vol. 5, pp. 249–410. Biographical information on prominent individuals in Colombian society is found in Joaquín Ospina, *Diccionario biográfico y bibliográfico de Colombia* (Bogotá, 1927); Gabriel Arango Mejía, *Geneologías de Antioquia y Caldas*, 2nd ed., 2 vols. (Medellín, 1942); and J.M. Cordóvez Moure, *Reminiscencias de Santa Fé y Bogotá* (Madrid, 1957).

4.   Richard Hyland, "A Fragile Prosperity: Credit and Agrarian Structure in the Cauca Valley, Colombia, 1851–87," *Hispanic American Historical Review* 62 (August 1982), 383–84.

5.   See McGreevey, pp. 119–21; and Palacios, *Coffee in Colombia*, pp. 35–37.

6.   See Hyland, "Secularization of Credit," pp. 166–73, 203–14.

7.   See descriptions of the land booms in Yolombó (Antioquia) in the 1890s when a new railroad was built and in the United Fruit Company banana zone in the 1920s, in LeGrand, "From Public Lands," pp. 145–50 and 225.

220 Notes

8.   See Paul W. Gates, *Landlords and Tenants on the Prairie Frontier: Studies in American Land Policy* (Ithaca, 1973).

9.   See A. López, *Problemas colombianos*, pp. 66–82.

10.   Until the 1950s, labor generally accounted for more than 75 percent of the cost of coffee production in Colombia. See Charles Bergquist, "Colombia," in *Labor in Latin America* (Stanford, 1986). p. 318.

11.   For the references to this survey, see Chapter 2, note 26 above.

12.   See Galindo, pp. 257–59; Gates, p. 11; and Magnus Morner, "The Spanish American Hacienda: A Survey of Recent Research and Debate," *Hispanic American Historical Review* 53 (May 1973), 192–93.

13.   *Boletín Industrial* (8 May 1875); *El Agricultor* 2 (6 October 1879) 77; ibid. 2 (8 December 1879), 109; ibid. 4 (November 1882), 516; and ibid. 14 (May 1898), 213; Brew, "Economic Development," p. 29; and Fabio Zambrano et al., "Colombia: desarrollo agrícola, 1900–1930" (Tesis de grado, Universidad Jorge Tadeo Lozano, 1974), Chapter 2.

14.   Whereas the population of Colombia stood at somewhat less than 3 million in 1870, by 1938 it had increased to 8.7 million, and by 1973 to 20.7 million. See Colombia, Contraloría General de la República, *Anuario general de estadística* (Bogotá, 1938); and Colombia, Departamento de Antioquia, *Anuario estadístico de Antioquia*, 1976 (Medellín, 1977).

15.   Sidney Mintz, "The Caribbean Region," *Daedalus* 103 (Spring 1974), 46.

16.   See Taussig, "Evolution"; and Malcolm Deas, "A Colombian Coffee Estate: Sta. Barbara, Cundinamarca, 1870–1912," in *Land and Labour in Latin America*, ed. Kenneth Duncan and Ian Rutledge (Cambridge, England, 1977), pp. 269–98.

17.   The type of labor recruitment called *enganche* in Colombia has not been systematically investigated. It appears to have resembled the enganche system employed by coastal sugar plantations in Peru to obtain rural workers from the Andean highlands during the same period. See Peter Klaren, "The Social and Economic Consequences of Modernization in the Peruvian Sugar Industry, 1870–1930," in *Land and Labour in Latin America*, ed. Kenneth Duncan and Ian Rutledge (Cambridge, England, 1977), pp. 229–52; Peter Blanchard, "The Recruitment of Workers in the Peruvian Sierra at the Turn of the Century: The *Enganche* System," *Inter-American Economic Affairs* 33 (Winter 1979), 63–84; and Michael Gonzales, "Capitalist Agriculture and Labor Contracting in Northern Peru, 1880–1905," *Journal of Latin American Studies* 12 (1980), 291–315.

18.   For theoretical discussions of this point, see Evsey D. Domar, "The Causes of Slavery or Serfdom: A Hypothesis," *Journal of Economic History* 30 (1970), 18–32; Martin Katzman, "The Brazilian Frontier in Comparative Perspective," *Comparative Studies in Society and History* 17 (July 1975), 274–75; and Castro de Rezende, "Plantation Systems," pp. 9–131.

19.   This point is suggested by Barraclough and Domike, pp. 98, 105, 127; McGreevey, pp. 387–89; Morner, "Spanish American Hacienda," pp. 192–93; Friede, *Indio en la lucha*, pp. 36, 101; Kalmanowitz, "El régimen . . . colonial,"

pp. 387–98; and Salomón Kalmanowitz, *Desarrollo de la agricultura en Colombia* (Bogotá, 1978), pp. 23–24.

20.   AC, "Leyes autógrafas de 1882 (Senado)," vol. 2 folios 250, 266.

21.   ANCB v. 42 f. 177. See also ANCB v. 12 f. 193, v. 44 fs. 335 and 345, and v 69 f. 581.

22.   See *Memoria de Hacienda*, 1873, p. 59; and AC, "Leyes autógrafas de 1913," vol. 13, folio 312.

23.   OFISEL, pp. 85–86. See also Bushnell, pp. 276–78; López Toro, pp. 39–40; *Memoria de Industrias*, 1931, vol. 5, pp. 13-14; and INBN v. 1 fs. 138–62.

24.   See ANCB v. 9 f. 21, v. 19 f. 235, v. 36 f. 268, v. 37 f. 478; and LeGrand "From Public Lands," pp. 102–03 and 164–67.

25.   See *Memoria de Industrias*, 1931, vol. 5, pp. 249–410. This list contains detailed information on more than 5,900 grants including the name of the grantee, the number of hectares awarded, and the name of the municipality in which each grant was located. For an analysis of problems in using this data, see LeGrand "From Public Lands," pp. 77–78.

26.   By certificate-holders and large-scale cultivators, I mean those referred to elsewhere as land entrepreneurs. People so classified include all grantees who received land grants larger than 100 hectares in size.

27.   Parsons, pp. 84–85; and Christie, "Antioqueño Colonization: A Reappraisal," 264.

28.   *Memoria de Hacienda*, 1870, p. LIII.

29.   *Memoria de Hacienda*, 1874, pp. 54–55.

30.   Emiliano Restrepo, *Una excursión al territorio de San Martín* (Bogotá, 1952) describes the hopes of one of these entrepreneurs for the economic development of the region. The book was first published in 1870. See also Jane M. Loy, "The Llanos in Colombian History: Some Implications of a Static Frontier," U. of Massachusetts Program in Latin American Studies, Occasional Papers Series No. 2, 1976.

31.   Parsons, pp. 93–94, 130–33; Cecilia de Rodríguez, *La Costa Atlántica: algunos aspectos socio-económicos de su desarrollo* (Bogotá, 1973), pp. 154–57; Ospina Vásquez, pp. 297, 426; Brew, "Economic Development", pp. 183–85, 195; and Orlando Fals Borda, "El 'secreto' de la acumulación originaria de capital: una aproximación empírica," *Revista de Extensión Cultural* [Universidad Nacional de Colombia, Medellín] 7 (n.d.), 28–39.

32.   See Christie, "Oligarchy and Society," pp. 23–46; and Sánchez Reyes.

33.   See Hyland, "Fragile Prosperity," for an excellent description of Valle in this period.

34.   See Botero and Guzmán Barney, pp. 337–55; LeGrand, "From Public Lands," pp. 144–50; and reports from the Special Public Lands Commission of the Banana Zone in ANCB vs. 52, 53, 56, 59, 60, 61, and 66.

35.   See Fals Borda, *Capitalismo*, pp. 51–62.

36.   The acerage that constitutes a large, medium, or small property in any country or region depends on the quality of the land, its potential (and actual) economic

use, its access to markets, and the level of available technology. In Colombia in the late nineteenth and early twentieth centuries, 10 to 20 hectares planted in coffee with markets nearby might comfortably support a family with a margin of profit, while in the Llanos, a cattle ranch of 500 hectares might be counted small and yield fewer returns. Given such considerations, any attempt to designate for all of Colombia the meaning of large, medium, and small holdings in hectares is necessarily schematic. In this book the following convention will be used: "large" refers to grants of more than 500 hectares, "medium" refers to grants of between 100 and 500 hectares, and "small" designates grants of less than 100 hectares. In fact, given the difficulty of clearing most public lands, colono families working by themselves could expect to form holdings of only 10 to 30 hectares. Once the land was cleared, a family might be able to exploit up to 100 hectares without hired workers if a significant proportion of the holding were devoted to cattle. Subsistence properties in Colombia generally comprise 1 to 10 hectares. The calculations on size distribution in the text were derived from *Memoria de Industrias*, 1931, vol. 5, pp. 249–410.

37.   See Palacios, *Coffee in Colombia*, p. 171. Multiple grants to large-scale entrepreneurs were particularly common in Antioquia and the Llanos.

38.   See ANCB v. 41 f. 17, v. 44 f. 362, v. 47 f. 295, v. 48 f. 79; and García, *Caldas*, p. 237.

39.   ANCB v. 44 f. 216, v. 69 f. 398, v. 70 f. 218, v. 71 fs. 86 and 194. A delay of five to ten years was not unusual.

40.   ANCB v. 13 f. 123, v. 14 f. 360, v. 15 f. 58, v. 17 f. 381, v. 19 f. 305, v. 25 f. 210, v. 26 f. 326, v. 45 f. 633, v. 46 f. 284, v. 55 f. 456, v. 57 f. 154.

41.   ANCB v. 9 fs. 16–17. See also ANCB v. 19 f. 350 and v. 20 f. 8.

42.   ANCB v. 13 f. 123, and v. 15 f. 58.

43.   AC, "Leyes autógrafas de 1882," vol. 2 folio 260. See also ANCB v. 5 f. 269, v. 9 f. 22, v. 22 f. 373, and v. 29 f. 164.

44.   ANCB v. 26 f. 326. See also ANCB v. 34 f. 366, v. 43 f. 273, v. 47 f. 302, v. 70 f. 75, v. 75 f. 295, and v. 76 f. 113.

45.   ANCB v. 32 f. 452, v. 33 fs. 394 and 471, v. 43 f. 283, v. 46 f. 22, v. 47 f. 392, v. 48 f. 79, v. 54 f. 424, v. 60 f. 170, v. 61 f. 186, v. 74 f. 106, and v. 75 fs. 229 and 258.

46.   ANCB v. 30 f. 237. See also v. 46 f. 375, and v. 56 f. 1.

47.   Francisco García Carbonell to President Reyes, 25 March 1907, in ANCB v. 42 f. 485.

48.   Smith, p. 103.

49.   See Law 75 of 1887 in AC, "Leyes autógrafas de 1887," vol. 10 folio 125; and *Memoria de Industrias*, 1932, p. 72.

50.   See ANCB v. 12 f. 87, v. 25 f. 657, v. 26 f. 2, v. 30 f. 190, v. 46 fs. 358 and 392, v. 47 f. 225, v. 48 f. 58, v. 50 f. 136, v. 62 f. 98, and v. 72 fs. 189 and 256. Also, *Memoria de Industrias*, 1930, anexos, pp. 115–18.

51.   See ANCB v. 11 f. 11, v. 26 f. 326, v. 44 f. 326, v. 46 f. 235, v. 55 f. 476, v. 56 fs. 4 and 15, v. 60 fs. 164 and 216; *Memoria de Agricultura*, 1923, pp.

14–15; and *Boletín de la Oficina General de Trabajo* 4 (October-December 1933), 1523–47 and 1641–62.

52.   ANCB v. 24 f. 335.

53.   See ANCB v. 13 f. 48, v. 24 fs. 335 and 336, v. 25 f. 210, v. 35 f. 595, v. 45 f. 624, and v. 55 f. 148.

54.   ANCB v. 4 f. 1, v. 21 f. 348, v. 25 f. 302, v. 32 f. 438, v. 37 f. 328, v. 44 f. 326, v. 55 f. 476, v. 69 f. 25, and v. 71 fs. 317–50.

55.   The following account is drawn from the reports of the treasurer of Tolima to the Ministry of Finance in 1881, in ANCB v. 3 fs. 181 and 183–88.

56.   See ANCB v. 13 f. 48 and v. 42 f. 365. For Mexico, too, John Coatsworth has discovered a direct correlation between the construction of railroads, rising land values, and the tendency of large landowners to expand their holdings. See Coatsworth, "Railroads, Landholding, and Agrarian Protest in the Early Porfiriato," *Hispanic American Historical Review* 54 (February 1974), 48–71.

57.   See Fals Borda, *Capitalismo*. The Public Land Correspondence (ANCB) also contains much information on landholding and land use on the Caribbean coast.

58.   ANCB v. 46 f. 220, v. 50 f. 351, v. 54 f. 540, v. 56 f. 65, v. 58 f. 535, v. 60 f. 164, v. 61 f. 84, v. 70 f. 169, and v. 72 f. 241.

59.   On these transactions, see ANCB v. 14 f. 373, v. 34 fs. 78 and 350, v. 46 f. 262, v. 49 fs. 50 and 90, v. 50 f. 40, v. 54 fs. 595 and 598, v. 55 fs. 41, 202, and 408, v. 57 f. 501, v. 75 f. 197, v. 77 fs. 280 and 423; *Memoria de Industrias, 1931*, vol. 5, pp. 313–14; and Orlando Fals Borda, *Historia doble de la costa,* vol. 3: *Resistencia en el San Jorge* (Bogotá, 1984), pp. 168b–71b. According to the Caja de Crédito Agrícola, Industrial y Minero, "Informe sobre la propiedad de la American Colombian Corporation en el Departamento de Bolívar, República de Colombia," Bogotá, 1960 (mimeographed), the properties of the American Colombian Corporation eventually came to encompass 600,000 hectares. Other foreign companies that owned land in Colombia included the Lancashire General Investment Company of Great Britain, a ranching enterprise in Magdalena; American mining firms in northeastern Caldas (ANCB v. 37 f. 476); the East Magdalena Exploitation Company in Puerto Wilches (Santander) (ANCB v. 33 f. 320 and v. 50 f. 187); the Lobitos Oilfields Corporation in Bolívar (Santander) (ANCB v. 57 f. 187); and the Union Oil Company, which purchased from the Colombian firm of Herrera y Uribe approximately 160,000 hectares of land including many baldíos, it was claimed, in Cundinamarca, Huila, and Meta (ANCB v. 50 f. 504). For a map showing the location of foreign companies with land in the department of Bolívar, see Fals Borda, *Capitalismo*, p. 53. Detailed information on foreign holdings in Colombia in the 1920s is also to be found in Arno S. Pearse, *Colombia, With Special Reference to Cotton (Being the Report of the International Cotton Mission Through the Republic of Colombia)* (Manchester, England, 1926).

60.   See LeGrand, "From Public Lands," pp. 136–50 for a more detailed analysis of the Colombian government's response to the usurpation of public lands.

61.   Law 48 of 1882, article 9; Decree 832 of 1884, articles 5 and 6; Circular

No. 94 of 1884 (Secretario de Estado del Despacho de Hacienda); and Decree 678 of 1890 in, respectively, Colombia, Consejo de Estado, *Codificación nacional de las leyes de Colombia desde el año de 1821*, vol. 32 (Bogotá, 1951), pp. 93–95; Vicente Olarte Camacho, *Recopilación de leyes y disposiciones administrativas* (Bogotá, 1901), pp. 299–305; ibid, pp. 313–17; and ibid., pp. 306–07.

62.   ANCB v. 18 fs. 26, 420 and 452, v. 21 f. 172, v. 32 f. 584, v. 41 f. 451, v. 58 f. 535, and v. 70 fs. 36 and 138. See also AC, "Proyectos pendientes, 1924–25 (Cámara)," vol. 9 folio 135.

63.   See ANCB v. 11 fs. 184, 188 and 245, v. 16 fs. 93 and 251, v. 38 fs. 99, 375, 417, and 425, and v. 44 f. 332.

64.   ANCB v. 2 f. 312. Underlining in the original.

65.   See ANCB v. 14 f. 285, v. 38 f. 194, v. 39 fs. 57–8 and 255, and v. 45 f. 589.

66.   ANCB v. 15 f. 375, v. 10 f. 94, v. 14 f. 335, v. 15 fs. 342 and 378, v. 26 f. 698 and v. 34 f. 34; and AC, "Leyes autógrafas de 1917," vol. 6 folio 148.

67.   ANCB v. 3 f. 130. In this case the government ordered that the grant be nullified and the hamlet protected (v. 3 f. 126).

68.   See ANCB v. 7 f. 175, v. 14 fs. 342 and 348, v. 18 fs. 463 and 495, v. 22 f. 392, v. 26 fs. 326 and 625, v. 28 f. 240, v. 30 fs. 126 and 225, v. 37 fs. 63 and 122, v. 41 f. 227, and v. 63 f. 353.

69.   See ANCB v. 5 f. 302, v. 15 fs. 246 and 253, v. 20 f. 131, v. 24 f. 336, v. 25 f. 707; Cauca, *Informe del Secretario de Hacienda*, 1935, p. 39; and Colombia, Valle del Cauca, *Mensaje del Gobernador del departamento a la Asamblea Departamental en el año de 1936* (Cali, 1936), p. 11. Hereafter the annual reports of the governor of a department to the assembly of that department will be cited as *Mensaje del Gobernador*, preceded by the name of the department and followed by the date.

70.   ANCB v. 22 f. 320, v. 23 f. 133, v. 24 fs. 242 and 581, and v. 25 f. 281.

71.   ANCB v. 45 f. 626.

72.   It should be noted that mining companies in isolated regions of Colombia often increased their labor supply by requiring colonos settled on the surrounding territory to sign tenancy contracts in which the colonos agreed to pay rent on their subsistence plots by working as miners. See Alvaro Tirado Mejía, *Colombia en la repartición imperialista (1870–1914)* (Medellín, 1976), pp. 80, 99.

73.   ANCB v. 18 f. 452, v. 33 fs. 507, 509 and 511, and v. 63 f. 238.

74.   See ANCB v. 26 fs. 276 and 291, v. 29 f. 164, v. 34 f. 366, v. 35 f. 595, v. 41 f. 148, v. 43 f. 254, and v. 70 fs. 75 and 264.

75.   See ANCB v. 13 fs. 30, 219 and 287, and v. 14 fs. 356, 365 and 367.

76.   See Brew, "Economic Development," pp. 156–81; Christie, "Oligarchy and Society," pp. 13–60; Christie, "Antioqueño Colonization," pp. 160–68; and López Toro. The primary actors in these real estate transactions were the Villegas family, the Aranzazu family, González, Salazar i Cía., and the Burila Land Company.

77.   The Antioqueño pattern of frontier development resembled in many ways

the development of the mid-western part of the United States and of the Paraná coffee frontier in Brazil. (See Gates; and Katzman, "Brazilian Frontier," 278–79). The subdivision of large holdings also occurred in the Missiones district of Argentina in the 1920s and 1930s (Eidt, p. 203). According to Katzman, "The key to a pattern of subdivision on export-propelled frontiers lies in the existence of a wide range of financial instruments which would provide landowners with alternative investments once their holdings were liquidated" (p. 284). Owing to the exceptional dynamism of the Antioqueño regional economy that originated in mining, alternative investment opportunities seem to have been present in that part of the country, while they were generally lacking elsewhere in Colombia during the nineteenth century. This hypothesis may help to explain the peculiar forms that frontier development took in the Antioqueño colonization area.

78. ANCB v. 26 fs. 67 and 282, v. 33 fs. 156, 159, 543 and 546, v. 34 f. 28, v. 37 f. 491, and v. 41 f. 414.

Chapter 4: The Struggle for Land and Labor

1. The Antioqueño controversies have been discussed at length elsewhere. See Parsons, pp. 72–95; Luis Duque Gómez, Juan Friede, and Jaime Jaramillo Uribe, *Historia de Pereira* (Bogotá, 1963), pp. 361–66; López Toro, pp. 37–63; Christie, "Oligarchy and Society," pp. 16–25, 50–56; and Guillermo Duque Botero, *Historia de Salamina* (Manizales, 1974), vol. 1, pp. 110–39.

2. See Colmenares, *Historia económica*, p. 213; Kalmanowitz, "El régimen agrario . . . colonia," pp. 423–24; Sierra, pp. 67-93, 147; and *Memoria de Industrias*, 1931, vol. 6, p. 356.

3. This interpretation of settler ideology is drawn from the numerous colono petitions in ANCB that constantly refer to the laws of 1874 and 1882 in their protests against land entrepreneurs.

4. Most colonos who could not write requested a neighbor to sign for them using the annotation *a ruego de*. Signatures on the petitions provide one good indication of the level of illiteracy among settlers.

5. See ANCB vs. 1–78 and Appendix C.

6. ANCB v. 4 fs. 267 and 270.

7. ANCB v. 41 fs. 451–52.

8. ANCB v. 37 f. 488.

9. ANCB v. 11 f. 185.

10. ANCB v. 41 f. 208.

11. Boyacá, *Mensaje del Gobernador*, 1934, anexos, pp. 39–40. See also ANCB v. 24 f. 373 and v. 64 f. 155. Large claimants sometimes resorted to this tactic too. Samuel Haskell of the American Colombian Corporation persuaded the tax committee of San Martín de Loba (Bolívar) in 1923 to inscribe the immense "Terrenos

de Loba" under his name. He intended in this way to counter a ministerial resolution in 1919 that overruled his claim to the territory. The protests of the citizens of
San Martín make it clear that they regarded the payment of property taxes to signify
an overt assertion of landownership. See ANCB v. 54 f. 540.

12.   See ANCB v. 14 f. 285, v. 30 f. 99, v. 39 f. 353, and v. 65 f. 471.

13.   See ANCB v. 20 f. 131 and v. 43 f. 473.

14.   ANCB v. 36 f. 346. See also ANCB v. 34 f. 353. Several booklets and
pamphlets produced by colonos engaged in disputes with land claimants are deposited in the Public Land Archives (ANCB v. 14 fs. 246–47, v. 44 f. 435bis, v. 55 fs.
477bis and 502, and v. 78 f. 437).

15.   See, for example, William B. Taylor, *Landlord and Peasant in Colonial
Oaxaca* (Stanford, 1972), pp. 82–89; Hobsbawm, "Peasant Land Occupations"; and
Woodrow Borah, *Justice by Insurance: The General Indian Court of Colonial Mex-
ico and the Legal Aides of the Half-Real* (Berkeley, 1983).

16.   For this reason, local authorities as a preventative measure usually set the
settlers' huts afire in evictions. See Cundinamarca, *Informe del Secretario de Gobierno*, 1937, pp. 62–3.

17.   ANCB v. 25 f. 31.

18.   ANCB v. 28 fs. 336, 340–41.

19.   ANCB v. 35 f. 529.

20.   ANCB v. 35 f. 41.

21.   ANCB v. 28 f. 385.

22.   ANCB v. 43 f. 123. See also ANCB v. 2 f. 201 and v. 24 fs. 242–43.

23.   Salvador Camacho Roldán, *Escritos varios* (Bogotá, 1893), p. 505.

24.   See ANCB v. 5 f. 95.

25.   *Boletín de la Oficina General de Trabajo* 5 (January-June 1934), 152–54.

26.   ANCB v. 34 f. 355. See also ANCB v. 14 f. 342.

27.   ANCB v. 25 f. 657.

28.   See INBN v. 21 f. 944, ANCB v. 10 f. 100, v. 14 fs. 342 and 347, v. 28 f.
341, v. 50 f. 363, v. 62 f. 282, v. 63 fs. 4 and 174, v. 64 f. 63, and v. 65 fs. 233
and 471. For a detailed account of the efforts of one tinterillo and tailor to defend
the inhabitants of Jegua on the Caribbean coast between 1892 and 1930, see Fals
Borda, *Resistencia*, pp. 117–31.

29.   See ANCB v. 55 f. 477bis for a copy of this pamplet, entitled "La Justicia
Llega, Pero Tarde". For other examples, see ANCB v. 10 f. 99 and v. 43 f. 483.

30.   ANCB v. 49 f. 215.

31.   ANCB v. 10 f. 100. See also ANCB v. 4 fs. 188 and 274, v. 10 fs. 6, 20,
22 and 29, v. 25 f. 596, v. 26 f. 80, and v. 31 f. 317.

32.   See Law 60 of 1905 in Colombia, Congreso Nacional, *Actos legislativos de
1905* (Bogotá, 1905), pp. 328–31. For the colono reaction, see ANCB v. 29 f. 739
and v. 30 fs. 246 and 588.

33.   ANCB v. 30 fs. 71 and 117. See ANCB v. 30 fs. 73–75 for the municipal

ordinance dealing with this issue and v. 54 f. 536 for examples of rental contracts signed with colonos in Ataco.

34.   ANCB v. 47 f. 276. Friction between the colonos of Sur de Atá and the municipality continued unabated in 1932, by which time the settlers not only refused to pay rent, but also declined to perform obligatory road repair and police services, to answer summonses, and to sell their produce in the town of Ataco. See Tolima, *Informe que rinde el Visitador Fiscal del departamento a la H. Asamblea Departamental en la legislatura de 1932* (Ibagué, 1932), pp. 17–18. During La Violencia in the 1950s this area became a Communist stronghold and a focal point of army repression (see Darío Fajardo M., *Violencia y desarrollo: transformaciones sociales en tres regiones cafetaleras del Tolima, 1936–1970* (Medellín, 1978), pp. 125–35).

35.   The following material is drawn from ANCB v. 55 fs. 22–33, 291–304, and 320.

36.   ANCB v. 55 f. 22.

37.   ANCB v. 55 f. 303.

38.   See ANCB v. 9 f. 21, v. 15 f. 375, v. 19 f. 235, v. 22 f. 373, v. 33 f. 272, v. 36 f. 268, v. 37 f. 478, v. 38 f. 181, and v. 43 f. 254.

39.   See ANCB v. 25 f. 656 for Torres' own explanation of the role he played. Petitions written by Torres from prison on behalf of the settlers are to be found in ANCB v. 25 fs. 656, 661, 663 and 665.

40.   ANCB v. 44 f. 435bis. As these examples make clear, educated individuals who sided with the settlers for whatever reasons often risked retaliation from the landlords they opposed. A report concerning Caparrapí (Cundinamarca) in 1920 is revealing of the methods used by influential entrepreneurs to remove the colonos' allies from the scene: "Out of benevolence and a sense of justice, Sr. General Ramón Marín supported those Colonos; as a result, the attorney of the caciques of Palenquero . . . charged the General with being the chief of a band of malefactors and the authorities sided with the accusers and jailed Gen. Marín" (ANCB v. 55 f. 477bis p. l9). An Antioqueño of African descent who had worked as a straw boss in the mines, Ramón Marín had been a popular Liberal guerrilla leader during the War of a Thousand Days. (See Bergquist, *Coffee and Conflict*, p. 191.)

41.   Some insight into Colombian local politics is provided by Henderson, "Origins," Chapters 7–9; Malcolm Deas, "Algunas notas sobre la historia del caciquismo en Colombia," *Revista del Occidente* 127 (October 1973), 118–40; Humberto Rojas Ruiz, "Peasant Consciousness in Three Rural Communities" (Ph.D. diss., University of Wisconsin, 1974), pp. 82–116; Deas, "A Colombian Coffee Estate," pp. 285–90; Keith H. Christie, "Gamonalismo in Colombia: An Historical Overview," *North-South: Canadian Journal of Latin American Studies* 4 (1979), 42–59; and Oquist, pp. 211–21.

42.   *Memoria de Agricultura*, 1920, anexos, p. 94.

43.   See, for example, ANCB v. 38 f. 485 and v. 65 f. 465. Of particular importance in Latin America, *compadrazgo* signifies the strong social ties of respect

and obligation established between the godparents and the parents of a child. Individuals who stand in such a relationship to one another call themselves and are referred to by others as *compadres* (M.) or *comadres* (F.).

44. See Annie Caputo, "Las luchas agrarias en Sumapaz" (Tesis de grado, Universidad de los Andes, 1974), pp. 26–27.

45. See LeGrand, "From Public Lands," pp. 256–58.

46. Medardo Rivas, *Los trabajadores de tierra caliente*, 2nd ed. (Bogota, 1972), p. 63.

47. See Gonzalo Sánchez, *Los 'Bolsheviques del Líbano' (Tolima)* (Bogotá, 1976) for insight into the role artisans played in local politics in one coffee municipality.

48. ANCB v. 29 f. 774. See also ANCB v. 13 f. 287, v. 19 fs. 8 and 10, v. 35 f. 591, v. 39 f. 199, v. 41 f. 425, and v. 44 f. 390.

49. ANCB v. 15 f. 267 and v. 47 f. 132.

50. See ANCB v. 25 f. 41, v. 43 f. 283, v. 46 f. 235, and v. 57 f. 50.

51. ANCB v. 44 f. 69. Faced with a similar situation, the officials and citizens of Barranco de Loba (Bolívar) together organized a "committee dedicated to the defense of the territory which Dr. Pantaleón G. Ribón is trying to steal from us by selling it unlawfully to some North Americans" (ANCB v. 32 f. 451). With the exception of the banana zone, where the influence of the United Fruit Company was predominant, the attempts of foreigners to invest in public lands often accentuated the tendency of local authorities to identify with colonos. British mining entrepreneurs Christopher Dixon and William Welton encountered strong resistance when they sought to obtain land grants in northern Tolima and Caldas. Where larger enterprises such as the Lancashire General Investment Company were involved, local officials sometimes tried to interfere with their operations in the hope of eliciting pay-offs. See ANCB v. 48 fs. 438 and 472, v. 49 f. 90, v. 58 f. 136, and v. 64 f. 480.

52. See ANCB v. 26 fs. 67, 282, and 284, v. 33 fs. 156, 159, 543 and 546, v. 34 f. 28, v. 37 f. 491, and v. 41 f. 414. For a list of forest concessions granted by the Colombian government, see Joelle Diot, "Estadísticas históricas: concesiones forestales, 1900–1968," *Boletín Mensual de Estadística* [DANE] 285 (April 1975), 92–93. *Memoria de Industrias*, 1931, vol. 6, pp. 9-100 contains a compilation of the most important laws and government rulings pertaining to the Colombian national forests from 1821 through 1931.

53. ANCB v. 28 f. 372.

54. ANCB v. 36 f. 233. The central government replied that the municipal council of Prado had no right to defend the colonos on its own initiative, and it directed the councilors to support the mayor in matters relating to administrative law.

55. The municipal advocate, or personero, is an official elected by the municipal council to act as its spokesman in the local executive branch. Among other duties, the advocate is charged with the protection of all property belonging to the national government within municipal boundaries, including public lands. For ex-

amples of municipal advocates and a few mayors supporting colonos, see ANCB v. 9 fs. 76 and 86, v. 11 f. 111, v. 16 f. 69, v. 28 f. 122, v. 29 f. 633, v. 33 f. 503, v. 35 f. 591, v. 39 f. 199, v. 44 f. 390, and v. 45 f. 629. Only in mining municipalities were local authorities almost always irrevocably set against colonos because the authorities depended on the mining companies for their salaries (see INBN v. 21 f. 944; and Tirado Mejía, *Colombia en la repartición*, pp. 84–85, 90–91).

56.   A petition written by cultivator Santiago M. Alvarez of Magangué (Bolívar) in 1907 is particularly revealing of this effect:

> By means of a lower court ruling, the Sres. Viñas have notified us to dispose of our hogs and pay tenancy obligations or sell out. I am pained by this decision because it involves an injustice, not only against me, but also against the poor and illiterate people of three rural pueblos. These people are so angry with the judge that I must restrain them. I will not permit them to take violent action, first, because it is not right and, second, because people would say that since I am their leader, I am responsible. I have told the colonos time and again: there are judges in Cartagena and Bogotá, and as long as President Reyes is alive, injustice will not be allowed in Colombia. Have confidence in General Reyes and you will see that this ruling is annulled by a higher court. . . . (ANCB v. 28 fs. 389–90).

57.   See LeGrand, "From Public Lands," pp. 500-03; and ANCB v. 20 f. 131, v. 36 f. 233, v. 41 f. 208, v. 43 fs. 121, 123, 208, and 440, v. 49 f. 194, and v. 68 f. 168.

58.   See LeGrand, "From Public Lands," pp. 495–99.

59.   See ANCB v. 31 f. 57, v. 33 fs. 507–15, v. 37 fs. 195 and 330, v. 47 fs. 343 and 383, v. 47 f. 404, and v. 58 f. 136; and Fals Borda, *Resistencia*, pp. 164–82. For additional information on settler-land entrepreneur confrontations, their location, and the number of settlers involved, see appendixes C and D.

60.   Law 61 of 1874, article 6, and Law 48 of 1882, articles 2, 4, and 5 in Colombia, Consejo de Estado, *Codificación nacional de todas las leyes de Colombia desde el año de 1821* (Bogotá, 1951), vol. 27, pp. 119–22 and vol. 32, pp. 93–95.

61.   ANCB v. 14 f. 307.

62.   ANCB v. 15 f. 246. On Sixto Durán's rural investments and the Junín controversy, see also Bergquist, *Coffee and Conflict*, pp. 27, 29, 34.

63.   For examples of these tactics, see ANCB v. 12 fs. 245 and 286, v. 15 fs. 342 and 378, v. 18 fs. 115 and 468, v. 27 fs. 125 and 132, v. 28 fs. 336, 340 and 341, v. 36 f. 452, and v. 45 fs. 626 and 674.

64.   ANCB v. 11 f. 190.

65.   Law 61 of 1874, article 6, and Law 48 of 1882, article 2. Administrative jurisprudence in Colombia referred to settled doctrines and practice developed by officials dependent on the executive branch. At the local level, the mayors were the primary agents of the executive power of the central government. In rural municipalities, administrative procedures permitted individuals involved in disputes to seek redress from the mayor rather than initiating a court case. For an explication

of administrative law in Colombia, see Richard C. Backus and Phanor J. Eder, *A Guide to the Law and Legal Literature of Colombia* (Washington, 1943), pp. 89–99.

66.   García, *Caldas*, p. 238.

67.   ANCB v. 49 f. 194; and *Boletín de la Oficina General de Trabajo* 4 (October–December 1932), 1159.

68.   Colombia, Congreso Nacional, *Leyes de 1905* (Bogotá, 1906), pp. 302–303.

69.   *Boletín de la Oficina General de Trabajo* 1 (June 1930), 433.

70.   Groups of colonos frequently reported that they had been deprived of their holdings through Law 57. See ANCB v. 29 f. 622, v. 36 f. 148, v. 39 fs. 452 and 578, v. 43 f. 416, v. 44 f. 435, v. 50 f. 436, and v. 55 fs. 477 and 477bis; and Cundinamarca, *Informe del Secretario de Gobierno*, 1937, pp. 62–63.

71.   See, respectively, ANCB v. 35 fs. 522 and 528, and v. 55 f. 477bis (pp. 9–11).

72.   ANCB v. 55 f. 477bis (p. 10).

73.   ANCB v. 29 f. 637.

74.   ANCB v. 20 f. 130. Colonos from Caparrapí (Cundinamarca) reported a similar situation there in 1918 (see ANCB v. 43 f. 473). In tenancy contracts it was often stipulated that the tenants pledge to defend the hacienda against "invaders": this term appears to refer to squatters and colonos.

75.   ANCB v. 63 fs. 355–56. It appears that landlords occasionally used the public land legislation to take over not only settlers' holdings, but also Indian communal lands. See LeGrand, "From Public Lands," pp. 67–68; Friede, *El indio en la lucha*, pp. 41–2, 127–233; and Fals Borda, *Resistencia*, pp. 96–131.

76.   ANCB v. 7 f. 113 and v. 10 fs. 296–97.

77.   See ANCB v. 10 fs. 219 and 249, v. 19 f. 200, v. 21 f. 297, v. 41 f. 182, and v. 43 fs. 133, 175 and 194. Bogotá's procolono attitude led landowners occasionally to portray themselves as settlers in petitions seeking government support. Used in conjunction with other influences, the government's compliance helped them to win land disputes with other proprietors or colonos. Conflicting testimony presented in a quarrel over the property "Finlandia" in Gachetá (Cundinamarca) in 1898 illustrates this strategy. One side argued that a number of colono families settled on baldíos were being disturbed by an adjacent landowner, David Guzmán. Guzmán, however, maintained that these were not true colonos, but hirelings of a neighboring proprietor who was trying to encroach on his land. The judge was unable to determine the truth of the matter (see ANCB v. 19 f. 450). Similarly the United Fruit Company instructed workers it sent to plant bananas illegally within a national public land reserve to pose as independent colonos. It also used such colono-workers to counter the efforts of true settler families to obtain land grants (ANCB v. 59 fs. 13 and 21, and v. 60 f. 237).

78.   See Resolución del Ministerio de Hacienda, 22 February 1893, in *Memoria de Industrias*, 1931, vol. 3 , p. 190.

79.   See ANCB v. 26 f. 680, and v. 46 f. 374. Sometimes, also, Bogotá authorized a state's attorney *(fiscal)* to represent the settlers' interests in judicial suits
affecting their rights.
80.   See ANCB v. 62 f. 282, v. 63 fs. 4 and 174, v. 64 f. 63, and v. 65 fs. 465
and 471.
81.   ANCB v. 46 f. 419.
82.   ANCB v. 25 fs. 709 and 714.
83.   ANCB v. 44 f. 636, and v. 45 f. 672.
84.   ANCB v. 41 f. 10. See also ANCB v. 18 f. 189.
85.   ANCB v. 45 f. 631.
86.   ANCB v. 50 f. 436, v. 54 fs. 583 and 601, and v. 63 f. 355.
87.   ANCB v. 38 fs. 32–3. See also ANCB v. 43 fs. 208 and 440.
88.   Keith Christie explores the causes and effects of the debility of the Colombian national government before 1920 in "Gamonalismo," 43–9. He attributes the
narrow radius of national power to the penury of the central government, the poorly
developed transportation network, and the lack of a well-trained, effective military.
See also Malcolm Deas, "Poverty, Civil War, and Politics: Ricardo Gaitán Obeso
and his Magdalena River Campaign in Colombia, 1885," *Nova Americana* [Turin]
2 (1979), 263–303.
89.   Cauca, *Informe del Secretario de Hacienda*, 1935, p. 84.
90.   See ANCB v. 54 f. 566.
91.   See ANCB v. 45 fs. 669–70.
92.   See Coatsworth; Hobsbawm, "Peasant Land Occupations"; Katzman, "The
Brazilian Frontier," 279, 283; Dean, *Rio Claro*, pp. 1–23; and Castro de Rezende,
"Plantation Systems," pp. 132–56. For Mexico the process is not yet entirely clear.
In Yucután and Morelos, henequen and sugar haciendas encroached on communal
lands during the late nineteenth century, provoking a strong popular reaction. In
the same period in the north, thousands of hectares of public lands were distributed
in vast blocks to foreign and native entrepreneurs, but the social effects of such
grants remain, to my knowledge, unexplored.
93.   Little empirical research has been done on the history of Colombian rural
labor relations. Scattered information on the topic may be found in Salvador Camacho Roldán, *Notas de viaje* (Bogotá, 1890), p. 52; Salvador Camacho Roldán, *Mis
memorias* (Bogotá, 1923), p. 94; Sierra, pp. 132–63; Anteo Quimbaya, *El problema
de la tierra en Colombia* (Bogotá, 1967), pp. 2–17; Smith, pp. 114–38; Roger Soles,
"Rural Land Invasions in Colombia: A Study of the Macro- and Micro-Conditions
and Forces Leading to Peasant Unrest" (Ph.D. diss., University of Wisconsin, 1972),
pp. 121–31; Christie, "Oligarchy and Society," pp. 211, 213; DeRoux, pp. 275–
79; Fals Borda, *Historia de la cuestión agraria*, pp. 93–114; Alejandro Reyes Posada, "Aparcería y capitalismo agrario," *Controversía* [Centro de Investigación y
Educación Popular] 38 (1975), 2–67; Hermes Tovar Pinzón, *El movimiento campesino en Colombia durante los siglos xix y xx* (Bogotá, 1975), pp. 18–35; Gloria

Gaitán de Valencia, *Colombia: la lucha por la tierra en la década del treinta* (Bogotá, 1976), pp. 29–38; Kalmanowitz, "El régimen agrario . . . colonia," 377, 396, 404–11; Deas, "A Colombian Coffee Estate"; Taussig, "Evolution"; Machado C., *El café;* Arango, pp. 141–72; Fajardo M., *Violencia y desarrollo,* pp. 7–23; Jesús Antonio Bejarano, *El régimen agrario de la economía exportadora a la economía industrial* (Bogotá, 1979), pp. 67–77, 164–222; Palacios, *Coffee in Colombia,* pp. 77–120; Victor Negrete B., *Origen de las luchas agrarias en Córdoba* (Montería, 1981), pp. 9–62; Fals Borda, "El 'secreto,' " 28–39; and Michael Jiménez, "Red Viotá: Rebellion in a Colombian Coffee Municipality, 1900–1938" (Ph.D. diss. Harvard University). For copies of tenancy contracts from various parts of the country, see ANCB v. 30 f. 559, v. 60 f. 266, v. 65 f. 405, and AC, "Informes, memoriales, telegramas, 1932 (Cámara)," vol. 7 folios 65–6. A survey of agricultural activities by department carried out by the Ministry of Agriculture in 1916–1918 also contains some relevant material. See ANCB v. 43 fs. 47, 62, 165, 172, 183, 196, 212, 242, and 246.

94.   Arnold J. Bauer summarizes the work on Mexico, Peru, and other countries in "Rural Workers in Spanish America: Problems of Peonage and Oppression," *Hispanic American Historical Review* 59 (February 1979), 34–63. See also Brian Loveman, "Critique of Arnold J. Bauer's 'Rural Workers in Spanish America: Problems of Peonage and Oppression'" and Bauer's "Reply," *Hispanic American Historical Review* 59 (August 1979), 478–89; and Friedrich Katz, "Labor Conditions on Haciendas in Porfirian Mexico: Some Trends and Tendencies," *Hispanic American Historical Review* 54 (February 1974), 1–47.

95.   During the 1920s some service tenants managed to expand their holdings by promising to provide landlords with more labor which they did, not by sending their own families, but by hiring unrelated wage workers. Such "kulak" tenants developed a certain productive autonomy within the haciendas of the province of Tequendama in Cundinamarca. See Palacios, *Coffee in Colombia,* pp. 98–99, 112–20; and Jiménez, "Red Viota." More research is needed to clarify the living conditions—and attendant opportunities and constraints—of Colombian hacienda labor in the various regions.

96.   See A. López, *Problemas colombianos;* Fabio Lozano T., *Con los agricultores de Colombia* (Lima, 1927); International Bank for Reconstruction and Development, *The Basis of A Development Program for Colombia* (Washington, D.C., 1950), pp. 61–64; Eduardo Jiménez Neira, "Bases para una tecnificación de la agricultura," *Economía Colombiana* 2 (September 1954), 289–93; and Smith.

97.   For descriptions of poverty in the Colombian countryside today, see R. Albert Berry, "Rural Poverty in Twentieth Century Colombia," *Journal of Interamerican Studies and World Affairs* 20 (November 1978), 355–76; and Wayne R. Thirsk, "Some Facets of Rural Poverty in Colombia," General Working Document No. 2, Rural Development Division, Bureau for Latin America and the Caribbean, Agency for International Development, Washington, D.C., 1978.

Chapter 5: Transformation of the Conflicts

1.   See Darío Mesa, "Treinta años de historia colombiana (1925–1955)," in *Colombia: estructura política y agraria*, ed. Gonzalo Cataño (Bogotá, 1972), pp. 22–25.

2.   The most informative works dealing with these changes are J. Fred Rippy, *The Capitalists and Colombia* (New York, 1931); Kathryn Wylie, *The Agriculture of Colombia* (Washington, 1942); United Nations, Economic Commission for Latin America, *Analyses and Projections of Economic Development: III. The Economic Development of Colombia* (Geneva, 1957); Oscar Rodríguez S., *Efectos de la gran depresión sobre la industria colombiana* (Bogotá, 1973); Hugo López C., "La inflación en Colombia en la década de los veintes," *Cuadernos Colombianos* 5 (1975), 41–140; Bejarano, "Fin de la economía (II)," 363–427; José Antonio Ocampo and Santiago Montenegro, "La crisis mundial de los años treinta en Colombia," *Desarrollo y Sociedad* 7 (January 1982), 35–96; and Albert Berry, ed., *Essays on Industrialization in Colombia* (Tempe, 1983). See also Vernon Lee Fluharty, *Dance of the Millions* (Pittsburgh, 1957); Carmenza Gallo, *Hipótesis de la acumulación originaria de capital en Colombia* (Medellín, 1974); and Zambrano P. et al., "Colombia: desarrollo agrícola".

3.   See Rodríguez Salazar, pp. 31–38; Jorge Villegas, *Petroleo colombiano, ganancia gringa*, 4th ed. (Bogotá, 1976); and Stephen J. Randall, *The Diplomacy of Modernization: Colombian-American Relations, 1920–1940* (Toronto, 1978). For a breakdown of U.S. loans and investments in Colombia, see Rippy, *The Capitalists*, pp. 152–76. U.S. and European investments in Colombia in earlier years are detailed in United States, Department of Commerce and Labor, *Report on Trade Conditions in Colombia* (Washington, 1907).

4.   See J. Fred Rippy, *Latin America and the Industrial Age*, 2nd ed. (Westport, Connecticut, 1971), pp. 198–207. At the same time that Mexico, following the Revolution of 1910, began to assert more direct control over her oil resources, relations between the United States and Colombia were improving. The key to more congenial relations was the U.S. government's payment of $25 million to Colombia in 1921 in reparation for Colombia's loss of Panama in 1903. The settlement opened the way for the oil companies and other U.S. investors. See Rippy, *The Capitalists*, pp. 103–22.

5.   Additional U.S. enterprises included electrical plants, telegraph and telephone systems, construction companies, sugar and coffee plantations, and a meatpacking plant. See Rippy, *The Capitalists*, pp. 172–76.

6.   Diot, "Colombia económica 1923-1929," 169–71.

7.   H. López, pp. 71–72.

8.   Ospina Vásquez, p. 429. Statistics on coffee exports for this period can be found in H. López, p. 64; United Nations, pp. 378–83; and Diot, "Colombia económica," 215–16.

9. H. López, pp. 65–66.

10. See Rodríguez Salazar, p. 47; and A. López, *Problemas colombianos*, p. 75. Unfortunately, accurate statistical data on Colombian land values is as scarce for this period as for earlier times.

11. See Parsons, pp. 174–88; Rodríguez Salazar, pp. 49–61; Ospina Vásquez, pp. 463–99; Diot, "Colombia económica," 141–51; and Carlos Dávila Ladrón de Guevara, "Dominant Classes and Elites in Economic Development: A Comparative Study of Eight Urban Centers in Colombia," (Ph.D. diss., Northwestern University, 1976), pp. 100–106.

12. See Ospina Vásquez, pp. 432–60 for a detailed discussion of this development.

13. See Bernardo Tovar Zambrano, *La intervención económica del estado en Colombia, 1914–1936* (Bogotá, 1984), pp. 61–62. Between 1919 and 1929 annual government income expanded from 16 to 75 million pesos. Customs duties accounted for one third to one half of all government revenues during this period.

14. See, for example, Charles W. Anderson, *Politics and Economic Change in Latin America* (New York, 1967), pp. 42–45, 207–08; William Glade, *The Latin American Economies: A Study in Their Institutional Evolution* (New York, 1969), pp. 349–402; Joseph Love, *Rio Grande do Sul and Brazilian Regionalism, 1882–1930* (Stanford, 1971); and Werner Baer, Isaac Kerstenetzhy, and Annibal Villela, "The Changing Role of the State in the Brazilian Economy," *World Development* 1 (November 1973), 23–34.

15. *Memoria de Industrias*, 1934, p. 365. The inflation problem and its impact are discussed in A. López, *Problemas colombianos*, pp. 134–41; Guillermo Torres García, *Historia de la moneda en Colombia* (Bogotá, 1945), pp. 357–59; Rodríguez Salazar, pp. 43–44; H. López, pp. 84–92, 104; and Tovar Zambrano, *Intervención*, pp. 43–47.

16. See Bejarano, "Fin de la economía (II)," p. 402; and Kalmanowitz, *Desarrollo*, pp. 21–22.

17. See Rodríguez Salazar, pp. 44–45; Daniel Pécaut, *Política y sindicalismo en Colombia* (Bogotá, 1973), p. 83; and Bejarano, "Fin de la economía (II)," pp. 401–03.

18. See A. López, *Problemas colombianos*; Lozano T.; Alejandro López, *Idearium Liberal* (Paris, 1931); Carlos Uribe Echeverrí, *Nuestro problema: producir* (Madrid, 1936); and various reports in the *Memorias de Industrias*, 1925–1935.

19. Statement of Minister of Industries Francisco José Chaux in *Boletín de la Oficina General de Trabajo* 4 (July-September 1933), 1438. See also AC, "Proyectos de ley de 1926," vol. 8, folios 36–39; *Memoria de Industrias*, 1926, anexos, p. 257; *Memoria de Industrias*, 1928, p. 146; Colombia, Procurador General de la Nación, *Informe al Presidente de la República*, 1931, p. 8; and Antonio García, *Gaitán y el camino de la revolución colombiana*, 2nd ed. (Bogotá, 1974), pp. 201–08. Hereafter the annual reports of the attorney general to the president of Colombia will be cited as *Informe del Procurador General*, followed by the date.

20. *Memoria de Industrias*, 1930, p. 36. See also *Memoria de Industrias*, 1934,

p. 29; and Caldas, *Informe del Secretario de Gobierno*, 1932, p. 8. Darío Mesa discusses the evolution of this outlook in *El problema agrario en Colombia, 1920–1960* (Bogotá, 1972). Policy-makers in Chile and Peru in the 1920s similarly stressed the desirability of fostering the emergence of a rural middle class. See George M. McBride, *Chile: Land and Society* (New York, 1936); and Colin Harding, "Land Reform and Social Conflict in Peru," in *The Peruvian Experiment: Continuity and Change Under Military Rule*, ed. Abraham F. Lowenthal (Princeton, 1976), pp. 226–27.

21. *Boletín de la Oficina General de Trabajo* 4 (July-September 1933), 1431.

22. *Memoria de Industrias*, 1930, p. 35.

23. See *Memoria de Industrias*, 1931, vol. 3, pp. 336–39; and Law 47 of 1926 in Colombia, Congreso Nacional, *Leyes expedidas por el Congreso Nacional en su legislatura del año de 1926* (Bogotá, 1926), pp. 106–08.

24. See Instituto Colombiano de la Reforma Agraria, *La colonización*, vol. 2, pp. 391–400.

25. Reports on the penal colonies can be found in the departmental *Informes* of the 1920s, particularly those of Antioquia and Tolima. Authorized by Decrees 839, 1110, and 1321 of 1928, most of the agricultural colonies were not actually founded because of budgetary cutbacks stemming from the economic crisis of 1929.

26. *Memoria de Industrias*, 1930, anexos, p. 119. See also Antioquia, *Informe del Secretario de Hacienda*, 1928, p. 42; *Informe del Procurador General*, 1932, pp. 35–36; and *Memoria de Industrias*, 1934, p. 370.

27. See, for example, AC, "Leyes autógrafas de 1917," vol. 4, folio 80 and vol. 6, folio 148; *Memoria de Agricultura*, 1918, p. 103; and AC, "Proyectos de ley de 1924–25 (Cámara)," vol. 9, folio 132.

28. Sentencia de la Sala de Negocios Generales de la Corte Suprema, April 15, 1926 in Colombia, Corte Suprema, *Jurisprudencia*, vol. 3, p. 357.

29. *Informe del Procurador General*, 1931, p. 10.

30. See *Memoria de Industrias*, 1928, pp. 27–42.

31. See *Memoria de Industrias*, 1935, anexos, pp. 184–95 for a list of these lawsuits.

32. See *Memoria de Industrias*, 1928, p. 38–42.

33. See *Memoria de Industrias*, 1935, anexos, p. 272; and ibid., 1936, anexos, p. 90. For a list by municipality of the proprietor and size of each grant nullified from 1931 through 1935, see ibid., 1935, anexos, pp. 273–79.

34. See *Memoria de Industrias*, 1935, anexos, pp. 151–52, 221–28; Tolima, *Informe del Secretario de Hacienda*, 1936, anexos, pp. 124–25; and Santander, *Informe del Secretario de Hacienda*, 1936, pp. 125–29.

35. See Decree 992 of 1930 in *Memoria de Industrias*, 1933, anexos, pp. 416–19.

36. AC, "Proyectos de ley de 1926 (Cámara)," vol. 8, folio 39.

37. See, for example, Jeffrey M. Paige, *Agrarian Revolution: Social Movements and Export Agriculture in the Underdeveloped World* (New York, 1975), p. 44.

38. See Henry A. Landsberger, ed., *Latin American Peasant Movements* (Ith-

aca, 1969); Paul Friedrich, *Agrarian Revolt in a Mexican Village* (Englewood Cliffs, N.J., 1970); Gerit Huizer, *The Revolutionary Potential of Peasants in Latin America* (Lexington, Mass., 1972), pp. 88–95; James Petras and Hugo Zimelman Merino, *Peasants in Revolt: A Chilean Case Study, 1965–1971* (Austin, 1972), p. 23; Wasserstrom, "Revolution in Guatemala"; Heather Salamini, *Agrarian Radicalism in Veracruz, 1920–38* (Lincoln, Nebraska, 1978); and James V. Kohl, "Peasants and Revolution in Bolivia, April 9, 1952–August 2, 1953," *Hispanic American Historical Review* 58 (May 1978), 238–59.

    39.   See Figure 2, p.48. The increase in grants smaller than twenty-one hectares is, however, partly illusory. During the 1920s, the Colombian government received many complaints that large and medium cultivators were using Law 71 of 1917 to acquire free grants of public lands. Such people split their holdings into twenty hectare segments and asked relatives and friends to seek grants of the land under Law 71. Once the grants were received, the original holdings were reconstituted through fictitious documents of sale. (See *Memoria de Industrias*, 1926, anexos, p. 191; and ANCB v. 44 f. 403, v. 46 f. 320, v. 47 f. 339, v. 50 f. 455, v. 67 f. 429, v. 68 f. 267, and v. 71 f. 189.) The list of grants published by the Ministry of Industries (1931, vol. 5, pp. 249–410) lends credence to these complaints. Not only did extended families collaborate in piecing together large grants, but some individuals obtained two or more grants of less than twenty-one hectares each, often in different areas of the same municipality. Thus, although the government awarded 2,503 grants of one to twenty hectares between 1918 and 1931, the number of individuals who obtained such grants was only 1,935. It should be noted that large entrepreneurs, middle-sized farmers, and peasants in Colombia all tended to acquire scattered properties. For discussions of dispersed landownership in coffee areas, see Jaime Arocha, *La Violencia en el Quindío* (Bogotá, 1979), pp. 56–57; and María Errazuriz, "'Cafeteros' et 'cafetales' de Líbano (Colombie): innovation technique et encadrement rural," (Thèse de IIIeme cycle de géografie, Université de Toulouse Le Mirail, l983), pp. 287–97. Such patterns are almost impossible to pick up in the Colombian agricultural censuses published since 1950, which enumerate productive units and shed little light on the concentration of landownership.

    40.   See A. López, *Problemas colombianos*, p. 133, and *Idearium Liberal*, pp. 38–42. The rural origins of many of the construction workers were underlined in a progress report from the Cauca railroad: "At present work has slowed down owing to a shortage of laborers, for many peons have left temporarily to harvest their crops at home." Antioquia, *Mensaje del Gobernador*, 1926, pp. 33–34.

    41.   H. López, 73–75. On rural-urban migration in this period, see also Pécaut, *Política y sindicalismo*, pp. 81–83.

    42.   On the issue of rural labor scarcity, see A. López, *Problemas colombianos*, pp. 132–41; Zambrano et al., Chapter 3; Rodríguez Salazar, pp. 45–46; H. López, 102–03; and Kalmanowitz, *Desarrollo*, pp. 19–21. See also Cundinamarca, *Informes de las oficinas dependientes de la Secretaría de Gobierno*, 1929, pp. 300, 347.

    43.   See H. López, 98, 101; Bejarano, "Fin de la economía (II)," 407–08; and

Kalmanowitz, *Desarrollo*, pp. 19–20. During the 1920s the exchange rate stood at approximately one peso to the U.S. dollar.

44. See Gonzalo Sánchez G., *Las ligas campesinas en Colombia* (Bogotá, 1977), pp. 29–60; *Memoria de Industrias*, 1928, pp. 144–47; ibid., l929, p. 167; ibid., 1930, anexos, pp. 372–75; and ibid., 1934, pp. 284–324.

45. Studies of Colombian labor organization in the 1920s and 1930s include Robert J. Alexander, *Communism in Latin America* (New Brunswick, N.J., 1957), pp. 243–53; Miguel Urrutia Montoya, *Development of the Colombian Labor Movement* (New Haven, 1969); Edgar Caicedo, *Historia de las luchas sindicales en Colombia* (Bogotá, 1971); Ignacio Torres Giraldo, *María Cano: mujer rebelde* (Bogotá, 1972); Pécaut, *Política y sindicalismo;* Ignacio Torres Giraldo, *Los inconformes: historia de la rebeldía de las masas en Colombia*, vols. 3 and 4 (Bogotá, 1974); Partido Comunista de Colombia, *Treinta años de lucha del Partido Comunista de Colombia* (Bogotá, n.d.); Medófilo Medina, *Historia del Partido Comunista de Colombia*, vol. 1 (Bogotá, 1980); and Mauricio Archila, "Los movimientos sociales entre 1920–1924: una aproximación metodológica," *Cuadernos de Filosofía y Letras* 3:3 (July–September 1980), 181–230. Gerardo Molina, *Las ideas liberales en Colombia, 1915–1934* (Bogotá, 1974) deals with the relations between labor groups and the Liberal party.

46. See Gabriel García Márquez, *One Hundred Years of Solitude*, trans. Gregory Rabassa (New York, 1971). More information on the banana strike is to be found in *Memoria de Industrias*, 1929, pp. 171–208; Alberto Castrillón R., *120 dias bajo el terror militar* (Bogotá, 1974); Judith White, *Historia de una ignominia: La United Fruit Co. en Colombia* (Bogotá, 1978); Carlos Cortés Vargas, *Los sucesos de las bananeras*, 2nd ed. (Bogotá, 1979); and Jorge Eliécer Gaitán, *1928: la masacre en las bananeras (documentos y testimonios)* (Medellín, n.d.).

47. Nicolás Buenaventura, "Movimiento obrero: líder agrario," *Estudios Marxistas* 2 (1969), 35.

48. The works of Ignacio Torres Giraldo are particularly informative concerning these activities.

49. See Torres Giraldo, *Los inconformes*, vol. 4, pp. 6, 8, 50, 56, 60, 72, 77, 150–51.

50. For a fascinating account of the rebellion in Tolima, see Sánchez G., *Los 'Bolsheviques.'*

51. *Boletín de la Oficina General de Trabajo* 4 (July–September 1933), 1423.

52. See *Memoria de Industrias*, 1930, anexos, p. 367; and Pécaut, pp. 122–23.

53. See Caldas, *Informe del Secretario de Gobierno*, 1929, p. 26; Caldas, *Mensaje del Gobernador*, 1930, pp. 5–6; Valle del Cauca, *Mensaje del Gobernador*, 1930, p. 19; Valle del Cauca, *Informe del Secretario de Gobierno*, 1931, p.4; and Partido Comunista de Colombia, *Treinta años*, pp. 24–25.

54. See *Memoria de Industrias*, 1933, p. 49; and ibid., 1934, p. 56.

55. See *Memoria de Industrias*, 1932, anexos, pp. 278–82, 296–304; ibid.,

238   Notes

1934, pp. 29, 130, 283; ibid., 1935, anexos, p. 266; and ibid., 1936, anexos, pp. 199, 222, 231.

56. *Memoria de Industrias*, 1930, p. 41.

57. Ibid., anexos, pp. 367–71.

58. See ibid., anexos, p. 371; and Cundinamarca, *Informe del Secretario de Gobierno*, 1930, p. 6.

59. *Memoria de Industrias*, 1934, p. 365.

60. See Boyacá, *Informe del Secretario de Gobierno*, 1929, p.98; Valle del Cauca, *Mensaje del Gobernador*, 1930, pp. 10–12; Marco Palacios, *El café en Colombia, 1850–1970*, 2nd ed. (Bogotá, 1983), pp. 353–72; and Jiménez, "Red Viotá." The impact of the depression on the Colombian countryside has received little attention. As Palacios and Jiménez show for Cundinamarca, analysis of the economic effects of the depression on large landowners in various regions would add much to our understanding of rural conflict in those years.

61. This point is stressed by Antonio García in *Caldas*, p. 237. See also Santander, *Informe del Secretario de Hacienda*, 1932, p. 150; *Memoria de Industrias*, 1932, anexos, p. 279; ibid., 1938, vol. 1, p. 21; and García, *Gaitán*, p. 238.

62. See, for example, Henry Landsberger, "Peasant Unrest: Themes and Variations," in *Rural Protest: Peasant Movements and Social Change* (New York, 1973), pp. 1–66.

63. See Anibal Quijano Obregón, "Contemporary Peasant Movements," in *Elites in Latin America*, ed. Seymour Martin Lipset and Aldo Solari (New York, 1967), pp. 301–42; John Duncan Powell, "Venezuela: The Peasant Union Movement," in *Latin American Peasant Movements*, ed. Henry A. Landsberger (Ithaca, 1969), pp. 62–100; and Kenneth Evan Sharpe, *Peasant Politics: Struggle in a Dominican Village* (Baltimore, 1977).

Chapter 6: The Peasants Take the Initiative

1. On these conflicts, see Hirschman, pp. 101–06; Urrutia Montoya, pp. 129–36; Pierre Gilhodes, "Agrarian Struggles in Colombia," in *Agrarian Problems and Peasant Movements in Latin America*, ed. Rodolfo Stavenhagen (Garden City, N.Y., 1970), pp. 407–52; Castrillón Arboleda; Quintín Lamé; Tovar Pinzón, *El movimiento campesino*, pp. 35–88; Gaitán de Valencia, *Colombia: la lucha*; Elias Sevilla Casas, "Lamé y el Cauca indígena," in *Tierra, tradición y poder en Colombia: enfoques antropológicos*, ed. N.S. Friedemann (Bogotá, 1976), pp. 85–106; Sánchez G., *Las ligas*; Bejarano, *El régimen agrario*, pp. 260–308; Bergquist, "Colombia"; and Jiménez, "Red Viota".

2. See Cundinamarca, *Informe del Secretario de Gobierno*, 1934, pp. 4, 28, 31; ibid., 1935, p. 41; *Boletín de la Oficina General de Trabajo* 4 (October-December 1933), 1700–01; and "1930–1933 Chaparral Tolima: luchas de los proletarios del

campo. Entrevista con un viejo campesino de Chaparral. Enero de 1969," *Estudios Marxistas* l (1969), 98–99.

3.   See Archivo Nacional de Colombia, Ministerio de Industrias, Copiador de Oficios, v. 210 fs. 330–32; and "Entrevista con un viejo campesino," 99. At times tenants who had assumed colono status encouraged wage laborers on the same haciendas to occupy additional land. On the Hacienda El Chocho in Fusugasugá (Cundinamarca), arrendatarios who had declared themselves colonos fostered an invasion of the unused mountain area of the property by the day workers *(voluntarios)* they employed so as to widen opposition to the landlords. See Cundinamarca, *Informe del Secretario de Gobierno*, 1934, pp. 32–33.

4.   *Memoria de Industrias*, 1933, vol. 1, p. 415. In this and subsequent chapters, the term "squatter" is used to refer to people who, calling themselves colonos, purposefully settled unused land within the borders of haciendas they knew were claimed as private property, but which they had reason to believe had been illegally usurped from the public domain.

5.   Unfortunately, petitions concerning the new land conflicts of the 1930s were not deposited in the Public Land Correspondence. The most informative sources on the rural conflicts of these years are the reports of departmental officials, a collection of which is located in the library of the Ministry of Government in Bogotá.

6.   Cundinamarca, *Informe del Secretario de Gobierno*, 1937, p. 48. The province of Sumapaz included the municipalities of Pandi, San Bernardo, Arbalaez, Pasca, Fusugasugá, Iconozco, and Cunday. In recent years the municipalities of Ospina Pérez and Cabrera have been carved from the territory of Pandi and the municipality of Villarica from the territory of Cunday.

7.   The following description of Sumapaz is drawn from Colombia, Departamento de Cundinamarca, *Visita del gobernador del departamento de Cundinamarca a las provincias de Sumapaz, Girardot y Tequendama* (Facatativá, 1906); Rivas; Diego Monsalve, *Colombia cafetera: información general de la república y estadísticas de la industria* (Barcelona, 1927); *Boletín de la Oficina General de Trabajo* 4 (July–September 1933), 1546–47; *Claridad* November 19, 1934; Caputo; Villegas, *Colonización de vertiente*; Velandia; and Carlos Enrique Pardo, "Cundinamarca: hacienda cafetera y conflictos agrarios" (Tesis de grado, Universidad de los Andes, 1981).

8.   See ANCB v. 36 f. 352, v. 47 fs. 413 and 416, v. 48 f. 536, v. 63 f. 367, v. 64 f. 156, v. 65 f. 404, v. 67 f. 105, v. 68 f. 456, and v. 77 f. 385; and Cundinamarca, *Informe del Secretario de Gobierno*, 1928, anexos, pp. 216–50.

9.   See Pardo, pp. 93–101.

10.   See Decree 1100 of 1928 in *Memoria de Industrias*, 1932, p. 120.

11.   On the repercussions of Decree 1100 in the Sumapaz area, see especially *Memoria de Industrias*, 1932, pp. 120–235; ibid., 1934, p. 337; Tolima, *Informe del Secretario de Gobierno*, 1932, pp. 28–35; and AHOH, box 2 folder 37, fs. 80–85, 116, 129, 229. The affected estates, many of which were devoted in part to coffee, included the Hacienda de Doa, Hacienda Guatimbol, Hacienda Castilla, and Ha-

cienda San Francisco, as well as several properties belonging to the Companía Cafetera de Cunday.

12.   The owners of this estate were the Sons of Juan Francisco Pardo Roche. For tenancy obligations on the Hacienda de Sumapaz and events leading to the tenant rebellion, see AHOH, box 3 folder 21, f. 4; and *Boletín de la Oficina General de Trabajo* 4 (October–December 1933), 1663–64.

13.   On the occupation of these haciendas and that of Sumapaz, see *Boletín de la Oficina General de Trabajo* 4 (October-December 1933), 1532–36, 1635–41, 1663–73; Cundinamarca, *Informe del Secretario de Gobierno*, 1931, pp. 31–33; ANCB v. 75 fs. 274 and 275; and AHOH, box 2 folder 37, fs. 33–39, and box 3, folder 21, "Informe presentado por el Jefe de la Sección de Justicia a los Sres. Gobernador y Secretario de Gobierno de Cundinamarca alrededor del problema agrario existente en la Hacienda de Sumapaz," October 1931.

14.   See *Memoria de Industrias*, 1933, pp. 146–47; AHOH, box 2, folder 37, fs. 33–39; *Informe del Procurador General*, 1932, p. 41, AC, "Informes, memoriales, telegramas (Cámara)," 1932, vol. 7, fs. 35–71 ("Informe de la comisión que investigó los sucesos sangrientos de 'Paquiló,' municipios de Pandi y San Bernardo, y estudió el problema de los colonos de Sumapaz"); and *Claridad* June 5, 1933, December 31, 1933, and November 19, 1936.

15.   See *Boletín de la Oficina General de Trabajo* 4 (October–December 1933), 1523–32, 1538–47, 1641–62; and *Memoria de Industrias*, 1933, pp. 434–40. The Leiva titles also were found deficient.

16.   AHOH, box 3, folder 21, "Informe presentado por el Jefe de la Sección de Justicia," and box 2, folder 37, f. 85.

17.   The province of Sinú in 1930 covered approximately the same area as the contemporary department of Córdoba. Information on the historical development of this region may be found in Antolín Díaz, *Sinú: pasión y vida del trópico* (Bogotá, 1935); Eugene Havens, Eduardo Montero, and Michel Romieux, *Cereté: un area de latifundio (estudio económico y social)* (Bogotá, 1965); Bossa Herazo; Theodore Nichols, *Tres puertos de Colombia* (Bogotá, 1973); de Rodríguez; Fals Borda, *Capitalismo*; Fals Borda, "El 'secreto'"; Bottía G. and Escobedo D.; and Negrete.

18.   See ANCB v. 46 f. 427, v. 55 f. 479, v. 64 f. 83, and v. 65 f. 458; Bolívar, *Informe del Secretario de Gobierno*, 1932, p. 273; and ibid., 1933, p. 36.

19.   See *Boletín de la Oficina General de Trabajo* 1 (September 1930), 550–54; and Bolívar, *Informe del Secretario de Gobierno*, 1932, pp. 3–5 for excellent descriptions of the living conditions of peasant cultivators in Bolívar.

20.   See Antioquia, *Informe del Secretario de Gobierno*, 1933, pp. 106–07.

21.   On Lomagrande and the role of Vicente Adamo, see Bolívar, *Informe del Secretario de Gobierno*, 1932, pp. 6–7; Asociación Nacional de Usuarios Campesinos de Córdoba, *Lomagrande—el baluarte del Sinú* (Montería, 1972); and Negrete. In collaboration with Adamo, the market women of Montería played an important role in organizing workers and peasants. Juana Julia Guzmán, a small store owner of peasant origins, became the second most important organizer in the region. In

1919 she founded the *Sociedad de Obreras Redención de la Mujer* with a membership of street venders, market women, domestic servants, and washerwomen who, among other activities, supported the colonos in their land reclamations (See Negrete, pp. 59–61). Orlando Fals Borda describes later offshoots of the agrarian movement in Sinú in "Sentido político del movimiento campesino en Colombia," *Estudios Rurales Latinoamericanos* 1 (May–August 1978), 169–76.

22. Bolívar, *Informe del Secretario de Gobierno*, 1927, anexos, pp. 30–31.

23. See Bolívar, *Informe del Secretario de Gobierno*, 1932, pp. 7–10.

24. Bolívar, *Informe del Secretario de Gobierno*, 1932, pp. 264, 272–73.

25. See ibid., pp. 325–26; AHOH, box 3, folder 20, f. 19; and ANCB v. 14 f. 373, v. 46 f. 236, v. 47 fs. 379 and 387, v. 49 f. 92, v. 63 f. 233, v. 70 f. 236, v. 75 f. 197, and v. 77 f. 280. Land occupations also occurred in Tinajones, Sicará, Lorica, Alto Sinú, and San Jorge in the department of Bolívar *(Lomagrande*, p. 18). Agrarian problems surfaced too in the municipality of San Onofre at this time. See AHOH, box 3, folder 20, f. 15.

26. The history of the United Fruit Company in Colombia is recounted in Pierre Gilhodes, "La Colombie et l'United Fruit Company," *Revue Française de Science Politique* 18 (April 1967), 307–17; Botero and Guzmán Barney; and White.

27. ANCB v. 54 f. 255. See also LeGrand, "From Public Lands," pp. 145–50.

28. For the history of colonos and colono movements in the banana zone, see Catherine LeGrand, "Colombian Transformations: Peasants and Wage Labourers in the Santa Marta Banana Zone," *Journal of Peasant Studies* 11: 4 (July 1984), 178–200.

29. For descriptions of these conflicts, see ANCB v. 21 f. 381, v. 46 f. 425, v. 47 fs. 81 and 85, v. 48 fs. 530 and 538, v. 49 f. 219, v. 50 fs. 324, 351, 354, 505 and 513, v. 54 fs. 485 and 509, v. 55 fs. 185, 453 and 544, v. 58 f. 342, v. 63 f. 368, v. 64 fs. 145, 560 and 582, v. 65 fs. 361 and 380, v. 68 f. 430, v. 69 fs. 334 and 365, v. 70 fs. 48, 51 and 53, v. 72 f. 278, v. 73 fs. 213 and 215, and v. 75 f. 371.

30. ANCB v. 60 f. 168.

31. See Colombia, Congreso Nacional, *Informes que rindió a la honorable Cámara de Representantes la comisión designada para visitar la zona bananera del Magdalena* (Bogotá, 1935).

32. ANCB v. 72 f. 293.

33. On the development of the Quindío frontier in the late nineteenth and early twentieth centuries, see Christie, "Oligarchy and Society," pp. 37–59; Sánchez Reyes; and Ortiz, "Fundadores y negociantes".

34. AHOH, box 3, folder 30, f. 6.

35. These estates included the Haciendas of Nápoles, El Orinoco, San Pablo, San José, La Quinta, Playa Azul, La Española, El Jazmín, La Judea, La Argentina, Palonegro, and El Jordán. See Caldas, *Informe del Secretario de Gobierno*, 1932, p. 65; and Christie, "Oligarchy and Society," p. 189.

36. For information on the squatter movement in Quindío, see Caldas, *In-*

forme del Secretario de Gobierno, 1932, pp. 7–8, 65–84, and anexos, p. 43; ibid., 1935, pp. 50–51; ibid., 1936, pp. 31–32; ibid., 1937, pp. 19–25; Caldas, *Mensaje del Gobernador,* 1932, pp. 17–19; García, *Caldas,* pp. 237–42; and Christie, "Oligarchy and Society," pp. 189–96.

37. On the economic history of Valle, see Crist; Michael T. Taussig, "Rural Proletarianization: A Social and Historical Enquiry into the Commercialization of the Southern Cauca Valley, Colombia," 2 vols. (Ph.D. diss., U. of London, 1974); Nina S. Friedemann, "Negros: monopolio de tierra, agricultores, y desarrollo de plantaciones de caña de azúcar en el Valle del Río Cauca," in *Tierra, tradición, y poder en Colombia,* ed. N.S. Friedemann (Bogotá, 1976), pp. 143–68; and Hyland, "Secularization".

38. See AC, "Leyes autógrafas de 1917," vol. 4, folios 74–80; and ANCB v. 37 f. 621, v. 43 fs. 95, 99 and 416, v. 49 fs. 205 and 222, v. 50 f. 139, v. 55 fs. 9, 53, 444 and 471, v. 58 f. 158, v. 63 fs. 143, 156 and 369, v. 64 fs. 51, 510, 549, 553, 555, 558, 559 and 578, v. 65 fs. 41, 280, 344, 428, 432 and 469, v. 68 fs. 243, 393, 396 and 453, v. 69 fs. 205A, 12 and 16, v. 70 f. 14, v. 71 fs. 317 and 323, v. 72 f. 216, and v. 75 f. 315; and *La Humanidad* [Cali] 1:20 September 26, 1925.

39. Valle del Cauca, *Mensaje del Gobernador,* 1932, pp. 14–17. For the impact of the depression on Valle, see ibid., 1931, pp. 8–12; ibid., 1933, p. 11; and Valle del Cauca, *Informe del Secretario de Gobierno,* 1931, pp. 2–3.

40. See Valle del Cauca, *Informe del Secretario de Gobierno,* 1930, pp. 6–7, 51; ibid., 1932, p. 4; and Valle del Cauca, *Mensaje del Gobernador,* 1930, pp. 14–16. Also, ANCB v. 71 f. 272. In the municipalities of El Zarzal, Sevilla, and Caicedonia, the squatters' initiative was precipitated by a ministerial resolution that withdrew government recognition from the titles of the "Terrenos de Burila." The last of several enormous colonial grants located within the area of Antioqueño colonization, the Burila territory, covering 125,000 hectares, had been opened for real estate development by a Manizales-based land company late in the nineteenth century. The attempts of the more than 20,000 colonos in the area to obtain legal grants of their parcels had been blocked for two decades by the state's support for the company's titles. Interpreted as a triumph by the settlers, the shift in official policy in 1930 triggered the occupation by squatters of several haciendas that had been purchased from the Burila Company in previous years. See *Memoria de Industrias,* 1930, pp. 163–77; ANCB v. 71 f. 357; and Christie, "Oligarchy and Society," pp. 50–59.

41. See ANCB v. 10 fs. 77 and 94, v. 24 f. 336, v. 25 f. 387, v. 26 f. 338, v. 27 fs. 60 and 250, v. 38 f. 352, v. 39 f. 379, v. 46 f. 437, v. 48 f. 104, v. 49 f. 208, v. 54 fs. 335, 391 and 392, v. 57 f. 316, v. 58 fs. 591, 594 and 597, v. 68 f. 277, v. 69 f. 44, v. 71 f. 265, and v. 74 f. 266.

42. See *Informe del Procurador General,* 1931, p. 8; and Huila, *Informe del Secretario de Gobierno,* 1934, p. 81.

43. Huila, *Mensaje del Gobernador,* 1936, p. 5.

44.   ANCB v. 62 f. 162.

45.   See Santander, *Informe del Secretario de Hacienda*, 1932, p. 150; and Santander, *Informe del Secretario de Gobierno*, 1936, pp. 20–29.

46.   Santander, *Informe del Secretario de Gobierno*, 1936, p. 15.

47.   Similar conflicts occurred in scattered municipalities in other regions too, including San Eduardo (Boyacá), Chaparral and Ibagué (Tolima), Plato (Magdalena), and Nare (Antioquia). See AC, "Memoriales, oficios, notas (Cámara)," 1932, vol. 5 folio 217; *Claridad* October 30, 1935; Tolima, *Mensaje del Gobernador*, 1935, p. 28; Antioquia, *Informe del Secretario de Gobierno*, 1935, anexos, p. 44; ANCB v. 74 f. 361; "Entrevista con un viejo campesino"; and Darío Fajardo, "La Violencia y las estructuras agrarias en tres municipios cafeteras del Tolima: 1936–1970," in *El agro en el desarrollo histórico colombiano* (Bogotá, 1977), pp. 283–93.

48.   Hobsbawm, "Peasant Land Occupations," 124. Eric Hobsbawm uses this phrase with reference to the somewhat different Indian land occupations of highland Peru.

49.   *Boletín de la Oficina General de Trabajo* 4 (July–September 1933), 1333.

50.   *Memoria de Industrias*, 1931, vol. 1, p. 53. See also Tolima, *Informe del Secretario de Gobierno*, 1932, pp. 31–34; Cundinamarca, *Mensaje del Gobernador*, 1933, p. 10; and *Memoria de Industrias*, 1934, p. 337.

51.   See AC, "Memorias (Cámara)," 1930–33, vol. 6 folio 437; and *Memoria de Industrias*, 1933, vol. 1, p. 62.

52.   See *Memoria de Industrias*, 1932, pp. 127–29; *Boletín de la Oficina General de Trabajo* 4 (October-December 1933), 1665; Cundinamarca, *Informe del Secretario de Gobierno*, 1934, pp. 21–32; and ibid., 1937, p. 59.

53.   *Memoria de Industrias*, 1932, pp. 127–29.

54.   See *Memoria de Industrias*, 1933, p. 420; *Boletín de la Oficina General de Trabajo* 4 (October-December 1933), 1535–36, 1633, 1636, 1639, 1667, 1669; Cundinamarca, *Informe del Secretario de Gobierno*, 1934, pp. 21–23; Valle del Cauca, *Informe del Secretario de Gobierno*, 1932, p. 5; and AC, "Informes, memoriales, telegramas (Cámara)," 1932, vol. 7 folios 38, 55, 64. Only under unusual circumstances did local officials take the colonos' side. One such occasion occurred in Sumapaz in the early 1930s in connection with a boundary dispute between the municipalities of Pandi and San Bernardo. When squatters invaded territory claimed by hacendado Jénaro Torres Otero in the region of Paquiló, the authorities of San Bernardo backed Torres Otero. The mayor of Pandi, however, promised to hand the land over to the squatters, seeking in this way to win popular support for annexation of the region to his municipality. On this incident, see Cundinamarca, *Informe del Secretario de Gobierno*, 1933, p. 5; and AC, "Informes, memoriales, telegramas (Cámara)," 1932, vol. 7 folios 42–52.

55.   See Cundinamarca, *Informe del Abogado del departamento al Sr. Gobernador*, 1933, pp. 6–8; AHOH, box 3, folder 20, f. 6; AC, "Informes, memoriales, telegramas (Cámara)," 1932, vol. 7 fs. 36–37, 41; Bolívar, *Informe del Secretario de Gobierno*, 1932, p. 6; Caldas, *Mensaje del Gobernador*, 1932, p. 17; Cundina-

marca, *Mensaje del Gobernador*, 1933, p. 11; Cundinamarca, *Informe del Secretario de Gobierno*, 1934, pp. 32–33; and Valle del Cauca, *Informe del Secretario de Gobierno*, 1931, pp. 71–72.

56.   Cundinamarca, *Informe del Secretario de Gobierno*, 1932, p. 9; ibid., 1937, pp. 221–42; *Claridad* October 10, 1932; and AC, "Informes, memoriales, telegramas (Cámara)," 1932, vol. 7, fs. 40–41, 62, 69.

57.   Valle del Cauca, *Mensaje del Gobernador*, 1930, p. 19; ibid., 1933, pp. 11–13; ibid., 1935, p. 12; and Valle del Cauca, Informe del Secretario de Gobierno, 1934, p. 19.

58.   On these extralegal tactics, see AC, "Informes, memoriales, telegramas (Cámara)," 1932, vol. 7 fs. 35–39; *Boletín de la Oficina General de Trabajo* 4 (October–December 1933), 1636–37, 1665–72, 1679–88; ANCB v. 60 f. 169; *Unirismo* January 31, 1935 and March 28, 1935; *Claridad*, 1933–37, most issues; Tovar Pinzón, *El movimiento campesino*, pp. 63–88; and Gaitán de Valencia, *Colombia: la lucha*, pp. 39–46.

59.   AHOH, box 3 folder 21, "Informe presentado por el Jefe de la Sección de Justicia," fs. 4–8; AC, "Informes, memoriales, telegramas (Cámara)," 1932, vol. 7 fs. 38–40; Tolima, *Informe del Secretario de Gobierno*, 1932, p. 33; and *Boletín de la Oficina General de Trabajo* 4 (October–December 1933), 1635–37, 1665–71. On violent confrontations in the Sumapaz region, see *Claridad* October 10, 1932, June 5, 1933, October 31, 1934, November 19, 1934, and August 12, 1935; and *Unirismo* April 25, 1935.

60.   *Boletín de la Oficina General de Trabajo* 4 (July–September 1933), 1417–18.

61.   On this type of colono leader, see Bolívar, *Informe del Secretario de Gobierno*, 1931, anexos, p. 79; ibid., 1932, p. 326; *Boletín de la Oficina General de Trabajo* 4 (July–September 1933), 1416; Cundinamarca, *Mensaje del Gobernador*, 1933, p. 4; AHOH, box 6 folder 12, petition from Comité de Cafeteros de Cundinamarca to President Olaya Herrera, 1/1/1934; Cundinamarca, *Informe del Secretario de Gobierno*, 1936, pp. 18–20; and ibid., 1937, p. 101. The kind of profits to be made by supporting colonos is illustrated by the following examples. In Santander, the colonos of "La Peña" were represented by tinterillos who demanded as payment one-half of the land obtained in grants from the government. These lawyers also employed a hired killer to take control of valuable forests within the hacienda, an objective facilitated by the colono occupation that they had encouraged. Meanwhile in Cunday (Tolima) Antonio José Pantoja, a lawyer who uncovered grave irregularities in the titles of the Leiva family properties, prompted tenant farmers there to disavow their contracts. Once the arrendatarios had assumed colono status, Pantoja charged them elevated fees to write their petitions and monopolized the marketing of their crops. At the same time, he entered into covert negotiations with the Leiva family, intending to purchase the occupied land cheaply and resell it to the squatters for a profit. See *Memoria de Industrias*, 1935, p. 184; Santander, *Informe del Secretario de Gobierno*, 1936, pp. 22, 29–30; AHOH, box 2, folder 37, fs. 33–39; Archivo Nacional de Colombia, Ministerio de Industrias, Copiador de ofi-

cios, fs. 1, 220 and 280; and Victor J. Merchán, "Datos para la historia social, económica y del movimiento agrario de Viotá y el Tequendama: testimonio," *Estudios Marxistas* 9 (1975), 106.

62. Studies of the emergence of the laboring people into political life in Latin America and the attendant growth of populist political movements between 1920 and 1940 include Torcuato Di Tella, "Populism and Reform in Latin America," in *Obstacles to Change in Latin America*, ed. Claudio Véliz (London, 1965), pp. 47–74; Francisco Weffort, "El populismo en la política brasileña," in *Brazil: hoy*, by Celso Furtado et al. (Mexico City, 1970), pp. 54–84; A. E. Van Nierkerk, *Populism and Political Development in Latin America* (Rotterdam, 1974); Paul Drake, *Socialism and Populism in Chile, 1932–52* (Urbana, Ill., 1978); Steve Stein, *Populism in Peru* (Madison, 1980); and Michael Conniff, ed., *Latin American Populism in Comparative Perspective* (Albuquerque, 1982).

63. On Gaitán and the Revolutionary Leftist National Union, see F. López Giraldo, *El apostol desnudo: o dos años al lado de un mito* (Manizales, 1936); J.A. Osorio Lizarazo, *Gaitán: vida, muerte y permanente presencia* (Buenos Aires, 1952); Jorge Eliécer Gaitán, *Los mejores discursos de Jorge Eliécer Gaitán, 1919–1948* (Bogotá, 1958); García, *Gaitán;* Sánchez G., *Las ligas*, pp. 78–85; Richard E. Sharpless, *Gaitán of Colombia: A Political Biography* (Pittsburgh, 1978); David Moreno and Elsy Marulanda, "La UNIR: primera táctica del Gaitanismo," Paper presented to the I Seminario Nacional Sobre Movimientos Sociales: "Gaitanismo y 9 de Abril", Departamento de Historia, Universidad Nacional and Centro Jorge Eliécer Gaitán, Bogotá, April 15–17, 1982; and Herbert Braun, "The 'Pueblo' and the Politicians of Colombia: The Assassination of Jorge Eliécer Gaitán and the 'Bogotazo' (Ph.D. diss., U. of Wisconsin-Madison, 1983).

64. *Unirismo* April 13, 1935, and June 6, 1935.

65. See Cundinamarca, *Informe del Abogado del departamento*, 1933, p. 4; Cundinamarca, *Informe del Secretario de Gobierno*, 1936, p. 27; *Claridad* July 21, 1933, December 26, 1933, February 5, 1934, May 6, 1935, and September 11, 1935; *Unirismo* February 14, 1935, February 28, 1935, and March 14, 1935; and Caputo, pp. 7, 20.

66. Partido Comunista de Colombia, *Treinta años*, p. 22.

67. On Communist party efforts in rural areas in the 1930s, see Tolima, *Informe del Secretario de Gobierno*, 1932, pp. 42–44; Buenaventura, pp. 6–58; Partido Comunista de Colombia, *Treinta años*, pp. 22–31; Merchán, 105–17; Sánchez G., *Las ligas*, pp. 86–93; Medina, pp. 169–230, 322–25; Pardo; and Jiménez, "Red Viota." Indicative of its rural orientation at this time, the Communist party nominated a full-blooded Indian, Eutiguio Timoté, for president of Colombia in the national elections of 1934. One year later the party complained to the International that its members were mostly peasants and Indians, not urban workers. See Urrutia Montoya, p. 124; and Eric Hobsbawm, "Peasant Movements in Colombia," *International Journal of Economic and Social History* 8 (1976), 183.

68. *El Bolshevique* August 4, 1934, October 20, 1934, and December 8, 1934; and Merchán, 114–15.

69. See *El Bolshevique* December 8, 1934; *Tierra* June 24, 1938; and Fajardo, "La Violencia," pp. 283–84. On the tactic of *autodefensa* espoused by the Communist party at this time, see Merchán, 110–11.

70. *El Bolshevique*, a collection of which is located in the National Library in Bogotá, began publishing around 1934. Subscription lists printed in the paper provide some indication of the breadth of circulation. *El Bolshevique* was superseded by *Tierra* in 1936 and by *Diario Popular* in 1942.

71. Torres Giraldo, *Los inconformes*, vol. 4, p. 11.

72. Numerous issues of *Claridad* for the years 1930–1937 can be found in the newspaper collection of the National Library in Bogotá. On its impact, see AHOH, box 2, folder 37, f. 82.

73. *Claridad* May 10, 1935, and October 5, 1935.

74. See *Claridad* June 17, 1935, October 30, 1935, and March 3, 1936; and Sánchez G., *Las ligas*, pp. 94–98.

75. See Terrence B. Horgan, "The Liberals Come to Power in Colombia 'Por Debajo de la Ruana': A Study of the Enrique Olaya Herrera Administration, 1930–1934" (Ph.D. diss., Vanderbilt University, 1983).

76. Cundinamarca, *Informe del Secretario de Gobierno*, 1937, p. 68. See also ibid., 1936, pp. 18–20; and AHOH, box 2 folder 37, fs. 71–79, 116.

77. Urrutia Montoya, pp. 118–19.

78. See *Memoria de Industrias*, 1933, vol. 2, p. 187; ibid., 1934, pp. 316, 324–26; *Nueva Era* [Cali] May 4, 1935; Sánchez G., *Las ligas*, pp. 63–77; and Michael Jiménez, "Social Crisis and Agrarian Politics in Colombia, 1930–1936 (The Making of Law 200 of 1936)" (M.A. thesis, Stanford University, 1971), pp. 69, 73. Distinguished by their affiliation with the Casas Liberales, leftist Liberals at this time expressed their desire to emulate the Mexican government in integrating peasants into the ruling party through officially sponsored unions. Published throughout the 1930s, the journal *Acción Liberal* provides a clear picture of the reformist orientation of the Liberal left in Colombia during this period.

79. On the cooperativist movement, see *Memoria de Industrias*, 1933, vol. 2, pp. 203–46; ibid., 1934, pp. 35, 267; ibid., 1938, vol. 1, p. 204; and vol. 3 pp. 239–314.

80. See Tolima, *Informe del Secretario de Gobierno*, 1932, p. 37; ANCB v. 60 f. 201; and AHOH, box 3, folder 21, f. 6.

81. See AHOH, box 3, folder 21, fs. 6, 11, and box 2, folder 37, fs. 82, 86; Cundinamarca, *Informe del Secretario de Gobierno*, 1931, p. 33; ibid., 1937, p. 109; Tolima, *Informe del Secretario de Gobierno*, 1932, p. 37; Caldas, *Informe del Secretario de Gobierno*, 1932, pp. 79, 82; ibid., 1936, p. 31; ibid., 1937, pp. 20–24; and Valle del Cauca, *Informe del Secretario de Gobierno*, 1932, p. 5.

82. AHOH, box 2, folder 37, f. 105. See also *Claridad* May 1, 1932; *Boletín de la Oficina General de Trabajo* 4 (October-December 1933), 1640, 1693; Tolima,

Informe del Secretario de Gobierno, 1933, pp. 5-6; ANCB v. 60 f. 201; and AHOH, box 3, folder 21, fs. 10–11.

83.   *Informe del Procurador General,* 1932, p. 34.

84.   See *Memoria de Industrias,* 1929, pp. 180–82; Gaitán de Valencia, *Colombia: la lucha,* pp. 63–77; Sánchez G., *Las ligas,* pp. 61–64; and Fals Borda, *La resistencia,* pp. 177b–78b.

85.   See *Memoria de Industrias,* 1933, vol. 2, p. 187; *Unirismo* February 14, 1935; Tolima, *Informe del Secretario de Agricultura y Industrias,* 1936, anexos, pp. 177, 200; Tolima, *Mensaje del Gobernador,* 1937, p. 47; and Cundinamarca, *Informe del Secretario de Gobierno,* 1937, p. 104. The role, support base, and political affiliations of the various rural leagues and unions of these years are difficult to sort out. It is not yet clear whether the membership of each organization generally was confined to one occupational group or whether instead colonos, tenant farmers engaged in contract disputes, and day laborers collaborated. In any case, tenants on the great coffee estates of western Cundinamarca and eastern Tolima who challenged the terms of their work contracts also formed rural leagues and unions during this period (see Sánchez G., *Las ligas,* pp. 61–100). Some municipal self-help organizations founded during the 1920s may have supported the colonos in their struggles. In 1926, the newly formed Worker's Society *(Sociedad de Obreros)* of Cunday petitioned the Ministry of Industries to protect colonos in that municipality against landowners intent on extending their boundaries. ANCB v. 65 f. 404 contains the statutes of this group and their petition. Similarly, in 1933 the colonos of "El Chocho" received letters supporting their cause from the Tailors' Union *(Sindicato de Obreros Sastres)* and a Burial Society *(Sociedad de Auxilio Postumo)* in Bogotá (see *Claridad* December 26, 1933).

86.   ANCB v. 60 f. 169bis, and v. 72 f. 293.

87.   Extensive information on the Colony of Sumapaz can be found in *Informe del Procurador General,* 1932, pp. 39–43; Cundinamarca, *Informe del Secretario de Gobierno,* 1931, pp. 31–34; Tolima, *Informe del Secretario de Gobierno,* 1932, pp. 34–37; AHOH, box 2, folder 37, f. 82 and box 3, folder 21, "Informe del Jefe de la Sección de Justicia," pp. 4–10; Merchán, 114–15; and *Claridad,* 1932–37, all issues.

88.   See Richard Gott, *Guerrilla Movements in Latin America* (London, 1970), pp. 169–94. During the 1930s, the Communist party also organized a peasant enclave in the coffee municipality of Viotá (Cundinamarca) that remained essentially independent of the Colombian government for twenty-five years. Tenant farmers dissatisfied with their work contracts, rather than colonos, formed the popular base of this insurgency. See José Gutiérrez, *La rebeldía colombiana: observaciones psicológicas sobre la actualidad política* (Bogotá, 1962), pp. 84–96; Pardo; and Jiménez, "Red Viota."

89.   AHOH, box 3, folder 21, f. 4.

90.   Cundinamarca, *Informe del Secretario de Gobierno,* 1931, p. 33.

91.   The four original sections were 1) Pandi; 2) Iconozco and Cunday; 3) Bogotá (corregimiento of Nazaret), Arbaláez, Pasca, and San Bernardo; and 4) Fusuga-

sugá and Soacha. Branches of the colony also existed in Colombia (Huila) and San Eduardo (Boyacá). See *Claridad* February 5, 1934.

92. Tolima, *Informe del Secretario de Gobierno*, 1932, p. 37.

93. See *Claridad* May 17, 1936 and June 30, 1936.

94. *Claridad* May 16, 1932.

95. On the El Salvadoran case, see Thomas P. Anderson, *Matanza: El Salvador's Communist Revolt of 1932* (Lincoln, Neb., 1971).

96. Caldas, *Informe del Secretario de Gobierno*, 1932, p. 83; and ANCB v. 75 f. 30.

97. AHOH, box 6, folder 46, report from the attorney general to the minister of industries, 8/3/l933. See also *Boletín de la Oficina General de Trabajo* 4 (July–September 1933), 1428, 1535–36.

98. On the history of the National Labor Bureau *(Oficina General de Trabajo)*, see *Boletín de la Oficina General de Trabajo* 2 (March–April 1931), 781, 816–20; ibid. 9 (1937), 3–8; and Tovar Zambrano, *La intervención*, pp. 148–52.

99. See AC, "Informes, memoriales, telegramas (Cámara)," 1932, vol. 7, fs. 35–71; Tolima, *Informe del Secretario de Gobierno*, 1932, pp. 27–38; Tolima, *Mensaje del Gobernador*, 1935, pp. 28–29; and Santander, *Mensaje del Gobernador*, 1936, pp. 9–10.

100. For examples of these pacts, see *Memoria de Industrias*, 1932, p. 346; ibid., 1933, vol. 2, p. 197; Valle del Cauca, *Mensaje del Gobernador*, 1930, pp. 14–15; Tolima, *Informe del Secretario de Gobierno*, 1934, pp. 28-30; Cundinamarca, *Informe del Secretario de Gobierno*, 1934, p. 21; Huila, *Informe del Secretario de Gobierno*, 1936, pp. 7–10; and Caldas, *Informe del Secretario de Gobierno*, 1937, p. 20.

101. See Tolima, *Informe del Secretario de Gobierno*, 1934, p. 28.

102. *Boletín de la Oficina General de Trabajo* 4 (July–September 1933), 1321; and AHOH, box 2, folder 37, f. 7 and box 6 folder 12, petition from the Comité de Cafeteros de Cundinamarca to President Olaya Herrera, 5/1/1934.

103. See AHOH, box 6, folder 46, f. 75; Jiménez, "Social Crisis", pp. 71–78; and Gaitán de Valencia, *Colombia: la lucha*, pp. 77–78.

104. Cundinamarca, *Informe del Secretario de Gobierno*, 1936, pp. 17–20.

105. See Tolima, *Informe del Secretario de Gobierno*, 1929, p. 37; *Informe del Procurador General*, 1931, p. 11; *Memoria de Industrias*, 1931, vol. 1, pp. 32, 35; ibid., 1934, pp. 370, 384; *Boletín de la Oficina General de Trabajo* 4 (July–September 1933), 1432; and Cundinamarca, *Informe del Secretario de Gobierno*, 1935, p. 35.

Chapter 7: The State and the Agrarian Problem

1. *Memoria de Industrias*, 1934, p. 359.

2. *Boletín de la Oficina General de Trabajo* 4 (July-September 1933), 1424.

See also *Memoria de Industrias*, 1934, p. 367; ibid., 1935, p. 206; ibid., 1936, anexos, pp. 64, 152; ibid., 1938, vol. 1, p. 21; *Informe del Procurador General*, 1931, pp. 8–9; and AC, *Anales del Congreso*, 1934, p. 367.

3. *Memoria de Industrias*, 1932, pp. 118, 124; and ibid., 1933, vol. 1, pp. 59–60, 433–34.

4. See *Memoria de Industrias*, 1933, vol. 1, pp. 436–37; and ibid., 1935, pp. 200–03, 206. In the case of the "Terrenos de Paquiló, La Cascada, y El Pilar," of which Jenaro Torres Otero was the principal owner, eighty-seven other part-owners were involved. Very little has been written on the form of landholding known as indiviso in Colombia. Some information can be found in Crist, pp. 32–33. In 1931, the governor of Valle noted as one of several impediments to rural development "the vast extension of properties called 'indivisos', each of which belongs to a multitude of owners. This form of proprietorship impedes the exploitation and valorization of the land and is ineligible for agricultural credit." AHOH, box 1, folder 23, f. 136.

5. *Memoria de Industrias*, 1935, p. 197.

6. Ibid., pp. 184–97.

7. Cundinamarca, *Informe del Secretario de Gobierno*, 1934, p. 22.

8. See *Memoria de Industrias*, 1930, p. 37; ibid., 1934, p. 383; ibid., 1936, p. 154; *Boletín de la Oficina General de Trabajo* 4 (July–September 1933), 1410–16; *Boletín de la Oficina General de Trabajo* 4 (October–December 1933), 1523–32, 1538–47, 1641–62; and Cundinamarca, *Informe del Secretario de Gobierno*, 1934, p. 17.

9. The parcelization program was based on Laws 74 of 1926 and 87 of 1928, which permitted the expropriation with indemnity of centrally located latifundia so that the land could be redistributed to cultivators.

10. Cundinamarca, *Informe del Secretario de Gobierno*, 1934, p. 24.

11. See *Memoria de Industrias*, 1930, pp. 376–77; and ibid., 1933, pp. 41, 63.

12. See Palacios, *Coffee in Colombia*, pp. 49–53; and Palacios, *El café en Colombia*, pp. 363–66.

13. For justifications of the parcelization program, see *Memoria de Industrias*, 1930, pp. 374–75; ibid., 1931, vol. 2, p. 238; Caldas, *Informe del Secretario de Gobierno*, 1929, p. 35; Antioquia, *Mensaje del Gobernador*, 1931, p. 14; Cundinamarca, *Informe de Obras Públicas*, 1932, p. 60; Cundinamarca, *Informe del Secretario de Gobierno*, 1934, pp. 16–17; Tolima, *Informe del Secretario de Hacienda*, 1936, p. 12; Santander, *Informe del Secretario de Gobierno*, 1936, p. 29; AC, "Memoriales, oficios, notas (Cámara)," 1932, vol. 4, folio 366; AHOH, box 1, folder 24, f. 137; and ANCB v. 60 f. 169.

14. On the division of these haciendas, see *Memoria de Industrias*, 1933, p. 37; ibid., 1934, pp. 29, 146–50; ibid., 1935, pp. 201, 218–19, 264; ibid., 1936, anexos, p. 222; *Boletín de la Oficina General de Trabajo* 5 (January–June 1934), 152–70; and Cundinamarca, *Informe del Secretario de Gobierno*, 1934, p. 23.

15.   The government paid 45,000 pesos ($36,000 U.S.) for these properties *(Ministerio de Industrias*, 1936, anexos, p. 145).

16.   The Agricultural Mortgage Bank *(Banco Agrícola Hipotecario)*, the first bank to dispense agricultural credit on a national scale, was established in 1923 as part of the reorganization of the Colombian banking system recommended by the Kemmerer Mission. Paul Drake describes the impact of this U.S. mission in "The Origins of United States Economic Supremacy in South America: Colombia's Dance of the Millions, 1923–33," Paper presented at the Woodrow Wilson International Center, Washington, D.C., December 10, 1979. In 1932 a second banking institution, the *Caja de Crédito Agrario*, was created to service the Colombian rural sector. The role the Agricultural Mortgage Bank played in land parcelization is discussed in Banco Agrícola Hipotecario, *La parcelación de tierras en Colombia* (Bogotá, 1937).

17.   The following description of the subdivisions of "El Chocho" and "El Soche" is drawn from *Memoria de Industrias*, 1928, p. 145; *Informes de los Sres. Gobernadores, Intendentes, y Comisarios Especiales, 1930 a 1934* (Bogotá, 1934); Cundinamarca, *Informe del Secretario de Gobierno*, 1934, p. 36; ibid., 1937, pp. 123–35, 278–79; Cundinamarca, *Informe del Secretario de Hacienda*, 1935, pp. 48–58; and *Claridad* June 12, 1933, June 21, 1933, and August 24, 1936.

18.   See Colombia, Contraloría General de la República, *Anuario general de estadística de 1934* (Bogotá, 1935), p. 569. In 1934 rural salaries in Cundinamarca ranged from 35 centavos to 1 peso per day for men; they were somewhat less for women. In U.S. currency, the equivalent value was 22 to 62 cents.

19.   *Claridad* May 15, 1934.

20.   See *Unirismo* May 25, 1935 and June 6, 1935; *Claridad* May 15, 1934, October 31, 1934, November 30, 1934, May 13, 1935, September 4, 1935, and October 30, 1935; and Bejarano, "Fin de la economía (I)," 724–27. The departmental government admitted the validity of some of these accusations (see Cundinamarca, *Informe del Secretario de Hacienda*, 1935, p. 55; and Cundinamarca, *Informe del Secretario de Gobierno*, 1937, p. 125).

21.   See *Claridad* October 2, 1930, December 31, 1933, and May 15, 1934; and *Unirismo* June 6, 1935.

22.   See AC, "Memoriales, oficios, notas (Senado)," 1930–31, vol. 16, folio 15; Cundinamarca, *Informe del Secretario de Gobierno*, 1934, p. 36; ibid., 1936, p. 24; ibid., 1937, pp. 78, 104, 132–35, 278–79; Cundinamarca, *Informe del Secretario de Hacienda*, 1935, pp. 56–57; *Memoria de Industrias*, 1936, anexos, p. 134; and *Claridad* May 10, 1935 and August 12, 1935.

23.   See Caldas, *Informe del Secretario de Gobierno*, 1934, p. 16; Cauca, *Informe del Secretario de Hacienda*, 1936, p. 25; and Huila, *Mensaje del Gobernador*, 1936, p. 21.

24.   Properties purchased for subdivision through the end of 1936 included a total of 41,910 hectares for which 1,216,618.13 pesos ($775,716 U.S.) were paid. By December 31, 1936, 18,989 hectares of this land had been sold to peasants in

3,206 parcels. Colombia, Contraloría General de la República, *Anuario general de estadística de 1936* (Bogota, 1937), p. 139.

25.   *Memoria de Industrias*, 1934, p. 377. See also ibid., 1935, p. 10. The relatively high capital outlay required by parcelization projects also limited the extent of their applicability.

26.   *Memoria de Industrias*, 1930, pp. 376–77.

27.   See *Memoria de Industrias*, 1932, pp. 130, 136–49; ibid., 1934, p. 341; and AHOH, box 2, folder 37, folios 129–35. Those who supported the landowners called the Supreme Court's action arbitrary and ahistorical. They argued that, in requiring original titles, the 1926 decision unfairly penalized landowners because it disregarded both the previously accepted criterion of thirty years chain of title and the notorious disorganization of the Colombian notarial and registry systems.

28.   *Memoria de Industrias*, 1933, p. 57.

29.   See Absalón Machado C., "Políticas agrarias en Colombia," Bogotá, 1979 (typewritten).

30.   See *Memoria de Industrias*, 1931, p. 53; ibid., 1933, p. 9; Valle del Cauca, *Mensaje del Gobernador*, 1932, p. 14; ibid., 1936, p. 12; Tolima, *Mensaje del Gobernador*, 1932, pp. 6-7; Cauca, *Informe del Secretario de Hacienda*, 1935, p. 38; and *Boletín de la Oficina General de Trabajo* 4 (July-September 1933), 1536.

31.   AHOH, box 6, folder 46, folios 10–13. See also AC, "Leyes autógrafas de 1936," vol. 18, folios 89–90. A recurrent theme in the Spanish-American legal tradition, the idea that the right of property should be contingent on its economic use was occasionally advanced by Colombian statesmen concerned with the development of the agrarian economy in the nineteenth and early twentieth centuries. See, for example, Aníbal Galindo, *Estudios económicos y fiscales* (Bogotá, 1880), p. 258; and Villegas, "Historia de la propiedad agraria," Chapter 12. A movement to put this concept into effect began to take form in the 1920s in response to the domestic economic factors discussed in Chapter 5. The Mexican Constitution of 1917, which similarly set out to define and limit the exercise of private property, probably also influenced the evolution of Colombian thought on agrarian reform.

32.   See *Memoria de Industrias*, 1934, p. 367; ibid., 1936, pp. 2–3; Cundinamarca, *Informe del Secretario de Gobierno*, 1933, anexos, p. 4; ibid., 1937, pp. 40, 69; Cundinamarca, *Mensaje del Gobernador*, 1933, p. 4; Caldas, *Mensaje del Gobernador*, 1932, p. 80; Santander, *Informe del Secretario de Gobierno*, 1936, pp. 18–19; and AHOH, box 6, folder 46, communication from the attorney general to the minister of industries, 8/4/1933.

33.   *Memoria de Agricultura*, 1938, p. 70. See also *Memoria de Industrias*, 1932, p. 149.

34.   *Memoria de Industrias*, 1933, vol. 1, pp. 442–44. The individuals on the Olaya Herrera Land Commission were Francisco José Chaux, Esteban Jaramillo, Guillermo Amaya Ramírez, Luis Felipe Latorre, Miguel Velandia, Jorge Eliécer Gaitán, and Rafael Escallón.

35.   The bill of 1933 and its antecedents are to be found in AC, "Proyectos de

1933 (Cámara)," vol. 2, folios 160ff. The bill was reprinted in *Memoria de Indus-trias*, 1934, pp. 344–87. For explications of the proposal, see ibid.; *Boletín de la Oficina General de Trabajo* 4 (July-September 1933), 1412–47; Justo Díaz Rodrí-guez, "Política agraria y colonización," *Tierras y Aguas* 4 (July–August 1943), 3–63; and Nestor Madrid Malo, "Génesis e ineficacia de la reforma sobre tierras," *Revista Trimestral de Cultura Moderna* 1 (October 1944), 399–420.

36.   *Boletín de la Oficina General de Trabajo* 4 (January–June 1934), 137.

37.   *Memoria de Industrias*, 1934, p. 372.

38.   Ibid., pp. 369–70.

39.   See *Memoria de Industrias*, 1930, p. 41; Tolima, *Informe del Secretario de Hacienda*, 1936, p. 12; and AHOH, box 1, folder 24, f. 136. It was generally agreed that large cattle ranches should continue to exist in the more remote areas.

40.   Madrid Malo, 409.

41.   Jiménez, "Social Crisis" provides a detailed analysis of the political fac-tors that gave rise to Law 200. See also Mesa, *El problema agrario*, pp. 62–88. Alvaro Tirado Mejía presents an overview of the López government in *Aspectos polí-ticos del primer gobierno de Alfonso López Pumarejo, 1934–38* (Bogota, 1981).

42.   Sharpless, pp. 82–83.

43.   Partido Comunista de Colombia, *Treinta años*, pp. 32–38; and Medina, *Partido Comunista*, pp. 263–99.

44.   See Palacios, *El café en Colombia*, pp. 372–430; and Bergquist, "Colombia."

45.   See Cundinamarca, *Informe del Secretario de Hacienda*, 1935, pp. 56–57; Cundinamarca, *Informe del Secretario de Gobierno*, 1937, p. 104; and Gaitán de Valencia, *Colombia: la lucha*, pp. 86–91. According to Vernon Fluharty, much real estate in the early years of the depression passed into the hands of the bankers, "creating a new landed aristocracy" (Fluharty, p. 44).

46.   On López's labor policy, see Urrutia Montoya, pp. 121–26, 169–76; and Pecaut, *Política y sindicalismo*, pp. 131–61.

47.   Jiménez, "Social Crisis," pp. 76–77. The Society of Colombian Agricultur-alists was founded in 1906; the Federation of Coffee Growers emerged out of it in 1928. Machado C., *El café*, pp. 71–81 traces the history of the SAC. On FEDECA-FE, see Bennett Eugene Koffman, "The National Federation of Coffee-Growers of Colombia" (Ph.D. diss., University of Virginia, 1969); and Hector Melo and Ivan López Botero, *El imperio clandestino del café* (Bogotá, 1976). María Errazuriz ex-plores the impact of FEDECAFE on one coffee municipality in " 'Cafeteros' et 'cafetales.' "

48.   Little has been written on this pressure group of proprietors. The syndicate is mentioned in AC, "Memoriales, oficios, notas (Cámara)," 1932, vol. 5, folio 283; *Claridad* November 30, 1934; Jiménez, "Social Crisis," pp. 73–76; Gaitán de Valencia, *Colombia: la lucha*, p. 77; and Machado C., *El café*, p. 282.

49.   On this tendency, see Anderson, pp. 42–61; Glade, pp. 349–402; and Baer et al., 23–24.

50.   Analyses of the López reform program are to be found in Fluharty, pp.

46–58; Robert H. Dix, *Colombia: The Political Dimensions of Change* (New Haven, 1967), pp. 82–91; Anderson, pp. 208–22; Francisco Posada, *Colombia: violencia y subdesarrollo* (Bogotá, 1969), pp. 95–99; Pécaut, *Política y sindicalismo*, pp. 131–41; Rodríguez Salazar, pp. 98-104; and Sharpless, pp. 19–28.

51.   The Apenistas published two newspapers, *La Razón* and *La Acción*, both of which can be found in the National Library in Bogotá. For additional information, see *Unirismo* March 28, 1935, April 4, 1935, April 13, 1935, and April 25, 1925; *Claridad* April 16, 1935; Dix, pp. 322, 356; Urrutia Montoya, p. 123; Jiménez, "Social Crisis," pp. 76–79; Machado C., *El café*, p. 282; and Tirado Mejía, *Aspectos políticos*, pp. 56–58, 103–15.

52.   *La Acción* May 11, 1935, quoted in Gaitán de Valencia, *Colombia: la lucha*, p. 77.

53.   See *Boletín de la Oficina General de Trabajo* 4 (July–September 1933), 1412–13; *Memoria de Industrias*, 1936, pp. 2–3, 64; and Cundinamarca, *Informe del Secretario de Gobierno*, 1937, p. 40.

54.   *Memoria de Industrias*, 1935, pp. 6–7, 12; *Claridad* February 11, 1937; and Sánchez G., *Las ligas*, pp. 126–29.

55.   Members of the López agrarian committee were Darío Echandía, Benito Bustos Hernández, Eduardo Zuleta Angel, Antonio Rocha, Guillermo Amaya Ramírez, and Alfonso López Michelsen. (See Jiménez, "Social Crisis," p. 79.)

56.   For Law 200 and its antecedents, see AC, "Leyes autógrafas de 1936," vol. 18, folios 1–354. Marco A. Martínez, ed., *Régimen de tierras en Colombia (antecedentes de la Ley 200 de 1936 'sobre régimen de tierras' y decretos reglamentarios)*, 2 vols. (Bogotá, 1939) presents a useful compilation of all official documents relating to Law 200 including the various drafts of the bill, congressional debates, and committee reports.

57.   For this viewpoint, see Fluharty, p. 53; Hirschman, pp. 107–13; Anderson, p. 210; Ernest A. Duff, *Agrarian Reform in Colombia* (New York, 1968), pp. 7–13; Dix, p. 88; Posada, pp. 95–97; Urrutia Montoya, pp. 125, 233; Joseph R. Thome, "Title Problems in Rural Areas: A Colonization Example," in *Internal Colonialism and Structural Change in Colombia*, ed. A. Eugene Havens and William L. Flinn (New York, 1970), p. 147; Pécaut, *Política y sindicalismo*, pp. 135–36; and Rodríguez Salazar, pp. 103–04. Recently a few Colombian scholars have begun to reinterpret the law in a more critical light. See Mesa, *El problema agrario*; Victor M. Moncayo C., "La ley y el problema agrario en Colombia," *Ideología y Sociedad* 14–15 (July-December 1975), 7–46; Gaitán de Valencia, *Colombia: la lucha*, p. 99; and Sánchez G., *Las ligas*, pp. 125–29.

58.   Article 22 of Law 200 defined more concretely than any previous statute the elements included under the term "improvements" for which compensation was mandatory (see LeGrand, "From Public Lands," p. 430). The final stipulation on reimbursement and purchase rights applied only to settlers who had never recognized the owners' claims to the land: Law 200 left the rights of tenants who later said they were colonos unclear.

59. Colombia, Alfonso López Pumarejo, *Mensajes del Presidente López al Congreso Nacional, 1934–38* (Bogotá, 1939), p. 51.

60. The history and activities of the important federations of coffee, sugar, cotton, rice, and livestock producers are detailed in Pierre Gilhodes, *La Questión agraire en Colombie, 1958–71* (Paris, 1974).

61. See Machado C., *El café*, pp. 334–35, 341; and Jiménez Neira, 289–93.

62. See Feder, p. 246; and Guillermo Benavides Melo, "Tierras para la reforma agraria," *Tierra: Revista de Economía Agraria* 3 (January–March 1967), 11–53.

63. See Martínez, *Régimen de tierras*, pp. 87–113.

64. See Dix; R. Albert Berry, "Some Implications of Elitist Rule for Economic Development in Colombia," in *Government and Economic Development*, ed. Gustav Ranis (New Haven, 1971), pp. 3–29; Francisco Leal Buitrago, "Social Classes, International Trade, and Foreign Capital in Colombia: An Attempt at Historical Interpretation of the Formation of the State, 1819–1935" (Ph.D. diss., University of Wisconsin, 1974); Fernando Guillén Martínez, *El poder político en Colombia* (Bogotá, 1979); and Oquist.

Chapter 8: Epilogue

1. On the Colombian rural economy since 1936, see United Nations; Mario Arrubla, *Estudios sobre el subdesarrollo colombiano* (Bogotá, 1963); Comité Interamericano de Desarrollo Agrícola, *Tenencia de la tierra y desarrollo socio-económico del sector agrícola colombiano* (Washington, D.C., 1966); R. Albert Berry, "The Development of Colombian Agriculture" (Ph.D. diss., Yale University, 1971); World Bank, *Economic Growth of Colombia: Problems and Prospects* (Baltimore, 1972), pp. 273–88; Gonzalo Cataño, ed., *Colombia: estructura política y agraria* (Bogotá, 1972); Hugo E. Vélez, *Dos ensayos acerca del desarrollo capitalista en la agricultura colombiana* (Medellín, 1973); Estanislao Zuleta and Asociación Nacional de Usuarios Campesinos, *La tierra en Colombia* (Medellín, 1973); Salomón Kalmanowitz, "Desarrollo capitalista en el campo colombiano," in *Colombia, hoy*, by Mario Arrubla et al., 3rd ed. (Bogotá, 1978), pp. 271–330; Kalmanowitz, *Desarrollo*; and Santiago Perry, *La crisis agraria en Colombia, 1950–1980* (Bogotá, 1983).

2. See Jesús Antonio Bejarano, "Contribución al debate sobre el problema agrario," in *El agro en el desarrollo histórico colombiano* (Bogotá, 1977), pp. 33–84; Jorge Vallejo Morillo, "Problemas de método en el estudio de la cuestión agraria," in ibid., pp. 85–128; and Mario Arrubla, ed., *La agricultura colombiana en el siglo xx* (Bogotá, 1976).

3. See Germán Guzmán Campos et al., *La Violencia en Colombia*, 2nd ed. (Bogotá, 1962), vol. 1, pp. 23–37; Hirschman, pp. 113–16; Bejarano, "Contribución al debate," p. 35; and Sánchez G., *Las ligas*, pp. 129–34.

4. See Gilhodes, "Agrarian Struggles," pp. 417–18.

5. Sánchez G., *Las ligas*, pp. 65–78, 134–35.
6. Articles 25-32 of Law 200 of 1936 dealt with the duties of the land judges. See *Memoria de Industrias*, 1938, vol. 1, pp. 162–64.
7. *Memoria de Industrias*, 1938, vol. 1, p. 23. In 1943 the land judges were abolished and a national police force established to deal with rural disturbances (Madrid Malo, 408).
8. See Gerardo Cabrera Moreno, "La reforma agraria de 1936," *Revista Jurídica* 4–5 (November 1944), 522–29; Colombia, Contraloría General de la República, *Geografía económica de Colombia*, vol. 8: *Santander* (Bucaramanga, 1947), p. 225; Fluharty, pp. 56–57; Christie, "Oligarchy and Society," pp. 192–93; and Reyes Posada, "Aparcería," 32–33. Additional information on the activities of the land judges can be found in the annual reports of the Ministry of National Economy to Congress after 1936.
9. See *Claridad* August 19, 1937; *Tierra* January 7, 1938, May 13, 1938, June 10, 1938, June 24, 1938, August 13, 1938, September 17, 1938, September 30, 1938, October 7, 1938, and December 2, 1938; and Crist, pp. 36–38. Sánchez G., *Las ligas*, pp. 137–38 notes that some landlords in Chaparral (Tolima) used Law 200 to take over Indian communal lands.
10. See *Claridad* August 24, 1936, January 14, 1937, April 2, 1937, and May 1, 1937; and Reyes Posada, *Latifundio*, pp. 71–77. The annual reports of the Ministry of National Economy and, within it, the Department of Land and Water, shed some light on the concrete effects of Law 200. See also this department's bulletin, *Tierras y Aguas*.
11. In the municipalities of Ciénaga, Aracataca, and Pueblo Viejo (Magdalena), for example, colonos who had invaded United Fruit Company properties in 1930–31 were still squatting there thirty years later when the Colombian Agrarian Reform Institute sent a team of experts to investigate their situation. See Pedro Padilla B., and Alberto Llanos O., "Proyecto Magdalena 4: zona bananera," Instituto Colombiano de la Reforma Agraria, Bogotá 1964 (mimeographed).
12. See Medófilo Medina, "La resistencia campesina en el sur del Tolima, 1949–1953," Paper presented to the I Simposio Internacional y II Seminario Nacional Sobre Movimientos Sociales: "La Violencia en Colombia," Departamento de Historia, Universidad Nacional and Centro Jorge Eliécer Gaitán, Bogotá, June 24–30, 1984, p. 16.
13. See *Claridad* September 30, 1936; and *Tierra* June 10, 1938, November 4, 1938, and November 18, 1938.
14. Colombia, Contraloría General de la República, *Anuario general de estadística de 1940* (Bogotá, 1941), pp. 174–75. These estates totalled 223,132 hectares in area. By December of 1940, 11,315 parcels had been sold, covering 84,047 hectares. Of the 240 estates purchased by the government, 173 were located in the departments of Tolima and Cundinamarca.
15. See Caputo, pp. 28–42; Palacios, *El café en Colombia*, pp. 341–430; Bergquist, "Colombia"; and Jiménez, "Red Viota." In the municipalities of Pasca and

San Bernardo (Cundinamarca), the breakup of the land was acompanied by a shift in voting patterns from Conservative to Liberal in the 1930–42 period.

16.   Originally it was thought that the agrarian conflicts of the 1930s produced the dissolution of the great estates in this region. According to Mariano Arango (pp. 155–57) and Absalón Machado C., *(El café,* pp. 329, 338–39), however, the real shift in landholding patterns occurred in the 1945–55 period, and not before. Recent work emphasizes the importance of economic factors: the fact that Colombian coffee production involved no economies of scale and was not mechanizable contributed to the decline of large coffee haciendas in the Santanders as well as in Cundinamarca and Tolima after 1930. Peasant farmers who relied primarily on family labor were better able to resist economic recession than estate owners who had to make large outlays on hired workers. In the coffee zones of Brazil, too, large estates tended to give way to smaller production units in the period between 1905 and 1940. See Thomas Holloway, *Immigrants on the Land: Coffee and Society in São Paulo, 1886–1934* (Chapel Hill, 1980).

17.   See *Claridad* May 15, 1934, April 13, 1935, and August 12, 1935; and *Unirismo* June 6, 1935.

18.   *Claridad* October 31, 1934 and September 4, 1935. See also Gloria Gaitán de Valencia "Guatimbol: formación y desintegración de un latifundio cafetero," Universidad de los Andes [CEDE], Bogotá, 1969 (mimeographed).

19.   *Claridad* August 24, 1936; Gaitán de Valencia, *Colombia: la lucha,* p. 92; and Mesa, *El problema agrario,* p. 107 raise this problem. See also Tolima, *Informe del Secretario de Agricultura y Industrias,* 1935, pp. 47, 139. Data on parcelization in the government's statistical yearbooks indicate that over 90 percent of parcels sold were between 1.3 and 32 hectares in size.

20.   See *Memoria de Industrias,* 1931, vol. 2, p. 238; ibid., 1938, vol. 3, p. 275; Caldas, *Informe del Secretario de Gobierno,* 1932, p. 10; and *Unirismo* April 13, 1935 and June 6, 1935.

21.   See Jorge Quiñonez and Gustavo Jaramillo Z., "Informe sobre la zona bananera del Magdalena," Instituto Colombiano de la Reforma Agraria, 1962 (mimeographed); Marco Palacios, "Las haciendas cafeteras de Cundinamarca, 1870–1970" Bogotá, 1975 (mimeographed); and "Reforma agraria burguesa: un estudio de caso," *Estudios Marxistas* 11 (1976), 32.

22.   Within the government, responsibility for parcelization projects passed from the Ministry of Industries to the Department of Land and Water *(Departamento de Tierras y Aguas)* of the Ministry of Agriculture in 1938. This department later was transferred to the Ministry of National Economy. In the early 1940s, the Caja de Crédito Agrario supplanted the Banco Agrícola Hipotecario in financing and supervising the projects. For a good case study of the impact of parcelization on one estate, see "Reforma agraria burguesa."

23.   Smith, pp. 40, 117–18, 122. Apart from the problem of social agitation, the incentive of rising land prices also motivated some proprietors to sell part of their domains so as to resolve credit problems or raise capital for farm improve-

ments. Instead of selling the properties intact, frequently they chose to break them down into smaller parcels for the simple reason that this method yielded greater profits. In this way, some tenants may have obtained title to the fields they worked. See Christie, "Oligarchy and Society," p. 195; and Campo, pp. 39–54.

24. Recently research has focused on economic explanations for the continuing existence of peasant subsistence producers in rural Latin America. The new work stresses that these peasants should not be viewed as ignorant remnants of the traditional past, completely divorced from the modern or capitalistic agricultural sector. Rather, such peasants are integrated into the larger economic system as providers of the cheap food and labor necessary, within the context of dependent development, to fuel both industrial growth and the expansion of the plantation economy. Thus, although they remain poor, peasant producers play an important role within the national economy. For this reason, resistance to structural change in the rural sector is very strong. For research dealing with these kinds of questions, see Alain de Janvry, "The Political Economy of Rural Development in Latin America: An Interpretation," *American Journal of Agricultural Economics* 57 (August 1975), 490–99; Sorj; Castro de Rezende, "Estrutura agrária"; Alain de Janvry, *The Agrarian Question and Reformism in Latin America* (Baltimore, 1981); and papers by Roger Bartra, Eugene Havens, and David McCreery presented at the panel "The Development of Capitalism and the Peasantry: Theoretical Perspectives," Meetings of the Latin American Studies Association, Pittsburgh, Pennsylvania, April 6, 1979.

25. See Pearse, Chapter 1.

26. See Gaitán de Valencia, *Colombia: la lucha*, pp. 89–90, 101; and Sánchez G., *Las ligas*, pp. 129, 142 for peasant attitudes toward Law 200. Congruent upper class interpretations of the statute can be found in Cundinamarca, *Informe del Secretario de Gobierno*, 1937, pp. 64, 70; Mesa, *El problema agrario*, pp. 81–84; Sánchez G., *Las ligas*, p. 127; and Vallejo Morillo, "Problemas," p. 93.

27. See Machado C., *El café*, pp. 320–23. Machado's chapter entitled "Cambio de relaciones sociales de producción de 1920 a 1950," pp. 292–348 is particularly informative on the transition from tenant to wage labor in coffee areas.

28. See Pedro Bernal, "Costos de producción en la agricultura," *Revista Nacional de Agricultura* (July 1957), quoted in ibid., pp. 322–23; and Colombia, Departamento de Tierras [Ministerio de Economia Nacional], *Informe de las labores realizadas en 1946–47* (Bogotá, 1948), p. 5. Also, Colombia, Contraloría General, *Geografía: Santander*, pp. 279–80; Fals Borda, *El hombre y la tierra*, pp 103–04; and Arango, p. 152.

29. Land invasions took place in Bitaco (Valle) in July of 1937 (Sánchez G., *Las ligas*, p. 140); in Fusugasugá (Cundinamarca) in January of 1938 (Gilhodes, "Agrarian Struggles," p. 419); in Guicán (Boyacá) (Fals Borda, *El hombre y la tierra*, p. 104); and in Ortega, Coello, and Saldaña de Sur (Tolima) (Machado C., *El café*, p. 289). In 1941 approximately one thousand colonos occupied the estates "Colombia" and "Alejandría" near the intersection of the municipalities Anserma, Maniza-

les, and Neira (Caldas) (Christie, "Oligarchy and Society," p. 196). Orlando Fals Borda refers to generalized colono problems in Boyacá after the passage of Law 200 *(El hombre y la tierra,* pp. 102–06). T. Lynn Smith, who worked in Colombia with the Departamento de Tierras y Aguas and with the Caja de Crédito Agrario in these years, asserts that serious clashes occurred in Aracataca, El Playón, El Colegio, Sumapaz, Fusugasugá, Río Negro, Chaparral, Coyaima, Chicaque, Otún, Pubenza, and Cartago in the late 1930s and 1940s. He maintains that the colono problem was especially acute along the western slope of the eastern cordillera from fifty miles south of Bogotá to the north of Norte de Santander. Disputes also took place along the slopes of the central cordillera from Cauca to Caldas (Smith, p. 142). See also Cundinamarca, *Informe del Secretario de Gobierno,* 1937, pp. 221–42; Ministerio de Economía Nacional, *Memoria al Congreso,* 1939, pp. 61–62; Gilhodes, "Agrarian Struggles," pp. 419, 422; Mesa, *El problema agrario,* p. 90; Oquist, p. 98; Betancourt, pp. 33–34, 38–40; and Medina, "La resistencia," pp. 18–21.

30.   See Smith, p. 76; Duff, p. 15; Gilhodes, "Agrarian Struggles," p. 418; Mesa, *El problema agrario,* p. 108; Rojas Ruiz, p. 89; Arango, pp. 152–53; Machahado C., *El café,* pp. 324–27; Sánchez G., *Las ligas,* pp. 138, 140, 142, 146; and Kalmanowitz, *Desarrollo,* p. 19. Also Cundinamarca, *Informe del Secretario de Gobierno,* 1935, pp. 40–41; ibid., 1937, p. 77; and Huila, *Informe del Secretario de Gobierno,* 1938–39, p. 109. Hirschman, pp. 112–13 presents a somewhat different interpretation of this period.

31.   Hirschman, pp. 113–14; Mesa, *El problema agrario,* pp. 92–93; and Oquist, p. 98. Darío Mesa suggests that to explain why rural production on large estates did not expand significantly in the late 1930s and early 1940s, it is also important to consider the impact of economic factors unrelated to Law 200 (Mesa, *El problema agrario,* pp. 94–95. See also Dix, pp. 93–94).

32.   See Colombia, Contraloría General, *Geografía: Santander,* p. 225; Madrid Malo, 417-18; Machado C., *El café,* pp. 324–27; and Sánchez G., *Las ligas,* pp. 143–44.

33.   Cabrera Moreno, 527–28.

34.   Colombia, Contraloria General, *Geografía: Santander,* pp. 279–80; Cabrera Moreno, 527–28; Machado C., *El café,* p. 341; and Sánchez G., *Las ligas,* pp. 142–44.

35.   The text of Law 100 and related documents are to be found in AC, "Leyes autógrafas de 1944," vol. 10, folios 1–64. On the significance of the law, see Hirschman, pp. 114–15; Duff, pp. 17–18; Mesa, *El problema agrario,* pp. 101–02; Reyes Posada "Aparcería," 34–39; Machado C., *El café,* pp. 331–43; and Sánchez G., *Las ligas,* pp. 144–46.

36.   See Machado C., *El café,* p. 343.

37.   Smith, pp. 85, 141.

38.   The best general works on La Violencia are Guzmán Campos et al.; and Oquist.

39.   Excellent reviews of interpretations of La Violencia are to be found in

Oquist, pp. 129–53; and Gonzalo Sánchez G., "La Violencia in Colombia: New Research, New Questions," *Hispanic American Historical Review* 65: 4 (November 1985).

40. The best of the new work on La Violencia includes Daniel Pécaut, "Reflexiones sobre el fenómeno de la Violencia," *Ideología y Sociedad* 19 (1976), 71–79; Gonzalo Sánchez G., "La Violencia y sus efectos en el sistema político colombiano," *Cuadernos Colombianos* 9 (January–April 1976), 1–44; Darío Fajardo, *Violencia y desarrollo*; Jaime Arocha, *La Violencia en el Quindío*; Darío Fajardo, "La Violencia 1946–1964: su desarrollo y su impacto," *Estudios Marxistas* 21 (1981); Russell W. Ramsey, *Guerrilleros y soldados* (Bogotá, 1981); Winston Horacio Granados, "La Violencia en Urrao, Antioquia, 1948–1953" (Tesis de grado, Universidad de Antioquia, Departamento de Sociología, Medellín, 1982); Gonzalo Sánchez G., *Los dias de la revolución: gaitanismo y 9 de abril en provincia* (Bogotá, 1983); James D. Henderson, *When Colombia Bled: A History of the 'Violencia' in Tolima* (Alabama, 1985); and Medina, "La resistencia." Particularly outstanding works are Gonzalo Sánchez and Donny Meertens, *Bandoleros, gamonales y campesinos: el caso de La Violencia en Colombia*, prologue by Eric Hobsbawm (Bogotá, 1983); and Carlos Ortiz, "La Violence en Colombie: le cas du Quindío" (Doctorat Ecole des Hautes Etudes en Sciences Sociales, Université de Paris, 1983). See also Richard Maullin's stimulating essay, "The Fall of Dumar Aljure, A Colombian Guerrilla and Bandit," Rand Memorandum 5750–1SA (Santa Monica, 1969).

41. See Gilhodes, "Agrarian Struggles," p. 432; Gott, pp. 169–94; Caputo, pp. 35–66; Oquist, pp. 222–25; Medina, "La resistencia," p. 59; and Carlos Arango Z., *FARC veinte años: de Marquetalia a la Uribe* (Bogotá, 1984), pp. 148–49. The Sumapaz region was also subject to massive army bombing in the early 1960s. See Clara Inés López Mejía and Clara Inés Ordoñez Súarez, "Violencia en la región de Sumapaz," (Tesis de grado, Universidad Nacional, Departamento de Historia, 1983).

42. Juan de la Cruz Varela's career has been a most interesting one. An agrarian leader in the colono struggles of the 1930s, he was elected in 1934 to the municipal council of Iconozco and in 1942 to the departmental assembly of Tolima as a Gaitanista. Around 1950 he joined the Communist party and was elected to the departmental assembly of Cundinamarca in 1958 and to the House of Representatives in 1960. During the 1950s, he organized the Communist defense of the Sumapaz region. See Caputo, p. 46. On southern Tolima, see Medina, "La resistencia," p. 34.

43. See Smith, pp. 41–42; Gilhodes, "Agrarian Struggles," pp. 425–26; Germán Castro Caicedo, *Colombia amarga* (Bogotá, 1976), pp. 3–6; Oquist, pp. 225–28; and Campo.

44. Much of the Violencia concentrated in public land regions. Dix, p. 366, quotes agrarian scholar Luis Duque Gómez, writing in 1954 as follows:

It is curious to note that besides favorable topographical conditions, the zones affected by political violence coincide exactly with the fronts of modern

colonization which in recent years have been pushing ahead in the regions of
the Carare, the northeast of the department of Antioquia, the north of Tolima,
the border zone between the latter department and Valle del Cauca, some areas
along the banks of the Magdalena, and in the eastern plains.

See also Hobsbawm, "Peasant Movements," 166–86 for some trenchant observations on the earlier frontier conflicts and their relation to La Violencia.
  45. See Campo; and Betancourt.
  46. See Bottía G. and Escobedo D..
  47. See Gilhodes, "Agrarian Struggles," pp. 432, 438; Oquist, pp. 227–28;
and Alfredo Molano Bravo, "De la Violencia a la colonización: un testimonio colombiano," *Estudios Rurales Latinoamericanos* 4 (September–December 1981), 257–
86. Guzmán Campos et al., vol. 1, contains maps showing the main centers of violence and the directions of the migrations (pp. 47, 64, 82, 86, 91, 119, 127, and
132).
  48. See Joelle Diot, "Estadísticas históricas: baldíos, 1931–1973, legislación
y adjudicaciones," *Boletín Mensual de Estadística* [DANE] 296 (March 1976), 89–
136. The government's allocation of public land increased markedly during La
Violencia: whereas in the 1931–45 period, the rate of allocation averaged 60,000
hectares a year, it rose to 150,000 hectares annually in the 1946–54 period and to
375,000 hectares a year from 1955 through 1959. Information on the size and location of the grants awarded since 1931 is available on computer at the Colombian
Departamento Administrativo Nacional de Estadística (DANE) in Bogotá.
  49. Oquist, p. 225. Studies of colonization areas show that the tactics used
today by cattle ranchers and speculators to extend their control over the land differ
little from the methods employed a half-century ago. For information on the contemporary process and the conflicts it engenders, see Carlos Lleras Restrepo et al.,
Tierra: diez ensayos sobre la reforma agraria en Colombia (Bogotá, 1961), pp. 45–47;
Comite Interamericano de Desarrollo Agrícola, appendix, p. 413; Thome, pp. 156–
58; Soles, pp. 138–46; Friede, *La explotación indígena*, pp. 43–44; and *El Tiempo*
June 8, 1977.
  50. Partido Comunista de Colombia, "Contra la represión oficial en Cimitarra,"
Cuadernos Políticos 10 (1976), 1–16.
  51. For an analysis of current conflicts involving colonos, landlords, guerrillas, the army, and a right wing death squad (MAS) in the central valley of the Magdalena River, see Gloria Lucy Zamora, *En el Magdalena medio: los moradores de
la represión* (Bogotá, 1983); and Gilma López Cardenas and Daniel Acosta Muñoz,
"Violencia capitalista en el Magdalena medio," in Comité de Solidaridad con los
Presos Políticos, ed., *La realidad del 'si se puede': demagogía y violencia* (Bogotá,
1984), pp. 153–247.
  52. See Gilhodes, "Agrarian Struggles," pp. 437–38, 444; Gott, pp. 183–230;
and Richard Maullin, *Soldiers, Guerrillas, and Politics in Colombia* (Lexington,
Mass., 1973). The leader of the Liberal Revolutionary Movement was Alfonso López

Michelsen (son of President Alfonso López Pumarejo) who was to become president of Colombia in 1974.

53.   See Bruce Bagley and Fernando Botero, "Organizaciones campesinas contemporaneas en Colombia: un estudio de la Asociación Nacional de Usuarios Campesinos (ANUC)," *Estudios Rurales Latinoamericanos* 1 (January-April 1978), 59–96.

54.   See Gilhodes, "Agrarian Struggles," pp. 446–47; Comité de Solidaridad con los Presos Políticos, *Libro negro de la represión* (Bogotá, 1974); and Sarah Ganitsky Guberek, "Luchas agrarias, 1920–1974" (Tesis de grado, Universidad de los Andes, 1976), pp. 178–200.

55.   See Segundo Bernal, Oswaldo Rico, and Guillermo Olano, "Informe de la Comisión Segunda: Cunday Alto," Instituto Colombiano de la Reforma Agraria, 1962 (mimeographed); Cesar Alonso M., "Informe de la Provincia de Sumapaz," Instituto Colombiano de la Reforma Agraria, September 1965 (mimeographed); Urrutia Montoya, p. 134; and Caputo, pp. 61, 66.

56.   See Quiñónez and Jaramillo, pp. 3–5; and William L. Partridge, "Banana Country in the Wake of United Fruit: Social and Economic Linkages," *American Ethnologist* 6 (1975), 491–509.

57.   Soles, pp. 62, 81–82, 90–95, 142–46, 150–54.

58.   Ernesto Parra E., *La investigación-acción en la costa atlántica: evaluación de la Rosca, 1972–74* (Cali, 1983), p. 121. This is a fascinating account of the successes and failures of the agrarian movement in the Sinú during the 1970s and of Colombian sociologist Orlando Fals Borda's effort to help the peasants become more politically conscious by recovering the history of their own struggles.

59.   Guido Taborda, Abel Ronderos, and Ernesto Díaz, "Informe y recommendaciones del Ariguaní y Hato del Monquezano," Instituto Colombiano de la Reforma Agraria, n.d. (mimeographed), p. 4.

60.   The agrarian reform effort of the 1960s and its outcome is explored in Lleras Restrepo et al.; Oscar Delgado, ed., *Reformas agrarias en la América Latina: procesos y perspectivas* (Mexico City, 1965), pp. 307–16, 615–74; Comité Interamericano de Desarrollo Agrícola, pp. 267–99; Colombia, Departamento Administrativo Nacional de Estadística, *Debate agrícola: documentos* (Bogotá, 1971); Oscar Delgado, ed., *Ideologías políticas y agrarias en Colombia* (Bogotá, 1973); and Bruce Michael Bagley, "Power, Politics, and Public Policy in Colombia: Case Studies of the Urban and Agrarian Reform during the National Front, 1958–74" (Ph.D. diss., University of California at Los Angeles, 1978).

61.   See Berry, "Rural Poverty"; Kalmanowitz, *Desarrollo*; Taussig, "Peasant Economics"; and Palacios, *Coffee in Colombia*, pp. 227–58.

62.   See Bruce M. Bagley, "The State and the Peasantry in Contemporary Colombia," Paper presented at the Meetings of the Latin American Studies Association, Washington, D.C., March 3–6, 1982, pp. 63–74. Other estimates of guerrillas in arms range as high as 16,000.

63.   See W. Ramírez Tobón, "La guerrilla rural en Colombia: ¿una vía hacía la colonización armada?" *Estudios Rurales Latinoamericanos* 4 (May–August 1981),

199–209; and Julian Vargas Lesmés, "Estudio de base para el desarrollo del oriente colombiano," Informe de avance (versión preliminar), Departamento Nacional de Planeación, Bogotá, 1983 (mimeographed), pp. 93–95. Vargas Lesmés suggests that in the eastern plains guerrilla fronts not only help colonos with self defense (autodefensa), but also provide for public order and the development of infrastructure and act as quasi-legal instruments of pressure on the government. They fulfill such functions even in frontier areas where there are few conflicts over land.

64. E. P. Thompson, *Whigs and Hunters: The Origins of the Black Act* (New York, 1975), p. 267. This study of the origins of a repressive piece of social legislation in eighteenth century England provides an illuminating analysis of the significance and operation of law within a broader societal context.

65. Bergquist, "Colombia."

66. See Barraclough and Domike, pp. 96–102; and Kalmanowitz, *Desarrollo*, pp. 16–59.

67. For an analysis of the use and significance of amnesties in Colombian history, see Gonzalo Sánchez G., "Raíces históricas de la amnistía o las etapas de la guerra en Colombia," *Revista de Extensión Cultural* [Universidad Nacional de Colombia, Medellín] 15 (1983), 23–44.

68. See Eric J. Hobsbawm, "Peasants and Rural Migrants in Politics," in *The Politics of Conformity in Latin America*, ed. Claudio Véliz (Oxford, 1970), pp. 54–55; Juan Martínez Alier, *Haciendas, Plantations and Collective Farms: Agrarian Class Societies—Peru and Cuba* (London, 1977), pp. 18–20; Conferência Nacional dos Bispos do Brasil, *Igreja x governo: documentos oficiais da CNBB* (São Paulo, 1977); Vera L.G. da Silva Rodrigues and José Gomes da Silva, "Conflitos de terra no Brasil: uma introdução ao estado empírico da violência no campo—período 1971/76," *Reforma Agrária* 7 (January–February 1977), 3–24; and Foweracker, pp. 106–27.

69. See Browning, pp. 225–70, 292–303; William H. Durham, *Scarcity and Survival in Central America* (Stanford, 1979), pp. 155–69; and Francisco Barahona Riera, *Reforma agraria y poder político* (San José, 1980).

A Note on Sources

1. The reader is also referred to Jesús Antonio Bejarano, "Campesinado, luchas agrarias e historia social: notas para un balance historiográfico," *Anuario Colombiano de Historia Social y de la Cultura* 11 (1983), 251–304. This is an excellent survey of the major issues in Colombian agrarian history.

2. Some potentially rich material of this sort has yet to be located— for example, the records of the Land Courts established by Law 200 of 1936. The Land Court records should illuminate the practical effects of the law and the process of agrarian change in the years immediately preceding La Violencia. Pioneers in the use of local archives in Colombian agrarian history are Fernando López G., Marco Palacios, Jaime Arocha, Gonzalo Sánchez G., Richard Hyland, and Michael Jiménez.

3. The information on the INCORA archive and on the Caja de Crédito Agrario (below) comes from French political scientist Pierre Gilhodes.

4. Gonzalo Sánchez G. and Donny Meertens in *Bandoleros* make innovative use of congressional debates to elucidate shifts in the government's interpretations of La Violencia and its policies to deal with it.

5. For an overview of the development of the historical profession in Colombia, see Jaime Jaramillo Uribe, "An Interview with Jaime Jaramillo Uribe," Introduction by Frank Safford, *Hispanic American Historical Review* 64:1 (February 1984), 1–15.

6. For full references, see bibliography.

7. A good selection of the new Colombian historical writing is Jaime Jaramillo Uribe, ed., *Manual de Historia de Colombia*, 3 vols., 3rd ed. (Bogotá, 1984).

8. Several Colombian historians have received doctorates under Professor Malcolm Deas at St. Anthony's College, Oxford University. The University of California at Berkeley and the State University of New York at Stony Brook have also hosted Colombian graduate history students. Professor Daniel Pécaut at the Ecole des Hautes Etudes en Sciences Sociales in Paris has trained several Colombian sociologists, as have the University of Florida and the Land Tenure Center of the University of Wisconsin.

9. For a review of recent Colombian works on coffee, see Jesús Antonio Bejarano, "Los estudios sobre la historia del café en Colombia," *Cuadernos de Economía* 2 (1980).

10. Marco Palacios' book on coffee in Colombia, first published by Oxford University, was reissued in 1983 by El Colegio de México and El Ancora Editores in Bogotá in a revised and expanded Spanish edition.

11. An important collection of critical essays on William P. McGreevey's economic history of Colombia is Luis Ospina Vásquez, ed., *Historia económica de Colombia: un debate en marcha* (Bogotá, 1979).

12. T. Lynn Smith's association with Colombia is explored in Francine Cronshaw, "Exporting Ideology: T. Lynn Smith in Colombia," *North-South: Canadian Journal of Latin American and Caribbean Studies* 7 (1982), 95–110.

13. For an explanation of Fals Borda's approach to "militant social investigation," see Victor D. Bonilla et al., *Causa popular, ciencia popular: una metodología del conocimiento científico a través de la acción* (Bogotá, 1972). Other Colombian sociologists who have contributed much to our understanding of the rural scene include Darío Mesa, Virginia Gutiérrez de Pineda, Roberto Pineda, Soledad Ruíz, and Humberto Rojas Ruíz, a founder of the Oficina Para Investigaciones Socioeconómicas y Legales (OFISEL), the independent research group that publishes *Estudios Rurales Latinoamericanos*. This journal disseminates the best work on the Latin American rural economy and society being done in Latin America, North America, and Europe.

14. Bernardo Tovar Zambrano, professor of history at the Universidad Nacional, is writing a study of government intervention in the Colombian economy from 1936 to the present.

9.   For a review of recent Colombian works on coffee, see Jesús Antonio Bejarano, "Los estudios sobre la historia del café en Colombia," *Cuadernos de Economía* 2 (1980).

10.   Marco Palacios' book on coffee in Colombia, first published by Oxford University, was reissued in 1983 by El Colegio de Mexico and El Ancora Editores in Bogotá in a revised and expanded Spanish edition.

11.   An important collection of critical essays on William P. McGreevey's economic history of Colombia is Luis Ospina Vásquez, ed., *Historia económica de Colombia: un debate en marcha* (Bogotá, 1979).

12.   T. Lynn Smith's association with Colombia is explored in Francine Cronshaw, "Exporting Ideology: T. Lynn Smith in Colombia," *North-South: Canadian Journal of Latin American and Caribbean Studies* 7 (1982), 95-110.

13.   For an explanation of Fals Borda's approach to "militant social investigation," see Victor D. Bonilla et al., *Causa popular, ciencia popular: una metodología del conocimiento científico a través de la acción* (Bogotá, 1972). Other Colombian sociologists who have contributed much to our understanding of the rural scene include Darío Mesa, Virginia Gutierrez de Pineda, Roberto Pineda, Soledad Ruíz, and Humberto Rojas Ruíz, a founder of the Oficina Para Investigaciones Socio-económicas y Legales (OFISEL), the independent research group that publishes *Estudios Rurales Latinoamericanos*. This journal disseminates the best work on the Latin American rural economy and society being done in Latin America, North America, and Europe.

14.   Bernardo Tovar Zambrano, professor of history at the Universidad Nacional, is writing a study of government intervention in the Colombian economy from 1936 to the present.

Glossary

aparcero   Sharecropper: a rural cultivator who pays rent for the use of a plot of land within a large estate with a portion of his or her crop

arrendatario   Service tenant: a rural cultivator who pays rent for the use of a plot of land within a large estate by providing labor for the landlord. Also called *concertados, agregados, terrazgueros* in some regions of Colombia

baldíos (terrenos baldíos)   Public domain land, the ownership of which is vested in the nation

campesino   A peasant

caserío   A small rural village that has no administrative status

colono   An individual who farms or grazes cattle on public lands with no legal title to the territory

colono a partido   Tenant-colono: a rural cultivator who receives the use of a plot of undeveloped land within a large estate on the condition that he or she turn the territory over to the landlord in two or three years planted in pastures or cash crops

corregimiento   The smallest administrative unit in the Colombian countryside, a subdivision of a municipality. The political authority of a corregimiento is called a corregidor.

fieles   Tenant farmers who remained loyal to the great proprietors of Cundinamarca during the peasant land invasions of the early 1930s

hectare   A metric measurement of land area:
1 hectare = 2.471 acres

latifundio/hacienda   A large landed estate

latifundista/hacendado   The owner of such an estate

latifundismo   The general problem of the excessive concentration of landholding in large, underutilized estates

Llanos   The great plains that cover the eastern half of Colombia and stretch into Venezuela

mejoras   Improvements introduced onto a tract of land that increase the value of the land, such as buildings, fences, roads, crops, etc.

mestizo   A person of mixed Indian and white ancestry

minifundio   A very small landholding, generally less than three hectares in size, too small to support a peasant family comfortably

minifundista   The owner of such a holding

minifundismo   The general problem of overly fragmented landholdings

municipio (municipality)   A rural county governed by a mayor and municipal council who reside in the county seat *(cabecera)*

parcelario   A rural cultivator who received rights to a plot of land through the government-mediated parcelization program by which some large estates were subdivided after 1930

poblaciones   Planned frontier settlements, generally composed of 200 to 300 families, that received corporate grants of public lands from the national government during the nineteenth century. The founding of poblaciones was an integral aspect of the Antioqueño colonization movement.

resguardos   Tracts of land owned in common by Indian communities. Confirmed by the Spanish Crown during the colonial period, this form of landholding persisted in Colombia and other parts of Latin America into the nineteenth and twentieth centuries.

tinterillo   A country lawyer, generally self-educated

Bibliography

Archival Sources

Academia Colombiana de Historia, Bogotá
    Archivo de Enrique Olaya Herrera

Archivo del Congreso, Bogotá
    Leyes Autógrafas
    Proyectos de Ley
    Informes, Memoriales, Telegramas

Archivo del Instituto Colombiano de la Reforma Agraria, Bogotá
    Bienes Nacionales, 35 vols.

Archivo Nacional de Colombia, Bogotá
    Ministerio de Industrias, Correspondencia de Baldíos, 78 vols.

Published Government Documents

Colombia. Alfonso López Pumarejo. *Mensajes del Presidente López al Congreso Nacional*, 1934–38.

Colombia. Banco Agrícola Hipotecario. *La parcelación de tierras en Colombia* (1937).

Colombia. Concejo de Estado (Sala de Negocios Generales). *Codificación nacional de todas las leyes de Colombia desde el año de 1821 hecha conforme a la ley 13 de 1912*. vols. 1–24.

Colombia. Congreso Nacional. *Actos legislativos de 1905*.

Colombia. Congreso Nacional. *Informes que rindió a la honorable Cámara de Representantes la comisión designada para visitar la zona bananera del Magdalena* (1935).

Colombia. Congreso Nacional. *Ley 110 de 1912 (el Código Fiscal)*.

Colombia. Congreso Nacional. *Leyes expedidas por el Congreso Nacional* (1921, 1922, 1923, 1926).

Colombia. Congreso Nacional. *Leyes y disposiciones de terrenos baldíos* (n. d.).

Colombia. Contraloría General de la República. *Geografía económica de Colombia*. vol. 8: *Santander*, by Mario Galán Gómez (1947).

Colombia. Contraloría General de la República. *Anuario general de estadística* (1934, 1936, 1938–40).

Colombia. Corte Suprema. *Jurisprudencia*. vol. 3 (1926).

Colombia. Departamento Administrativo Nacional de Estadística. *Debate agrícola: documentos* (1971).

Colombia. Departamento de Antioquia. *Anuario estadístico de Antioquia (1976)*.

Colombia. Departamento de Antioquia. *Informe del Secretario de Agricultura y Fomento al Gobernador* (1931).

Colombia. Departamento de Cundinamarca. *Informe del Abogado del departamento al Sr. Gobernador* (1933).

Colombia. Departamento de Cundinamarca. *Informes de las oficinas dependientes de la Secretaría de Gobierno* (1929).

Colombia. Departamento de Cundinamarca. *Visita del gobernador del departamento de Cundinamarca a las provincias de Sumapaz, Girardot y Tequendama*. Facatativá, (1906).

Colombia. Departamento de Tolima. *Informe del Secretario de Agricultura y Industrias al Sr. Gobernador* (1934–36).

Colombia. Departamentos varios. *Informe del Secretario de Gobierno al Gobernador del departamento* (1925–38).

Colombia. Departamentos varios. *Informe del Secretario de Hacienda al Gobernador del departamento* (1925–38).

Colombia. Departamentos varios. *Mensaje del Gobernador del departamento a la H. Asamblea Departamental* (1925–38).

Colombia. *Informes de los Sres. Gobernadores, Intendentes y Comisarios Especiales, 1930 a 1934*.

Colombia. Instituto Colombiano de la Reforma Agraria y Instituto Interamericano de Ciencias Agrícolas. *La colonización en Colombia: evaluación de un proceso* (1974). 2 vols.

Colombia. Ministerio de Agricultura y Comercio. *Memorias al Congreso Nacional* (1917–23).

Colombia. Ministerio de Agricultura. *Memoria al Congreso Nacional* (1938).

Colombia. Ministerio de Hacienda. *Memorias al Congreso Nacional* (1870–92).

Colombia. Ministerio de Industrias. *Memorias al Congreso Nacional* (1925–37).

Colombia. Procurador General de la Nación. *Informes al Presidente de la República* (1930–31).

United States. Department of Commerce and Labor. *Report on Trade Conditions in Colombia* (1907).

Newspapers and Magazines

El Agricultor (Bogotá, 1879, 1882–83, 1898)
Boletín de la Oficina General de Trabajo (Bogotá, 1929–35)
Boletín Industrial (Bogotá, 1875)
El Bolshevique (Bogotá, 1934–35)
Claridad (Bogotá, 1932–37)
Nueva Era (Cali, 1935)
Revista Nacional de Agricultura (Bogotá, 1906–09, 1915–20)
El Tiempo (Bogotá, 1977)
Tierra (Bogotá, 1938)
Unirismo (Bogotá, 1934–35)

Books, Articles, Papers, Theses, and Dissertations

Acosta Ayerbe, Alejandro. "Aspectos generales de los territorios nacionales: perspectivas y requísitos para absorver un volumen grande de población." *Enfoques Colombianos* 2 (1975), 44–80.

Adams, Dale. "The Land-Tenure System: Antecedents and Problems." *Internal Colonialism and Structural Change in Colombia*. Ed. A. Eugene Havens and William L. Flinn, New York, 1970, 128–245.

Alonso M., Cesar. "Informe de la Provincia de Sumapaz." Instituto Colombiano de la Reforma Agraria, September 1965. (mimeographed)

Alexander, Robert J. *Communism in Latin America*. New Brunswick, N.J., 1957.

Anderson, Charles W. *Politics and Economic Change in Latin America: The Governing of Restless Nations*. New York, 1967.

Anderson, Thomas P., *Matanza: El Salvador's Communist Revolt of 1932*. Lincoln, Neb., 1971.

Arango, Mariano. *Café e industria, 1850–1930*. Bogotá, 1977.

———. *El café en Colombia, 1930–1958: producción, circulación y política*. Bogotá, 1982.

Arango Mejía, Gabriel. *Geneologías de Antioquia y Caldas*. 2nd ed. 2 vols. Medellín, 1942.

Arango Z., Carlos. *FARC veinte años: de Marquetalia a la Uribe*. Bogotá, 1984.

Archila, Mauricio. "Los movimientos sociales entre 1920–1924: una aproximación metodológica." *Cuadernos de Filosofía y Letras* 3:3 (July–September 1980), 181–230.

Arévalo-Salazar, Luis. "The Legal Insecurity of Rural Property in Colombia: A Case Study of the Notarial and Registry Systems." Ph.D. Dissertation, University of Wisconsin, 1970.

Arocha, Jaime. *La Violencia en el Quindío: determinantes ecológicos y económicos del homocidio en un municipio cafucultur*. Bogotá, 1979.

Arrubla, Mario. *Estudios sobre el subdesarrollo colombiano*. Bogotá, 1963.

————, ed. *La agricultura en Colombia en el siglo xx*. Bogotá, 1976.

Asociación Nacional de Usuarios Campesinos de Córdoba. *Lomagrande—el baluarte del Sinú*. Montería, 1972.

Backus, Richard C., and Eder, Phanor J. *A Guide to the Law and Legal Literature of Colombia*. Washington, D.C., 1943.

Baer, Werner, Kerstenstzky, Isaac, and Villela, Annibal. "The Changing Role of the State in the Brazilian Economy." *World Development* 6 (November 1973), 23–34.

Bagley, Bruce M. "Power, Politics and Public Policy in Colombia: Case Studies of the Urban and Agrarian Reform During the National Front, 1958–74." Ph.D. dissertation, University of California at Los Angeles, 1978.

————. "The State and the Peasantry in Contemporary Colombia." Paper presented at the Meetings of the Latin American Studies Association. Washington, D.C. March 3–6, 1982.

Bagley, Bruce M., and Botero, Fernando. "Organizaciones campesinas contemporaneas en Colombia: un estudio de la Asociación Nacional de Usuarios Campesinos (ANUC)." *Estudios Rurales Latinoamericanos* 1 (January–April 1978), 59–96.

Barahona Riera, Francisco. *Reforma agraria y poder político*. San José, 1980.

Barraclough, Solon, and Domike, Arthur. "Agrarian Structure in Seven Latin American Countries." *Latin America: Problems In Economic Development*. Ed. Charles T. Nisbet. New York, 1969, pp. 91–131.

Bauer, Arnold J. "Rural Workers in Spanish America: Problems of Peonage and Oppression." *Hispanic American Historical Review* 59 (February 1979), 34–63.

Bejarano, Jesús Antonio. "Campesinado, luchas agrarias e historia social: notas para un balance historiográfico." *Anuario Colombiano de Historia Social y de la Cultura* 11 (1983), 251–304.

————. Contribución al debate sobre el problema agrario." *El agro en el desarrollo histórico colombiano*, by F. Leal Buitrago et al. Bogotá, 1977, pp. 33–84.

————. "Los estudios sobre la historia del café en Colombia." *Cuadernos de Economía* 2 (1980).

————. "El fin de la economía exportadora (I)." *La nueva historia de Colombia*. Ed. Darío Jaramillo Agudelo. Bogotá, 1976, pp. 673–740.

————. "El fin de la economía exportadora y los orígenes del problema agrario (II)." *Cuadernos Colombianos* 7 (1975), 363–427.

————. *El régimen agrario de la economía exportadora a la economía industrial*. Bogotá, 1979.

Benavides Melo, Guillermo. "Tierras para la reforma agraria." *Tierra: Revista de Economía Agraria* 3 (January–March 1967), 11–53.

Bergquist, Charles W. *Coffee and Conflict in Colombia, 1886–1910*. Durham, N.C., 1978.

————. "Colombia" in *Labor in Latin America: Comparative Essays on Chile, Argentina, Venezuela, and Columbia*. Stanford, 1986, 274–375.

Bernal, Segundo, Rico, Oswaldo, and Olano, Guillermo. "Informe de la Comisión Segunda: Cunday Alto." Instituto Colombiano de la Reforma Agraria, 1962. (mimeographed)

Berry, R. Albert. "The Development of Colombian Agriculture." Ph.D. dissertation, Yale University, 1971.

————, ed. *Essays on Industrialization in Colombia*. Tempe, 1983.

————. "Land Distribution, Income Distribution and the Productive Efficiency of Colombian Agriculture." *Food Resource Institute Studies in Agricultural Economics, Trade, and Development* [Stanford University] 3 (1973), 199–231.

————. "Rural Poverty in Twentieth Century Colombia." *Journal of Interamerican Studies and World Affairs* 20 (November 1978), 355–76.

————. "Some Implications of Elitist Rule for Economic Development in Colombia." *Government and Economic Development*. Ed. Gustav Ranis. New Haven, 1971, 3–29.

Betancourt, Darío. "Los 'Pájaros' en el Valle del Cauca: colonización, café y violencia." Tesis de grado, Universidad Santo Tomás, 1984.

Beyer, Robert. "The Colombian Coffee Industry: Origins and Major Trends, 1740–1940." Ph. D. dissertation, University of Minnesota, 1947.

————. "Transportation and the Coffee Industry in Colombia." *Inter-American Economic Affairs* 2 (1948), 17–30.

Blanchard, Peter. "The Recruitment of Workers in the Peruvian Sierra at the Turn of the Century: The *Enganche* System." *Inter-American Economic Affairs* 33 (Winter 1979), 63–84.

Bonilla, Victor D., Castillo, Gonzalo, Fals Borda, Orlando, and Libreros, Augusto. *Causa popular, ciencia popular: una metodología del conocimiento científico a través de la acción*. Bogotá, 1972.

Bonilla, Victor Daniel. *Servants of God or Masters of Men: The Story of a Capuchín Mission in Amazonia*, Trans. Rosemary Sheed. Harmondsworth, England, 1972.

Borah, Woodrow. *Justice by Insurance: The General Indian Court of Colonial Mexico and the Legal Aides of the Half-Real*. Berkeley, 1983.

Bossa Herazo, Donaldo. *Cartagena independiente: tradición y desarrollo*. Bogotá, 1967.

Botero, Fernando, and Guzmán Barney, Alvaro. "El enclave agrícola en la zona bananera de Santa Marta." *Cuadernos Colombianos* 11 (1977), 309–90.

Bottía G., Luis F., and Escobedo D., Rudolfo. "La Violencia en el sur del departamento de Córdoba." Tesis de grado, Universidad de les Andes, 1979.

Braun, Herbert, "The 'Pueblo' and the Politicians of Colombia: The Assassination of Jorge Eliécer Gaitán and the 'Bogotazo.' Ph.D. diss., University of Wisconsin-Madison, 1983.

Brenner, Robert. "Agrarian Class Structure and Economic Development in Pre-
Industrial Europe." *Past and Present* 70 (February 1976), 30 75.
Brew, R.J. "The Economic Development of Antioquia, 1820–1920." D. Phil. dis-
sertation, Oxford University, 1975.
Browning, David. *El Salvador: Landscape and Society*. Oxford, 1971.
Brücher, Wolfgang. *La colonización de la selva pluvial en el piedemonte amazónico
de Colombia*. Trans. Gerda Westendorp de Núñez. Bogotá, 1974.
Buenaventura, Nicolás. "Movimiento obrero: líder agrario." *Estudios Marxistas* 2
(1969), 6–58.
Bushnell, David. *The Santander Regime in Gran Colombia*. 2nd ed. Westport, Conn.,
1970.
Cabrera Moreno, Gerardo. "La reforma agraria de 1936." *Revista Jurídica* 4–5 (No-
vember 1944), 522–29.
Caicedo, Edgar. *Historia de las luchas sindicales en Colombia*. Bogotá, 1971.
Caja de Crédito Agrícola, Industrial y Minero. "Informe sobre la propiedad de la
American Colombian Corporation en el Departamento de Bolívar, República
de Colombia." Bogotá, 1960. (mimeographed)
Camacho Roldán, Salvador. *Artículos escogidos*. Bogotá, n.d.
———. *Escritos varios*. Bogotá, 1893.
———. *Mis memorias*. Bogotá, 1923.
———. *Notas de viaje*. Bogotá, 1890.
Campo, Urbano. *Urbanización y violencia en el Valle*. Bogotá, 1980.
Caputo, Annie. "Las luchas agrarias en Sumapaz." Tesis de grado, Universidad de
los Andes, 1974.
Cárcano, Miguel Angel. *Evolución histórica del régimen de la tierra pública,
1810–1916*. 3rd ed. Buenos Aires, 1972.
Cardoso, Ciro F.S. "The Formation of the Coffee Estate in Nineteenth Century Costa
Rica." *Land and Labour in Latin America*. Ed. Kenneth Duncan and Ian Rut-
ledge. Cambridge, England, 1977, pp. 165–202.
Castrillón Arboleda, Diego. *El indio Quintín Lamé*. Bogotá, 1973.
Castrillón R., Alberto. *120 días bajo el terror militar*. Bogotá, 1973.
Castro Caycedo, Germán. *Colombia amarga*. Bogotá, 1976.
Castro de Rezende, Gervasio. "Estrutura agrária, produção e emprêgo no nordeste:
uma visão geral." Rio de Janeiro, 1978. (mimeographed)
———. "Plantation Systems, Land Tenure, and Labor Supply: An Historical Anal-
ysis of the Brazilian Case with a Contemporary Study of the Cacao Regions of
Bahia, Brazil." Ph.D. dissertation, University of Wisconsin, 1976.
Cataño, Gonzalo, ed. *Colombia: estructura política y agraria*. Bogotá, 1972.
Chiriboga, Manuel. "Conformación histórica del régimen agro-exportador de la costa
ecuatoriana: la plantación cacaotera." *Estudios Rurales Latinamericanos* 1
(January–April 1978), 111–43.
Christie, Keith H. "Antioqueño Colonization in Western Colombia: A Reappraisal."
Hispanic American Historical Review 58 (May 1978), 260–83.

————. "Gamonalismo in Colombia: An Historical Overview." *North South: Canadian Journal of Latin American Studies* 4 (1979), 42–59.

————. "Oligarchy and Society in Caldas, Colombia." D. Phil. dissertation, Oxford University, 1974.

Coatsworth, John. "Railroads, Landholding, and Agrarian Protest in the Early Porfiriato." *Hispanic American Historical Review* 54 (February 1974), 48–71.

Colmenares, Germán. *Cali: terratenientes, mineros y comerciantes, siglo xviii.* Cali, 1976.

————. "La economía y la sociedad coloniales, 1550–1800." *Manual de Historia de Colombia.* Ed. Jaime Jaramillo Uribe. 3rd ed. vol. 1. Bogotá, 1984, pp. 223–300.

————. *Haciendas de los Jesuitas en el Nuevo Reino de Granada, siglo xviii.* Bogotá, 1969.

————. *Historia económica y social de Colombia, 1537–1719.* 2nd ed. Medellín, 1975.

————. *Partidos políticos y clases sociales en Colombia.* Bogotá, 1968.

Comité de Solidaridad con los Presos Políticos. *Libro negro de la represión, Frente Nacional 1958–1974.* Bogotá, 1974.

Comité Interamericano de Desarrollo Agrícola. *Tenencia de la tierra y desarrollo socio-económico del sector agrícola—Colombia.* Washington, D.C., 1966.

Conferência Nacional dos Bispos do Brasil. *Igreja x governo: documentos oficias da CNBB.* São Paulo, 1977.

Coniff, Michael, ed. *Latin American Populism in Comparative Perspective.* Albuquerque, 1982.

Cordóvez Moure, J.M. *Reminiscencias de Santa Fé y Bogotá.* Madrid, 1957.

Cortés Conde, Roberto. *The First Stages of Modernization in Spanish America.* New York, 1974.

Crist, Raymond E. *The Cauca Valley: Land Tenure and Land Use.* Baltimore, 1952.

Cronshaw, Francine. "Exporting Ideology: T. Lynn Smith in Colombia." *North South: Canadian Journal of Latin American and Caribbean Studies* 7 (1982), 95–110.

Curry, Glenn. "The Dissappearance of the *Resguardos Indígenas* of Cundinamarca, Colombia, 1800–1863." Ph. D. dissertation, Vanderbilt University, 1981.

da Silva Rodrigues, Vera L.G., and Gomes da Silva, José. "Conflitos de terra no Brasil: uma introdução ao estado empírico da violência no campo—período 1971/76." *Reforma Agrária* 7 (January–February 1977), 3–24.

Dávila Ladrón de Guevara, Carlos. "Dominant Classes and Elites in Economic Development: A Comparative Study of Eight Urban Centres in Colombia." Ph.D. dissertation, Northwestern University, 1976.

Dean, Warren. "Latifundia and Land Policy in Nineteenth Century Brazil." *Hispanic American Historical Review* 51 (November 1971), 606–25.

————. *Rio Claro: A Brazilian Plantation System, 1820–1920.* Stanford, 1976.

Deas, Malcolm. "Algunas notas sobre la historia del caciquismo en Colombia." *Revista del Occidente* 127 (October 1973), 118–40.

————. "A Colombian Coffee Estate: Sta. Barbara, Cundinamarca, 1870–1912." *Land and Labour in Latin America*. Ed. Kenneth Duncan and Ian Rutledge. Cambridge, England, 1977, pp. 269–98.

————. "The Fiscal Problems of Nineteenth-Century Colombia." *Journal of Latin American Studies* 14 (November 1982), 287–328.

————. "Poverty, Civil War, and Politics: Ricardo Gaitán Obeso and His Magdalena River Campaign in Colombia, 1885." *Nova Americana* [Turin] 2 (1979), 263–303.

De Janvry, Alain. "The Political Economy of Rural Development in Latin America: An Interpretation." *American Journal of Agricultural Economics* 57 (August 1975), 490–99.

De Janvry, Alain, and Garramón, Carlos. "The Dynamics of Rural Poverty in Latin America." *Journal of Peasant Studies* 4 (April 1977), 206–16.

De la Haye, Olivier. "Formación de la propiedad y renta de la tierra: un análisis regional en Venezuela." Universidad Central de Venezuela, Facultad de Agronomía, Comisión de Información y Documentación, Maracay, Serie Ciencias Sociales, No. 3 (June 1980).

De la Pedraja Tomán, René. "Los cosecheros de Ambalema: un esbozo preliminar." *Anuario Colombiano de Historia Social y de la Cultura* 9 (1979), 39–62.

Delgado, Oscar, ed. *Ideologías políticas y agrarias en Colombia*. Bogotá, 1973.

————. *Reformas agrarias en la América Latina: procesos y perspectivas*. Mexico City, 1965.

Delpar, Helen. *Red Against Blue: The Liberal Party in Colombian Politics, 1863–1899*. Alabama, 1981.

De Rodríguez, Cecilia. *La Costa Atlántica: algunas aspectos socio-económicos de su desarrollo*. Bogotá, 1973.

De Roux, Gustavo Ignacio. "The Social Basis of Peasant Unrest: A Theoretical Framework with Special Reference to the Colombian Case." Ph.D. dissertation, University of Wisconsin, 1974.

De Souza Martins, José. *Capitalismo e tradicionalismo: estudos sôbre as contradições da sociedade agrária no Brasil*. São Paulo, 1975.

Díaz, Antolín. *Sinú: pasión y vida del trópico*. Bogotá, 1935.

Díaz Rodríguez, Justo. "Política agraria y colonización." *Tierras y Aguas* [Organo del Departamento de Tierras y Aguas] 4 (July–August 1943), 3–63.

Diot, Joelle. "Colombia económica 1923–1929: estadísticas historicas." *Boletín Mensual de Estadística* [Departmento Administrativo Nacional de Estadística] 300 (July 1976), 122–35.

————. "Estadísticas históricas, baldíos 1931–1973, legislación y adjudicaciones." *Boletín Mensual de Estadística* 296 (March 1976), 89–136.

————. "Estadísticas históricas: concesiones forestales 1900–1968." *Boletín Mensual de Estadística* 285 (April 1975), 89–155.

Di Tella, Torcuato. "Populism and Reform in Latin America." *Obstacles to Change in Latin America*. Ed. Claudio Véliz. London, 1965, pp. 47–74.

Dix, Robert H. *Colombia: The Political Dimensions of Change*. New Haven, 1967.

Domar, Evsey D. "The Causes of Slavery or Serfdom: A Hypothesis." *Journal of Economic History* 30 (1970), 18–32.

Domínguez Ossa, Camilo A. "Problemas generales de la colonización amazónica en Colombia." *Enfoques Colombianos* 5 (1975), 25–42.

———. "El proceso de colonización en la Amazonia y su incidencia sobre el uso de los recursos naturales." *Revista Colombiana de Antropología* 18 (1975), 293–304.

Drake, Paul. "The Origins of United States Economic Supremacy in South America: Colombia's Dance of the Millions, 1923–33." Paper presented at the Woodrow Wilson International Center. Washington, D.C., December 10, 1979. (mimeographed)

———. "La primera misión Kemmerer: prosperidad al debe." *Economía Colombiana* (October, 1983), 56–75.

———. *Socialism and Populism in Chile, 1932–52*. Urbana, Ill., 1978.

Duff, Ernest A. *Agrarian Reform in Colombia*. New York, 1968.

Duncan Baretta, Silvio R., and Markoff, John. "Civilization and Barbarism: Cattle Frontiers in Latin America." *Comparative Studies in Society and History* 20 (October 1978), 587–620.

Duque Botero, Guillermo. *Historia de Salamina*. Manizales, 1974.

Duque Gómez, Luis, Friede, Juan, and Jaramillo Uribe, Jaime. *Historia de Pereira*. Bogotá, 1963.

Durham, William Haynes, *Scarcity and Survival in Central America*. Stanford, 1979.

Eidt, Robert C. *Pioneer Settlement in Northeast Argentina*. Madison, 1971.

Errazuriz, María. " 'Cafeteros' et 'cafetales' de Líbano (Colombie); innovation technique et encadrement rural." Thèse de IIIème cycle de géografie, Université de Toulouse Le Mirail [France], 1983.

Escorcia, José. *Sociedad y economía en el Valle del Cauca*. vol. 3: *Desarrollo político, social y económico 1800–1854*. Bogotá, 1983.

Fajardo M., Darío. *Violencia y desarrollo: transformaciones sociales en tres regiones cafetaleras del Tolima, 1936–1970*. Bogotá, 1978.

———. "La Violencia y las estructuras agrarias en tres municipios cafeteros del Tolima: 1936–1970." *El agro en el desarrollo histórico colombiano*. Bogotá, 1977, pp. 265–300.

———. "La Violencia 1946–1964: su desarrollo y su impacto." *Estudios Marxistas* 21 (1981).

Fajardo M., Darío et al. *Estudio socio-económico del valle alto del río Tunjuelo*. Bogotá, 1975.

Fals Borda, Orlando. *Capitalismo, hacienda, y poblamiento en la Costa Atlántica*. Bogotá, 1976.

———. *Historia de la cuestión agraria en Colombia*. Bogotá, 1975.

———. *Historia doble de la costa*. vol. 1: *Mompox y Loba*. Bogotá, 1980. vol. 2:

El presidente Nieto. Bogotá, 1981. vol. 3: *Resistencia en el San Jorge*. Bogotá, 1984.

———. *El hombre y la tierra en Boyacá: desarrollo histórico de una sociedad minifundista*. 2nd ed. Bogotá, 1973.

———. "Influencia del vecindario pobre colonial en las relaciones de producción de la Costa Atlántica colombiana." *El agro en el desarrollo histórico colombiano*. Bogotá, 1977, pp. 129–60.

———. "El 'secreto' de la acumulación originaria de capital: una aproximación empírica." *Revista de Extension Cultural* [Universidad Nacional de Colombia, Medellín] 7 (n.d.), 28–39.

———. "Sentido político del movimiento campesino en Colombia." *Estudios Rurales Latinoamericanos* 2 (May–August 1978), 169–76.

Feder, Ernest. *The Rape of the Peasantry: Latin America's Landholding System*. Garden City, N.Y., 1971.

Fluharty, Vernon Lee. *Dance of the Millions: Military Rule and the Social Revolution in Colombia, 1930–1956*. Pittsburgh, 1957.

Fonnegra, Gabriel. *Bananeras: testimonio vivo de una epopeya*. Bogotá, 1980.

Foster, George M. "Peasant Society and the Image of Limited Good." *Peasant Society: A Reader*. Ed. Jack Potter, May Díaz, and George Foster. Boston, 1967, pp. 300–23.

Foweracker, Joe. *The Struggle for Land: A Political Economy of the Pioneer Frontier in Brazil from 1930 to the Present Day*. Cambridge, England, 1981.

Friede, Juan. "Colonos alemanes en la Sierra Nevada de Santa Marta." *Revista Colombiana de Antropología* 12 (1963), 401–11.

———. *La explotación indígena en Colombia bajo el gobierno de las misiones: el caso de los Aruacos de la Sierra Nevada de Santa Marta*. 2nd ed. Bogotá, 1973.

———. *El indio en la lucha por la tierra: historia de los resguardos del macizo central colombiano*. 3rd ed. Bogotá, 1976.

Friedemann, Nina S. de. "Negros: monopolio de tierra, agricultores y desarrollo de plantaciones de caña de azucar en el Valle del Río Cauca." *Tierra, tradición, y poder en Colombia*. Ed. N.S. Friedemann. Bogotá, 1976, pp. 143–68.

Friedrich, Paul. *Agrarian Revolt in a Mexican Village*. Englewood Cliffs, N.J., 1970.

Furtado, Celso. *The Economic Growth of Brazil*. Trans. Richardo W. de Aguiar and Eric Charles Drysdale. Berkeley, 1963.

Gaitán, Jorge Eliécer. *Los mejores discursos de Jorge Eliécer Gaitan, 1919–1948*. Bogotá, 1958.

———. *1928: la masacre en las bananeras (documentos y testimonios)*. Medellín, n.d.

Gaitán de Valencia, Gloria. *Colombia: la lucha por la tierra en la década del treinta*. Bogotá, 1976.

———. "Guatimbol: formación y desintegración de un latifundio cafetero." Universidad de los Andes (CEDE), Bogota, 1969. (mimeographed)

Galindo, Anibal. *Estudios económicos y fiscales*. Bogotá, 1880.

Gallo, Carmenza. *Hipótesis de la acumulación originaria de capital en Colombia*. Medellín, 1974.

Ganitsky Guberek, Sarah. "Luchas agrarias, 1920–1974." Tesis de grado, Universidad de los Andes, 1976.

García, Antonio. *Gaitán y el camino de la revolución colombiana*. 2nd ed. Bogotá, 1974.

———. *Geografía económica de Colombia: Caldas*. Bogotá, 1937.

García Márquez, Gabriel. *One Hundred Years of Solitude*. Trans. Gregory Rabassa. New York, 1971.

Gates, Paul W. *Landlords and Tenants on the Prairie Frontier: Studies in American Land Policy*. Ithaca, N.Y., 1973.

Gilhodes, Pierre. "Agrarian Struggles in Colombia." *Agrarian Problems and Peasant Movements in Latin America*. Ed. Rodolfo Stavenhagen. Garden City, N.Y., 1970, pp. 407–52.

———. "La Colombie et l'United Fruit Company." *Revue Française de Science Politique* 18 (April 1967), 307–17.

———. *La Question agraire en Colombie, 1958–71*. Paris, 1974.

Giraldo Samper, Giraldo and Ladrón de Guevara, Laureano. *Desarrollo y colonización: el caso colombiano*. Bogotá, 1981.

Glade, William P. *The Latin American Economies: A Study of Their Institutional Evolution*. New York, 1969.

Gómez Rodríguez, Carmen, and Camacho Zavala, Antonieta. *Materiales para el estudio de la cuestión agraria en Venezuela 1829–1860: enajenación y arrendamiento de tierras baldías*. Caracas, 1971.

Gonzáles, Michael, "Capitalist Agriculture and Labor Contracting in Northern Peru, 1880–1905." *Journal of Latin American Studies* 12 (1980), 291–315.

González, Margarita. "La hacienda colonial y los orígines de la propiedad territorial en Colombia." *Cuadernos Colombianos* 12 (March 1979), 567–90.

Gott, Richard. *Guerrilla Movements in Latin America*. London, 1970.

Granados, Winston Horacio, "La Violencia en Urrao, Antioquia, 1948–1953." Tesis de grado, Universidad de Antioquia, Departamento de Sociología, Medellín, 1982.

Graziano da Silva, José F. et al. *Estrutura agrária e produção de subsistência na agricultura brasileira*. São Paulo, 1977.

Guhl, Ernesto. *Colombia: bosquejo de su geografía tropical*. 2 vols. Bogotá, 1975.

Guillén Martínez, Fernando. *El poder político en Colombia*. Bogotá, 1979.

Guilmore, Robert L. and Harrison, John P. "Juan Bernardo Elbers and the Introduction of Steam Navigation on the Magdalena River." *Hispanic American Historical Review* 28 (August 1948), 325–59.

Gutiérrez, José. *La rebeldía colombiana: observaciones psicológicas sobre la actualidad política*. Bogotá, 1962.

Guzmán Campos, Germán, Fals Borda, Orlando, and Umaña Luna, Eduardo. *La*

Violencia en Colombia: estudio de un proceso social. 2 vols. 2nd ed. Bogotá, 1962.

Hagen, Everett. "How Economic Growth Begins: A Theory of Social Change." *The Journal of Social Issues* 19 (January 1963), 20–34.

Hale, Charles A. *Mexican Liberalism in the Age of Mora, 1821–1853.* New Haven, 1968.

Hamon, James L., and Niblo, Stephen R. *Precursores de la revolución agraria en México.* Mexico City, 1975.

Harding, Colin. "Land Reform and Social Conflict in Peru." *The Peruvian Experiment: Continuity and Change Under Military Rule.* Ed. Abraham F. Lowenthal. Princeton, 1976, pp. 220–53.

Havens, A. Eugene, Montero, Eduardo, and Romieux, Michel. *Cereté: un area de latifundio (estudio económico y social).* Bogotá, 1965.

Henderson, James D. *When Colombia Bled: A History of the 'Violencia' in Tolima.* Alabama, 1985.

———. "Origins of the *Violencia* in Colombia." Ph.D. dissertation, Texas Christian University, 1972.

Hennessy, Alistair. *The Frontier in Latin American History.* Albuquerque, 1978.

Henríquez, Demetrio Daniel. *Monografía completa de la zona bananera.* Santa Marta, 1939.

Hirschman, Albert O. "Land Use and Land Reform in Colombia." *Journeys Towards Progress.* Garden City, N.Y., 1965, pp. 93–158.

Hobsbawm, Eric J. "Peasant Land Occupations." *Past and Present* 62 (February 1974), 120–52.

———. "Peasant Movements in Colombia." *International Journal of Economic and Social History* 8 (1976), 166–86.

———. "Peasants and Rural Migrants in Politics." *The Politics of Conformity in Latin America.* Ed. Claudio Véliz. Oxford, 1970, pp. 43–65.

Holloway, Thomas. H. *Immigrants on the Land: Coffee, Labor, and Agrarian Society in Western São Paulo, 1886–1934.* Chapel Hill, N.C., 1980.

Horgan, Terrence B. "The Liberals Come to Power in Colombia 'Por Debajo de la Ruana': A Study of the Enrique Olaya Herrera Administration, 1930–1934." Ph.D. dissertation, Vanderbilt University, 1983.

Horna, Hernán. "Transportation Modernization and Entrepreneurship in Nineteenth Century Colombia." *Journal of Latin American Studies* 14 (May 1982), 33–53.

Huizer, Gerrit. *The Revolutionary Potential of Peasants in Latin America.* Lexington, Mass., 1972.

Huizer, Gerrit, and Stavenhagen, Rodolfo. "Peasant Movements and Land Reform in Latin America: Mexico and Bolivia." *Rural Protest: Peasant Movements and Social Change.* Ed. Henry A. Landsberger. New York, 1973, pp. 378–410.

Hyland, Richard P. "A Fragile Prosperity: Credit and Agrarian Structure in the Cauca Valley, Colombia, 1851–87." *Hispanic American Historical Review* 62 (August 1982), 369–406.

―――. "The Secularization of Credit in the Cauca Valley, Colombia, 1851–1880."
Ph.D. dissertation, University of California at Berkeley, 1979.

International Bank for Reconstruction and Development. *The Basis of a Development Program for Colombia*. *(Report of a Mission headed by Lauchlin Currie
and sponsored by the International Bank for Reconstruction and Development
in collaboration with the Government of Colombia)*. Washington, D.C., 1950.

James, Preston. *Latin America*. New York, 1942.

Jara, Alvaro, et al. *Tierras nuevas: expansión territorial y ocupación del suelo en
América (siglos xvi-xix)*. Mexico City, 1969.

Jaramillo Uribe, Jaime. "An Interview with Jaramillo Jaramillo Uribe." Introduction by Frank Safford. *Hispanic American Historical Review* 64:1 (Feburary
l984), 1–l5.

―――, ed. *Manual de Historia de Colombia*. 3rd ed. 3 vols. Bogotá, 1984.

―――. *El pensamiento colombiano en el siglo xix*. Bogotá, 1964.

Jiménez, Michael., "Red Viota: Authority and Rebellion in a Colombian Coffee
Municipality, 1900–1938." Ph.D. dissertation, Harvard University.

―――. "Social Crisis and Agrarian Politics in Colombia, 1930–1936 (The Making
of Law 200 of 1936)." M.A. paper, Latin American Studies Program, Stanford
University, 1971.

Jiménez Neira, Eduardo. "Bases para una tecnificación de la agricultura." *Economía Colombiana* 2 (September 1954), 289–93.

Johnson, David Church. "Social and Economic Change in Nineteenth Century Santander, Colombia." Ph.D. dissertation, University of California at Berkeley,
1975.

Kalmanowitz, Salomón. *Desarrollo de la agricultura en Colombia*. Bogotá, 1978.

―――. "Desarrollo capitalista en el campo colombiano." *Colombia: hoy*. 3rd ed.
Bogotá, 1978, pp. 271–330.

―――. "El régimen agrario durante la colonia." *La nueva historia en Colombia*.
Ed. Darío Jaramillo Agudelo. Bogotá, 1976, pp. 367–454.

―――. "El régimen agrario durante el siglo xix en Colombia." *Manual de historia
de Colombia*. Ed. Jaime Jaramillo Uribe. 3rd ed., vol. 2. Bogotá, 1984, pp.
211–324.

Katz, Friedrich. "Labor Conditions on Haciendas in Porfirian Mexico: Some Trends
and Tendencies." *Hispanic American Historical Review* 54 (February 1974),
1–47.

Katzman, Martin. "The Brazilian Frontier in Comparative Perspective." *Comparative Studies in Society and History* 17 (July 1975), 266–85.

―――. *Cities and Frontiers in Brazil: Regional Dimensions of Economic Development*. Cambridge, Mass., 1977.

Klarén, Peter F. "The Social and Economic Consequences of Modernization in the
Peruvian Sugar Industry, 1870–1930." *Land and Labour in Latin America*. Ed.
Kenneth Duncan and Ian Rutledge. Cambridge, England, 1977, pp. 229–52.

Knowlton, Robert J. "Expropriation of Church Property in Nineteenth Century Mexico and Colombia. A Comparison." *The Americas* 24 (April 1969), 387–401.

Koffman, Bennett E. "The National Federation of Coffee Growers of Colombia." Ph.D. dissertation, University of Virginia, 1969.

Kohl, James V. "Peasants and Revolution in Bolivia, April 9, 1952–August 2, 1952." *Hispanic American Historical Review* 58 (May 1978), 238–59.

Lambert, Jacques. *Os dois Brasís*. Rio de Janeiro, 1959.

———. *Latin America: Social Structure and Political Institutions*. Trans. Helen Katel. Berkeley, 1967.

Landsberger, Henry A., ed. *Latin American Peasant Movements*. Ithaca, N.Y., 1969.

———. "Peasant Unrest: Themes and Variations." *Rural Protest: Peasant Movements and Social Change*. New York, 1973, pp. 1–66.

———. *Rural Protest: Peasant Movements and Social Change*. New York, 1973.

Leal Buitrago, Francisco. "Social Classes, International Trade, and Foreign Capital in Colombia: An Attempt at Historical Interpretation of the Formation of the State, 1819–1935." Ph.D. dissertation, University of Wisconsin, 1974.

LeGrand, Catherine C. "Colombian Transformations: Peasants and Wage Labourers in the Santa Marta Banana Zone." *Journal of Peasant Studies* 11 (July 1984), 178–200.

———. "De las tierras públicas a las propiedades privadas: acaparamiento de tierras y conflictos agrarios en Colombia, 1870–1930." *Lecturas de Economía* 13 (January-April 1984), 13–50.

———. "From Public Lands into Private Properties: Landholding and Rural Conflict in Colombia, 1850–1936." Ph.D. dissertation, Stanford University, 1980.

———. "Labor Acquisition and Social Conflict on the Colombian Frontier, 1850–1936." *Journal of Latin American Studies* 16:1 (May 1984), 27–49.

———. "Perspectives for the Historical Study of Rural Politics and the Colombian Case: An Overview." *Latin American Research Review* 12 (Spring 1977), 7–36.

León de Leal, Magdalena, et al. *Mujer y capitalismo agrario: estudio de cuatro regiones colombianas*. Bogotá, 1980.

Lleras Restrepo, Carlos, et al. *Tierra: diez ensayos sobre la reforma agraria en Colombia*. Bogotá, 1961.

López, Alejandro. *Idearium Liberal*. Paris, 1931.

———. *Problemas colombianos*. Paris, 1927.

López C., Hugo. "La inflación en Colombia en la década de los veintes." *Cuadernos Colombianos* 5 (1975), 41–140.

López Cardenas, Gilma and Acosta Muñoz, Daniel. "Violencia capitalista en el Magdalena Medio." *La realidad del "si se puede": demagogía y violencia*. Ed. Comité de Solidaridad con Los Presos Políticos. Bogotá, 1984, pp. 153–245.

López Giraldo, Fermín. *El apostol desnudo: o dos años al lado de un mito*. Manizales, 1936.

López G., Fernando. *Evolución de la tenencia de la tierra en una zona minifundista*. Bogotá, 1975.

López Mejía, Clara Inés and Ordóñez Súarez, Clara Inés. "Violencia en la región de Sumapaz, 1953–57." Tesis de grado, Universidad Nacional, 1983.

López Toro, Alvaro. *Migración y cambio social en Antioquia durante el siglo diez y nueve*. Bogotá, 1970.

Love, Joseph. *Rio Grande do Sul and Brazilian Regionalism, 1882–1930*. Stanford, 1971.

Loveman, Brian. "Critique of Arnold J. Bauer's 'Rural Workers in Spanish America: Problems of Peonage and Oppression.' " *Hispanic American Historical Review* 59 (August 1979), 478–89.

Loy, Jane M. "The Llanos in Colombian History: Some Implications of a Static Frontier." University of Massachusetts Program in Latin American Studies, Occasional Papers Series No. 2, 1976.

Lozano T., Fabio. *Con los agricultores de Colombia*. Lima, 1927.

McBride, George M. *Chile: Land and Society*. New York, 1936.

McCreery, D.J. "Coffee and Class: The Structure of Development in Liberal Guatemala." *Hispanic American Historical Review* 56 (August 1976), 438–60.

McGreevey, William Paul. *An Economic History of Colombia*. Cambridge, England, 1971.

Machado C., Absalón. *El café: de la aparcería al capitalismo*. Bogotá, 1977.

———. "Políticas agrarias en Colombia." Bogotá, 1979, (typewritten).

Madrid Malo, Nestor. "Génesis e ineficacia de la reforma sobre tierras." *Revista Trimestral de Cultura Moderna* [Universidad Nacional de Colombia] 1 (October 1944), 399–420.

Martínez, Marco A., ed. *Régimen de tierras en Colombia (Antecedentes de la Ley 200 de 1936 'sobre régimen de tierras' y decretos reglamentarios)*. 2 vols. Bogotá, 1939.

Martínez-Alier, Juan. *Haciendas, Plantations, and Collective Farms: Agrarian Class Societies—Cuba and Peru*. London, 1977.

Maullin, Richard. "The Fall of Dumar Aljure, A Colombian Guerrilla and Bandit." Rand Memorandum 5750-1SA. Santa Monica, Cal., 1969.

———. *Soldiers, Guerrillas and Politics in Colombia*. Lexington, Mass., 1973.

Medina, Medófilo. *Historia del Partido Comunista de Colombia*. vol. 1. Bogotá, 1980.

———. "La resistencia campesina en el sur del Tolima 1949–1953." Paper presented at the I Simposio Internacional y II Seminario Sobre Movimientos Sociales: "La Violencia en Colombia." Sponsored by the History Department of the Universidad Nacional and the Centro Jorge Eliécer Gaitán. Bogotá, June 24–30, 1984. (mimeographed)

Melo, Hector, and López Botero, Ivan. *El imperio clandestino del café*. Bogotá, 1976.

Melo, Jorge Orlando. "La economía colombiana en la cuarta década del siglo xix." *Sobre historia y política*. Bogotá, 1979, pp. 99–140.

————. *Historia de Colombia: el establecimiento de la dominación española*. Medellín, 1977.

Merchán, Victor J. "Datos para la historia social, económica y del movimiento agrario de Viotá y el Tequendama: testimonio." *Estudios Marxistas* 9 (1975), 105–16.

Mesa, Darío. *El problema agrario en Colombia, 1920–1960*. Bogotá, 1972.

————. "Treinta años de historia colombiana (1925–1955)." *Colombia: estructura política y agraria*. Ed. Gonzalo Cataño. Bogotá, 1972, pp. 19–62.

Meyer, Jean. *Problemas campesinos y revueltas agrarias (1821–1919)*. Mexico City, 1973.

Mina, Mateo (pseud. for M. Taussig and A. Rubbo). *Esclavitud y libertad en el valle del río Cauca*. Bogotá, 1975.

Mintz, Sidney. "The Caribbean Region." *Daedalus* 103 (Spring 1974), 45–72.

Molano Bravo, Alfredo. "De la Violencia a la colonización: un testimonio colombiano." *Estudios Rurales Latinoamericanos* 4 (Sepember–December 1981), 257–86.

Molina, Gerardo. *Las ideas liberales en Colombia, 1849–1914*. Bogotá, 1970.

————. *Las ideas liberales en Colombia, 1915–1934*. Bogotá, 1974.

Moncayo C., Victor M. "La ley y el problema agrario en Colombia." *Ideología y Sociedad* 14–15 (July–December 1975), 7–46.

Monsalve, Diego. *Colombia cafetera: información general de la república y estadísticas de la industria*. Barcelona, 1927.

Morales Benítez, Otto. *Testimonio de un pueblo*. Bogotá, 1962.

Moreno, David, and Marulanda, Elsy. "La UNIR: primera táctica del Gaitanismo." Paper presented to the I Seminario Nacional Sobre Movimientos Sociales: "Gaitanismo y el 9 de Abril." Sponsored by the History Department of the Universidad Nacional and Centro Jorge Eliécer Gaitán. Bogotá, April 15–17, 1982. (mimeographed)

Mörner, Magnus. "The Spanish American Hacienda: A Survey of Recent Research and Debate." *Hispanic American Historical Review* 53 (May 1973), 183–216

Negrete B., Victor. *Origen de las luchas agrarias en Córdoba*. Montería, 1981.

Nichols, Theodore E. *Tres puertos de Colombia*. Bogotá, 1973.

Nieto Arteta, Luis Eduardo. *El café en la sociedad colombiana*. 2nd ed. Bogotá, 1971.

————. *Economía y cultura en la historia de Colombia*. 6th ed. Bogotá, 1975.

"1930–1933 Chaparral, Tolima: lucha de los proletarios del campo. Entrevista con un viejo campesino de Chaparral. Enero de 1969." *Estudios Marxistas* 1 (1969), 98–99.

OCampo, José Antonio. "Desarrollo exportador y desarrollo capitalista colombiano en el siglo xix (una hipótesis)." *Desarrollo y Sociedad* 1 (January 1979), 135–44.

————. "Desarrollo exportador y desarrollo capitalista colombiano en el siglo xix." *Desarrollo y Sociedad* 8 (May 1982), 37–75.

————. "Las exportaciones colombianas en el siglo xix." *Desarrollo y Sociedad* 4 (July 1980), 163–226.

————. "El mercado mundial del café y el surgimiento de Colombia como un país cafetero." *Desarrollo y Sociedad* 5 (January 1981), 125–56.

OCampo, José Antonio and Montenegro, Santiago. "La crisis mundial de los años treinta en Colombia." *Desarrollo y Sociedad* 7 (January 1982), 35–96.

OCampo, José Fernando. *Dominio de clase en las cuidad colombiana*. Medellín, 1972.

Oficina Para Investigaciones Socio-económicas y Legales (OFISEL). "La acción del estado en Colombia y sus beneficiarios, 1820–1931. Tres aspectos de política en el sector agropecuario:—adjudicación de baldíos,—desamortización de bienes de manos muertos, —resguardos indígenas." Bogotá, 1975. (mimeographed)

Olarte Camacho, Vicente. *Recopilación de leyes y disposiciones administrativas*. Bogotá, 1901.

Oquist, Paul. *Violence, Conflict and Politics in Colombia*. New York, 1980.

Orozco, Winstano Luis. *Legislación y jurisprudencia sobre terrenos baldíos*. 2 vols. Mexico City, 1895.

Ortega Díaz, Alfredo. *Ferrocarriles colombianos: legislación ferroviaria*. Bogotá, 1949.

————. *Ferrocarriles colombianos: resumen histórico*. Bogotá, 1923.

————. *Ferrocarriles colombianos: la última experiencia ferroviaria del país*. Bogotá, 1932.

Ortiz, Carlos. "Fundadores y negociantes en la colonización del Quindío." *Lecturas de Economía* [Universidad de Antioquia] 13 (January–April 1984), 105–40.

————. "La Violence en Colombie: le cas du Quindío." Doctorat, Ecole des Hautes Etudes en Sciences Sociales, Universite de Paris, 1983.

Osorio Lizarazo, J. A. *La cosecha*. Manizales, 1935.

————. *Gaitán: vida, muerte y permanente presencia*. Buenos Aires, 1952.

Ospina, Joaquín. *Diccionario biográfico y bibliográfico de Colombia*. Bogotá, 1927.

Ospina Vásquez, Luis, ed. *Historia económica en Colombia: un debate en marcha*. Bogotá, 1979.

————. *Industria y protección en Colombia, 1810–1930*. Bogotá, 1955.

Ots Capdequí, José María. *El régimen de la tierra en la América española durante el periodo colonial*. Cuidad Trujillo, 1946.

Padilla B., Pedro, and Llanos O., Alberto. "Proyecto Magdalena 4: zona bananera." Instituto Colombiano de la Reforma Agraria. Bogotá, 1964. (mimeographed)

Paez Courvel, Luis E. *Historia de las medidas agrarias antiguas. Legislación colonial y republicana y el proceso de su aplicación en las titulaciones de tierras*. Bogotá, 1940.

Paige, Jeffrey M. *Agrarian Revolution: Social Movements and Export Agriculture in the Underdeveloped World*. New York, 1975.

Palacios, Marco. *El café en Colombia, 1850–1970: una historia económica, social y política*. 2nd ed. Mexico and Bogotá, 1983.

———. *Coffee in Colombia (1850–1970): An Economic, Social and Political History*. Cambridge, England, 1980.

———. "La fragmentación regional de las clases dominantes en Colombia: una perspectiva histórica." *Revista Mexicana de Sociología* 42 (October–December 1980), 1663–89.

———. "Las haciendas cafeteras de Cundinamarca, 1870–1970." Bogotá, 1975. (mimeographed)

Pardo, Carlos Enrique. "Cundinamarca: hacienda cafetera y conflictos agrarios." Tesis de grado, Universidad de los Andes, 1981.

Parra E., Ernesto. *La investigación-acción en la costa atlántica: evaluación de La Rosca, 1972–74*. Cali, 1983.

Parsons, James. *Antioqueño Colonization in Western Colombia*. Berkeley, 1949.

Partido Comunista de Colombia. "Contra la represión oficial en Cimitarra." *Cuadernos Políticos* 10 (1976), 1–16.

———. *Treinta años de lucha del Partido Comunista de Colombia*. Bogotá, n.d.

Partridge, William L. "Banana Country in the Wake of United Fruit: Social and Economic Linkages." *American Ethnologist* 6 (1975), 491–509.

Pearse, Andrew. *The Latin American Peasant*. London, 1975.

Pearse, Arno S. *Colombia, With Special Reference to Cotton (Being the Report of the Journey of the International Cotton Mission Through the Republic of Colombia)*. Manchester, 1926.

Pécaut, Daniel. "Classe ouvrière et systeme politique en Colombie, 1930–1953." Doctorat d'état, Ecole des Hautes Etudes en Sciences Sociales, Université de Paris, 1979.

———. *Política y sindicalismo en Colombia*. Bogotá, 1973.

———. "Reflexiones sobre el fenómeno de La Violencia." *Ideología y Sociedad* 19 (1976), 71–79.

Perry, Santiago. *La crisis agraria en Colombia, 1950–1980*. Bogotá, 1983.

Petras, James, and Zimelman Merino, Hugo. *Peasants in Revolt: A Chilean Case Study, 1965–1971*. Austin, 1972.

Pompermayer, Malori. "The State and The Frontier in Brazil: A Case Study of the Amazon." Ph.D. dissertation, Stanford University, 1979.

Poppino, Rollie E. *Brazil: The Land and People*. New York, 1968.

Posada, Francisco. *Colombia: violencia y subdesarrollo*. Bogotá, 1969.

Powell, John Duncan. "Venezuela: The Peasant Union Movement." *Latin American Peasant Movements*. Ed. Henry Landsberger. Ithaca, N.Y., 1969, pp. 62–100.

Quijano Obregón, Anibal. "Contemporary Peasant Movements." *Elites in Latin America*. Ed. Seymour Martin Lipset and Aldo Solari. New York, 1967, pp. 301–41.

Quimbaya, Anteo. *El problema de la tierra en Colombia*. Bogotá, 1967.

Quiñónez, Jorge, and Jaramillo A., Gustavo. "Informe sobre la zona bananera del

Magdalena." Instituto Colombiano de la Reforma Agraria. Bogotá, 1962. (mimeographed)

Quintín Lamé, Manuel. *Las luchas del indio que bajó de la montaña al valle de la 'civilización'*. Bogotá, 1973.

Ramírez Tobón, W. "La guerrilla rural en Colombia: una vía hacia la colonización armada?" *Estudios Rurales Latinamericanos* 4 (May–August 1981, 199–209.

Ramsey, Russell W. *Guerrilleros y soldados*. Bogotá, 1981.

Randall, Stephen J. *The Diplomacy of Modernization: Colombian-American Relations, 1920–1940*. Toronto, 1978.

Rausch, Jane M. *A Tropical Plains Frontier: The Llanos of Colombia, 1531–1831*. Albuquerque, 1984.

"Reforma agraria burguesa. Un estudio de caso." *Estudios Marxistas* 11 (1976), 18–34.

Reinhardt, Nola. "The Independent Family Farm Mode of Production: El Palmar, Colombia, 1890–1978. A Study of Economic Development and Agrarian Structure." Ph.D. dissertation, University of California at Berkeley, 1981.

Restrepo, Emiliano. *Una excursión al territorio de San Martín*. 2nd ed. Bogotá, 1952.

Restrepo, Vicente. *Estudio sobre las minas de oro y plata de Colombia*. Bogotá, 1952.

Reyes Posada, Alejandro. "Aparcería y capitalismo agrario." *Controversia* [Centro de Investigación y Educación Popular] 38 (1975), 2–67.

———. *Latifundio y poder político: la hacienda ganadera en Sucre*. Bogotá, 1978.

Rippy, J. Fred. *The Capitalists and Colombia*. New York, 1931.

———. *Latin America and the Industrial Age*. 2nd ed. Westport, Conn., 1971.

Rivas, Medardo. *Los trabajadores de tierra caliente*. 2nd ed. Bogotá, 1972.

Rivas Groot, José María. *Asuntos económicos y fiscales*. Bogotá, 1909.

Rodríguez Córdoba, Clara Inés and Moreno Coronado, Aydée Esmeralda. "Desintegración del resguardo y consolidación de la propiedad privada en Natagaima, siglo xix." Tesis de grado, Universidad Nacional, 1983.

Rodríquez Plata, Horacio. *La inmigración alemana al estado soberano de Santander en el siglo xix*. Bogotá, 1968.

Rodríquez R., Jorge E., and McGreevey, William P. "Colombia: comercio exterior, 1835–1962." *Compendio de estadísticas históricas de Colombia*. Ed. Miguel Urrutia M. and Mario Arrubla. Bogotá, 1970, pp. 106–208.

Rodríguez Salazar, Oscar. *Efectos de la gran depresión sobre la industria colombiana*. Bogotá, 1973.

Rojas Ruíz, Humberto. "Peasant Consciousness in Three Rural Communities." Ph.D. dissertation, University of Wisconsin, 1974.

Safford, Frank. "Commerce and Enterprise in Central Colombia, 1821–70." Ph.D. dissertation, Columbia University, 1964.

———. *The Ideal of the Practical: Colombia's Struggle to Form a Technical Elite*. Austin, 1976.

————. "Social Aspects of Politics in Nineteenth Century Spanish America: New Granada, 1825–1850." *Journal of Social History* 5 (1972), 344–70.

Sánchez G., Gonzalo. *Los 'Bolsheviques del Líbano' (Tolima)*. Bogotá, 1976.

————. *Los días de la revolución: gaitanismo y 9 de abril en provincia*. Bogotá, 1983.

————. *Las ligas campesinas en Colombia*. Bogotá, 1977.

————. "Raices históricas de la amnistía o las etapas de la guerra en Colombia." *Revista de Extension Cultural* [Universidad Nacional de Colombia, Medellín] 15 (1983), 23–44.

————. "La Violencia in Colombia: New Research, New Questions." *Hispanic American Historical Review* 65: 4 (November 1985).

————. "La Violencia y sus efectos en el sistema político colombiano." *Cuadernos Colombianos* 9 (January–April 1976), 1–44.

Sánchez G., Gonzalo, and Meertens, Donny. *Bandoleros, gamonales y campesinos: el caso de la Violencia en Colombia*. Prologue by Eric Hobsbawm. Bogotá, 1983.

Sánchez Reyes, Joel Darío. "Colonización quindiana: proceso político-ideológico en la conformación del campesinado cafetero, 1840–1920." Tesis de masters, Universidad de los Andes, 1982.

Santa Eduardo. *Arrieros y fundadores: aspectos de la colonización antioqueña*. Bogotá, 1961.

Seligson, Mitchell. *Peasants of Costa Rica and the Development of Agrarian Capitalism*. Madison, 1980.

————. "Agrarian Policies in Dependent Societies: Costa Rica." *Journal of Interamerican Studies and World Affairs* 19 (May 1977), 201–32.

Sevilla Casas, Elias. "Lamé y el Cauca indígena." *Tierra, tradición y poder en Colombia: enfoques antropológicos*. Ed. N.S. Friedemann. Bogotá, 1976, pp. 85–106.

Sharp, William Frederick. *Slavery on the Spanish Frontier: The Colombian Chocó, 1680–1810*. Norman, Oklahoma, 1976.

Sharpe, Kenneth Evan. *Peasant Politics: Struggle in a Dominican Village*. Baltimore, 1977.

Sharpless, Richard E. *Gaitán of Colombia: A Political Biography*. Pittsburgh, 1978.

Sierra, Luis Fernando. *El tobaco en la economía colombiana del siglo xix*. Bogotá, 1961.

Smith, T. Lynn. *Colombia: Social Structure and the Process of Development*. Gainsville, 1967.

Solberg, Carl E. "A Discriminatory Frontier Land Policy: Chile 1870–1914." *The Americas* 26 (October 1969), 115–33.

Soles, Roger E. "Rural Land Invasions in Colombia. A Study of the Macro- and Micro-Conditions and Forces Leading to Peasant Unrest." Ph.D. dissertation, University of Wisconsin, 1972.

Sorj, Bernardo. "Estructura agrária e dinâmica política no Brasil atual." London, 1977. (mimeographed)

Stein, Stanley. *Vassouras: A Brazilian Coffee County, 1850–1890*. 2nd ed. New York, 1974.

Stein, Stephen. *Populism in Peru: The Emergence of the Masses and the Politics of Social Control*. Madison, 1980.

Taborda, Guido, Ronderos, Abel, and Díaz, Ernesto. "Informe y recommendaciones del Ariguani y Hato del Monquezano." Instituto Colombiano de la Reforma Agraria, n.d. (mimeographed)

Tannenbaum, Frank. *The Mexican Agrarian Revolution*. Washington, D.C., 1929.

———. *Ten Keys to Latin America*. New York, 1962.

Taussig, Michael. "The Evolution of Rural Wage Labor in the Cauca Valley of Colombia, 1700–1970." *Land and Labour in Latin America*. Ed. Kenneth Duncan and Ian Rutledge. Cambridge, England, 1977, pp. 409–21.

———. "Peasant Economics and the Development of Capitalist Agriculture in the Cauca Valley, Colombia." *Latin American Perspectives* 5 (Summer 1978), 62–91.

———. "Rural Proletarianization: A Social and Historical Enquiry into the Commercialization of the Southern Cauca Valley." 2 vols. Ph.D. dissertation, University of London, 1974.

Taylor, Carl C. *Rural Life in Argentina*. Baton Rouge, 1948.

Taylor, William B. *Landlord and Peasant in Colonial Oaxaca*. Stanford, 1972.

Thirsk, Wayne. "Some Facets of Rural Poverty in Colombia." General Working Paper No. 2. Rural Development Division. Bureau for Latin America and the Caribbean. Agency for International Development. Washington, D.C. 1978.

Thome, Joseph R. "Title Problems in Rural Areas: A Colonization Example." *Internal Colonialism and the Structural Change in Colombia*. Ed. A. Eugene Havens and William Flinn. New York, 1970, pp. 146–67.

Thompson, E.P. *Whigs and Hunters: The Origins of the Black Act*. New York, 1975.

Tirado Mejía, Alvaro. *Aspectos políticos del primer gobierno de Alfonso López Pumarejo, 1934–38*. Bogotá, 1981.

———. *Aspectos sociales de las guerras civiles en Colombia*. Bogotá, 1976.

———. *Colombia en la repartición imperialista (1870–1913)*. Medellín, 1976.

———. *Introducción a la historia económica de Colombia*. 3rd ed. Bogotá, 1974.

Torres García, Guillermo. *Historia de la moneda en Colombia*. Bogotá, 1945.

Torres Giraldo, Ignacio. *Los inconformes: historia de la rebeldía de las masas en Colombia*. vols. 3 and 4. Bogotá, 1974.

———. *María Cano: mujer rebelde*. Bogotá, 1972.

Tovar Pinzón, Hermes. *Grandes empresas agrícolas y ganaderas, su desarrollo en el siglo xviii*. Bogotá, 1980.

———. *El movimiento campesino en Colombia durante los siglos xix y xx*. Bogotá, 1975.

———. "Orígenes y características de los sistemas de terraje y arrendamiento en la sociedad colonial durante el siglo xviii: el caso neogranadino." *Desarrollo y Sociedad* 8 (May 1982), 15–34.

Tovar Zambrano, Bernardo. *La colonia en la historiografía colombiana*. Bogotá, 1984.

———. *La intervención económica del estado en Colombia, 1914–1936*. Bogotá, 1984.

Twinam, Ann. *Miners, Merchants, and Farmers in Colonial Colombia*. Austin 1982.

United Nations. Economic Commission for Latin America [ECLA]. *Analyses and Projections of Economic Development: III. The Economic Development of Colombia*. Geneva, 1957.

Uribe de H., María Teresa and Alvarez, Jesús María. "Regiones, economía, y espacio nacional en Colombia, 1820–1850." *Lecturas de Economía* 13 (January–April 1984), 155–222.

Uribe Echeverrí, Carlos. *Nuestro problema, producir*. Madrid, 1936.

Urrutia Montoya, Miguel. *The Development of the Colombian Labor Movement*. New Haven, 1969.

Vallejo Morillo, Jorge. "Los colonos del Putumayo." *Enfoques Colombianos* 5 (1975), 59–78.

———. "Problemas de método en el estudio de la cuestión agraria." *El agro en el desarrollo histórico colombiano*. Bogotá, 1977, pp. 85–126.

Van Nierkerk, A.E. *Populism and Political Development in Latin America*. Rotterdam, 1974.

Vargas Lesmés, Julian. "Estudio de base para el desarrollo del oriente colombiano." Informe de avance (versión preliminar). Departamento Nacional de Planeación. Bogotá, 1983.

Vassberg, David. "The Sale of Baldíos in Sixteenth Century Castile." *Journal of Modern History* 47 (December 1975), 629–54.

———. *La venta de tierras baldías: el comunitarismo agrario y la corona de Castilla durante el siglo xvi*. Madrid, 1983.

Velandia, Roberto. *Encyclopedia histórica de Cundinamarca*. vol. 2. Bogotá, 1979.

Vélez M., Hugo. *Dos ensayos acerca del desarrollo capitalista en la agricultura colombiana*. Medellín, 1975.

Vergara y Velasco, Francisco. *Nueva geografía de Colombia*. 3 vols. Bogotá, 1901.

Villamarín, Juan A., "Haciendas en la sabana de Bogotá, Colombia en la época colonial: 1539–1810." *Haciendas, latifundios y plantaciones en América Latina*. Ed. Enrique Florescano. Mexico City, 1975, pp. 327–45.

Villegas, Jorge. *Colombia: colonización de vertiente en el siglo 19*. Medellín, 1977.

———. *Colombia: enfrentamiento iglesia-estado, 1819–1887*. Medellín, 1977.

———. "Historia de la propiedad agraria en Colombia, 1819–1936." Bogotá, 1976. (typewritten)

———. *Petroleo colombiano, ganancia gringa*. 4th ed. Bogotá, 1976.

Warman, Arturo. *"We Come to Object": The Peasants of Morelos and the National State*. Trans. Stephen K. Ault. Baltimore, 1980.

Wasserstrom, Robert. "Revolution in Guatemala: Peasants and Politics Under the Arbenz Government." *Comparative Studies in Society and History* 17 (October 1975), 410–42.

Weffort, Francisco. "El populismo en la política brasileña." *Brasil: hoy*. Ed. Celso Furtado et al. Mexico City, 1970, pp. 54–84.

West, Robert C. *The Pacific Lowlands of Colombia: A Negroid Area of the American Tropics*. Baton Rouge, 1957.

White, Judith. *Historia de una ignominia: La United Fruit Co. en Colombia*. Bogotá, 1978.

Womack, Jr., John. *Zapata and the Mexican Revolution*. New York, 1968.

World Bank [International Bank for Reconstruction and Development]. *Economic Growth of Colombia: Problems and Prospects*. Baltimore, 1972.

Wylie, Kathryn. *The Agriculture of Colombia*. Washington, D.C., 1942.

Zambrano, Fabio, et al. "Colombia: desarrollo agrícola, 1900–1930." Tesis de grado, Universidad Jorge Tadeo Lozano, 1974.

———. "La navegación a vapor por el río Magdalena." *Anuario Colombiano de Historia Social y de la Cultura* 9 (1979), 653–77.

Zambrano, Gloria Lucy. *En el Magdalena Medio: los moradores de la represión*. Bogotá, 1983.

Zuleta, Estanislao, and Asociación Nacional de Usuarios Campesinos. *La tierra en Colombia*. Medellín, 1973.

Index

Adamo, Vicente, 114, 165, 240
Administrative divisions of Colombia, 212
Agrarian bill of 1933, 143–46, 160, 251
Agrarian reform: *See* Agrarian bill of 1933;
    Law 200 of 1936; Law 135 of 1961;
    Supreme Court decision of 1926
Agricultural Mortgage Bank, 139, 141, 250
Agustín Codazzi Geographical Institute,
    173
Alvarez, Santiago M., 229
American Colombian Corporation: purchase
    of "Terrenos de Loba", 55; land conflicts
    and, 77; opposed by colono leagues,
    128; size of holdings, 223; methods of
    asserting land claims, 225–26
Antioqueño colonization: geographical area,
    xv; revisionist interpretations of, xv; and
    positive image of peasants, 17; and land
    tenure patterns, 89; in Sumapaz, 112; in
    Valle del Cauca, 116; reasons for land
    subdivision, 224–25; in Burila territory,
    242. *See also* Antioqueño settlements;
    Antioquia
Antioqueño settlements (*poblaciones*):
    creation of, 13; land grants to (figures),
    31, 41, 48, 49, 50, 219; disputes with
    land entrepreneurs, 63; mentioned, 14,
    43, 169. *See also* Antioqueño
    colonization
Antioquia (department of): Medellín, xv,
    11, 60, 77, 131, 147; colonial economy,
    2; coffee production, 7, 19; *palenques*,
    19; conditions in the highlands, late
    19th century, 21; colonization
    companies, 22; Támesis, 22; Urabá, 25,

    60, 164; Turbo, 29, 86; early land
    grants in, 41; Caramanta, 41; ranching,
    42; usurpation of public land, 53, 54;
    Yolombó, 59–60, 84, 219; Puerto
    Berrío, 60, 128; forest concessions, 75;
    migration from Sinú into, 113; work of
    historians on, 174–75; Nare, 243;
    mentioned, 34, 35, 57, 70, 88, 260
Aranzazu family, 224
Arce, Laureano, 72
Argentina: location of public land, xiv;
    attitude to native peasants, 17;
    immigrant settlements, 17; populism,
    122; patterns of frontier development,
    225; mention, 105
Artisans: as colono leaders, 121, 226, 228
Asociación Nacional de Usuarios
    Campesinos, linea Sincelejo (ANUC):
    164, 166
Asociación Patronal Económica Nacional
    (APEN). *See* Employers' National
    Economic Association

Baldíos. *See* Public lands; Public land
    policy
Bananas: export of, 7; hot country crop, 9;
    and frontier expansion, 35–36; mention,
    93
Banana zone: in-migration, 1930's, 107;
    conflicts over land, 110, 114–16;
    Communist influence in, 124; peasant
    leagues, 128–29; designated agrarian
    reform area, 172; Public Land
    Commission reports on, 172. *See also*
    Bananas; United Fruit Company

Sumapaz, Agrarian Colony of;
Parcelization program
Communist Party of Colombia (PCC):
involved in agrarian conflicts, 123–24;
forms peasant leagues and unions, 128;
opposes parcelization, 140; popular front
policy, 146, 156; supports parcelization
after 1936, 157; in La Violencia, 163,
164; in Cimitarra (Santander), 164;
supported by Indians and peasants, 245;
organizes independent enclave in Viotá,
247; Juan de la Cruz Varela and, 259;
mention, 125, 126
Compañía Cafetera de Cunday, 240
Conflict over public land: relation to export
economy, xii; laws concerning, 15;
among colonos, 28
—1874–1928: colonos resist expropriation,
63–68; role of tinterillos, 69–70; rent
disputes, 70–72, 227; role of large
cultivators, 70–73; role of municipal
authorities, 73–76; landlords' tactics to
evict colonos, 77–83; location of, 79,
80, 95; response of national government,
83–87; impact of, 89–90; in the 1920s,
93, 94
—1928–36: squatters invade haciendas,
91, 109–10; reasons for squatter
occupations, 107–08; regionalization of
land invasions, 109–18; peasant
ideology, 118–19; landlord opposition,
119–21; government response, 131–34,
135–53; intervention of National Labor
Bureau, 132; political impact, 133,
152–53; economic effects, 134; squatter
occupations diminish after 1936, 156;
tenant farmers encourage wage workers
to invade haciendas, 239; squatters
invade "Terrenos de Burila", 242
—1936–46: 160–61, 257–58
—Post–1960: 164–65, 166. See also
Colonos; Land entrepreneurs; Public
land policy; La Violencia
Conservative party: formation of, 10; land
policy, 15, 97, 102–03; attitude to
industrialization, 94; rural mobilization,
125; opposition to land reform, 147,

148, 165–66; in Córdoba, during La
Violencia, 164; mention, xv, 70, 168
Convers, Sergio, 42
Córdoba (department of): during La
Violencia, 164; Montelíbano, 218;
Tierralta, 218. See also Bolívar
Costa Rica: public land policy, compared
to Colombia, 17, 214; squatter
movements, 170
Cotton, 6, 9, 165
Cruz E., Antonio A., 72
Cuadrillas: used by landlords to evict
colonos, 83; used by colonos in
self-defense, 164
Cuba, 170
Cundinamarca (department of): coffee
production, 7; Tequendama, 19,
123–24; breakdown of Indian
communities, 20; Pandi, 75, 77, 86,
113, 125, 243; San Bernardo, 77, 125,
165, 218, 243, 255; Junín, 80;
Caparrapí, 85, 227; tenant protests, 104;
in-migration in 1930s, 107; Usme, 113;
Gutiérrez, 113; response to squatter
occupations, 120; Gaitán studies
hacienda titles, 123; Fusugasugá, 125,
257, 258; Pasca, 125, 255; peasant
leagues, 128; pacts between landlords
and squatters, 132; rise in number of
small coffee farms, 146; landlords
organize against colonos, 147; effects of
parcelization program, 157, 255; Ospina
Pérez, 165; Cabrera, 218; Gachetá, 230;
Viotá, 247; Pubenza, 258; El Colegio,
258; mention, 42, 48, 66, 88, 93. See
also Sumapaz; Sumapaz, Agrarian
Colony of

Dávila Pumarejo, Manuel, 35
De La Cruz Varela, Juan, 129, 163, 259
Debt: and colonos, 216
Departamento Nacional Administrativo de
Estadística (DANE), 173
Depression of 1929: social impact,
106–07; government response to,
106–07; impact in banana zone, 115;

221; mention, 32. *See also* Conflicts over
public land; Merchants; Speculation;
Usurpation of public land

Land grants: obtained with certificates of
public debt, 11–12, 14; and economic
use requirement, 14, 101, 213; limits on
size of, 16, 211, 213; to Antioqueño
settlements (figures), 31, 48, 49, 219; to
colonos (figures), 31, 48, 49, 219; ways
to acquire, 40; to land entrepreneurs
(figures), 41 ,48, 49; geographical
distribution, 41–46; breakdown by size,
43, 48, 49, 50, 221–22; use of front
men, 50; multiple grants, acquired by
one person, 50, 236; government
revocation of, 100–01, 137; increase in
small grants (1920s), 103, 236;
1931–71 (figures), 164; to sovereign
states, 211; consolidation of small grants
into large properties, 236; during *La
Violencia* (figures), 260

Land invasions. *See* Conflict over public
land, 1928–36, post–1960

Land judges, 156–57, 160, 255, 262

Land policy. *See* Public land policy

Land surveying. *See* Surveying practices

Land values: and speculation, 37; and
usurpation of public land, 54; and
advent of land entrepreneurs, 75; rise in
1920s, 93, 94; in banana zone, 115; in
1933–34, 139–40

Latifundia: defined, xi; effects, xi;
formation of, in colonial period, 2;
government critique of, 16, 89, 97;
specialization of production, 29; reasons
for consolidation of, 35–39; formed
through usurpation of public land,
50–56; challenged by squatter
movement, 133; mortgaged to banks,
138; sanctioned by Law 200 of 1936,
151; modernization of, 166; formed
through privatization of public lands,
167; reasons output did not increase
(late 1930s), 258

Latifundia/minifundia system: and
underdevelopment, xi, 89; economic
explanations for persistence of, 218, 257

La Violencia: interpretations of, 162;
disputes over public land and, 163–64;
writings on, 176; in Sumapaz, 259; in
frontier regions, 259–60; public land
grants during (figures), 260; mentioned,
xviii, 155, 168, 174

Law 61 of 1874: explication of 14–15;
provisions protecting colonos, 56–57,
80; circumvented by landlords, 57, 83;
and peasant resistance against
expropriation, 64

Law 48 of 1882: explication of, 14–15;
provisions protecting colonos, 15,
56–57, 80; limits maximum grant size,
16; requires economic use of land
grants, 16, 101; and peasant resistance
against expropriation, 64; circumvented
by landlords, 57, 83; provisions on
grants to cultivators, 218; mention, 52

Law 57 of 1905: used to evict *colonos*, 82,
85; revision of, 101–02

Law 200 of 1936 (the Land Act):
significance of, xvii, 143–44, 155;
response to shift in political forces, 146;
explication of, 149–53; as solution to
land disputes, 152; mechanisms for
settling land disputes, 156; hastened
proletarianization of rural labor, 159–61;
peasant interpretation of, 160; definition
of "improvements", 253; authors of, 253;
used to appropriate Indian land, 255.
See also Land judges; López Pumarejo,
Alfonso

Law 100 of 1944, 161–62

Law 135 of 1961, 159, 165–66

Lawyers. *See Tinterillos*

Leiva family, 68, 76, 77, 112, 113, 244

Leiva M., Uldarico, 6, 83

Liberal party: formation of, 10; land policy,
15, 97, 103; attitude to industrialization,
94; and labor movement, 105; attitude to
colonization, 106; Jorge Eliécer Gaitán
splits from, 122; return of Gaitán, 124;
rural mobilization, 125–26; forms
peasant unions, 126, 156; opposes land
reform, 147, 148, 165–66; in Córdoba,
during La Violencia, 164; reformists